Centaurs and Snake-Kings

Griffins, centaurs and gorgons: the Greek imagination teems with wondrous, yet often monstrous, hybrids. Jeremy McInerney discusses how these composite creatures arise from the entanglement of humans and animals. Overlaying such enmeshment is the rich cultural exchange experienced by Greeks across the Mediterranean. Hybrids, the author reveals, capture the anxiety of cross-cultural encounter, where similarity and incongruity were conjoined. Hybridity likewise expresses the instability of identity. The ancient sea, that most changeable ancient domain, was viewed as home to monsters like Skylla, while on land the centaur might be hypersexual yet also hypercivilized, like Cheiron. Medusa may be destructive, yet also alluring. Wherever conventional values or behaviours are challenged, the hybrid gives that threat a face. This absorbing work unveils a mercurial world of shifting categories that offer an alternative to conventional certainties. Transforming disorder into images of wonder, Greek hybrids, McInerney suggests, finally point to other ways of being human.

JEREMY MCINERNEY is Professor of Classical Studies at the University of Pennsylvania. He is the author of *The Folds of Parnassos* (1999), *The Cattle of the Sun* (2010) and *Greece in the Ancient World* (2018), and the editor of *A Companion to Ethnicity in the Ancient Mediterranean* (2014).

Centaurs and Snake-Kings

Hybrids and the Greek Imagination

JEREMY MCINERNEY
University of Pennsylvania

Shaftesbury Road, Cambridge CB2 8EA, United Kingdom

One Liberty Plaza, 20th Floor, New York, NY 10006, USA

477 Williamstown Road, Port Melbourne, VIC 3207, Australia

314–321, 3rd Floor, Plot 3, Splendor Forum, Jasola District Centre, New Delhi – 110025, India

103 Penang Road, #05–06/07, Visioncrest Commercial, Singapore 238467

Cambridge University Press is part of Cambridge University Press & Assessment, a department of the University of Cambridge.

We share the University's mission to contribute to society through the pursuit of education, learning and research at the highest international levels of excellence.

www.cambridge.org
Information on this title: www.cambridge.org/9781009459105

DOI: 10.1017/9781009459068

© Jeremy McInerney 2024

This publication is in copyright. Subject to statutory exception and to the provisions of relevant collective licensing agreements, no reproduction of any part may take place without the written permission of Cambridge University Press & Assessment.

First published 2024

Printed in the United Kingdom by CPI Group Ltd, Croydon CR0 4YY

A catalogue record for this publication is available from the British Library

A Cataloging-in-Publication data record for this book is available from the Library of Congress

ISBN 978-1-009-45910-5 Hardback

Cambridge University Press & Assessment has no responsibility for the persistence or accuracy of URLs for external or third-party internet websites referred to in this publication and does not guarantee that any content on such websites is, or will remain, accurate or appropriate.

This book is dedicated to Pamela Zinn, with love and gratitude.

Contents

List of Figures [*page* viii]
Preface [xi]
Acknowledgements [xv]
Spelling and Orthography [xvi]

1 Introduction: Encountering the Sphinx [1]

2 'Welcome to Athens': Theories of Hybridity [24]

3 Hybrids around the Corrupting Sea [57]

4 Hybrids, Contact Zones and Margins [92]

5 Heads or Tails: Gorgons, Satyrs and Other Composites [136]

6 Centaurs and Other Horses [171]

7 Snakes and the Perils of Autochthony [202]

8 Hermaphrodites and Other Bodies [231]

9 *Adynata*, Ethnography and Paradox [260]

10 Conclusions [291]

Bibliography [297]
Index [348]

Figures

P.1 Argos centaur   [*page* xii]
1.1 Oedipus and the Sphinx   [2]
1.2 Marble capital and finial in the form of a sphinx   [4]
1.3 Red granite Sphinx of Ramses II   [6]
1.4 Ivory plaque with striding sphinx   [6]
1.5 The Lion-man ('Löwenmensch')   [10]
1.6 Chimbu woman breastfeeding a piglet   [12]
2.1 Bronze figure of winged horse   [25]
2.2 The Education of Achilles by Chiron   [27]
2.3 'Welcome to Athens'   [30]
2.4 Patricia Piccinini, *No Fear of Depths*   [41]
2.5 Low relief bucrania, Tomba A ('domus de janas'), Anghelu Ruju, Alghero, Sardinia   [49]
3.1 Mušḫuššu bas-relief from the Ishtar Gate   [62]
3.2 Zeus aiming his thunderbolt at a winged and snake-footed Typhoeus   [67]
3.3 Carnelian seal depicting the killing of Humbaba   [69]
3.4 Two dog palette   [72]
3.5 Gold foil diadem with sphinxes and spiral patterns   [74]
3.6 Ivory furniture panels from Ugarit   [76]
3.7 A. Gold signet ring from Tiryns. B. Limestone votive stela with Taweret and Mut   [79]
3.8 Satirical papyrus depicting animals behaving as humans. Deir el-Medina, Egypt   [80]
3.9 Cup of Arkesilas. Laconian black-figure *kylix*   [84]
3.10 Book of the Dead. The Weighing of Ani's Soul   [84]
3.11 Steatite bull's head rhyton. Knossos   [89]
3.12 Apulian red-figure *kylix*. Pasiphai and the Minotaur   [90]
4.1 Relief map of the Mediterranean Basin   [93]
4.2 Skylla. Terracotta plaque, Melos   [98]
4.3 Herakles and Triton wrestling. Attic black-figure hydria   [101]

List of Figures

4.4 Perseus and Medusa Metope. Temple C, Selinus   [102]
4.5 Abduction of Thetis by Peleus. Calyx krater by the Niobid Painter   [103]
4.6 Thetis seated on a hippocampus. Eretria, House of Mosaics   [108]
4.7 Minoan seals depicting hybrids   [110]
4.8 Detail of black-figure dinos by Sophilos   [113]
4.9 Aristonothos Krater   [114]
4.10 Bronze statuette of a woman. Ionian   [122]
4.11 Bronze repoussé relief. North Syrian   [124]
4.12 Figure with mask. Cyprus   [128]
4.13 Hematite cylinder seal. Cyprus   [129]
4.14 Terracotta centaur figurine. Agia Irini, NW Cyprus   [131]
5.1 Winged snake-tailed demon in an animal frieze. Oversized Corinthian kylix   [137]
5.2 Terracotta olla with griffin protomes standing on terracotta olmos (stand). Ficana   [138]
5.3 Proto-Attic amphora showing Gorgon. Eleusis   [139]
5.4 Perseus killing Medusa. Cycladic relief pithos   [143]
5.5 Terracotta gorgon mask, Tiryns   [146]
5.6 Gorgon head decoration on volute handle. Vix krater   [148]
5.7 White-ground kyathos. Girl riding a *phallos*-bird   [155]
5.8 Sexually excited satyr facing the viewer. Terracotta kylix by the Oakeshott Painter   [157]
5.9 Satyr masturbating. Attic red-figure kalpis fragment attributed to Kleophrades painter   [159]
5.10 The metamorphosis of the Tyrrhenian pirates by Dionysos   [160]
5.11 Bronze figurine of one of Odysseus' men undergoing transformation   [166]
5.12 Circe giving a potion to Odysseus' men: black-figure kylix   [167]
6.1 Battle between the Lapiths and centaurs (detail). The François Vase   [172]
6.2 Cypriot terracotta figurine depicting horse and rider   [177]
6.3 Krater with horse-leader flanked by two horses. Tiryns   [178]
6.4 Herakles and Pholos reclining. Early fifth century   [184]
6.5 Boiotian terracotta centaur   [186]
6.6 Centauro de Royos, bronze   [187]
6.7 Bronze man and centaur. Mid-eighth century BC   [189]

List of Figures

6.8 Bronze statuette of a centaur [191]
6.9 Drawing of a painted alabastron depicting a centaur and a woman [192]
6.10 Two centaurs (Cheiron and Centaur×) [193]
6.11 Bellerophon and Pegasos slaying the Chimaira. Attributed to Boreads painter [200]
6.12 A. Silver drachma (Sikyon) with Chimaira. B. Silver stater (Corinth) with Pegasos [201]
7.1 Gaia, Athena and Kekrops. Melian relief [210]
7.2 Kekrops and the nymph of Marathon (detail). Pella hydria [220]
7.3 Man wrestling a human-headed snake (detail). Black-figure vase, Perachora [221]
7.4 'Bluebeard', from the Hekatompedon pediment, Akropolis, Athens [222]
8.1 Statuette of hermaphrodite, second century BC [235]
8.2 Kaineus attacked by centaurs. Hammered bronze sheet [250]
8.3 Cock-headed anguiped (Abrasax), jasper, first–sixth century AD [254]
8.4 Sleeping hermaphrodite. Marble, second century AD [255]
9.1 Venus crowned by two centaurides. Mosaic [286]
9.2 Mosaic depicting a pair of centaurs fighting cats of prey from Hadrian's Villa [288]
9.3 Mosaic depicting a tigress–griffin eating a lizard, Istanbul [289]

Preface

> In fact, when I was very little, I wanted to marry a horse. I'd heard of an Englishwoman who had married her dog because she didn't like humans. So I thought, Why can't I marry my horse? But I grew out of that.
>
> (Interviewer): That was probably for the best.
>
> My father said to me, 'You do realize your children will be centaurs, don't you?'
>
> Prue Leith, *New Yorker*, 23 October 2022

This is a book that grew out of a slightly less charming episode than Prue Leith's memory of girlish naiveté, but one that also involved centaurs. In 2013, while teaching in Athens, I had occasion to visit the Argos Museum before it closed for remodelling. In a vitrine devoted to Archaic material I saw a figurine that was really eye catching: a terracotta centaur about 30 cm tall, unmistakeably equipped with human genitalia (see Figure P.1).

It soon turned out that my colleagues in art history were familiar with this composition, and that the Argive centaur was not especially noteworthy to experts, but to someone coming to the object from the point of view of human/animals relations the idea of a centaur that was human all the way to its feet was a revelation. A thousand questions, most of them imponderable and unanswerable, arose, and the centaur began to assume a decidedly less familiar mien in my mind's eye. I was aware that they were a part of the mythic stratum that underpinned Greek culture, depicted on vases and referred to in stories, but the Argive centaur prodded me into asking questions about what fits and what doesn't, about harmony and discordance, about what we expect and what we take for granted and, most of all, about the place of monsters and their less threatening cousins, hybrids. This book grew out of a somewhat inchoate investigation of these categories until, in the course of being written, it became more of an investigation into the very idea of categories, their boundaries, their purpose and their function.

Figure P.1 Centaur. Terracotta. Argos, 6th century BC. Photo: J. McInerney

Since my 'road to Damascus' moment in Argos, I have presented some preliminary forays into the topic at various venues. A talk at the American School of Classical Studies in Athens early on alerted me to some truly significant dangers. A too-casual reference to the threat of bestiality making the threat of rape worse once centaurs became genitally equine – centaurs are never far from these threats – elicited a firm corrective from a friend who observed that one couldn't talk about degrees of rape. A conference on animals held at NYU in the middle of a snowstorm and hosted imperturbably by Phil Mitsis soon followed, as well as a colloquium on animals and the sacred held at St Andrews, hosted by Sam Newington and Sian Lewis. Also during these early investigations, a panel at the annual meeting of the Classical Association gave me a chance to rehearse ideas and refine them still further. Anyone who has spent years on a book will understand how important these try-outs were, even if at the time the presentations were patchy and undercooked. All of these were among the most satisfying scholarly experiences I have enjoyed, thanks to the participants, speakers and interlocutors who all played a vital part in helping me to refine and develop the theses of the book. Something about centaurs and other hybrids seems to excite just about every audience. As the blurb for a recent exhibition ('Animalistic! Animals and Hybrid Creatures in Antiquity') in Basel modestly claimed, 'Monsters, beasts and chimaeras have always inspired the human imagination.' That excitement has continued to propel me further into the subject. Why do they matter so?

The cutting, shaping and working out of one's ideas are the stuff of writing a book, but I also found there was a parallel experience that complemented the formal procedures of research in ways I hadn't expected: hybrids are everywhere, and are easy to take for granted. A walk through a Dallas airport took me past a clothing store where the mannequins were human bodies with bulls' heads. Well, it was Texas, I suppose. A catalogue in the mail declared the arrival of hybrid shoes that could be worn at work and on the weekend. And, as ever, one of the ghastly after-effects of the coronavirus pandemic was the rise of hybrid teaching and, worse, hybrid conferences. As I began to take stock of these casual encounters, where hybrids seemed ubiquitous and increasingly part of the background hum of daily life, hybridity, ironically, came to assume a greater significance than I had previously suspected in my engagement with the ancient Greeks. The shock of this recognition was similar to the experience of encountering childhood stories and fairy tales as an adult. When I introduced my children to Norman Lindsay's *The Magic Pudding*, an Australian classic, I was at first as delighted as I had been thirty years earlier by the wild imagination that could conjure a world in which a pudding, 'always anxious to be eaten', could magically renew itself. But the adventures of Bunyip Bluegum and his mates in search of their stolen pudding, Albert, become increasingly weird and, for the adult reader at least, disturbing. Albert's taste for self-cannibalization (and his irascibility) are unsettling and defy comprehension, while Lindsay's amusing Aesopic world, in which wombats and koalas dress in top-hats and sport Victorian whiskers, occasionally veers off in very strange directions; in one episode, Sam the Penguin saves the 'Hearl of Buncle' in a shipwreck and gets to marry his very lovely (and very human) niece. It may be, as Bruno Bettelheim believed, that children learn to handle their fears by being exposed to the cruelty and malice woven into fairy tales, but very little in *The Magic Pudding* would really terrify a child. Instead, the ingredients are peculiarity and oddity, and they leave a slightly 'off' taste. The odd hybrids of the Greek imagination work in a similar way: sphinxes, gorgons, centaurs and snake-kings are everywhere, and by their ubiquity they seem unremarkable, yet once you really start to pay attention they appear to be anything but ordinary. Their significance masquerades behind a taken-for-grantedness. Collectively, they mark a culture that was alert to the possibility that the stuff of daily life might also contain traces of other ingredients, with the potential to cause a more violent reaction than expected. It is that tension – I won't exaggerate by calling it a paradox, or even a contradiction – that I hope to explore in this book: a tension between the familiar and the unexpected that was so crucial to the shape of the culture of the Greeks.

Acknowledgements

A great many people have contributed to this book through conversations, suggestions, questions and disagreements. I am very happy to acknowledge as many of them here as I can recall: Ioannis Akamatis, Emma Aston, Bill Beck, Dan Ben-Amos, Grace Boyle, Madeleine Brown, Ann Brownlee, Cynthia Damon, Joe Day, Joe Farrell, Marian Feldman, Maria Fragoulaki, Chelsea Gardiner, Anne Lee, Sian Lewis, James McInerney, Lucy McInerney, Timothy McNiven, Irad Malkin, Thomas Metzinger, Philip Mitsis, Sam Newington, Jenifer Niels, Monty Ngan, Michael Padgett, Nassos Papalexandrou, Maciej Paprocki, Brian Rose, Claudio Sansone, Dallas Simons, Ann Steiner, Andrew Stewart, Fabio Tutrone and last (in alphabetical order only) Pamela Zinn.

I have benefitted from strong institutional and collegial support that I must recognize here. The American School of Classical Studies, where I served as Whitehead Professor in 2013–14, is in a real sense the cradle in which this project was nurtured during its infancy. The Department of Classical Studies at the University of Pennsylvania has been my academic home for my entire career and I offer my sincerest thanks to the colleagues who have always shared their intelligence and knowledge with such unfailing generosity. They, and the many, many students, undergraduate and graduate, who have suffered through this book's slow growth to maturity, have been its nurses, for better or for worse. The University of Pennsylvania also generously contributed to the project by granting two dean's leaves and supplementing my sabbatical time. These proved invaluable.

Most importantly, I must thank the two anonymous readers for Cambridge University Press, who took a shamefully self-indulgent manuscript and provided the necessary guidance for rewriting it top to bottom. What is good in the rewritten version you hold in your hands is due to their unmatched professionalism. All else is my sole responsibility.

Spelling and Orthography

I generally prefer spelling that stays close to the Greek: hence, 'Sikyon' not 'Sicyon' and 'Kleisthenes' not 'Cleisthenes'. Sometimes this is mildly jarring, as in 'Herodotos' which I prefer to 'Herodotus'. When hypercorrect forms render familiar names unfamiliar or unrecognizable to an English-speaking reader, I stick to the recognizable forms: hence, 'Circe' not 'Kirke', 'Thucydides' not 'Thoukydides', 'Aeschylus' not 'Aiskhylos' and 'Plato' not 'Platon'. In Chapter 8 this means that readers will encounter (Latin) Salmacis, when I am treating Ovid's nymph and her love for Hermaphroditus, but they will also have to cope with Salmakis and Hermaphroditos when I discuss the episode's roots in Greek/Karian Halikarnassos. My aim has been intelligibility, not consistency. If the result is an odd hybrid, so much the better.

1 | Introduction

Encountering the Sphinx

> If you went hunting for tigers and encountered a centaur, you would start a revolution in zoology.
>
> Sábato, *Sobre héroes y tumbas*

The Riddle of the Sphinxes

Hybrids, such as centaurs, gorgons, sphinxes and satyrs, are among the most recognizable characters in Greek mythology and continue to turn up in popular culture. From the centaurs in *Harry Potter* to Pegasos in *Clash of the Titans*, Greek hybrids exert a hold on the popular imagination. This is a book about such hybrids, but it is also a book about hybridity. The two are not the same. The difference can be illustrated by looking at what is surely one of the most famous hybrids in Greek myth, the Sphinx. As imagined by Moreau in the middle of the nineteenth century, the encounter between Oidipous and the monster takes place in a gloomy landscape suffused with menace and laden with eroticism (Figure 1.1). 'The bane of the Thebans', as the Sphinx is called by Hesiod, is singularly focused on the handsome young hero.[1] As she gazes up at Oidipous, her body thrusts against him while she remains unnaturally suspended, as if the scene were set in a dream. Below her innocent face the Sphinx's paws cling to him, ready to tear off his carefully arranged garment. She is the focus of our attention even as we take in a profusion of other elements: the body parts of her previous victims, glimpsed at the bottom of the tableau, a belt of red beads around her waist, a vase decorated with griffins and a column in the lower right, around which curls a snake. But in the midst of all these visual cues suggesting sexual violence cloaked in classical serenity stand the hero and the monster, their eyes locked. The allegorical significance of the hybrid here is unmistakable. A composite of woman, eagle and lion, she unambiguously embodies the male fear of predatory female desire. All these elements combine to render the Sphinx a hybrid monster, horrifying and

---

[1] Hesiod, *Theog.* 326. Oidipous' encounter with the Sphinx is referred to in Aeschylus' *Septem* 773–5. The full story of the riddle is given by Apollodorus 3.52–5.

Figure 1.1 Oedipus and the Sphinx. G. Moreau. 1864. Oil. 81 1/4 × 41 1/4 in. Metropolitan Museum of Art, 21.134.1.

attractive, full of menace, a symbol of all that threatens male control. Ingres' 1808 painting of the same episode is less feverish, but takes on added significance when set against the artist's lifelong struggle to free himself from his father's influence. As Posèq has shown, the painting is an Oedipal treatment of an Oedipal subject.[2]

Do any of these factors shed light on the sphinx in Greek culture?[3] Moreau's and Ingres' sphinxes resemble their Greek antecedents in so far as each is composed of a lion's body, an eagle's wings and a woman's head, although the prominent breasts of the modern sphinxes are an addition that highlights a sexual threat only latent in the earlier figures. Since sexual threat is not an emphatic part of the ancient sphinx's make-up

---

[2] Posèq 2001.   [3] For the iconography of Greek sphinxes, see Tsiafakis 2003: 78–83.

(although Odysseus might disagree), we are forced to look elsewhere for the sphinx's place in Greek culture and for its sudden popularity in the sixth century. At that time, sphinxes proliferate in Greek decorative arts. They are found on vases as part of a larger composition, usually flanking vegetal motifs, gorgons, riders or '*Nikai*'. On the François vase, for example, there are in fact four such figures, heraldically facing each other with one paw raised, possibly an apotropaic gesture.[4]

They also appear on funerary monuments and on the roofs of temples. A sixth-century funerary marker now in the Met illustrates how imposing such funerary monuments could be (Figure 1.2). The sphinx sat atop a funeral stele commemorating a young man named Megakles. At a total height of more than four metres it was a dramatic statement of the status of the family – in this case, the Alkmeonids – that erected it.[5]

There have been many interpretations offered for the popularity of the sphinx in Archaic Greece, and Thierry Petit sums up modern attempts to explain the sphinx under these headings:

- Purely decorative. Acroteria are fantasy decorations that yield to no logic of meaning.
- Psychoanalytical explanations, in which the sphinx represents the 'bad mother'.
- The creation of liminal and sacred space. In this reading the sphinx marks the threshold between this world and the other.
- An apotropaic function. According to this interpretation the sphinx guards either the dead or the deity.
- Death demons, mastered by the deities of the temples they adorn.
- Tamed nature. Since many of the gods whose temples the sphinxes adorn are masters or mistresses of animals and nature, by extension the sphinxes symbolize that mastery.
- Hypostases. In this interpretation, the sphinxes are like satellites representing in miniaturized form the major deity with whom they are associated.[6]

The sheer range of these explanations alerts us to a significant hurdle to understanding these and other hybrids: the profusion of sphinxes resists attempts to infer a single meaning. Can the sphinx be apotropaic and a death demon at the same time? A fifth-century headstone from Pagasai

---

[4] For a description of the vase, see Petit 2019. For the *Schutzgestus*, see Petit 2011: 176–82.
[5] Attic grave stele with sphinx, 530 BC. Marble. total H. 4.23 m. Metropolitan Museum of Art (11.185a–c, f, g).
[6] Petit 2013: 211–14.

Figure 1.2 Marble capital and finial in the form of a sphinx, ca. 530 BC. Attic. Parian Marble. Height with acroterion 142.6 cm. Metropolitan Museum of Art, 11.185d, x.

carries an inscription addressed to the sphinx guarding the burial: 'Dog of Hades, whom do you watch over, sitting over the dead?'[7] This sphinx, at least, is a protector, but in the fifth century there were also depictions of Oidipous killing the sphinx. In this tradition, as in the literary accounts, the creature is an agent of death rather than a guardian. Nor can we solve the riddle of the sphinx by simply treating it as a Near Eastern figure transplanted to a Greek setting. Petit observes that 'We have long known that the Kerûbhîm ("cherubim") of the Bible are represented in the form of the hybrid called "sphinx" by the Greeks.'[8] But what prompted the Greeks to adopt the Cherubim, and did the Greek sphinx mean the same thing as its antecedents? Origin is not explanation. Furthermore, symbols can lose their meaning and become just images. When Kleitias arranged his

---

[7] Inscription: Volos 690. See Kurtz and Boardman 1971: 239 and Tsiafakis 2003: 82.
[8] Petit 2013: 217.

sphinxes on the François vase facing a vegetal motif he was employing a syntax of decoration that only dimly recalled the Near Eastern motif of the tree of life.

This is not to dismiss the hybrid's capacity to evoke awe. The Naxian Sphinx is proof, if any is needed, that a monumental hybrid will always be powerful.[9] At more than twelve metres tall, including the column on which it stood, it dominated the Aire in front of the Stoa of the Athenians in the sanctuary of Apollo at Delphi. It also offered visitors the opportunity to experience it up close from the temple terrace. On many temples, there are hybrids and monsters on metopes, as acroteria and in pedimental sculpture, where their dynamism complements the regularity and symmetry of the temple's underlying architecture. Together, the orderliness of the temple's design and non-figural elements combines with the liveliness of the hybrids and monsters found in the decorative elements to create a unique experience: comprehensible, and yet at the same time awe-inspiring.[10] It is at this general level that many Greek sphinxes reflect their ancestry, so to speak. The sphinxes that protected tombs in the Kerameikos are distant cousins of the red granite Sphinx of Ramses II. It stood outside the temple of Ptah at Memphis and, like many other ram- or goat-headed sphinxes placed along the avenues leading to Egyptian temple complexes, it was apotropaic and a statement of the pharaoh's power[11] (see Figure 1.3). The comparison with the Greek sphinxes (and Moreau's sphinx) reminds us that as hybrids move between cultures they may lose old meanings and acquire new ones, just as new stylistic details are added or changed.

As the sphinx motif moves from Egypt to Mari and Anatolia in the nineteenth and eighteenth centuries BC, the figure diminishes in size, first depicted on frescoes, then carved onto ivory plaques and finally into small seals cut from precious stone, such as jasper.[12] Along the way the sphinx acquires wings and becomes female. It is the last of these configurations, on the highly portable media of carved sealstones and ivory plaques that comes to Greece in the eighth century, where sphinxes are dedicated in temples and buried as apotropaic devices.[13] An example from the palace of Nimrud built by Ashurnasirpal II in the ninth century illustrates how elegant such pieces were, but also how easily portable they were (Figure 1.4). The range of forms and associations is a reminder that any explanation of hybridity (as opposed to the interpretation of a particular hybrid) must cast a very

[9] Amandry 1953: 26–32.
[10] Hölscher 2009 makes a powerful case for viewing the decorative elements (*kosmos*) of a temple as contributing to the temple's affirmation of order (also *kosmos*).
[11] Wegner and Wegner, 2015: 239.   [12] Sagiv 2018:130–1.   [13] Tsiafakis 2003: 82.

6   *Introduction: Encountering the Sphinx*

Figure 1.3 Red granite Sphinx of Ramses II (nineteenth dynasty, ca. 1293–1185 BC). Sacred enclosure of the temple of the god Ptah, Memphis. 362 × 145 cm. University of Pennsylvania Museum, E12326.

Figure 1.4 Openwork plaque with a striding sphinx. Neo-Assyrian, ninth–eighth centuries BC. Nimrud. H. 3 7/16 × W. 4 1/16 × Th. 13/16 in. (8.8 × 10.3 × 2.1 cm). Metropolitan Museum of Art, 64.37.1.

wide net. Some hybrids may be hideous monsters, but monstrosity is not an inevitable component of the hybrid. Some hybrids may be benign or protective, yet with a slight shift they can become menacing.

Further complicating any analysis of hybridity is that the Greeks encountered hybrids in a wide variety of media and settings. In the *Seven Against Thebes*, Aeschylus refers to the Sphinx as the 'ravenous, detested beast' and describes the shield of Parthenopaios adorned with an image of the monster. It serves as an emblem, designed to humiliate the Thebans by reminding them of their city's shame. These and other literary references guide our reading of the Theban sphinx: she is, as Aeschylus says, 'a deadly, man-seizing plague'. But it is highly unlikely that the sphinxes depicted on an Assyrian ivory pyxis from the thirteenth century BC were read precisely this way.[14] The pyxis was found in a royal tomb in (Greek) Thebes but the hybrid figures on it reflect an international style, and they should not be seen as early depictions of the Sphinx that would later be banished by Oidipous. The pyxis' precious material (ivory), expert craftsmanship and distant provenance confirm the object's exotic appeal and affirm the status of the member of the Mycenaean elite who acquired it. Unlike Aeschylus' fifth-century sphinx, the Assyrian import does not offer a clear reading of the sphinx as a pestilential threat; sometimes the foreignness and exoticism of the sphinx are its most telling features.

There are other dimensions to hybridity that call for caution. Aside from hybrids that are a mixture of parts that remain distinct, such as the sphinx with her leonine body and eagle's wings, there are other, real hybrids produced by breeding in which the hybrid is wholly new. The mule, crossbred from a horse and a donkey, is one such. It is as much a hybrid as the Theban Sphinx, but it is a dependable work animal and as helpful to humans as the Sphinx is threatening.[15] And there are other, 'real', hybrids that are benign and ubiquitous, but are also barely noticed: emmer, durum, and bread wheat, for example, are all hybridized grains responsible for increased yields of disease resistant crops.[16] Hybridization, in fact, has long been recognized to play an important role in plant evolution.[17] It is not clear, however, that the people of the ancient Mediterranean world were aware of naturally occurring hybridization.[18] Hybrids, then, exist on

---

[14] Ivory pyxis with sphinxes, from Thebes (Greece). LH IIIA-B, Archaeological Museum of Thebes 42459. For an image see Aruz et al. 2013: 249.

[15] On mules, see Griffith 2006.

[16] Many wheat hybrids occur naturally, and it is often claimed that Einkorn is the only unhybridized wheat. The deliberate hybridization of corn and rice is more recent, dating to the 1940s. The development of hybrid rice by Yuan Longping in the 1970s was perhaps the most significant step towards food security in modern times. See Schmalzer 2015: 73–99.

[17] Mehregan and Kadereit 2009: 36.

[18] As Robert Sallares (1991: 36) notes, 'Lucretius ... denied the possibility of plant hybridization'; Lucret., *DRN* 5.920–4: 'for the species of plants which even now spring abundantly from the

a continuum from the real to the imaginary and from the benevolent to the monstrous, from the Sphinx to the hinny. But this does not mean that hybridity is simply a matter of any kind of mixing. In each instance around the hybrid there lurks a host of questions: what bits have been mixed, how exactly are the parts combined, and is the mixture taxonomically fitting or anomalous? Each of these questions remains in the background, shaping our response to a hybrid, affirming the power of hybridity to challenge (or affirm) categories and taxonomies. And since taxonomies are the proof of our comprehending the world by classifying phenomena, hybridity represents a culture's uneasiness with the limits of its epistemology. If such things exist, even if only in our stories and imagination, how certain is certainty?

The Origins of Hybridity

Hybrids have a prehistory that lies in the human encounter with the animal. Most human societies which maintain an intimate relationship with the natural world contemplate what it means to be human by focusing on our deeply entangled relationship with animals.[19] A recent study puts it succinctly: '[Animals] helped us deal with questions of human existence while still appearing as themselves, speaking to us in their alterity.'[20] And it is a deeply intimate, symbiotic relationship. The white *scelera* around the dark iris of our eyes make it possible for the dog to track our gaze as we hunt. Consequently, as canids undergo the transition from wolf, a threat and competitor, to dog, companion and hunting partner, we adapt to a mutual reliance.[21] Animals guide us, threaten us, compete with us and,

---

earth, and the cereal crops and fruitful trees, cannot even so be crossed with each other, but each kind goes on its own way and all maintain their distinctions by a fixed pact of nature' (tr. Gale).

[19] Animal–human studies have mushroomed in recent years. For the Greek world, fundamental is Lonsdale 1979, updated and expanded by Calder 2011. Comprehensive bibliographies up to the early 2000s can be found in Kalof et al. 2004 and Fögen 2006. For a useful overview of recent work relating to the ancient Mediterranean, see Kindt 2017. Major contributions in the field more generally include Ingold 1988, Agamben 2004, Ingold 2007 and Calarco 2008. For attempts to write an animal history from the animal's point of view, see Baratay 2015 and the essays collected in Baratay 2019. The modern interest in animal welfare is only the most recent expression of the complexity of our relationship with animals, particularly as we continue to eat them. For a recent discussion of the notion of 'the Good Life' in relation to animals' quality of life, see Yeates 2017.

[20] Korhonen and Ruonakoski 2017: 191

[21] Shipman 2015: 218, notes that 'domestic dogs not only share the wolf's genetic ability to communicate through gazing, they also gaze at humans twice as long as wolves do on average – suggesting that duration of gaze may have been selected for during the domestication process'.

in some instances, create us. One aboriginal Dreaming captures this succinctly in the observation, 'Dingo makes us human.'[22] Similarly, Hemas Harvey Humchitt sums up the world view of the Heiltsuk people of the Pacific Northwest as 'Everything revolves around the herring'.[23] Nor is this an intimacy restricted to contemporary indigenous societies living close to nature. There is good reason to believe that early human communities shaped their entire world view through their experience of animals. In the Palaeolithic and the Neolithic, animals were the nearest category of living beings with whom we engaged. As hunters we looked at them as prey, yet poorly equipped as we are in the face of nature, red in tooth and claw, we were also sometimes preyed upon. Our relationship with animals is therefore subject to constant shifts, and we experience the animal universe as an insistent, polyvalent cosmos. It is worth exploring this further, not because every Greek hybrid is an evolutionary holdover from some imagined *Urzeit*, but because hybridity is a direct outgrowth of human–animal entanglement.

The blending of human and animal can be shown to go back at least to 35,000–40,000 years BP. Carved from the right tusk of a mammoth, the Löwenmensch from Hohlenstein reveals that already in the Aurignacian there existed a human capacity to imagine the possibilities created by merging parts of different species[24] (Figure 1.5). Is the hybrid creature a projection of the human hunter into another predator's body? Whether or not the Löwenmensch was a trophy commemorating the hunter's victory over the mammoth from which the tusk was taken, the figurine offers evidence not only of the hunter's imagination but of a symbolic engagement with the world, in which lion and human hunter are fused.[25] Figures such as the shaman depicted as a 'reindeer-man' in Les Trois Frères, the bird-headed female of Pech Merle and the bison-man from

---

[22] Rose 2000: 47, 104–5, 176–7. Readers unfamiliar with the concept of Dreaming should see Rose 2000: 43–7. The term encompasses both the place and time of creation, as well the creator beings and the telling of these in 'a poetic key to Reality' (Stanner 1979: 29).

[23] Gavreau et al. 2017.

[24] Beutelspacher et al. 2014: 13 refer to the figure as 'ein einzigartiges Zeugnis der fantasievollen Vorstellungswelt der Menschen im Aurignacien der Schwäbischen Alb' (a unique attestation to the rich imaginative world of the people who dwelt in the Swabian Alps during the Aurignacian period). For a cognitive neuroscientific discussion of the conceptual blending of animal and human in the figure, see Wynn et al. 2009.

[25] On the time needed to carve the piece, see Berger 2012: 37. A replica took 320 hours to carve using flint tools. Given the haptic qualities of the figurine it is also not unrealistic to imagine a use in shamanistic rituals. Such an identification with the animal's power is a deeply rooted practice: in the nineteenth century, King Glele of Dahomey received a divination sign (du) promising a full and prosperous reign, which the king chose to commemorate by adopting the hybrid of a man-lion as his personal device. See Blier 1993: 191–2.

Figure 1.5 The Lion-man ('Löwenmensch') from the Stadel cave in Hohlenstein in the valley of Lone (Germany) ca. 35,000–40,000 BP. Copyright Landesamt für Denkmalpflege im RP Stuttgart/Museum Ulm/Yvonne Mühleis (CC BY-NC-ND).

the Chauvet Cave show that the boundary of human and animal is not firmly fixed, but is forever breaking down.

Discussing the figures of the Chauvet Cave, for example, Gernot Grube has recently concluded that

> What we discover with this extremely cautious interpretation, very close to the visual findings, are a few basic attitudes. First, the psychological theme of the transformation of men into aggressive beings, who threaten the peace of the community. Second, a metaphysical theme: worship of a being that embodies the ideal community. Third, the association of man and bison. Fourth, the association of woman and lion ... Fifth, the association of the horse with a positive male role.[26]

---

[26] Grube 2020: 47.

Even the most cautious analysis of such images concludes that 'We can be rather sure that people reflected on the abilities and qualities of animals and compared some of these qualities with their own.'[27] Set against this universal phenomenon of humans interacting with animals, Bataille proposed seeing hybrids as a sign of humans fleeing their humanity, both resisting and endorsing their animal origins.[28] Similarly, Kristeva uses the abject as a means of explaining monsters by proposing that the early societies sought a clear demarcation between the animal and the human: 'The abject confronts us', she writes, 'on the one hand, with those fragile states where man strays on the territories of *animal*. Thus, by way of abjection, primitive societies have marked out a precise area of their culture in order to remove it from the threatening world of animals or animalism, which were imagined as representatives of sex and murder.'[29] Such claims rely on a highly simplified and problematic view of 'primitive' societies in which primal drives can be mechanically displaced. Yet the exuberance and complexity of non-Western cultures should lead us to pause for a moment and ask if there might not be a wider range of possibilities at play here.

There is, for example, a very different approach to what could be called humanimality among the Kujamaat Diola people of Senegal. Here, a human will defecate an animal, the *ewúúm*, which runs off into the bush.[30] This creature, a totemic double of the human, is usually some kind of common wild animal, such as an antelope, leopard or snake. The human and the *ewúúm* are in communication with each other, and are metonymically bound, sharing the same *yut* or soul. Social relationships, in fact, are constructed not simply around the individual and their lineage defined monadically, but around a series of dyadic relationships arising from the person and their *ewúúm*, mediated through their respective places of residence and the behaviours appropriate to their own and others' 'doubles'. This and other instances of human–animal relations show that it is a mistake to put human and animal experience into separate compartments: it utterly misses the richness of the entanglement of human and animal. Similarly, the practice of Chimbu women breastfeeding piglets arose neither from feelings of abjection nor as a response to a threat from the animal realm (see Figure 1.6). The pig was often nurtured by spells also used to protect humans. The keys to this relationship are proximity, value and affection.[31]

---

[27] Antl-Weiser 2018: 66.
[28] The theme of animality runs through Bataille's work. See Pawlett 2016: 1–19.
[29] Kristeva 1982: 12.   [30] Sapir 1977.   [31] Oliver 1989, Fowke 1995 and Sillitoe 2003.

Figure 1.6 Chimbu woman breastfeeding a piglet, 1939. Peter Skinner: Ian Skinner Collection/Science Source. 1494781.

As far as we can tell from ethnographic comparisons and from the testimony of rock art and other artefacts of early human culture, from the earliest times of human consciousness animals have been present as creators, ancestors, guides and sometimes competitors. The animal dimension of human experience is pervasive and finds expression in the deepest structures of human society, expressed in song, dance, figural art and combined performances. It is enormously powerful, because if humans exist in a here-and-now, we also exist in a there-and-then. In the Dreamtime animals crossed the land, leaving their traces in lake, stream, hill and cave, which we create afresh in dance, song, initiation and ritual. At the corroboree all these performances cohere. Peter Sutton sees this human incarnation of the Dreaming as temporary, in contrast with the Dreaming itself, which 'pre-exists and persists'.[32] The contrast, however, is potentially misleading. Animal and land spirits are channelled and accessed by human participants led by their shaman in the coroborree, For example, in an episode, recorded in 1938, the old barnmarn (poet, medicine man and shaman) Allan Balbungu teaches other Worrora men his songs, after which he passes into a trance described by one of the others present, Ngarinyin man David Mowaljarlai:

> Yeah. You see him breathing but he gone. He travelling. And that's how uh they compose corroborree there. Juunba. When they get all the story

---

[32] Sutton 2003: 117.

belong to every Wunggud, snake story, Wondjina story, any animal. We dance now. They teach us now. That how he go. It's all round the nature power. Power all belong nature. We get all the power from land. That's why it's important.[33]

Here there exists a consubstantiality, in which place, animal and human are intimately intermingled.

The oldest cave paintings recently discovered in limestone caves on the Indonesian island of Sulawesi also illustrate the deep antiquity of the human/animal encounter. The warty pig depicted on the wall of Leang Tedongnge dates to 45,500 years ago, while nearby at Leang Bulu' Sipong 4, a panel 4.5 m long depicts a hunting scene.[34] Various local animals, pigs and anoas (pygmy buffaloes), are being roped or speared by eight or more theriomorphic figures. The scene has been dated to at least 43,500 BP, and is the most recent evidence that the earliest figurative art created by humans arose in response to our complex relationship with animals. If the theriomorphs in these paintings represent humans draped in animal skins to approach their prey, it only goes further towards supporting the notion that hybridity is one of our most deeply rooted mechanisms for symbolically shaping the world around us. The Sumatran paintings confirm Jacques Cauvin's claim that the earliest figural representations were of women and animals, and that these are evidence for the beginnings of a richer engagement with the natural world that helped the shaping of early human consciousness.[35] As the objects of immensely stimulating experiences, especially hunting and killing, these animals are woven into the fabric of the human psyche grappling with life and death. Not coincidentally, the earliest repertoire of images created by early humans focuses on the locus of birth and life: the female body. Narration, allegory and symbolic thinking all have their source in these experiences, focused on the female and the animal. The constant repetition of these intense interactions with animals – tracking, chasing, lying in ambush, waiting, pouncing –

---

[33] See Lommel and Mowaljarlai 1994: 286–7. This is a remarkable account based first on the notes taken by a German anthropologist (Andreas Lommel) during his time in the Kimberleys in 1938. More than half a century later, in 1993, Lommel's draft was offered to David Mowaljarlai for comment. Mowaljarlai, a Ngarinyin man of the Brrejirad (Pink Hibiscus) clan, was thirteen years old at the time of Lommel's visit and had first-hand memories of the corroboree supervised by Allan Balbungu. See also Hume 2004. Wunggud may refer both to a creator earth snake and to places of concentrated earth power, usually marked by pools of fresh water. Wonjina (also Wandjina) refers to a Raingod creator, usually depicted as a white figure shrouded in cloud and mist.

[34] Leang Tedongnge: Brumm et al. 2021; Leang Bulu' Sipong 4: Aubert et al. 2019.

[35] Cauvin 1994. See also Helmer et al. 2004.

stimulates a range of responses from scanning and stalking to killing. This is a world before domestication.[36]

In Cauvin's scheme, animal and female figures are the first figural representations made by men, outgrowths of the symbolic thinking and consciousness taking shape in the Neolithic. The spectacular finds at Göbekli Tepe (ca. 9,000 BC) in south-eastern Turkey demonstrate conclusively that before farming, and even before the domestication of plants and animals, human groups were taking shape as cult communities for whom the proximity with animals was a stimulus for symbolic communication, probably aided by intoxicants such as early forms of beer and wine.[37] At Göbekli Tepe pillars are carved with bird-like creatures, some with the heads of raptors and with human-like legs, while at both Göbekli Tepe and Çatalhöyük, according to Ian Hodder and Lynn Meskell, 'the birds that are associated with the headless bodies have human traits or adopt a hybrid human/animal form'.[38] Rather than separating themselves from the animal realm, the people of Göbekli Tepe experienced a world in which the human and animal domains constantly overlapped. In this respect they continued the traditions that clearly go back into the Palaeolithic, where encounters with the animal had already produced hybrids. A similar picture can be seen at Karahan Tepe, approximately 80 km from Göbekli Tepe, where 266 T-pillars have been found, some of these are carved with anthropomorphic arms and animal legs.

One way of reading these pillars would be to view them as markers of affiliation to the land or as assertions of group identity employing totemic animals. Traditional societies frequently use animals such as the emu, leopard and raven as markers of expressing a group identity. In some instances these may serve as caste designations – leopard men, for example, being warriors and hunters. Or they define exogamous moieties; in the northern Kimberleys, the men of the Kuranguli (black crane) line only marry women of the Banar (bush turkey) moiety.[39] In yet other instances

---

[36] It is not credible that the development of symbolic thinking and communication occurred only among men. Marija Gimbutas postulated a complementary world of symbols and shapes that arose in a female sphere; see Gimbutas 1989. From 'female' symbols such as the chevron and triangle Gimbutas famously extrapolated an entire reconstruction of a peaceful matriarchal Neolithic European culture. Few archaeologists accept this system in its entirety, but for a sympathetic evaluation see Christ 1996.

[37] For animal images at Göbekli Tepe, see McGovern 2009, Schmidt 2010, Dietrich et al. 2012: 684, 687–98 and Clare et al. 2018. Wengrow 2014: 40 downplays the animal images from Göbekli Tepe, arguing that 'they make very little play on the possibilities of composite depiction.' Contra, see Gifford and Antonello 2015: 275, who claim 'that the association of animal and human is in fact present virtually, anticipating implicitly ... hybrid forms'.

[38] Hodder and Meskell 2011: 247.   [39] Lommel and Mowaljarlai 1994: 281.

the raven may bring sacred knowledge, the control of which is both significant for the status of the knowledge-keeper and helps maintain group solidarity through the orderly transmission of secret knowledge through initiation. Entire lodges organize and distribute resources such as whale hunting or salmon fishing in deliberate and rational ways for the continuing health of the community and the curating of the resources of the natural world on which we depend for survival.[40] All these cases, drawn from a variety of cultures, are examples of the different roles played by our animal awareness in the expression of group identities – a stunning range of operations lurking behind the single term 'totemism'.[41] If Karahan Tepe and Göbekli Tepe are the earliest examples of monumental architecture systematically deployed at a site of communal sacrifice and ritual, the presence of animals in both the faunal remains and in the iconographic programme proves that from the first moments when human societies grew beyond the limits of the hunting band, animals shaped our awareness of life, death, violence and the cycle of being that governs our lives.[42] Animals taught us to be human, and there is a persistent impulse to reaffirm our humanity by minimizing the difference between human and animals.[43] Instead of a barrier we see a bond so powerful that the boundary between human and animal frequently disappears.[44] As Elizabeth Grosz puts it, 'Animals continue to haunt man's imagination, compel him to seek out their habits, preferences and cycles, and provide models and formulae by which he comes to represent his own desires, needs and excitements.'[45]

The close entanglement of human and animal is especially evident in folklore, where the proximity of the animal extends well beyond pet cats

---

[40] On the intersection between animal stories and ecological awareness, see Pierotti 2020: 50, who notes that such stories 'demonstrate connection, respect, and how to live properly in a world filled with nonhuman beings'.

[41] The study of totemism has a long history. See Durkheim 1912, Lang 1911 and, more recently, Kuper 2005. For a description of various animal and hybrid forms as part of a coherent visual language appropriate to funerary rites across a swathe of Steppe cultures, see Andreeva 2018.

[42] On the symbolism and iconography of Göbleki Tepe, see Gifford and Antonello 2015. As they observe (266), the T-shaped pillars are carved with arms, hands and clothing, revealing their anthropomorphic character. On the totemic significance of this, see Peters and Schmidt 2004: 209.

[43] The animal-guardian has been a remarkably resilient figure in popular culture. In addition to dogs (Lassie and Rin Tin Tin), we have also had dolphins (Flipper) and kangaroos (Skippy).

[44] A Belgian Malinois, Kuga, was awarded a medal for bravery in 2018, having been shot in Afghanistan seven years earlier. The language used to describe the dog's actions are no different to a citation one would expect for a human combatant: 'Kuga's sacrifice was an ultimate sacrifice. The reason he got the Dickin Medal was he just was so courageous.' https://thenewdaily.com.au/news/national/2018/10/26/kuga-the-adf-war-dog-bravery-award/.

[45] Grosz 1995: 278. For animals in popular culture, see Baker 1993 and Chris 2006: 1–44.

and dogs. In an early twentieth-century work on the folklore of Florence, Rev. J. Wood Brown noted three kinds of monsters that might attack children born between 25 December and 6 January (the boundary between one year and the next): the *callicantzaros*, the werewolf and the vampire.[46] The first he describes as 'shaggy, black and wild, in whose name some vestige has been found of the classic centaur'. Like the *callicantzaros*, the werewolf too challenges the categories of human and animal, not by blending but by transformation, while the third, the vampire, breaks down the boundary between life and death. These are instances of hybrid monsters giving shape to a community's fears that boundaries are sites of danger, that they may collapse. Here, as elsewhere, the shape emerging from our imaginative response is frequently hybrid, because hybrids foreground boundaries. In the case of the *callicantzaros* and his cousins, their composite bodies destabilize the boundaries between categories.

The Plan of the Book

From the Neolithic to the Iron Age, cultures around the Mediterranean were deeply influenced by the intimate bonds between human and animal. The immediate result of this fundamental condition of connectedness was the prevalence throughout the eastern Mediterranean of hybrids, born of the merging of the human and the animal. These would appear in many guises in Greek culture, becoming one of its most characteristic features, yet, as the brief examination of the sphinx has demonstrated, hybrids are polymorphous, polysemic and polyvalent. In order to arrive at a better understanding of hybridity I suggest, therefore, approaching the phenomenon from various angles. In Part I explore some of the complications of defining hybrids and developing theories of hybridity. This may seem unnecessary; after all, most people can recognize a centaur by identifying its parts, but form and function are very different beasts. Hybrids aside, hybridity is a term used very loosely in cultural studies, where any aspect of cultural and individual identity characterized by mixing is a hybrid, from fusion cuisine to hip-hop sampling. A study of hybridity runs the risk of being about everything and nothing. Certainly, in classical studies and Mediterranean archaeology the term has often been used as a shorthand for many kinds of culture contact, and so I suggest greater care in how the term is applied. It is better to apply a rather literal interpretation

---

[46] Brown 1911: 287–8.

of hybridity, grounded in the history of hybrid figures combining animal and human parts, as a corrective to the flawed view that any mixture is a hybrid. For the most part I restrict this study to hybrids that are composites of human and animal, or male and female bodies. Not only does this clarify exactly what does and does not count as a hybrid, it also invites us to see hybrids evolving out of our earliest involvement with animals.

The need for both clarity of definition and a theoretical framework is addressed further in Chapter 2, which also asks whether a comprehensive theory of hybridity is even possible. I do not aspire, like *Middlemarch*'s Casaubon, to find a universal key to all hybrids, but rather to identify the various fields in which hybridity operated in the Greek world. At the same time, this should not be taken to mean that a study of hybridity in Greek culture amounts to no more than a catalogue of odd mythological creatures. In other words, I hope to respect the particularity of hybrids – Skylla, Medusa, Pegasos – while identifying the features that are common to hybrids as cultural products. (Hint: they're anomalies.) Recent work in monster theory offers some guidance, emphasizing the role of monsters in policing the borders of what is normative. Monsters have repeatedly been interpreted as threats to order. I suggest that hybrids, as anomalies, undermine the very categories from which order is constructed. As a mode of cultural production hybrids are a means of coping with that which defies neat classification. This may veer towards the monstrous, as in the case of the demonic female figure, the gorgon, but equally it can tend towards the curious and the wondrous, like Pegasos alighting at the Peirene Fountain in Corinth or the horses of Achilles grieving for the death of Patroklos. In trying to understand how and why the Greeks generated hybrids in their mythology it may seem that I am trying to put the Greeks on the psychiatrist's couch, but Freud's conception of the uncanny sheds some light, I hope to show, on how hybrids function. I navigate between the Skylla of reading every mixture as a hybrid and the Charybdis of treating hybridity as monster-lite by sticking to a narrow course: the path of anomaly.

Part II of the book opens the aperture of the study to bring non-Greek monsters and hybrids into focus. In Chapter 3, I examine the Near Eastern antecedents of the familiar hybrids of Greek myth and art. This may be thought of as a shallow dive into the deep history of hybrids in the Mediterranean world, going back to various cultures of the Ancient Near East, Egypt, Crete and Cyprus. The danger here, of course, is to confuse origin with explanation. Nevertheless, Greek hybrids do not simply pop up like mushrooms after a rain shower and a greater danger would be to consider them in isolation, as if they had emerged fully formed from the head of Zeus, like armed Athena. The disciplinary boundaries between the Classical World and the Ancient Near East have meant that Greek historians move into such territory at their own risk, but it is impossible to write about early Greek culture without giving some consideration to eastern antecedents. Walter Burkert, Martin West and Jan Bremmer, to name only three major scholars, have demonstrated that the Greek imagination was powerfully influenced by a creative engagement with eastern cultures.[47] I am not arguing for an earlier generation's notion of diffusionism, whereby eastern motifs are simply 'borrowed' by the Greek poets, but rather endorsing a view of the eastern Mediterranean as a place of endless fluid engagements characterized by bilingualism, intermarriage and the movement of artisans, traders, poets and itinerant religious practitioners.[48] Indeed, much of my writing about these processes of cultural transmission is meant to signal that hybrids were like vessels that could carry different contents depending on the audience or the market. I compare material from the Ancient Near East such as *Enuma Elish* and the *Gilgamesh* epic with Homeric and Hesiodic accounts of similar episodes to underscore the congruence of Greek and Near Eastern cosmogonies. And, just as often as an echo of Akkadian or Sumerian can be heard behind the Greek voices of the eighth and seventh centuries, I am also keen to show how and where Greek sensibilities respond creatively to source material, adapting it freely in new settings. As a complement to this attempt to situate Greek hybrids in a broader East Mediterranean setting, I also consider recent work on the so-called International Style of the Late Bronze Age, which relied heavily on hybrid motifs to fashion a shared visual language for the elites of Egypt and the Near East. Located on the edge of this culturally enmeshed zone, Greece and Crete were influenced by the cultural productions emanating from the power centres of Egypt and Mesopotamia, but wherever we find traces of cultural exchange, ideas and objects always take on new forms in Greek settings. This is not the result of innate genius, but rather a function of the differences between the imperial states of the eastern Mediterranean and the smaller communities of Greece and Crete. In fact, since hybrids are not restricted by having to correspond to a 'real' avatar, there is no simple line of transmission from either Mesopotamia or Egypt to Greece, and in each instance of a hybrid emerging in a Greek context it is testimony to the flexibility of hybrids to convey new meanings in new settings. The Minotaur, as we shall see, is not merely royal authority wearing a crown of horns.

---

[47] Burkert 1988 and 1992; West 1997; Bremmer 2008.   [48] López-Ruiz 2010: 23–47.

In Chapter 4, I move from this general discussion of hybridity in the cultures of the eastern Mediterranean to a more specific cluster of hybrids crucial to the Greeks and their setting: the sea. After looking at the Mediterranean as a zone of rich contact, characterized by the movement of goods, people and ideas, I examine the sea as the element from which hybrids arise, such as Skylla, Nereus, the Nereids and other, more monstrous figures in Hesiod's *Theogony*. These hybrids shape and give expression to the fears and aspirations of Greek speakers on the move. In this discussion, the existence of contact zones such as Sicily stimulates a powerful response from Greek speakers, who are compelled constantly to undergo confrontations with other people, other tongues, other styles. Hybridity emerges as a useful mechanism for envisaging otherness and rendering it manageable, either as monstrous threat or as something in a more muted register: recognizable, similar, yet at the same time different, like the prow of a Phoenician ship. It is this polarity of similarity and difference that is the pendulum swinging through Archaic Greek culture. Focusing on two places of particularly rich cultural encounters, Naukratis and Samos, I tease out the ways in which the categories of exotic and hybrid map onto each other, suggesting an eclecticism for which hybrid objects are a fitting expression. Even more complicated is Cyprus, which, in this reading of the Iron Age, demonstrates the most intense cultural layering in the eastern Mediterranean. It is hardly coincidental that where EteoCypriots, Mycenaean Greeks, Assyrians and Phoenicians all mingle and merge, hybridity should be a recurring feature of the island's culture.

In Part III, I turn to a series of case studies designed to illustrate the central importance of hybrids to the culture of Archaic and Classical Greece. Chapter 5 begins with griffins and gorgons, exploring the connections between wondrous objects and the depiction of hybrid creatures. At the same time, the clear connection between gorgons and the toxic demonization of women reintroduces gender into the study of hybrids, a theme going back to the earliest hybrid monsters of cosmogenic myth. Developing the theme of gendered hybridity, this chapter juxtaposes the demonic gorgon and the female demons threatening mothers and children with the satyr, an exaggerated figure of the man identified by and with his penis. These matched exaggerations, by turns horrific and comic, illustrate the function of the hybrid as a projection of certain human anxieties along the lines of thought experiments: what if the man were no more than his erection? What if the woman were as dangerous as she is beautiful? What if a mother devoured her children instead of protecting them? Each caricature exists as an alternative to the ordinary men and women encountered in our daily lives, but in recognizing these alternatives the Greeks are also using the contrafactual to ask what exactly it means to be human. For this reason, transformation is a recurring theme in early Greek culture, with a wide range of applications. The hybrids born of transformation appear on the stage, especially the comic stage, exuberantly breaking down the barrier between human and animal, but also in religious contexts, especially linked to initiation. Even the different forms and faces worn by the gods arise from our experience of the cosmos as a space of entanglement. If a human shares some characteristics with an animal, does the divine also partake of this mutability? When the gods resemble men and women, what is the significance of their animal avatars?

Chapter 6 focuses on the horse. Here is the best evidence for the distinction between the monster and the hybrid, since no horses or equine hybrids were considered entirely monstrous, with the exception of the flesh-eating Mares of Diomedes. Instead, the intimacy of horse and horseman resulted in a generally positive set of associations. Horse riding, as opposed to chariot driving, was actually a relatively recent development in Archaic Greece, and the hybrid figures of riders fused to their horses reveal that this was a psychologically charged experience. This is entirely understandable given that riding requires control of an animal much more powerful than the rider. Furthermore, as possibly the best-known hybrid in the Greek bestiary, the centaur is a perfect illustration of how in form and function hybrids can be immensely flexible. Some centaurs are human cap-a-pie, with a horse's rear end jutting out of the middle of the creature's human back. Others exhibit the more familiar human head and torso rising from the horse's withers. This might seem no more than a stylistic variation until one considers that the centaur is frequently used as a symbol of unrestrained lust. The change in form forces the audience or viewer to consider uncomfortable questions regarding sexuality and animality. There is also a greater complexity to horse hybrids than a simple externalization of sex drives, since the complete opposite of centaur behaviour is embodied in another centaur: Cheiron, the tutor of heroes. Pegasos, too, reflects a different way of imagining a horse hybrid: not with a human body but with wings. Here, the horse figure is the hero's companion and makes possible monster slaying. In all these ways, the horse emerges as much more than a beast firmly fixed one rung below humans in an Aristotelian chain of being. More powerful than the human, less civilized than the human, a symbol of sexual aggression challenging the human, matched with the human, the horse and its hybrid cousin, the centaur, capture the kaleidoscopic nature of being and identity in the Archaic Greek world: not fixed and categorically neat, but refracted, shifting, unstable.

Shifting associations and unstable meaning are also a feature of the class of hybrids studied in Chapter 7: snakes. Despite the appearance of snake deities in a variety of religious systems, no precise antecedents suggest an external point of origin for the snake hybrid figures of Athenian myth in the Archaic period. Rather, the presence of human/snake hybrids appears to have been an Athenian invention, the snake's connections with the earth and rebirth providing a suitable form for expressing the Athenian claim to autochthony. This was not an uncomplicated claim. For some aristocratic *gene*, such as the Eteoboutadai, autochthony marked them as superior to more recent arrivals, but the foundational myth of Athens, involving the birth of Erichthonios after Hephaistos' attempted rape of Athena, was tinged with incest and pollution, indicating a degree of ambivalence towards autochthony. A significant reason for this is that traditions of snake-bodied kings and daimons reflected a conception of the past that was conceptually both near and far from the present. The hybridity of the snake-figured ancestor connected them to a deep mythic past, but also bridged the gap that separated the present and connected past (recent, measurable, similar) from the plupast (long ago, primordial, aorist, alien). This was a particular concern in the sixth century, as new notions of national identity, place and embeddedness were taking shape. Bluebeard, the famous pedimental sculpture from the Archaic Akropolis, embodies this. This chapter argues for identifying Bluebeard as the Tritopatores, ancestral deities of the Athenians, who mark the emergence of the recent past from that primordial time of monsters that preceded it. These and other hybrids signify the continuous irruption of the deep past into the current world, a condition that produced a creative tension between order and chaos.

Chapter 8 is a discussion of another source of tension: the anxieties within (conventionally cisgendered) communities facing the complex realities of transgender identities, sexual binarism, dysphoria and other aspects of what Luc Brisson has termed 'sexual ambivalence'. While the underlying issues are complex and arise from the broad gamut of possibilities created by human sexuality, anatomy and cultural practices, ancient discourse tended to reduce this to a simple binary according to which conventional constructions of cisgendered bodies contrasted with a single representation of anomaly: the hermaphrodite. But the varieties of sexed bodies and gendered performances resist oversimplification, and a close analysis of the story of Hermaphroditos told in his hometown of Halikarnassos shows that different iterations of the story conveyed very different messages: from Hermaphroditos, the emasculated figure combining both male and female in a single epicene hybrid, to Hermaphroditos, the child of Hermes and Aphrodite, the perfect union of male and female and a model for the ideal married couple. Detecting another polarity embodied in the figure of Hermaphroditos, specifically the ethnic difference between indigenous Karian and exogenous Greek, we find sexual hybridity and ethnic categorization operating in tandem and recursively: one group's culture hero (as founder of marriage) becomes another's intersex monstrosity. Hermaphroditos is only one example of a body undergoing sexual transformation, and other figures such as Teiresias, Kaineus and even cross-dressing Achilles illustrate that in counterpoint to a normative understanding of sex and gender in Greek society there existed a space for imagining alternatives to the classes and categories of conventional thinking. At the same time, an imaginative space is not a revolutionary manifesto, and sexual anomaly (as it appears in ancient thinking) illustrates a trajectory of Greek culture beginning in the Classical period: hybrids and anomalous bodies become partly decorative and, in literary works, interesting paradoxes, while their power to shock is largely relegated to the sphere of magic. Here and in other spheres of social praxis, the category of the strangely familiar allowed Greeks to play with different constructions of being human.

In Part IV, two chapters take the discussion beyond the Archaic and Classical World to examine the later history of Greek hybrids and hybridity. Chapter 9 presents the argument that hybrids were an integral feature of the classificatory schemes that accompanied the acquisition and organization of information parallel to the control of territory in the wider Mediterranean world and beyond after Alexander. Texts produced by Hanno, Ktesias and Megasthenes reveal the slippage that allows ethnographic description to mutate into exercises in ordering hierarchies of both animals and humans, so attractive to readers that even authors sceptical of increasingly fantastic tales full of magical hybrid beasts nevertheless continued to spice up their histories and travel accounts with them. The fabulous assumed a life of its own thanks to the importance of marking out the farthest limits of certainty and imperial control by populating it with the incredible, the mutant and the monstrous. Literary accounts of exotic lands mirrored the menageries and displays of the Ptolemies, Seleukids and later Roman emperors. In these accounts, India played an especially significant role. It was a mirror image of the Mediterranean, yet far enough away to also generate anomalous wonders on its borders. It was not merely the exotic animals of distant lands, such as camels, leopards and giraffes, that astonished the Greek subjects of Hellenistic kings, but also the descriptions of anomalous humans, such as Blemmyes, Dog-Heads and Skiapods, that confirmed an orderly Mediterranean world of properly recognizable humanity, the edges of which were populated by the monstrous, the ugly and the deformed. Ethnography and paradoxography were therefore highly conservative genres that provided hierarchies structured on normality and anomaly to reinforce order. It was in philosophy and literary criticism that hybridity continued to represent both an opportunity and a challenge. As a contrafactual the hybrid invites reflection on what is fitting, what is appropriate to a genre and whether beauty and harmony can be found in forms that are mixed. And even more than these aesthetic questions are the ontological and epistemological quandaries posed by the hybrid: if a centaur never existed and could never have existed, how can we dream it up? Why do we imagine it? The contrafactuality of the hybrid proved to be a Trojan horse within the secure citadel of ancient philosophy.

There is, however, another aspect of the hybrid that deserves attention. Perhaps like other people, the Greeks created a culture that seemed secure and well ordered, in which status, gender and identity appeared to be if not fixed, then at least clear-cut. A free man knew his place and his privileges, a foreigner was aware of the disabilities under which he laboured, an enslaved woman had a fair idea of her lot, a worker in the mines of Laureion even more so. Yet, as I suggest in the final chapter, lived experience was in fact more precarious for all the Greeks than perhaps we recognize. The rich man could lose his fortune, the highborn girl could be shipwrecked and enslaved. These are not just the plot devices of Hellenistic novels; they are the possible experiences of men and women for whom vulnerability and impermanence were as real as wealth and good fortune. These conditions favoured expressions – stories and images in particular – that made change and anomaly part of the cultural repertoire of the Greeks. It is perhaps for this reason that the vivid, vibrant hybrids of the Greek imagination attracted so much attention from Christian writers of late antiquity and beyond. By raising the possibility of other ways of engaging with the world, and by offering alternatives to the settled order of things, hybrids would always be a threat to those attempting to impose their order on the world: demons that demanded to be slain.

2 | 'Welcome to Athens'

Theories of Hybridity

> The 'fox-goose' (vulpanser, shelduck) derives its name from the natural characteristics of each of these creatures, because while it looks like a goose, for trickery it really is most comparable to the fox.
>
> Aelian, *De Animal.* 5.30 (trans. McInerney)[1]

Hybrids and Monsters

Fans were delighted to find, during the Covid-19 outbreak of 2020, that Gary Larson, creator of *The Far Side*, had returned to producing his pithy evocations of the absurd. In one image, an artist suffering from artist's block sits in front his easel, waiting for inspiration before he applies the final strokes to a nearly finished painting. It is a painting of a cow – four legs, body, udder and tail – but the artist cannot decide which head should finish the composition. A thought bubble above his head shows a menagerie of Larsonesque possibilities: donkey, rhinoceros, duck, crocodile. The humour relies on incongruity, because we know exactly what should go on a cow's body: a cow's head.[2] None of the possibilities in the artist's head fit. Each would produce a weird hybrid. I begin with this description of a cartoon for a reason: incongruity is not inherently terrifying. Larson's hybrid possibilities are funny, not scary. Accordingly, hybrids do not neatly map on to the class of monsters. Of course, some do. In Hesiod's account of the creation of the earth, monsters are frequently the offspring of elemental forces like Night and Fear, their monstrosity connoted by their hybridity: Echidna is 'half fair-cheeked and bright-eyed nymph, and half huge and monstrous snake'.[3] Since many hybrids – such as Echidna, Medusa and Kerberos, to name only three – could be considered monstrous, the recent vogue for monster theory might seem

---

[1] Compare Kafka's *Crossbreed*: 'It has the restlessness of both beasts, that of the cat and that of the lamb, diverse as they are. For that reason its skin feels too tight for it'; Kafka 1971: 468.

[2] On the incongruity theory of humour, see Clark 1970 and Watson 2015.

[3] Hes. *Theog.* 297–8 (tr. Athanassakis). On the 'donna formosa, donna mostruosa', see Visintin 1997.

Figure 2.1 Bronze figure of winged horse. Northwestern Greece (perhaps Ambrakia), third quarter of the sixth century BC. From Dodona in Epirus. Louvre Br149 © Marie-Lan Nguyen/Wikimedia Commons. CC BY 3.0.

a plausible point of entry into the strange world of hybrids. But not all hybrids are monsters: the winged horse from Dodona is unlikely to have scared anyone (Figure 2.1). Accordingly, we should be careful not to treat monster theory and hybrid theory as interchangeable.

The most comprehensive study of monster theory is the influential study by Jeffrey Jerome Cohen, who begins with an uncontestable statement: 'We live in a time of monsters.'[4] To orient the reader towards an understanding of this ubiquitous phenomenon he advances seven theses:

- The Monster's Body is a Cultural Body
- The Monster always escapes
- The Monster is a Harbinger of Category Crisis
- The Monster dwells at the Gates of Difference
- The Monster polices the Borders of the Possible
- Fear of the Monster is really a Kind of Desire
- The Monster stands at the Threshold … of becoming

Monsters, it seems, do some pretty heavy lifting when it comes to cultural work.[5] At the same time, all seven theses recognize that monsters threaten what is normative and conventional. Richard Buxton reminds us

---

[4] Cohen 1996: vii. For his seven theses, see pp. 3–25. On monster theory, see also Weinstock 2020 and Wright 2013.
[5] See, for example, the various types catalogued by Gilmore 2003.

that 'a monster is chaotic, conforming to no existing class'.[6] Or, as Foucault put it, 'the transgression of natural limits, the transgression of classifications ... this is the real question of monstrosity'.[7] Monsters, in fact, reveal what we fear, especially that which threatens to up-end the order of things. Monsters patrol the boundaries of the permissible and the illicit. In the oath of Plataea, for example, the Athenians committed themselves to the defence of their city with the following imprecation:

> And if I keep true to what has been written in the oath may my city be free from sickness, if not, may it be sick; and may my city be unravaged, but if not may it be ravaged; and my [land] bear, but if not, may it be barren; and may the women bear children like their parents, but if not, monsters; and may the animals bear young like the animals, but if not, monsters.
>
> (Rhodes-Osborne *GHI* 88 39–45)[8]

Here the defence of territory is combined with the fecundity of the land and its people, as well as their proper ethical disposition; the opposites of this propriety are illness, barrenness and monstrosity. As we shall see, the problem of classification is central to the role of hybrids as well. If the monster is a 'taxonomical anomaly', the hybrid is a particular variant on this confusion, but one that would prove surprisingly useful for the Greeks and their imaginative response to the world around them.[9]

In part the hybrid's power arises from the very fact that hybridity is not identical to monstrosity: Cheiron, a centaur, famously tutors heroes such as Achilles, and depictions of him wearing chiton and himation with his horsey rump exposed behind emphasize his hybridity as a duality of form only. In behaviour and bearing he is a *kalos k'agathos*, the model of a gentleman *erastes* wooing his young charge, tutoring heroes in advanced arts such as medicine and music (see Figure 2.2). In the Herculaneum fresco the centaur's horsey parts are painted in shadow and deemphasized, while the skin tones of his human torso are closer to those of the young hero. As he gestures towards the lyre, coaching his mentee, their lower legs mirror each other, even down to the shape of foot and hoof. In another culturally charged setting, the symposium, centaurs such as Pholos recline

---

[6] Buxton 1994. [7] Foucault 2003.
[8] For discussion of the inscription, see Rhodes and Osborne 2003: 443–8. Krentz 2007 identifies this inscription as the Oath of Marathon, but see Cartledge 2013 for a more nuanced treatment of the inscription as a fourth-century invention.
[9] Lada-Richards 1998. Sperber (1975: 7) similarly notes that 'Hybrides, monstres ou hybrides monstrueux, les animaux fantastiques, par ailleurs si divers, ont tous en commun d'être des aberrations taxinomiques' (Hybrids, monsters, or monstrous hybrids, fantastic animals, no matter how different have this in common: they are taxonomic aberrations).

Figure 2.2 The Education of Achilles by Chiron, fresco from Herculaneum, first century AD (Museo Archeologico Nazionale, Naples, 9109) Photo: Public domain.

at a banquet. If the symposium is the height of culture, the centaur shows himself as capable of refinement, even as the smell of wine sends other centaurs crazy. Hybrids, therefore, are not a simple subset of monsters. They share with monsters the potential to serve as a counterpoint to our humanity, helping to define oppositionally the category we inhabit, yet at other times they blur the boundaries and suggest a space at a tangent to the conventional. This complexity is sometimes played out over generations: Pegasos, with the wings of an eagle and the body of a horse, is not a monster but is born of the blood of decapitated Medusa. Here the hybrid may be closer to the Derridean notion of the supplément: not a straightforward antithesis to the human as is the monster, but a *tertium quid* which may add to but also threaten the logic, categories and conventions that define the human.[10]

---

[10] Derrida 1998: 141–64. One might object that Derrida's exploration of this notion is primarily designed to tease out the relationship of writing to speech, and speech to thought, alluded to in Rousseau's *Confessions* and *Discourses*, but both Rousseau and Derrida deploy this as a heuristic device in a dazzling array of situations. See, for example, Rousseau's ruminations on mining: 'The wan faces of the unhappy people who languish in the poisonous vapors of mines, of black forgemen, of hideous cyclops, are the spectacle which the working of the mine substitutes, in the heart [womb] of the earth for that of green fields and flowers', Rousseau 1927: 145. The act of

The Anomalous

A useful way of identifying this third category is to consider hybrids, whether monstrous or not, as falling into a different class: they are anomalies. In her influential study of pollution and taboo, Mary Douglas addressed the existence of the anomalous, which she correctly saw as both inevitable and yet challenging: 'Any given system of classification must give rise to anomalies, and any given culture must confront events which seem to defy its assumptions. It cannot ignore the anomalies which its scheme produces, except at risk of forfeiting confidence.'[11] According to Douglas, societies respond in various ways to the threat embodied in the anomalous. Rituals and propitiatory actions are deployed to restore the natural order. So, for example, a monstrous birth might be construed as a threat to the boundary between human and animal, leading to the exposure of the child. Citing Evans-Pritchard's famous study of the Nuer, she notes that 'the Nuer treat monstrous births as baby hippopotamuses, accidentally born to humans and, with this labelling, the appropriate action is clear. They gently lay them in the river where they belong.'[12] In subsequent work Douglas recognized that the existence of the anomalous called for more than a simple functionalist explanation of challenge and response. Anomalies exposed the fundamental uncertainty of systems. This exposure is on display in two areas of communication: the joke and the insult. Regarding the former, Douglas argued that the power of the joke arose from giving expression to the realization 'that an accepted pattern has no necessity. Its excitement lies in the suggestion that experience may be arbitrary and subjective.'[13] Similarly, Edmund Leach drew attention to the classificatory in-betweenness of many animals used as insults in English.[14] Cristiana Franco has neatly summarized the point:

> In Leach's analysis it turned out that the insulting animal names come mainly from species that occupy an ambiguous position in the classification scheme, in a poorly defined space between one category and another: those animals closest to but not identical with humans and so not entirely friendly but not completely wild and hostile either. For being unclassifiable, such species are perceived with a certain anxiety and tension and are subject to taboo, whether explicit or unconscious.[15]

---

substitution referred to is precisely the broader notion of the supplement that we can apply to hybridity.
[11] Douglas 1966: 40. [12] Douglas 1966: 40. [13] Douglas 1968: 365. [14] Leach 1964: 23–63.
[15] Franco 2014: 11.

Cultures require space for uncertainty and for the free movement of ideas, images and forms that have at least the potential to subvert. Viewed from this perspective, an all-encompassing theory of hybridity comparable to the monster theory with which we began is going to be a challenge. Furthermore, leaving aside the metaphorical use of hybridity as a way of locating cultural production under unequal conditions of power, as does Bhabha, by limiting the hybrid to a more restricted and limited range of images and constructs, we find hybridity as a mental operation of unusual flexibility, expressing alternative realities, hinting at other types of existence, giving form to anxieties, fears and sometimes wonder. In short, the hybrid is the product and the proof of the rich entanglement of Greek speakers in an eastern Mediterranean world that moved fluidly from hostility to peaceful exchange of goods and ideas. If Greece was constantly exposed to a high degree of cultural contact and exchange, this can only have exposed the Greeks to many different ways of being in the world, further calling attention to the subjectivity of how we organize our social life. When Douglas identifies a strategy of using ambiguous symbols to enrich meaning and 'to call attention to other levels of existence', her remarks are a perfect encapsulation of why hybrids are a recurring element in Greek culture.[16] Whenever the otherness of the wider world impinged on the Greek world, hybrids were there to give shape to that alterity.

This is not to say that hybrids primarily exist to explain phenomena. Rather, their significance lies in their capacity to render phenomena into forms that elicit a variety of responses ranging from revulsion (Skylla) to wonder (Pegasos). They are arresting because they blend the familiar and the odd. They are, in fact, good examples of Freud's notion of the *Unheimlich*. They are dimly recognizable, yet they have a dreamlike quality that arrests without repelling. Freud defined the *Unheimlich* this way: 'The uncanny is that class of the frightening which goes back to what was once well known and had long been familiar.'[17] The uncanny is therefore not entirely alien. Beal puts it well: 'For Freud the unheimlich is only "outside the house" (the house of the self, the house of culture, the house of the cosmos) insofar as it is hidden within the house. It is a revelation not of the wholly other but of a repressed otherness within the self.'[18] The monster is

---

[16] Douglas 1966: 39–40. Sperber (1975: 7) acknowledges Douglas but applies a rigid structuralist reading, according to which hybrids are taxonomical anomalies and symbolic beings: '[I]l est tentant de mettre en rapport ces deux propriétés, d'expliquer la symbolicité par l'anomalie et d'étendre l'hypothèse aux animaux réels cette fois' (It is tempting to connect these two properties [anomaly and symbolism] to explain the symbolic significance of the hybrid by the anomaly and to extend the hypothesis to real animals this time).
[17] Freud 1919 (2003): 124.   [18] Beal 2002: 8.

a personification of the *Unheimlich*, as that which has broken out of the subterranean basement, but the hybrid, also *unheimlich*, while unsettling, is not always terrifying. To understand this dissonance (as opposed to horror) caused by the hybrid we can consider an example drawn from the recent wave of arresting images that cropped up in response to the economic crisis in Greece around 2014 (see Figure 2.3).

The viewer is immediately struck by an incongruity: an innocuous body, dressed in shorts and sneakers, is topped by a grotesque, grimacing head that resembles a ragdoll with yarn hair and heavy, Frankensteinian stitching. The effect is not unlike encountering Medusa. If it is hard to avoid looking at the head one nevertheless soon notices the Molotov cocktail in the figure's hand, and the burning welcome sign, both of which are placed on the wreckage of a (real) burned-out building. But while the image is arresting, it is only horrible in the way that a nightmare recalled in the light of day is shocking. Softened, weird, powerful, the image inspires awe but not horror.

Other promising approaches to hybridity have been explored by Bakhtin, Bhabha and, most recently, Werbner. From Bakhtin we have learned to see organic hybridity as, on the one hand, unintentional and unconscious, but also 'profoundly productive historically'. Hybrids 'are pregnant with potential for new world views, with new 'internal forms'

Figure 2.3 'Welcome to Athens'. Exarchia wall art, ca. 2014. Photo: J. McInerney.

for perceiving the world'.[19] In a similar vein, Bhabha has attempted to explore the colonial encounter as a location in which hybrid forms arise, serviceable for both colonizer and colonized.[20] Even so, Bhabha's approach has limitations. As Joseph Skinner correctly observes, 'If culture is best understood, in the words of Homi K. Bhabha, as an intrinsically 'hybrid' entity, then the discursive interplay of ideas of identity and difference emerges as a thoroughly mundane activity: a reflexive positioning that could find expression in any area of cultural production.'[21] Furthermore, we have to be careful not to shoehorn the eastern Mediterranean of the first millennium BC into a post-colonial form generated only yesterday, so to speak. There is, however, at least one compelling reason for exploring hybridity in Greek culture from this angle: erasure. Colonized cultures struggle in the face of the colonial encounter, and it is a feature of the Greek world that indigenous, non-Greek cultures tend to be demonized or exoticized. Herakles' adventures in the West, for example, involve a variety of beasts, monsters and indigenes to be tamed, tricked and beaten, from Geryon to Kakos.[22] Modern studies of hybridity can stimulate us to look at how the Greeks structured a world in which they continuously encountered similarity and difference in varying degrees. Werbner, for example, reads various festivals of reversed roles using hybrid figures as modes of expressing cultural change as well as resistance to these in migrant groups and post-colonial nations.[23] It is unlikely that we will ever have the data to perform such a comprehensive reading of wider Mediterranean culture in the first millennium, but as we examine the adoption of hybrid figures from Egypt and the Near East in early Greek culture it will be worth remembering that such 'appropriations' (as we may be inclined to label them) point to a Greek culture responding richly and imaginatively to the older cultures of the Ancient Near East. How they framed the encounter with people to the west was altogether different.

It is important to recognize the polyvalence of the Greek hybrid because globalism and modernity are constantly generating new hybrids that threaten to strip hybridity of its power to shock. Some recent hybrids are

---

[19] Bakhtin 1981: 360.   [20] Bhabha 1994.   [21] Skinner 2012: 29.
[22] On Greek myth encoding the arrival of Greek customs, especially modes of sacrifice, throughout the western Mediterranean, see Lincoln 1976; D'Agostino 1996; Braun 2004; Harari 2004; McInerney 2010: 102–12. A recent equivalent to Herakles' mission would be the zombie apocalypse. As Morrissette (2014: 2) has argued, 'the discourse of fighting the zombie apocalypse delegitimizes any effort to instead solve the zombie apocalypse'. The flow-over into the 'real world' of foreign policy privileges violent solutions to complex problems, just as the monster authorizes the slaughter of indigenes.
[23] Werbner 2001.

surprising curiosities, like Thai boxing by Moroccan girls in Amsterdam, Asian rap in London or Nigerian kung fu.[24] Each ingredient in these mixes is distinct; the new form is a mash-up. They are not hugely significant, except perhaps as evidence for a contemporary taste for eclecticism. Other forms of hybridity, however, may be less innocent. A Black man who regards his dreadlocks as a statement of cultural pride may see white dreadlocks as wholly inappropriate.[25] Similarly, in the context of racial inequality, hybrids such as blue-eyed soul and white funk perform what the dreadlocks signify. Accordingly, for some, Elvis Presley singing the blues is yet another example of cultural appropriation.[26] At the same time, condemning this hybridity as the theft of Black culture risks failing to recognize the rich cultural entanglement of Blacks and Whites, particularly in the American South, without which rock and roll would not exist. Hybrids and hybridity therefore present us with many challenges. Aside from identifying the elements that make up a hybrid, we should also be alert to the significance of hybrids marking points of tension and disquiet within a culture. The hybrid may alert us to a place of rupture but also signal the emergence of a new form in response to it.

At its core, the concept of hybridity is therefore far from straightforward. It is not new, and it has a troubled ancestry. Originally a biological term to describe the offspring of a tame sow and a wild boar, it did not take long to emerge as a racial descriptor, synonymous with 'half-breed' and 'mongrel', before being applied to languages such as kriol and Tok Pisin, and an ever-increasing number of cultural phenomena.[27] The term entered serious critical studies a generation ago when Homi Bhabha argued for hybrids as the product of the colonial encounter.[28] Since then, the hybrid can be found in virtually every area of cultural analysis. In fact, hybridity has been deployed across such a wide range that it is sometimes dismissed as virtually meaningless.[29] It is now often little more than a synonym for 'complex'. The sheer range of fields in which hybridity appears as either

---

[24] On Thai boxing in Amsterdam and Asian Rap in London, see Nederveen Pieterse 1994: 169. See also Frank and Stollberg 2004: 75.

[25] Ashe 2015.   [26] Demers 2006: 31.

[27] Kapchan and Strong 1999, Knoepflmacher 2008. For criticisms of hybridity as an analytical tool, see Ackermann 2012 and Heil 2018. For an assessment of attempts to revive the term, see Hutnyk 2005.

[28] Bhabha 1994.

[29] Marwan Kraidy (2017: 4) has recently argued that hybridity's time has come and gone: 'Now largely absent from book titles, conference themes and intellectual polemics, hybridity has taken residence in interdisciplinary venues like media studies, as a once-dominant concept now content with latent taken-for-grantedness and banal usage. We now assume rather than argue over hybridity.'

a descriptive label or metaphor means that the term and underlying concept risk losing any analytical power. Take, for example, this cluster of recent examples all drawn from one region: West Africa. Afropop is commonly viewed as a hybrid creation resulting from a 'return to sameness', as African hip-hop artists engage with music created by African-American artists in dialogue with African musical traditions.[30] One of the richest regions musically is Senegal, where the studios and equipment used for performing and recording this music are powered by 'solar hybrid systems', supplied by a German company, DHYBRID, selected by a French contractor.[31] The government of Senegal, which is behind these economic decisions and cultural products, is classified by the Economist Intelligence Unit as a 'hybrid regime'.[32] And, almost inevitably, the people who run everything from the generators to the government are described as affirming hybrid gender identities.[33] If the category of the hybrid encompasses power generation, sexual identity and everything in between, then the term is close to meaningless. This is the bleak conclusion of a recent study on the politics of cultural heritage. In a sceptical essay, David Lowenthal observes that 'every people are hybrid, every legacy multiple, every society heterogeneous, every tradition as much recent as ancient. All cultures are compage that amalgamate reworked fragments stemming from manifold antecedents. The farther back in time the more mixed is every ancestry.'[34] As Lowenthal uses it, the term 'hybrid' applies to everyone, and hybridity is a fundamental characteristic of every culture. Similarly, in a recent discussion of the use of analogies in archaeology and anthropology, Fahlander equates hybridity with the fluid and complex nature of existence, observing that 'Social life is far too complex and normally in [sic] continuous state of hybridity which makes it unfit to be submitted to the same laws as physical objects.'[35]

If hybridity is universal and ubiquitous, can it be rescued from banality? It can, provided we use the term carefully. In the first place, we have to be careful to distinguish discrete fields of operation. In his study *Hybrid*

---

[30] Appert 2016. The 19 December 2019 podcast of Afropop Worldwide announced itself as 'an hour of African music that points to the future: new styles, new hybrids, artists to watch, and glimpses of upcoming Afropop Worldwide projects and productions'. See www.pastimeapp.com/pod/Afropop-Worldwide#/.

[31] www.esi-africa.com/industry-sectors/renewable-energy/solar-hybrid-systems-to-power-senegalese-communities/.

[32] The Economist Intelligence Unit (8 January 2019). 'Democracy Index 2019'. www.eiu.com/topic/democracy-index/. Accessed 13 January 2019.

[33] On gender, see M'Baye 2019. On hybrid African identities, see Mbembe 2007 and Diouf 2008.

[34] Lowenthal 2005: 405.   [35] Fahlander 2017: 71.

Renaissance, for example, Peter Burke uses hybridity not as a mere label (as we do when we speak of a hybrid generator) but as a lens through which to examine afresh cultural production and performance. To take one example, the roiling shifts of power, territory and faith in the Spanish peninsula of the fifteenth century begin to look different when one encounters *mudéjar*-style geometric, calligraphic and floral designs typical of mosques continuing to be used to decorate churches after the Reconquista in 1492. As Burke observes, 'the tradition of the interpenetration of Islamic, Gothic and classical motifs continued well beyond that date'.[36] Hybridity here refers to more than a mélange of styles in architectural ornament, and points to a cultural response more complex than the shifting balance of political power would suggest. Also more granular is Burke's reading of the ways that physicians influenced by Renaissance humanists tried to exclude the Arab tradition of commentary from their reading of the classical texts of Hippokrates. The close connection between hybridity and notions of racial purity helps to explain this cultural development. In other words, Burke is not using hybrid just as a label for any cultural product of mixed provenance. Instead, hybridity points to a complexity potentially lost by relying on the fixity of older categories. In similar fashion, Carol Dougherty has recently explored nostalgia as more than just a theme or phenomenon in Homer (and modern literature), but as 'an interpretive framework, a mode of critical analysis'.[37] A similar case can be made for hybridity, but there remains the danger of using hybridity in a very loose sense to mean cultural blending, a usage so loose as to be misleading.

Hybridity and Thin Coherence

The strengths and weaknesses of using hybridity as a lens through which to look afresh at the Greeks is well illustrated in recent work on Herodotos. In one study, taking hybridity in its broadest sense leads to such claims as 'nothing serves a hybridizing function more than war'.[38] The author goes on to explain that in Herodotos we get many examples of war confusing cultural and political boundaries: 'one of the great themes of the History is the way in which the war ... transforms the Persians'. And, on the Greek side of the ledger, the same author finds in Herodotos an openness to the notion that hybridity gets at the truth of things: 'political practice requires a spirit of cross-cultural inquiry and openness to the revision of custom'.

---

[36] Burke 2016: 263.   [37] Dougherty 2019: 149–50.   [38] McWilliams 2013: 748.

Employed this way, hybridity amounts to little more than the recognition that Herodotos was a sensitive observer of cultural relativity, but that is hardly a revelation: if *The Histories* had an epigraph it would be Pindar's observation that 'Custom is King'.[39] A far more productive line of inquiry is to look at specific examples of hybrids in Herodotos and to ask what light they shed on his understanding of cultural difference. Such an approach begins not with hybridity *sensu lato* but with hybrids. Cyrus, for example, half-Mede, half-Persian, is famously referred to in an oracle given to Kroisos as a mule (*hemionos*).[40] Is it a successful hybridization? On the one hand he amasses enormous power and leads the Persians to greatness. One might say that he exhibits hybrid vigour. At the same time he is succeeded by Cambyses, who mocks religion, goes mad and with whom the dynasty dies out. Like a mule, which is usually infertile, Cyrus' line is doomed to extinction. Hybridity here is more than a metaphor for cultural relativism; it is a way of embodying a paradox of empire: dynasties contain the seeds of their own downfall. Another episode in Herodotos investigates the hold of *nomos* and the ambiguities of hybridity. This is the story of Skyles, son of the Skythian king Ariapithes and a Greek woman. Raised to speak and read Greek, he would spend a month each year living with a Greek wife in Borysthenes, dressing as a Greek, walking around the agora, worshipping the gods in Greek style and generally adopting a Greek way of life. When this is reported to the Skythians they revolt, and this brief flirtation with hybridizing Greek and Skythian modes of life ends with the beheading of Skyles. 'The Skythians are so conservative', concludes Herodotos, 'that this is how they treat people who adopt foreign ways'.[41] In fact, their aversion to any kind of métissage is so profound that the very land of Skythia will not produce either donkeys or mules.[42] In Herodotos, therefore, hybridity writ large can be seen as a challenge to the hard hold of *nomos*, but the threat varies enormously depending on the specifics of the hybrid and the elements being hybridized.

Hybridity, accordingly, is a slippery concept that should be used with some caution. The challenge, after reading Herodotos, is to think with hybridity

---

[39] Pindar fr. 169 Snell, quoted by Herodotos at 3.38 in the famous passage comparing the funeral practices of Greeks and Indians. The Greeks are horrified when asked how much money would convince them to eat their fathers' corpses. The Kalliatai are equally repelled when asked how much it would take to have them cremate their dead. For a comprehensive treatment of *nomos*, see Ostwald 2009: 93–124.
[40] Hdt 1.55.2.   [41] Hdt 4.78–80. For discussion, see Strong 2010: 461.
[42] Hdt 4.129. See Strong 2010: 463. Discussing Hdt 4.30, Strong claims, 'According to Herodotus, to breed mules the Scythians have to drive their mares over the Greek border in order to mate them with their neighbors' donkeys.' This is a mistake. Herodotos attributes this practice to the Elians.

while keeping an eye on particular hybrids. It is, nonetheless, a valuable exercise, offering us an opportunity to revisit and update some older interpretations of the Greek world. Take, for example, the perennial problem of Greek colonization. Building on nineteenth-century models of the European colonization of Africa, Asia and Oceania, many narratives of Greek colonization still rely on notions of coherent colonial expeditions dispatched from a mother-city to a colonial site. In these scenarios Greek colonists populate the Mediterranean like so many First Fleets arriving in Botany Bay. Hybridity, as 'an interpretive framework', to use Dougherty's phrase, suggests a different phenomenon.[43] Hybridity in this sense alerts us to new cultural forms arising from the combination of older elements. Gillian Shepherd, for example, has suggested that the contracted, acephalous burials found in the Greek colonies of Magna Graecia constitute coherent burial systems that are not exclusively Greek or indigenous, but 'part of an attempt to forge a unified and independent cultural identity'.[44] Shepherd's explanation reflects the recognition that exposure to different people and settings challenged the Greek speakers of the Aegean and wider diaspora. In the shadow of nineteenth-century colonialism, scholarship in the twentieth century treated the diaspora of Greek and Phoenician speakers and the encounter with indigenous people monadically: Phoenicians found Carthage, Euboians seize Cumae. In reaction to this anachronistic model, and influenced by post-colonial theory, the most recent studies of communities in the Greek-speaking diaspora have emphasized contingency and the episodic unfolding of what we refer to uniformly as Greek colonization. The colonial ground is constantly shifting and the identities of ethnic groups coalesce rather than emerge fully formed from the head of the oikist. Irad Malkin has argued that the contact between Greeks and Phoenicians can be viewed through the lens of middle ground theory, an approach borrowed from Richard White's ground-breaking study of cultural contact in early colonial America, and even scholars sceptical of post-colonial theory, such as Michael Sommer, have enthusiastically embraced hybridity, métissage and creolization as characteristics of the Greek diaspora experience.[45] The older scholarly construct of coherent Greek colonial expeditions planting themselves on Sicilian or Sardinian soil looks increasingly shaky. In its place is a model emphasizing fluidity and entanglement, in which identities are negotiated and only thinly coherent.[46]

---

[43] On the terms 'hybridism', 'hybridity' and 'hybridization', see Jiménez 2011: 199.
[44] Shepherd 2005: 115.   [45] Sommer 2012.
[46] On thin coherence, see Antonaccio 2003. On the move away from 'colonial' as a label for this diaspora, see De Angelis 2016. For the middle ground as an interpretive model suitable to the Greek diaspora, see Malkin 2011, Antonaccio 2013 and Malkin 2016. For a world systems

As valuable as this may be, however, as an explanation for the formation of communal identities, hybridity is also potentially misleading.[47] While laudably alive to the fluidity of colonial encounters, scholars using hybridity to characterize the worlds of the Greek and Phoenician diasporas risk over-correcting earlier models. To return to Shepherd's analysis of the burials from Archaic Sicily, she finds the evidence for acculturation and hybridity difficult to locate unequivocally at the level of the community and suggests that what looks like hybridity may be evidence for markers of elite status.[48] Even attempts to finesse 'hybridity' by speaking of 'hybridization' do little to clarify the process of acculturation.[49] Take, for example, Van Dommelen's work tracing the changes in western Sardinia following the arrival of the Phoenicians at Tharros and Orthoca as early as the seventh century. After a lengthy period of exchange of goods between the new arrivals and the indigenes, the Phoenicians embarked on a gradual territorial expansion into the hinterland through the establishment of rural settlements, culminating 'in the acculturation of the inhabitants of western-central Sardinia'.[50] Van Dommelen's reconstruction of cultural change over three centuries is far more sophisticated than a simple narrative in which colonists arrive and dispossess the locals, but if hybridity means no more than gradual acculturation then the term is still essentially meaningless. Van Dommelen argues that 'hybridization' avoids 'reducing colonial situations to abstract instances of "culture contact"' and focuses on the agency of the players who adopt new cultural forms.[51] This is a more dynamic view of how cultures change, yet the term still risks substituting a neat scheme of cultural exchange for a much messier, more chaotic reality. A more promising approach is to recognize that people on the edges of a settled community, namely rural dwellers living in remote areas, were more likely to experience hybrid identities precisely because of their marginal status.[52]

---

approach deconstructing the notion of Euboians driving Greek colonization, see Papadopoulos 1997. On the question of intermarriage between Greeks and indigenes, see Hodos 1999. On the inapplicability of modern parallels, see Osborne 1998. On identity and the material record see chapters by Burgers and Crielaard in Donnellan et al. 2016. On trade at sites of Middle Ground contact, see Demetriou 2012. On ethnic identity formation in diaspora settings, see the essays in Lomas 2004. On indigenous responses to Greek populations, see Antonaccio 2001.

[47] On this, see Jiménez 2011: 104: 'And if we abandon the thought of the existence of "essentialist cultures" for the idea of the essentially hybrid nature of all cultural productions, what is the point of even thinking about hybridism? At this point asserting that all cultures and languages are hybrids is at best a facile truism.'

[48] Shepherd 2009 and Shepherd 2011.   [49] Van Dommelen 2005: 117.
[50] Van Dommelen 2005: 117.   [51] Van Dommelen 2005: 137.   [52] Zuchtriegel 2017: 195.

The danger of equating hybridity with gradual acculturation is real. For a start, there remain the complications of power, inclusion and self-definition – all issues that risk being glossed over by appealing to hybridity. For example, Lin Foxhall has rightly drawn attention to the slippery business of inferring the identity of the inhabitants of the mountainous Bova region between Rhegion and Locri in Calabria, suggesting that 'It seems likely that the inhabitants of the Umbro Greek site considered themselves to be "Greek" but whether the citizens of Rhegion and Locri considered them to be "Greek", or even part of (or "having a share in", as Greeks would have expressed it) one of the two poleis, remains an open question.'[53] Did they have hybrid identities, or contingent identities, that jostled for prominence according to context: visits to town, encounters with shepherds, marriage negotiations, military service, religious performances and so forth? There is a temptation to appeal to hybridity to fill in blank spaces in our understanding, as is demonstrated by recent work on Roman Spain. In a study of statuary produced from the third to the first century BC in Spain, Alicia Jiménez has argued for hybridity as a model for understanding the local response to Rome. She consciously avoids essentialist models of hybridism which reduce hybrid artefacts to a simple fusion of Iberian and Roman elements. Instead, she sees the local artefacts 'partially recreating Roman items according to a local logic in sanctuaries and cemeteries that were sometimes in use well before the Roman conquest. These sculptures show us a representation of Rome and of pre-Roman traditions simultaneously in a local language and in a "single utterance"'.[54] This view of hybridization is dynamic and creative, but even here there is a danger. It is laudable to move beyond a classificatory grid that reproduces false notions of cultural purity, but the Roman conquest of the Spanish peninsula was immensely bloody, and Jiménez's conclusions risk obscuring this. Jiménez writes:

> Hybridism is fusion and rupture but not at random, as it builds up according to metaphors of similarity and difference, through metonymic representations of the part for the whole and through images of partial presence. In this metaphoric practice of substituting one term for another, the agents involved (sculptors and their patrons) explicitly express precious details about perceived external or internal similarities, tracing a path between hidden continuities, detecting underlying but essential relations, and establishing analogies between elements that may no longer have been considered contradictory.[55]

---

[53] Foxhall et al. 2007: 26.   [54] Jiménez 2011: 116–17.
[55] Jiménez 2011: 118. For the bloody history of Rome's wars and the Spanish resistance to the incorporation of Iberia into the Roman provincial structure, see Rosenstein 2012: 198–203.

It is worrisome that the attempt to give sculptors and patrons a greater agency in the production of culture should at the same time ignore the conditions of constant warfare, armed resistance and occupation that set the stage for this hybrid entanglement. The 4,000 children born of Roman soldiers and Spanish women in the first quarter of the second century are a more powerful example of hybridity – eloquent testimony to the sexual violence that was fundamental to the cultural exchange which occurred between the Spanish tribes and their new Roman overlords.[56]

Similar problems exist below the level of the community, where hybridity is also invoked to explain individual identities, as people pick and choose from a smorgasbord of objects and motifs to express a sense of self. In his recent study of what he calls 'hybrid go-betweens', whom he defines as individuals with multiple identities in cross-cultural settings, Jan Paul Crielaard offers a striking instance of this contingent identity formation and its relationship to hybridity.[57] Crielaard analyses four funerary assemblages, which he labels 'ambiguous', from Kourion-Kaloriziki (Cyprus, tomb 40), to Lefkandi (Euboia, Toumba shaft grave) and Lefkandi (Euboia, Toumba t. 79), to Fondo Artiaco (Kyme, Campania, t. 104). What makes them ambiguous is that, despite being widely separated in place and time, all four display a very similar combination of burial practices, such as secondary cremation, and a similar range of funerary objects that include urns, bowls and weapons as well as scales and weights. Faced with these distinctive assemblages, scholars have downplayed the wide-ranging provenance of the goods, instead identifying the individuals as an Achaean royal buried with a Mycenaean style sceptre (Cyprus), Cypriot immigrants (Lefkandi shaft grave), a Euboian warrior trader or Phoenician aristocrat (Lefkandi t. 79) and a local chief with connections to the Greeks of Pithekoussai and the Etruscans at Capua (Fondo Artiaco). In asserting these fixed and clearly defined identities, Crielaard notes, scholars are failing to engage with the mixed character of the grave goods and burial rites. Instead, scholars have preferred to assume that the individuals possessed one identity and that the scholar's task was to identify the individual as either Greek or Cypriot, Euboian or Phoenician, indigenous or Etruscan. Observing that at this micro-level individuals can move across cultural boundaries, being at one time and in one setting Greek (or Lycian, or Phoenician) and in another Egyptian (or Etruscan), Crielaard argues for hybrid identities.[58]

[56] Livy 43.3.1–4   [57] Crielaard 2018.
[58] We should be cautious before inferring too much with respect to individual identity from material goods. If pots do not equal people, neither does a variety of pots equal a fluid identity.

It is striking to find such similar assemblages across the central and eastern Mediterranean over a span of 300 years, but there are dangers in using hybridity to explain identity. One is the risk of confusing hybridity operating across a community and culture with the eclectic tastes of an individual. The assemblages analysed by Crielaard challenge the simple identifications of individuals as Phoenician, Cypriot or Euboian, but the ambiguity of the evidence speaks to our categories, not their realities. The experiences of exile, trade and migration favoured the adoption of bricolage identities, but every immigrant grapples with this. Using hybridity as a label for this avoids understanding the dynamic situation of identity formation and reduces hybridity to a synonym for complexity. Demaratos the Corinthian, often cited as an example of hybridity and code-shifting, had little to gain by aggressively asserting a Greek identity once he settled in Tarquinia. Marrying a local woman and giving his sons Etruscan names (Arruns and Lucumo) were eminently practical strategies for integration into his new world, but do not mean that 'Corinthian' or 'Etruscan' are meaningless labels, nor that switching from one to the other makes Demaratos, in any genuine sense, a hybrid.

Hybridity and Order

In response to the looseness with which hybridity has been employed, I suggest restricting discussion to actual hybrid bodies and to cultural products and processes that are focused on bodies. I propose doing so because hybrids are the product of an abrupt encounter between classes of bodies that, in conventional thinking, are not supposed to merge: the human and animal, and the male and female. Kristeva draws attention to this disruptive element: 'It is thus not lack of cleanliness or health that causes abjection but what disturbs identity, system, order. What does not respect borders, positions, rules. The in-between, the ambiguous, the composite.'[59] This is broadly correct, in that the composite violates borders and fixity. Abjection, however, is not the only product of encountering hybrids, as is demonstrated by the complex reactions elicited by Patricia Piccinini's *No Fear of Depths* (Figure 2.4).

Otherwise, we could drop all modern ethnic identifiers and call ourselves IKEAn. But just as owning a set of Billy bookshelves doesn't make the owner Swedish, it also doesn't nullify the owner's French, British or Indonesian identity.

[59] Kristeva 1982: 4.

Hybridity and Order 41

Figure 2.4 Patricia Piccinini, *No Fear of Depths*, 2019. Silicone, fibreglass, human hair, clothing. 150 × 150 × 110 cm. Courtesy of the artist, Tolarno Galleries and Roslyn Oxley9 Gallery.

The viewer is presented with a glabrous body with some human features (eyes, ears, hands, fingers, nails, shoulders, nipples) merged with bits from a dolphin (beak) and a pinniped (flipper-feet). Viewers often react to the work with an 'Oh my!', followed by the question 'what is that?', which in turn elicits an answer in which the different parts are listed separately. This hybrid, like many others, cannot be ignored, but it defies a specific logic: we can identify the parts but they do not add up to a coherent whole. Furthermore, while there may be nothing horrifying in the embrace of the hybrid dolphin-man, the intimacy of the two figures is startling. Piccinini's hybrid is a graphic reminder that hybridity is a direct outgrowth of the human/animal encounter, a place rich in feeling, from our love of pets to our appreciation of horses to our horror of sharks, and rich in imagination: what if we could merge with animals? There is a barrier separating us, but it only serves to highlight our desire to surmount the species barrier. We are entangled.[60] At the same time, this entanglement operates according to certain unwritten rules: the Greeks had no difficulty imagining a hybrid of man and horse or woman and eagle, but they did not imagine plant–men or rock–women.[61] This distinction reflects the complex way hybrids call attention to the boundaries of the human. Empirically, we do not experience centaurs or sirens in the mundane world, yet we and the Greeks have no difficulty imagining them. The proximity of the animal to the human means that there are always two questions implicit in these encounters: what is an animal, and what is a human?

Treating hybridity as a mode of cultural production necessitates looking at a range of hybrids from different periods and in different media. What they have in common is that all hybrids are composites, and the very idea of a composite raises the possibility of crossing of boundaries between categories. Depending on the categories involved, this can be exciting or threatening. Accordingly, one can approach any hybrid as an example of mixing, for better ('hybrid vigour') or for worse ('mongrelization'). Pegasos may be the hero's trusty companion, while the Chimaira is his mortal enemy. Each hybrid has its own particular *Sitz im Leben*, a specific context which informs meaning and function. Each hybrid is an example of hybridity, but at the same time each has its own unique history, so that Greek hybrids resist easy categorization.[62] This study will therefore have two goals: to clarify the significance of many hybrids, such as centaurs and gorgons, and also to elucidate the tensions and anxieties that found expression in these curious and unsettling figures.

Hybrid figures were a constant presence in Greek culture from the Bronze Age, through the Classical Age and well on into the Hellenistic and Roman

---

[60] McInerney 2021a.

[61] Evidence for belief among the Greeks for hybrids of animals and plants is elusive. Despite Ovid's exploration of a tree/nymph hybrid in the metamorphosed figure of Daphne, the Greeks do not generally present nature spirits such as the Dryads and Nereids as hybrids but as quasi-divine, wholly anthropomorphic figures, as when Zeus summons them to his house (Hom. *Il.* 20). The fullest description of their nature, in HH 5 *to Aphrodite*, has trees springing up with them at their birth and dying at the same time as the Dryads. Their fates are entwined, but not their forms. It is perhaps to be expected that the major exception to this is Ovid. When Erysichthon cuts down the tree sacred to Ceres, blood pours from the tree's wound like a sacrificial animal bleeding at the altar. See *Metamorph* 8.763–4, and Zatta 2016. Tree–mammal hybrids are mentioned in Lucretius *DRN* 2.702–3. Bailey's commentary (Lucretius 1986) suggests that Lucretius may have been 'thinking of such metamorphoses as those of Daphne, Philemon and Baucis, or the sisters of Phaëthon'. Woolerton 2010 argues that this is a Lucretian answer to a passage in Empedokles now lost. On imaginary creatures in Empedokles, Epicurus and Lucretius, see Gale 1994: 88–94. On plants as upside down animals, see Zatta 2019: 95–104.

[62] Aston 2014.

periods. Early in this long span of time, as culture flowed across the eastern Mediterranean, Greek speakers encountered the imaginative bestiaries of the older, sophisticated urban cultures of Egypt and the Near East, and freely and selectively adopted these forms to serve their own needs. The Greeks were always part of a rich, complex East Mediterranean cultural zone where social structures were constantly evolving and changing. At times contact was violent, marked by conquest and territorial acquisition. Plutarch, for example, pithily sums up Alexander's murderous expedition across Central Asia: 'Thus Alexander's new subjects would not have been civilized, had they not been vanquished.'[63] At other times cultural contact produced less bloody results. For every Alexander of Macedon bringing Greece to the Ganges through conquest and colonization there were dozens of men like Herakleides-Abdelmelqart from Kition, whose bilingual names advertised their movement between different worlds.[64] Similar double names borne by individuals who moved between Greek and Akkadian identity also occur in third-century Uruk, where the city administrator was named Anu-uballit-Nikarchos. Another member of the priestly elite was Anu-uballit/Kephalon. Both men came from families in which Greek or double names recur across five generations. Entire communities might exhibit a contingent approach to ethnicity, such as the people of Halikarnassos. A member of the Karian community, for example, Panamyes son of Kasbolis erected a dedication to Apollo, and in the epigraphy of the Halikarnassian community, Greek and Karian intermingle seamlessly.[65] Zenodoros, son of Aryassis, purchases land from Artemon, son of Panamyes. Again and again, family lineages point to a fluidity between Greek and Karian: Arbessios, son of Apollonides; Moschos, son of Arliômos and Panyassis, son of Idagygos, blending Greek and Karian across the generations.[66]

But fluidity was not to everyone's taste. In the Archaic period, in particular, the elites of the Greek world were obsessed with defining order (*eunomia*) and the right way of behaving (*themis*).[67] Similarly, the

---

[63] Plut. *De Fort. Alex.* 5: 'He educated the Hyrcanians to respect the marriage bond and taught the Arachosians to till the soil, and persuaded the Sogdians to support their parents, not to kill them, and the Persians to respect their mothers and not to marry them.'
[64] Herakleides-Abdelmelqart: Fraser 1970; Lane Fox 2008. On third-century Uruk, see Honigman 2014: 314.
[65] Panamyes: Svenbro 1993: 58. [66] *Halikarnassos* 31 (McCabe 1991).
[67] Andrewes 1938, Sanders 2010, Lombardini 2013. According to Aristotle, *Pol.* 5.6, 1306b 22, Tyrtaios' poem *Eunomia* dealt with class tensions in Lakonia at the time of the Messenian Wars. For Pindar, Corinth was the home of Eunomia and her sisters, Dike and Eirene, the daughters of Themis. Pi. *Ol.* 13.5–10. Xenophon, *Memorabilia* 8.3–10 recounts the sententious advice of Ischomachos to his young wife: 'nothing is more useful and good for mankind than good order [*taxis*]'.

threat to order, whether from Titans in Hesiod or profit-driven merchants in Theognis, was an abiding concern of early Greek culture.[68] In fact, a case can be made for seeing the Iron Age and the Archaic period as centuries during which the Greeks passed from proto-legal societies to communities committed to the rule of law.[69] This produced a mania for classification and taxonomy, assigning functions and roles to everything from gods and humans to natural forces. The significance of this for the establishment of a social order is clear, but the corollary to this mindset was a fascination with those symbols and images that either defied or challenged taxonomies. Not coincidentally, the longest catalogues of monsters and composite hybrids occur in the voice of the Archaic period, Hesiod. The countervailing pressures of 'order' and 'threat' produced responses ranging from wonder to anxiety and fear.[70] As we shall see, hybrids perfectly embody that ambiguity, giving expression to the uncertainty that accompanied encounters with other cultures. As the Greeks mixed with other cultures and languages, hybrids served as a useful means of negotiating similarity and difference, adding degrees of horror and monstrosity where necessary. So flexible was hybridity, in fact, that wherever the category of the normal was placed under pressure a hybrid emerged to give that threat a face: bold women, a threat to heterosexual order, appear as gorgons and Amazons; wild men, a challenge to civilized life, take the shape of centaurs and satyrs; indigenes, savage and dangerous, enter the Greek imaginary as Cyclopean monsters. The Greeks experienced a thin globalism, where hybrids gave a face to the alienness that lay beyond (and beneath) the Aegean. In this wider world, meeting with people speaking different languages and practicing different habits was transformed into encounters with fabulous creatures and odd quasi-humans whose appearance was both recognizable and unsettling. Hearing about the strange, alien inhabitants of far-off places – often jungles and deserts, the topographic opposites of Greece – was entertaining. As the horizons of the Classical World, largely synonymous with the Mediterranean, broadened in every direction, the figure of the

---

[68] According to Theognis 677, the Base 'have seized possessions by force and destroyed good order'.
[69] For proto-legal societies and the problem of lawlessness (*anomiē*) see Gagarin 1986: 21. The significance of the Rule of Law is a perennial subject of interest with regard to the Athenian democracy. See, inter alia, Sealey 1987 and Harris 2013. Most recently, Almog 2022 has emphasized that the shift from a lack of formal legal practices to institutionalized law informs the world of the Homeric poems.
[70] On the states of mind conveyed by 'tremendous', 'terrible, 'awful', 'awesome' and other terms conventionally used in the encounter with monsters, hybrids and other threats to order, see Warner 2007: 7–9.

hybrid contributed to the handling of this in the imagination of Greek artists: anomaly and peculiarity became literary tropes and genres, as writers collected paradoxical tales of monopods, basilisks and one-eyed Aramaspians. Hybridity was useful as a means of giving a recognizable shape to the oddities at the edges of culture.

Body Parts

Also contributing to the anomalous nature of the hybrid is a psychologically powerful aspect of the human/animal encounter: the phenomenon of disarticulation. At Çatal Hüyük (ca. 7500–6000 BC) in central Turkey, like Göbekli Tepe a site where occupation precedes the domestication of animals, wall paintings and decorations return incessantly to violent scenes of hunting and the disarticulation of the bodies of the hunted animals.[71] Explaining the recurring theme of violence, René Girard employs mimesis as a way of reading the scenes as expressions of disorder within the human community displaced onto the destruction of the animal. He observes:

> The explanation brought by mimetic theory to these pictures would suggest that there was probably internal disorder and violence inside this society; and the hunt, or at least the ritualized collective killing of these animals, was a measure invented to give back unity to the group. This procedure allowed the group to shift the violence internal to the community onto an external agent, which was ritually and collectively killed.[72]

It is a step too far to suggest that human social bands invented hunting to unify the group, since other primates (such as chimpanzees and bonobos) also live in packs and hunt meat.[73] Nevertheless, the representations of these events demonstrate that the people of Çatal Höyük invested immense symbolic capital in the hunt. The wall paintings from Çatal Höyük depict a world filled with deer, bulls and boars that dwarf the human domain, but the hunt scenes are composed with more than massive animals and miniscule humans. In each scene, one or at most two gigantic animals will be grabbed, taunted and eventually cut to pieces by a throng of small human figures. The animals as prey are solitary, divorced from any herd, while the humans are always part of a band. The cooperation needed to stalk the prey, the coordination needed to carry out the attack and the commensality

---

[71] For Çatalhöyük, see Hodder 2006.   [72] Girard 2015: 226.   [73] Surbeck and Hohmann 2008.

arising from a successful hunt all reinforced group cohesion. Our confrontation with animals makes us not just human, but a community.

Time and again, successful hunters would break the hunted animal down into parts, prior to sharing the meat of the hunt and consuming it. After the animal's death, the head and horns were used to demonstrate the power of a life force brought under control by humans. Accordingly, the hunted animal exists as both a single entity –auroch, caribou or kangaroo – but also as head, leg, haunch, ribs and tail. Most bits have a use – meat and marrow for eating, ligaments and sinews for binding, hide for clothing, horn for drinking – but the dismemberment of the hunted animal through butchery leads us to experience the animal as a composite as well as an integral figure. As soon as any body can be disarticulated, it can be rearticulated in new and shocking ways to convey an entire set of associations and meanings that do not reside in the integral body. These are actions full of significance, and a Natufian burial from Hilazon Tachtit in Israel (12,000 BP) underscores how body parts could serve as a metonymy for power. The woman buried here suffered deformations of the pelvis, os sacrum and various vertebrae; she was old, bent and walked with a pronounced limp, yet the goods buried with her prove her standing in the community: an auroch's tail, a marten's skull, the wing-tip of a golden eagle, the forearm of a wild boar and, most strikingly, more than fifty complete tortoise carapaces. These animals may have supplied the meat for a funerary feast (the plastrons had been fractured by a hammerstone and removed from the carapace). Such body parts from a range of exotic animals attest to the shaman's status and her capacity to access the spirit world of animals.[74]

This is not to suggest an unchanged continuity of shamanistic practice from the Neolithic Near East to Archaic Greece, but rather to draw attention to perceptions and practices whose influence persisted throughout the cultures of the eastern Mediterranean. Linking shamanism to the appearance of winged and bird-headed human figures in Assyrian art of the second and first millennium, Mehmet Ali Ataç proposes that 'They may have preserved the same trope of combining an animal capable of flying and the human body in visualizing superhuman beings with special magical and craftsmanship skills.'[75] The Greeks were heirs to this same set of associations. This is suggested by two sectors of Greek religious practice.

---

[74] Groszman et al. 2008. Habits of mind and practices associated with shamanism – animal power, transformation, even initiation – are not the same as arguments for a fully developed set of religious practices that should be identified as Greek shamanism. For an overview of the question, see Bremmer 2016.

[75] Ataç 2019: 532.

In the first place, the transformation into animal form was the source of an altered state of consciousness, as in the case of Dionysos' Bacchants, the Thyiades; in the second place, abstention from meat and other foods in some circles, such as the so-called Orphics, arose from an underlying feeling that human and animal were intertwined.[76]

The animal encounter challenges notions of bodily integrity. The presence of bucrania and other body parts in burials and mortuary contexts reminds us that our animal experiences repeatedly oscillate between the body as a whole and the body as an assemblage of parts, disintegrated by death or by human agency, or both. It is a lesson we did not unlearn for thousands of years. In fact, the assurance of corporeal integrity which is so deeply embedded in modern, western culture is much less firmly established in societies predating the rise of complex, hierarchical states.[77] In these early societies a process of enchainment appears to tie humans, animals and objects together in complex networks of meaning that arise as much from relations between parts as between integral bodies.[78] The replacement of a head by a similarly shaped pot or weight, the substitution of a pig's mandible for the human jaw, the addition of foxes and puppies to human burials and a variety of other 'deviant burials' in which bones are added, subtracted or substituted are all examples of breaking down and fragmenting bodies and objects.[79] Each challenges the notion of an integral, whole body expressing a unique human individuality and instead points towards societies in which the categories so familiar to us were emergent rather than fixed.

---

[76] On the Thyiades at Delphi, see McInerney 1999 and Ustinova 2022. For a short but judicious overview of conflicting definitions of Orphism, see Zhmud' 1992. On animals in Orphic rituals, see Fornari 2021. On abstention from meat in Orphic practice, see Bourgeaud 2013. I am not concerned with the question of whether or not Orphism was a coherent and organized religious movement. For instances of Greek religious practices that displayed shamanic elements in Minoan religion, see Morris and Peatfield 2022. For Mycenae, see Lupack 2022.

[77] Athanasiou 2003: 125 asks: 'How does one reckon the technologies of the human? But there is no such thing as the human. Instead, there is only the dizzying multiplicity of the cut human, the human body as interminably cut, fractured.'

[78] Chapman 2000: 140.

[79] Pots as head replacement objects: Croucher 2010: 9 (Domuztepe, Turkey); net weight as head replacement: Chapman 2010: 35 (Hódmezővásárhely, Hungary); pig's mandible as head replacement: Chapman 2010: 40–1 (Zengővárkony, Hungary). As Chapman observes, 'The pig mandible replacement of human skulls/skull parts raises the issue of hybrid pig-humans, who transgressed categorical boundaries and enabled thought about the differences and similarities between humans and other animals.' Prenatufian fox/human burial: Maher et al. 2011 ('Uyun al-Hammam, Jordan); old woman and puppy (Natufian): Valla 2019: 313 (Ain Mallaha, Israel); 'deviant' burials: Chapman 2010: 30–45 (Central and Southeastern Europe).

The most striking of these 'deviant burials' are those that employ addition, recombination and substitution of different limbs and body parts to create what Robert Chapman describes as 'a series of striking hybrid images … including pig-humans, half-children, half-adults and men-women'.[80] Even after death parts circulated, giving the dead a continued presence among the living, while mortuary rituals including the consumption of flesh, marrow and liquids were conducted in such ways that animal and human were equivalent and interchangeable. At Çayönü Tepesi, in south-eastern Anatolia, a Skull Building shows that the bodies of humans and aurochs were processed side by side for 1,000 years (7600–6600 BC).[81] The blood of both is found in the same places and contexts, as are their skulls and, in the case of the humans, long bones.[82] Later changes in burial practice can be tied to a growing emphasis on the integral body, buried individually with grave goods, but before this shift the dead belonged to a class that encompassed animal, object and human.[83] Similarly, in the so-called Death Pit at Domuztepe, also in south-eastern Turkey, in the middle of the sixth millennium, human and dog skulls were treated indiscriminately, while mirrors and pottery vessels were broken in the same way as the bones of the dead.[84] Fragmentation only reinforced the exchangeability of animal and human bodies, as well as objects.

Prominent in this lexicon of body parts is the bucranium. The bull's head, in fact, is one of the earliest components in the symbolic language of words and objects we use to express our encounter with the numinous. This is an experience that requires the separation of the ego from the limitlessness of eternity. But the longing to efface that separation and to immerse ourselves in the 'oceanic feeling' is based on the belief, rightly challenged by Freud, that there is an indissoluble bond between us and the world around us, that 'We cannot fall out of this world'.[85] We can; we do at death. The bucranium is a token of the passage that awaits us. In the guise of the bucranium, both real and carved, it will remain the most common religious image of the entire Mediterranean and adjoining areas, recurring from Sardinia to Sudan (see Figure 2.5).[86]

---

[80] Chapman 2010: 44. It might be worth considering the possibility that before death some of the bodies found in 'deviant' burials had been impacted by disease, such as dental caries, polio and leprosy. In such cases, the substitutions and additions made to the body would amount to a kind of compensation, anticipating the 'correct' and integral body in the afterlife.

[81] Özdoğan 1999.   [82] Özdoğan and Özdoğan 1998: 584.   [83] Croucher 2010: 10–11.

[84] Croucher 2010: 8–10.

[85] 'Ja, aus der Welt werden wir nicht fallen', a line from Grabbe's *Hannibal*, quoted by Freud in *Civilization and its Discontents* (Freud 1930) in his discussion of the 'oceanic feeling.'

[86] For Sardinia, see Demartis 1986. Tomba A is decorated with a series of engraved bucrania. In the tomb, robbed in antiquity, were found some sherds dating to the mid-fourth millennium (Ozzieri culture).

Figure 2.5 Low relief bucrania, Tomba A ('domus de janas'), Necropolis of Anghelu Ruju, Alghero, Sardinia, 3200–2800 BC (?) Photo J. McInerney.

The bucranium reminds us that an animal much more powerful than us has died, probably at our hands. The very skin covering it has been removed, either by human intervention or decay, laying bare the animal's mortality, a fitting reminder of the imminence of death. There is also a paradox in the bucranium: we consign to death other creatures and are nurtured by their dead flesh, yet we cannot avoid death ourselves. The bucranium is the first and perhaps most powerful metonym devised by humans.[87]

Compelling evidence for this comes from the Kerma culture of the Neolithic Sudan, where burials were often marked with rings of (real) bucrania.[88] The heads were cut from the body at the occipital bone and the lower jaw was removed. They were then arranged in rows according to a deliberate pattern, beginning with cows and juveniles. Behind them were

---

[87] The power of the bull's head crops up repeatedly in the Mediterranean world. Herodotus 2.39 describes the curses called down on a sacrificial bull's head by Egyptian priests before it is hurled into the Nile. Rehak 1995b calls attention to the ritual destruction of bull's head *rhyta*, amounting to a second killing of the sacrificial animal.

[88] Chaix, Dubosson and Honegger 2011. At approximately the same time as the Kerma pastoralists were commemorating the deaths of their rulers with displays of bucrania, at Mohenjo-Daro in the Indus valley bull's heads, bull-headed men (often tricephalic) and horned men begin to multiply on masks, vases and seals, part of a network of symbols combining fertility, power and the animal universe. See Srinivasan 1975/1976.

arrayed bulls, and behind them oxen. In the early classical Kerma period (KM I, ca. 2050 BC) some tombs were surrounded by hundreds of such bucrania. In one instance, (grave 253, sector CE 25), 4,069 bovine skulls were placed in front of the grave in an unparalleled display of power and prestige. At another cemetery in the central Sudanese Nile Valley (R 12) more than 250 burials were found in which typically a bucranium had been carefully placed by the human head.[89] Approximately one in eight of the bucrania found in the Kerma burials show signs of having been artificially deformed, and studies of contemporary practices among a variety of peoples in Ethiopia suggest this practice was associated with the marking out of the *Errewak* or favoured bull. Among the Hamar people this practice is regarded as enhancing the owner's *barjo* (life force, prosperity). So close is the identification of cattle-pastoralists with their herd animals that the Nuer draw a comparison between the suffering the animal feels when its horn is cut or broken and the incisions an adolescent receives on his forehead as he is initiated into manhood. Such rituals of body modification, both animal and human, firmly attest to the powerful identification we project onto our animals.[90]

Given the intensity of our persistent encounter with animals, what, then, does a theory of hybridity amount to? Arising from the profound connections between humans and animals, hybrid creatures challenge the firm boundaries between species. In turn, they raise questions about all boundaries: the body, sexual identity and social norms are all rendered more fluid once we start contemplating anomalies. The challenge that the hybrid poses is not a simple question of affirming or rejecting normativity; the gorgon may embody a monstrous version of the female just as the satyr may represent a chaotic but finally impotent version of the male agent. Both are examples of the hybrid's capacity to give expression to an alternative discourse in which each fixed category – human, man, woman, animal, Greek – is complemented by a variation that may verge on the monstrous or merely veer towards the curious. Across this spectrum, the hybrid provides a mute commentary on what is taken for granted, sometimes allowing, sometimes forcing the viewer to consider alternatives. The proximity of this animal world has resulted in the rich entanglement of humans with animals, and has also given shape and structure to a distinctive

---

[89] Wenger 2006: 56–7.
[90] The absolute entanglement of bovine and human culture in the world of the pastoralist was first studied by Evans-Pritchard 1940, who coined the expression 'the bovine idiom' to convey this intimacy. See McInerney 2010: 1–34.

thought-world wherein hybrids complicate and destabilize the separate categories of human and animal.

Proximity

This intense encounter with the animal is a staple of popular culture, from Lassie to Skippy, but philosophical reflection on the human/animal relationship tends to focus on a paradox: we feel so close to animals, yet we regularly kill them. Deleuze and Guattari claim that the conundrum is resolved by a kind of exchange: 'The agony of the rat or the slaughter of a calf remains present in thought not through pity but at the zone of exchange between man and animal in which something of one passes into the other.'[91] For Baudrillard this zone of exchange is where we destroy that aspect of the animal nature that keeps it separate from us: 'Bestiality, and its principle of uncertainty, must be killed in animals.'[92] Baudrillard drives the observer inward, forcing us to see ourselves picking up the knife, ready to kill, even as we contemplate that there is something fraternal between us and our prey. Consistent with this, contemporary thinkers have asserted an equivalence between human-on-animal violence and human-on-human violence, from Peter Singer deploring our carnivory as evidence of an unjustifiable exploitation of other species to Carol Adams' equally trenchant denunciation of the pornography of meat.[93] 'Do animals have a kind of moral intelligence?' ask Marc Bekoff and Jessica Pierce in a recent book.[94] 'Yes they do ... Animals display moral behavior, [and] they can be compassionate, empathetic, altruistic, and fair.' Few today would share Heidegger's confident distinction between humans and animals, whom he regarded as 'poor in world', compared with which 'man is world-forming'.[95]

The Greeks also experienced intense relationships with the animals around them, and this intimacy provides the foundation for Mediterranean hybridity.

---

[91] Deleuze and Guattari 1994: 109.   [92] Baudrillard 1994: 129.
[93] Singer 1989, Adams 2000. See also Donovan 1990. The field of animal ethics has grown enormously since the publication of Regan 1983. For a succinct summary of its recent history, see Ryan 2015: 119–52.
[94] Bekoff and Pierce 2009: 153. For a recent summary of animal culture studies, see Angier 2021.
[95] Heidegger 1995: 177–96. For an illuminating study of the shifts in Heidegger's thought on animals, see McMahon 2019: 42–5. A view more likely to win endorsement would be the observation 'Auschwitz begins whenever someone looks at a slaughterhouse and thinks they are only animals'. This is widely attributed to Adorno, but cannot, in fact, be found in his writings. For a concise discussion of the contemporary debate on the ethical treatment of animals, see Kuzniar 2011.

In both Greece and Rome stories abound of animals with an affection for humans that occasionally borders on erotic fixation. From Xenophon's hunting dogs devoted to their masters to episodes in Pliny and Aelian that tell of geese, rams, dogs, birds and even a snake in love with a shepherd, the people of the ancient Mediterranean experienced the world as a place inhabited by both humans and animals side by side.[96] The existence of these bonds of affection between human and animal is hardly in itself a revelation, but it does reveal a shortcoming in Aristotelian thought, a failure to grasp that the proximity of animals elicited nuanced and deeply felt emotions that made them 'good to think'.[97] Recently, this approach has emphasized the 'affordances' (qualities that the proximity of animals can offer human awareness) as critical components in our encounters. Maurizio Bettini, for example, has used this approach to identify the qualities of the weasel – motherly instincts, physical agility, flexibility and an ability to wriggle out of tight places – that recommend it to humans as a symbol of successful childbirth.[98] The result is given narrative form in the tale of the weasel that helped Alkmene give birth to Herakles. This is childbirth treated folklorically, with a good dose of sympathetic magic, a mixture of fable and myth that simply defies Aristotelian observation and logic.

Turning the animal encounter into narrative opened up enormous possibilities for exploring human nature. For example, one popular story was that of the elephant who pined for his beloved, a female flower seller, an episode that blends the exotic and the humble. If an animal can feel this way, then what, we are forced to ask, is the nature of attachment? Most of these stories of human/animal attachment stress the exceptional nature of the bond, yet they are almost always modelled on conventional Graeco-Roman sex roles: all ten of the dolphin tales we know of involve boys as the object of the animal's affections. It would be a mistake, therefore, to regard the ancient Mediterranean imagination as a Garden of Eden from which human exceptionalism had been banished. But when Aulus Gellius (*NA* 6.8) describes a boy as a dolphin's beloved (*delphineromenos*), it is

---

[96] Tales of 'cross-species enamourments' are listed in Konstan 2013: 16–17 and are dealt with in greater detail in Williams 2013. For Aelian's treatment of the same theme, see Smith 2013.

[97] See Lloyd 1997: 553. 'Le programme zoologique d'Aristote correspond donc à la recherche de ce qui est dans l'ordre, c'est-à-dire du noble et du beau. Mais il est facile de voir comment cela restraint ses intérêts' (Aristotle's zoological programme corresponds, then, to the search for what is orderly, that is to say, the noble and the beautiful. But it is easy to see how this limits his interests).

[98] Bettini 2013: 127 comments: 'Of course, this notion of metaphorical affordances presupposes that we as humans engage in a metaphorical project that depends on turning animals into symbols, basing specific beliefs on animals' affordances.'

clear that the human/animal barrier has been breached. Hybrids appear to collapse many of the comfortable binaries of Greek epistemology: part and whole, near and far, familiar and unknown, Greek and alien. At each of these points of contact, distinguishing hybrids from monsters is important. If monsters affirm boundaries by discouraging transgression and punishing it, hybrids play a gentler role: they create an imaginative space by replacing certitude with a much richer range of alternatives: uncertainty, possibility, ambiguity. The importance of such a space is illustrated in the rich discourse surrounding the relationship between humans and animals, where, once again, hybridity stands at the interstices.[99] In the broadest possible terms, philosophers treated both human and animal *gene* as parts of the class of living creatures, *zoa*. Within that general classification, philosophers from Demokritos to Aristotle operated with subdivisions that were clear-cut. There was the human realm, and an animal realm comprised of creatures collectively known as *ta aloga* (τὰ ἄλογα), usually rendered in older translations as 'dumb brutes'. For Demokritos, for example, living beings (*zoa*) were drawn to congregate with similar creatures: doves with doves, cranes with cranes and 'likewise in the case of other brute beasts (ἐπὶ ἄλλων ἀλόγων).'[100] The line of demarcation between humans who can talk and beasts that cannot was a hard distinction, so much so that in his treatment of the myth of Epimetheus, Plato has the titan distribute hides and claws to the beasts (*ta aloga*), leaving no protection for 'the human tribe'.[101] Similarly, Plato characterized the wise man as someone who refused to surrender himself to 'beastly and brutish pleasure'.[102] Going a step further, Aristotle framed the categorical difference between animals and humans as complete. Debra Hawhee refers to it as 'the *logos/alogos* distinction that so decisively cleaved humans from animals'.[103] Aristotle also framed the relationship of human and animal as adversarial. According to Aristotle, all relationships consist of either ruling or being ruled, an inflexible teleology which only varies according to the quality of the parties involved. The better the ruled, the better the domination created

---

[99] According to Newmyer 2014: 507, 'It is no exaggeration to state that, from their earliest philosophical musings on other species, the Greeks were preoccupied with determining whether the relationship between human and non-human animals involves more analogy than polarity and more sameness than differentness, and on what grounds such a determination is to be made.'

[100] Demokritos, DK 164: καὶ ἐπὶ ἄλλων ἀλόγων ὡσαύτως.

[101] Plato, *Prt* 321: καταναλώσας τὰς δυνάμεις εἰς τὰ ἄλογα: λοιπὸν δὴ ἀκόσμητον ἔτι αὐτῷ ἦν τὸ ἀνθρώπων γένος (he squandered various capabilities on the beasts, but this left the human race without resources).

[102] Plato, *Rpb* 9.591c: οὐχ ὅπως τῇ θηριώδει καὶ ἀλόγῳ ἡδονῇ ἐπιτρέψας.

[103] Hawhee 2017: 13. See also Heath 2005.

by the ruler. Accordingly, Aristotle infamously justified slavery by concluding that it is even better to dominate another human than to exercise mastery over an animal.[104] Implicit in this argument is the assumption of human superiority: other living creatures were inferior and that inferiority was marked by their inability to speak, their *alogia*. Furthermore, for Aristotle animals are fit for domination because they perceive through their emotions, not through *logos*.[105] Although classified as *aloga*, animals, Aristotle conceded, do have a voice. It can express pain and pleasure, but among living creatures only humans possess speech.[106]

Aristotle's categories underpin a long tradition of exploitation, both of animals and humans who are not free Greek men, but as a system of thought justifying domination Aristotle's arguments run the risk of collapsing under the weight of their own certitude. There will always be a woman to refuse the yoke of marriage, an enslaved person who resists being beaten, a bow that subverts it value as an *organon praktikon* by snapping. In the case of 'dumb beasts', and in our relationship with the horse, in particular, it is not so much a matter of a subaltern resistance to the Aristotelian system of subordination. It is simply that Aristotelian categories do not correspond to the lived experience (and imagination) of the Greeks. Men mourned the death of their favourite horses (and dogs), often immoderately according to Solon. In the case of Kimon, he commemorated the horses who had won at successive Olympics, erecting tombs in their honour opposite his own.[107]

This destabilization is especially prominent when reproduction is at stake. Hybrid creatures such as mules should not be able to reproduce. Deleuze makes much of this sterility, emphasizing that hybrids are 'born of

---

[104] Aristot., *Pol.* 1.1254a: καὶ ἀεὶ βελτίων ἡ ἀρχὴ ἡ τῶν βελτιόνων ἀρχομένων, οἷον ἀνθρώπου ἢ θηρίου (and the better type of domination results from domination over the better type of subjects just as control over a human being is superior to domination over an animal).

[105] Aristot., *Pol.* 1.1254b:. Aristotle makes explicit that division into 'wild' and 'tame' is not legitimate (*De Part. An.* 643b2). For a fuller exploration of humanity and the animality in Aristotelian thought, see Bodéüs 1997. Hawhee 2017 argues that Aristotle's neat binary is partially undone by his tendency to employ animals, particularly in metaphors or examples, to instill speeches with life and feeling: 'Sensing, feeling animals help to fill out the parts of rhetoric that are *alogos*.'

[106] Aristot., *Pol.* 1.1253a: λόγον δὲ μόνον ἄνθρωπος ἔχει τῶν ζῴων (The human alone of living creatures possesses speech). For the denial of reason to animals see Sorabji 1993: 7–16. The topic of animality, speech and rationality is vast, and we will return to it at various points throughout this study. A good point of entry into recent discussions is found in Verde 2020.

[107] For Solon's disapproval see Plut. *Sol.* 7.3–4. For Kimon's horses see Hdt 6.103. See also Lewis and Llewellyn-Jones 2018: 140–1 and Bodson 2000.

a sexual union that will not reproduce itself'.[108] This is not entirely true, of course, since there is a *race* of centaurs which includes Kentaurides (female centaurs), and in Greek theogonies hybrid monsters often produce offspring: the children of Pontos, including Phorkys and Keto, generate many monsters, such as Echidna and Skylla. Nevertheless, a hybrid such as the centaur is a powerful instantiation of Deleuze and Guattari's notion of becoming-animal, their term for the complex entity produced as humans engage with their animality. This animal presence has a long pedigree, going back at least to Empedokles' dictum 'For in truth I was born a boy and a maiden, and a plant and a bird, and a fish whose course lies in the sea.'[109] It also features in Platonic thought, particularly the *Timaeus*, in which the unenlightened soul is reborn in animal form.[110] But becoming-animal has a more specific resonance: the human can knowingly break down the human/animal boundary, creating a post-human hybrid. For Deleuze and Guattari this is not play or imitation, but something different, which they qualify with a concession: 'if becoming-animal does not consist in playing animal or imitating an animal, it is clear that the human being does not "really" become an animal any more than the animal "really" becomes something else'.[111] They do, however, insist that what is created is more than a role-play. Despite their insistence on reality as a supervention there are many contemporary practitioners of humanimality, referred to collectively as therianthropes, who would question where the boundaries of the 'real' lie.[112] For such people there are various ways of 'being' an animal, but they insist that the experience is real, however it is realized, and that it is not play-acting. The hybrid alerts us to a space in Greek culture where a similar polysemy operates.

In a zone of regular cultural contact with the alien, the foreign and the unknown, there is always uncertainty, of language, of food and of manners. The hybrid gives a form to those experiences that do not fit. It creates a manageable and therefore meaningful zone at the edge of the normal, the expected and the quotidian. Put another way, there are categories of regular cultural experience, and then there are exceptional experiences that defy categorization. As a contrafactual, the hybrid forces us to consider the existence of the non-existent. Every hybrid is an alternative to regularity,

---

[108] Deleuze and Guattari 1987: 241. [109] Hipp. *Phil.* 3; *Dox.* 558. [110] Morgan 2012: 325.
[111] Deleuze and Guattari 1987: 238.
[112] For a sympathetic overview of the contemporary therianthropy movement, see Robertson 2013. The sentiments of people exploring their animal nature are based on feelings of being other-than-human and are further evidence of the segmentation or multiplication of identities currently underway in WEIRD (Western, educated, industrialized, rich and democratic) societies.

to normality and therefore to normativity. We embrace them as a way of playing at subversion. Cryptozoology may classify creatures that do not exist, but the very process of investigating and classifying monsters is part of a quasi-Linnaean mindset that carves out a place for alternative facts. In this respect, the hybrid occupies a cultural space similar to Bakhtin's ludic sphere, like carnivals of inversion, such as northern Greece's *Gynaikokrateia*, where women spend the day sitting in the *kafeneion*, or the Roman Saturnalia, where masters served their slaves. The performances involve role reversals as participants adopt the dress and identity that are the opposite of normal. The temporary hybrids created by these inversions – the manly woman, the free slave – may release the tensions created by inequality, but the results are certainly not transgressive in any lasting way. The carnivalesque and the hybrid both point to a cultural pressure that is counter-directional, destabilizing categories and hence certainty without fundamentally undermining either. What lies at the heart of this is a creative uncertainty.

3 | Hybrids around the Corrupting Sea

> Humbaba, his voice is the deluge,
> his speech is fire, his breath is death.
> He hears the forest's murmur for sixty leagues.
> He who ventures into his forest [feebleness will seize him!]
> Who is there who would venture into his forest?
>
> *Gilgamesh* (Standard Babylonian Epic), Tablet II,
> 291–5 trans. A. R. George

Before Greece

Chapter 2 argued that hybridity, narrowly understood as combinations of body parts assembled to produce contrafactuals (lion-man, griffin, hermaphrodite and so forth) arose out of the deep entanglement of human and animal. The snapshots of human history provided in that chapter, taken together, serve as a collage showing human consciousness taking shape in the encounter with animals, real and imagined. In this chapter I wish to complement that survey of the deep roots of hybridity, once again episodically, by identifying the places and cultures in the eastern Mediterranean that supplied the Greeks with the source material for the hybrid images, motifs and ideas of Greek art and poetry. As Walter Burkert wrote twenty years ago, 'Classical scholars should no longer ignore the nearest parallels and partial antecedents of the oldest Greek poetry.'[1] Hybrids emerged with gusto as part of the culture of the Aegean world in the eighth and seventh centuries, but this emergence should be set in the context of centuries of earlier encounters between Greek speakers and other people and cultures around the eastern Mediterranean and lands adjacent. The nature of this contact has been debated continuously for more than 200 years, and over the last generation outdated notions of a unique Greek genius have yielded to a model of diffusionism. Twenty-five years ago Martin West expressed the hope that 'any illusions that the reader may have had about the

---

[1] Burkert 2004: 48.

autonomy of early Greek culture should have faded, or at any rate severely shrunk, in the wash of facts'.[2] In the wake of West's work, scholarship has uncovered numerous points of connection between the poetic imagination of Greece and the Near East. Bruce Louden's study of the *Odyssey*, for example, teases out many of the similarities between Homer's poetic world and its eastern antecedents. To give one example, a text from the Middle Kingdom entitled *The Shipwrecked Sailor* tells the story of a decent man whose entire crew is lost in a massive storm. Shipwrecked, the sailor washes upon the shore of a magical island where he encounters a beneficent divine spirit in the form of a great snake who prophesies a successful homecoming. The points of connection between the Egyptian text and the Circe episode of Odysseus' *nostos* are unmistakable and suggest more than generic similarities, but reading Homer as just a Greek translation of Egyptian or Near Eastern texts would underestimate the complexity of culture contact and its impact on poetic practice. Louden, for example, demonstrates that Homer's poetry combines material from a wide range of sources: Mesopotamian, Egyptian, Ugaritic and especially the Old Testament. More recently even this unidirectional approach, privileging the flow of culture to the west from the east, has come under pressure as scholars have begun to emphasize the back-and-forth exchange of ideas and motifs that circulated around the eastern Mediterranean, as well as local responses to imported goods and ideas.[3] In this formulation, the zone in which Egyptian, Assyrian, Phoenician and Greek interact is a network, with multiple nodes and the movement of cultural forms, objects, ideas and practices along the ties between them. The Aegean world was thus embedded in a much larger *oikoumene* of cultures.

---

[2] West 1997: 59. For a useful overview of changing approaches to the diffusionist model, see López-Ruiz 2010: 23–47. It may seem unnecessary to challenge the Glory-that-was-Greece school of thought, but Greek exceptionalism dies hard. In 1992 Bernard Knox wrote that 'The primacy of the Greeks in the canon of Western literature is neither an accident nor the result of a decision imposed by higher authority; it is simply a reflection of the intrinsic worth of the material, its sheer originality and brilliance' (p. 21). Similarly, Isaac et al. 2009 contains the remarkable claim that 'It is generally accepted that Greek civilization was the first to raise abstract, systematic thought to a level that we now recognize as approaching our own' (p. 9, with a footnote referencing Frankfort 1946). For a slightly more elegant formulation of the notion, though equally misguided, see Golder 2011.

[3] For recent pushback against a simple model of diffusion from east to west, see Haubold 2013, primarily concerning literature, and Arrington 2021: 88–98, regarding material culture. In a review written nearly seventy-five years ago, Norman O. Brown put the danger of diffusionism succinctly: 'The history of religion is conceived as a blind diffusion and collision of tribal traditions, with little or no regard for the functional interrelationship between religious institutions and the total culture of which they form a part.' See Brown 1949: 218.

The earliest levels of the stratigraphy of hybrid images in the setting of urban cultures go back to Mesopotamia. Emphasizing the innovations associated with urban settlements, David Wengrow attributes the spread of hybrid imagery to the new modes of information storage and dissemination arising in the bureaucratic record keeping of the new states. At this time, he notes, 'the trajectory toward standardization and modularity in material culture intensified markedly'.[4] With respect to record keeping, he further suggests that, 'In order for such a recording system to function, every named commodity – each beer or oil jar, each dairy vessel and their contents, and each animal of the herd – had to be interchangeable with, and thus equivalent to, every other of the same administrative class.'[5] This resulted in images of hybrids which Wengrow terms 'contrafactuals'. He concludes: 'Composites thus encapsulated, in striking visual forms, the bureaucratic imperative to confront the world, not as we ordinarily encounter it – made up of unique and sentient totalities – but as an imaginary realm made up of divisible subjects, each comprising a multitude of fissionable, commensurable, and recombinable parts.'[6] This may be giving too much credit to the imaginative powers of the scribes of Mesopotamia, but it does explain the emergence of a hybrid bestiary from the earlier strata of human/animal experiences, such as hunting, butchery and shamanism, as explored in Chapter 1.

Hybrids were a distinctive feature of life in Mesopotamia, where for three millennia people experienced regular fluctuations of growth and decline, marked by invasion, widescale destruction and a succession of dynasties.[7] Reflecting these conditions, beginning in Sumer, and radiating out from the Assyrians to the Hittites, successive west Asian cultures told stories of a continuous cycle of the breakdown and restoration of order. In these myths the endless succession of pestilence, conflict and upheaval afflicting human society was recast as a cosmic struggle between gods and monsters associated with primordial chaos – the so-called *Chaoskampf*.[8] In the texts and depictions of these stories, on seals and

---

[4] Wengrow 2014: 69.   [5] Wengrow 2014: 70.
[6] Wengrow 2014: 73. It is worth contrasting Wengrow's interpretation of hybrids as bureaucratic inventions with Nash and Pieszko 1982, whose study of preschoolers' reactions to different hybrid combinations points to a fundamental human response to human headedness versus animal headedness. There is a taxonomy of unpleasantness and incongruity.
[7] Thompson 2004: 617 offers a pithy summary: 'An empirical examination of Mesopotamia and Egypt for the 4000–1000 BCE period shows a statistically significant relationship between climate deterioration and river level fluctuations, hinterland incursions, trade collapses, and political regime changes.'
[8] The theme of *Chaosmythus* was first explored by Gunkel 1895 in his study of the historical and religious world in which the Hebrew Bible's narrative of creation was shaped. Gunkel identified

slate palettes, the evil that must be vanquished is usually a hideous hybrid dragon combining lion and serpent features.[9] It rages furiously; it threatens to overwhelm the earth and even challenges heaven. This primordial struggle is not unique to Mesopotamia, but it is here that we first glimpse the distant ancestors of Greek hybrids who also straddle the lines between divine, human and monster. As Wiggerman has conclusively demonstrated, in its earliest Near Eastern forms the polarities of the *Chaoskampf* were mapped on to the stark contrasts of the topography of Mesopotamia.[10] Monsters, like the merman *kulullû*, were composite creatures, agents of unpredictability, associated with the sea, mountains and distant places.[11] Gods, in contrast, were anthropomorphic, represented order and were associated with lowlands and dry land.[12] In Sumer, Akkad and Babylon where these gods had their homes, this cosmic worldview ideologically underpinned royalty. Order and right ritual action all validated kingship, framing it as a victory in the here and now of a battle which had raged across the cosmos. As T. J. Lewis puts it, 'the primary motif running through the *Chaoskampf* traditions about Tispak in Eshnunna, Marduk in Babylon, and Ba'lu at Ugarit was divine supremacy, and such pre-eminence was articulated via the language of royalty'.[13] In this scheme, the defeat of monsters (which in the Ancient Near East were overwhelmingly hybrids) was necessary for the movement from chaos to order to come about. As a result, ancient Mesopotamia teemed with lion-centaurs, goat-fish, and other *Mischwesen* ('mixed beings').[14] Most were malevolent, but some, like the fish-*apkallû*, were seen as benevolent beings

---

a Dragon-Tradition and a Primal Sea-Tradition as originally Babylonian. The term *Chaoskampf* does not occur in the work itself but is used as a convenient shorthand for the motif of cosmic struggle. Debate concerning the applicability of *Chaoskampf* to Biblical exegesis remains highly contested. See Batto 2013, Ayali-Darshan 2014 and Ballentine 2015. The significance of the theme to Mesopotamian cosmology, however, remains fundamental. For an ecological interpretation of the fluctuations encoded in the struggle, see Thompson 2004: 617.

[9] Lewis 2020: 433–7.   [10] Wiggermann 1992: 158.
[11] On the *kulullû* merman, see Wiggermann 1992: 76.
[12] The principal exception to the representation of Mesopotamian gods in fully anthropomorphic form is the depiction of Ereshkigal on the Burney Relief from Nippur in the early second millennium (British Museum 2003, 0718.1). The goddess wears a crown of horns, has wings attached to her shoulders, has dew claws growing from her calves, and has bird-claws with talons in place of feet. While her wings suggest divinity, her other attributes point towards her association with death. For discussion of the artefact's provenance, authenticity and identification, see Porada 1980, Collon 2005 and Collon 2007. For the notion that religion develops from the capacity to imagine things which do not exist, such as hybrids, see Mithen 2009.
[13] Lewis 2020: 454.   [14] Black and Green 1992: 53.

who could be enlisted through incantation and spells to protect houses and even help exorcise demons.[15]

The legacy of Babylonian cosmology as it spread across the Ancient Near East was a fundamental conception of the world as a battleground where monstrous hybrid creatures had to be kept at bay or enlisted for protection.[16] As part animals, these earliest Babylonian hybrids had access to powers that humans do not. As Constance Gane puts it, 'Many species of animals can do things and move in ways that humans cannot. Composite creatures, in which boundaries between species are crossed, possess superior combinations of capabilities that enable them to transcend boundaries of action and motion available to any one species.'[17] The longevity of this tradition is striking, but only very few general symbols, such as the horned helmet signifying divinity, remained unchanged from the Early Dynastic Period onwards.[18] Hybrid monsters of Babylonian myth were not repositories of fixed meaning, nor can they be read as precise allegories. Instead, hybridity served to mark one pole in the elemental opposition that was expressed in cosmogenic myths: anthropomorphic order versus hybrid monstrosity. Karen Sonik notes that 'the alterity of outsiders and enemies, regardless of whether these were ambiguously dangerous, potentially helpful, or explicitly harmful, might be marked by physical anomaly, a measure of bestiality or brutishness in appearance, or even explicit corporeal hybridity'.[19] Resisting the urge to assign precise meaning to particular hybrids, some scholars have returned to the notion of artistic style as a self-contained system in which change is generated independently of any supposed underlying meaning. The griffin, for example, was the most popular hybrid to enter the Aegean canon from the Near East, but whereas it was originally a personification of evil forces, in the Aegean its predatory power was linked to its role as a protector of divine power and royal authority.[20]

Similarly, Sebastiano Soldi has examined the antecedents of the Chimaira, the creature which Homer describes as having the forepart of a lion, a snake in the back and a goat in the middle. Acknowledging that the

---

[15] Ataç 2010: 150–8 and Geller 2016. In rituals designed to avert evil from houses, clay statuettes of the fish-*apkallū* were placed within the house facing east, after having been blessed, and were invoked in an elaborate ritual that culminated in the words 'Evil go out!' Handbooks containing various spells and incantations, sometimes referred to as the 'Exorcist's Vademecum', classified these figurines as statuettes of Ea and Marduk repelling Evil Ones.

[16] See Frey-Anthes 2007.   [17] Gane 2012: 228.   [18] Pongratz-Leisten and Sonik 2015: 31.

[19] Sonik 2015: 152.

[20] On the griffin's eastern origins, see Crowley 1989: 46–51. On its protective role, see Tamvaki 1974: 289.

Figure 3.1 Mušḫuššu bas-relief from the Ishtar Gate, Pergamon Museum. Glazed brick, ca. 575 BC. © Allie Caulfield/Wikimedia Commons.

Chimaira familiar from the Arezzo bronze is a product of the Greek imagination, he nevertheless identifies a series of antecedents from across the Ancient Near East: second millennium *kudurru* stones from Babylonia depicting a fish-goat hybrid, the lion-dragon from eighteenth-century Ebla, the scorpion-man on Neo-Assyrian seals and, of course, the *mušḫuššu* dragon, best known from the glazed bricks of the Ishtar Gate in Babylon (605–562 BC) (Figure 3.1). Since the body parts of these hybrids are subject to constant reconfiguration over the course of more than a millennium, Soldi quite properly does not ascribe a fixed meaning to these assemblages, instead drawing attention to mutation and recombination. He observes that

> The early experiments influenced by Mesopotamian art gave birth to a fully developed syntax where Anatolian and Syrian traditions melt in new original productions. This process of assembling different part of animals had further development in the Greek world, where the top of the wings of the winged lion became the head of the new Chimaera and a snake's head substituted the bird of prey's head at the end of the tail.[21]

A similar process operates in the case of the winged horse. Donald Matthews refuses to see a winged horse on a Middle Assyrian seal as a direct precursor of the Greek Pegasus, but rather 'as a reinterpretation

[21] Soldi 2012: 108.

by the engraver of his artistic inheritance, which resulted from a natural development in the rules governing the act of creation'.[22] Matthews adds:

> It may thus be misleading to identify the monsters on the contest seals with the repertory of supernatural beings, still less with denizens of unconnected mythic traditions such as the Greek Pegasus. On the contrary, nearly all monsters can be understood most economically as recombinations of elements which already existed separately in natural conjunctions of forms in the previous period.[23]

Near Eastern Cosmologies and Combat Myth

As objects, carved in glyptic, moulded as figurines or depicted in brick reliefs, Near Eastern hybrids embodied the fantastic and otherworldly powers that threatened urban life. It is possible to offer a more precise picture of how this package was received in the Aegean world of the early Iron Age because the poetry of the time is frequently concerned with the same theme: the defeat of monsters and the establishment of order, although it is clear that this theme and related motifs were altered in Greek settings. This is best seen in Hesiod's *Theogony*, where what Martin West called West Asiatic elements are now recognized as important influences. The *Theogony*, as Carolina López-Ruiz, puts it, 'sets out to exalt the enthronement of the Storm God (Zeus), a motif ... that runs through the mainstream of Near Eastern traditions *(Enuma Elish, Baal Cycle, Kumarbi Cycle)*'.[24] In the Song of Kumarbi, for example, often referred to as *Kingship in Heaven*, Anu, Kumarbi and Teššub succeed each other as violently as their Hesiodic equivalents: Ouranos, Kronos and Zeus. Anu's 'manhood' is bitten off by Kumarbi, much as Ouranos is castrated by Kronos. Kumarbi plans on preventing his displacement by eating his child, Teššub, but is given a lump of basalt to eat, just as Kronos is deceived into eating a rock instead of devouring Zeus. In both stories, the young storm god survives and finally supplants the father. Yet the Near Eastern version that so closely foreshadows the Greek theogony is a Hurro-Hittite version of the story that predates Hesiod by five hundred years, so the similarities point to a process more complicated than simple textual transmission. Furthermore, Hesiod's treatment of the birth of the gods also shows the influence of the Babylonian celebration of Marduk's ancestry

---

[22] Matthews 1992: 191. [23] Matthews 1992: 201. [24] López-Ruiz 2010: 177.

and victories, *Enuma Elish*. Composed in the second millennium BC and performed at the New Year festival, *Enuma Elish* linked Marduk's victory over Tiamat to the regeneration brought by the new year. The hymn describes how Marduk fills Tiamat's belly with the *imhullu* wind until it swells, before shooting her and standing over her corpse. Central to the story of Marduk's ascendancy is his triumph over a series of hybrid monsters: 'a horned serpent, a *Mušḫuššu* -dragon, and a *lahmu*-hero, an *ugallu*-demon, a rabid dog, and a scorpion-man, aggressive *umu*-demons, a fish-man and a bull-man bearing merciless weapons, fearless in battle'.[25] It is this broad pattern of anthropomorphic deities defeating elemental monsters that would be adapted in early Greek poetry, drawing on more than a single cosmogenic text.

Despite the similarities between Hesiod's cosmological account and its Near Eastern antecedents, there are significant differences as motifs are transferred. This becomes clear when the Babylonian cosmology is read in its environmental setting. Tiamat, the mother of monsters, is identified with the salt water of the deep sea. She is paired with Apsu, the sweet river waters. As sweet and salty water, they are dialogically linked, the former bringing life and the latter producing monsters. This reflects the ecology of Mesopotamia, where the increasing salinity of a rising water table, the intrusion of the sea onto the land, as it were, represents a real threat to the land's ability to grow crops and sustain life.[26] The two waters are therefore locked in a struggle that mirrors the experiences of the people of southern Mesopotamia in particular: the waters of the Gulf are brackish close to shore, where the sweet waters of the Tigris and Euphrates merge with the salty seawater. The only semi-divine creatures associated with this coastal zone of the Persian Gulf are the *Apkallū*, whose hybridity consists of a fish skin and tail that envelops their human form. They are neither full-fledged gods nor are they fish-garbed priests, but something in between, both man and fish.[27] Their fish component derives from the *purādu* fish

---

[25] *Enuma Elish* Tablet III (tr. S. Dalley). I follow here the text as printed in López-Ruiz 2017: 13.

[26] Among the monsters defeated by Marduk is *lahmu*, a demon often associated with Eridu. If, as has been suggested, his name means 'The Muddy One', his presence among Tiamat's forces may indicate that he personifies the threat of a rising water table and increasing salinity, problems which afflicted Eridu because of its transitional position between land and sea. See Bonatz 2019. On the ecology of Eridu, see Leick 2001: 1–3.

[27] Ataç 2010: 170, Wiggerman 1992: 76. Across Mesopotamia the *apkallū* appeared in different forms, and in incantations and reliefs it is possible to distinguish anthropomorphic, winged figures (*ūmu-apkallū*), bird-*apkallū*, and fish-*apkallū*. The bird-*apkallū* may have originated in Assyria as apotropaic spirits, but the fish-*apkallū* are regarded as genuinely Babylonian and do not display the combative character of the other groups. Altogether they occur frequently in Mesopotamian literature of the second and first millennium BC, and the fish-*apkallū* seem to

(carp). These are freshwater fish, capable of flourishing in brackish waters, and are not found in the deep waters of the Gulf. Accordingly, the *Apkallū* are not associated with Tiamat, the deep salt waters from which arose monsters. Instead, they straddle the sea and the land. Alien, strange, unsettling, yet not monstrous, the *Apkallū* are perfect examples of the benevolent hybrid. They serve as sage figures and royal advisors.[28] When the Babylonian priest Berossos wanted to explain the deep antiquity of his culture to the Seleucid dynasty he relied on a description of the *Apkallu* Oannes because, despite the alarming oddity of an amphibious creature who walked out of the sea each night to confer on humanity the gift of culture, it was a type of hybrid the Greeks could recognize: exotic and strange, yet ultimately a benefactor of mankind.[29] In Greece, the centaur Cheiron would come to serve a similar function.

The elemental polarities of the Babylonian creation story do not map well onto the more varied landscape of Greece and the Aegean world. Accordingly, in Hesiod's account of creation the simple monstrosity of Tiamat gives way to the more complex profile of Tethys: her partner is Okeanos, the deep water that surrounds the world, analogous to Apsu, but the rivers born from Tethys and Okeanos are deep-eddying, silver-swirling and divine, from the Nile to the Danube. They are not an elemental threat to mortals. Furthermore, the union of Tethys and Okeanos produces not only rivers, but also a catalogue of nymphs:

> For there are three thousand neat-ankled daughters of Ocean who are dispersed far and wide, and in every place alike serve the earth and the deep waters, children who are glorious among goddesses. And as many other rivers are there, babbling as they flow, sons of Ocean, whom queenly Tethys bare, but their names it is hard for a mortal man to tell, but people know those by which they severally dwell.
>
> Hesiod, *Theog.* 374–80

In place of Mesopotamian hybrid monsters – lion-men, scorpion-men, goat-fish – whose animal parts emphasize their anomaly, the Greek poet imagines entirely anthropomorphic semi-goddesses. Though the nymphs are interstitial figures existing between mortals and gods, as are the Babylonian hybrids, they are awesome rather than monstrous.

---

have particularly strong associations with the southern cities of Eridu, Bad-tibira, Larak and Sippar. See Streck 2003. Carp remain the largest component of Iraq's commercial fisheries. See Etheredge 2011: 37, and Kitto and Tabish 2004.

[28] See van Dijk 1962 and Dillery 2015: 66.

[29] On Berossos, the *Apkallu* and Oannes, see Lang 2013, Haubold 2013: 157; Dillery 2015 and McInerney 2017.

Hesiod's catalogues still resonate with the echo of monstrosity, but it is muted. Okeanos' daughter Electra bears the Harpies, Aello and Okypete ('Swift-Storm' and 'Swift-Flying') (*Theog.* 267), while other seaborn goddesses, Keto and Echidna, are the mothers of monsters. Tiamat has functionally been split into a series of lesser figures. There are other signs of adaption and modification in Hesiod's treatment of the earlier material. In *Enuma Elish* it is Tiamat who is defeated by her descendant of five generations later, Marduk, while in Hesiod it is Tethys' creation Typhon who is defeated by Zeus.[30] Once again, there are similarities in the cosmogenic poems of the Babylonians and Greeks, but a simple line of textual transmission, as if Hesiod were reading a translation of *Enuma Elish*, is implausible.[31] Instead, the relationship between the earlier hymn to Marduk and Hesiod's celebration of Zeus resembles a family photo album, in which some pages and some details are missing, but where broad similarities can still be made out. It is a relationship that occurred in other areas of cultural activity as well. In medicine, for example, it is possible to identify broad commonalities in the way Egyptian, Assyrian and Greek practitioners understood disease. As Markus Asper notes, 'all three traditions share the same concept of "disease" as an entity, defined by a set of observable symptoms, caused by external factors, having the same trajectory in all patients, which allows for a general prognosis'.[32] All three systems shared a common practice of listing symptoms, often noting their duration measured in days, and on occasion recording similar treatments, such as seizing the tongue before giving the patient medicine to drink. But it is perhaps not surprising that in mathematics, astronomy and medicine, all highly specialized areas based on observation, the transmission of precise knowledge could take place across hundreds of miles and even hundreds of years: linguistic and medical parallels between a twelfth-century Egyptian text and a fourth-century Hippokratic text dealing with pregnancy illustrate the transmission of specific knowledge.[33]

Hybrids, monsters and battling gods, however, are not the subject of technical treatises. So, while it is not the case that all or even most of the *Mischwesen* that populate Babylonian religion are wholly transferred into the Greek setting of Hesiod's poetry, when Zeus subdues Typhoeus (*Theog.* 820–80) he is repeating a basic, recurring pattern of Near Eastern religious thought, according to which chaotic and elemental forces are figured as

---

[30] West 1966: 24; López-Ruiz 2010: 90–1.
[31] For a subtle treatment of similarities and differences between Greek and Mesopotamian creation stories, see Haubold 2013: 18–73.
[32] Asper 2015: 26.   [33] Pommerening 2010.

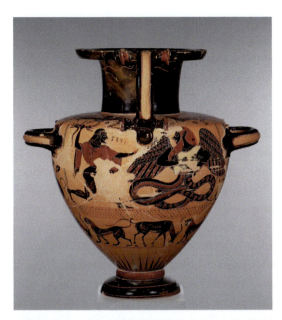

Figure 3.2 Zeus aiming his thunderbolt at a winged and snake-footed Typhoeus. Chalcidian black-figured hydria (ca. 540–530 BC), Staatliche Antikensammlungen (Inv. 596).

hybrids.[34] The depiction of Zeus's victory on black-figure vases not only conforms to Hesiod's rendering of the cosmogenic myth but also shows that Greek artists had picked up hybridity as part of a visual vocabulary to express elemental monstrosity (Figure 3.2). At this point, the literary and material evidence for the Near Eastern genealogy of Greek hybrids begin to converge.

Theogonies aside, there are other texts and genres where it is possible to trace the ancestry of Greek hybrids back to their Near Eastern forebears.[35] A good example of this is the story of Gilgamesh and later Greek hero stories. The Gilgamesh cycle goes back in one form or another to the third millennium, but tablets recounting the hero's adventures were in Ashurbanipal's library at Nineveh, so his tale was still being retold and rewritten as late as the seventh century BC. It is no surprise, therefore, that episodes originating with Gilgamesh should be reflected in Greek myth. Gilgamesh, like Odysseus and Herakles in Stesichorus' *Geryoneis*, travels to the Underworld. Like Odysseus, too, Gilgamesh must cope with the advances of a sex goddess, and in both poems angry gods threaten to overturn the natural order if the hero is not punished. (Ishtar will bring

---

[34] For the Typhoeus episode as part of a longer tradition with Sumerian, Akkadian and possibly Ugaritic version, see West 1997: 300–4. For the pattern of Storm-God versus Monster, see Lewis 1996.

[35] For an overview of recurring motifs and story patterns, see Burkert 2004: 21–48.

up the dead from the Underworld if Gilgamesh is not made to pay for spurning her; Helios will take the sun to the Underworld if Odysseus' men are not punished for eating the Cattle of the Sun.) Some episodes reflect broad similarities of plot, such as Gilgamesh embracing Enkidu in the Underworld and asking him about his parents, just as Odysseus tries to embrace his mother in the Underworld in Book 11 of the *Odyssey*. Other details suggest an even closer affinity: Achilles' lamentation over the body of Patroklos includes the forlorn gesture of touching the corpse's chest (*Il.* 18. 317) in precisely the same way that Gilgamesh reaches out to touch the heart of Enkidu (*Gilg.* VIII.iii).[36] These correspondences underscore the complexity of what used to be called the Orientalizing Period.[37] In the Greek response to the cultures of the eastern Mediterranean there are signs at times of a very close familiarity with the earlier poetic traditions, and at other times a much more attenuated presence of Near Eastern motifs, as if there have been other stages of transmission unknown to us.

In the Gilgamesh cycle, the episode that best illustrates the complex relationship between a Near Eastern and Greek monster is the tale of Humbaba, the Guardian of the Forest.[38] In Tablet V of the Standard Babylonian Version, Gilgamesh and Enkidu travel to the forest to do battle with Humbaba. This fearsome creature is described as a terror of the people. His shout is 'the flood weapon', his utterance 'is Fire', his 'breath is Death'. These expressions are broadly generic, fixing Humbaba's place in the category of foreign threat, but once the heroes engage the monster it is hard not to see the episode as a distant forerunner to Odysseus' encounter with the Cyclops.[39] Like Polyphemos, Humbaba is huge; he remarks that 'Enkidu is small fry ... You are so very small that I regard you as a turtle or a tortoise ... so I do not approach you.' Humbaba concludes dismissively, 'Even if I were to kill you, would I satisfy my stomach?' Like the Cyclops, Humbaba is a cannibal, and like Polyphemos he will be struck in the head by his assailant and left dazed. After overcoming Humbaba, Enkidu cuts down a mighty pine tree to serve as part of a raft, just as Odysseus will fashion a weapon from a piece of olive wood as big as a ship's mast. Gilgamesh's timber-raiding expedition to the pine forest will become in Homer the tale of a daring escape from a monster's cave.

[36] West 1997: 340–3.
[37] For the complex history of 'Orientalizing', see Arrington 2021: 27–61.
[38] For a useful introduction to the history of the text of the *Gilgamesh* epic and the Humbaba episode, see Forsyth 1987: 21–43.
[39] On similarities between Polyphemos, Humbaba and Gilgamesh, see Knox 1979. If Humbaba, whose terrible power is connected to his voice, is a distant prototype for Polyphemos, this might suggest that the Cyclops' name is closer to 'loud' than 'famous'. On Gilgamesh's name corresponding to 'Cyclops', see Oberhuber 1974.

Figure 3.3 Carnelian seal depicting the killing of Humbaba (centre) by Gilgamesh (left, in royal regalia) and Enkidu (right) eighth century BC (Neo-Assyrian) 1.30 × 2.80 cm. British Museum, 1613474571. © The Trustees of the British Museum.

But, as with the transformation of Marduk's victory over Tiamat into Zeus's victory over Typhoeus, text and visual media follow different trajectories and suggest a more complicated genealogy. Representations of Humbaba find a Greek parallel not in Polyphemos, but in the gorgon. In a Neo-Assyrian carnelian seal (see Figure 3.3) a gigantic Humbaba is shown between Gilgamesh and Enkidu in the *Knielauf* position, often also used for the gorgon, as in the pediment of the early sixth-century Temple of Artemis on Corfu.[40] Like the gorgon, Humbaba looks directly towards the viewer. The spiky hair, wide-open eyes and grimacing lower half of his face emphasize his grotesque appearance, just as the gorgon will have serpents for hair and is sometimes depicted bearded. And both creatures are beheaded, leaving a disembodied head to serve as a talisman. For this reason, Jane Carter has referred to the Gorgoneion as 'the spiritual descendent of Humbaba'.[41] The similarities are apparent when one compares a terracotta mask from Sippar from ca. 1700 BC and an Etruscan antefix fired more than a millennium later.[42] It would be absurd, of course, to suggest that the demonic figure was transferred from one cultural setting to

---

[40] For the Assyrian elements, including the Knielauf gorgon, see Hopkins 1934.
[41] Carter 1987: 382. Carter shows in detail the material connections linking the Ortheia sanctuary to Phoenicia: metal, ivory and, above all, terracotta masks. The relationship between the grimacing demons of Ortheia and Humbaba is not one of uncomplicated linear descent but of Near Eastern motifs redeployed.
[42] Compare a fired clay mask of the demon Humbaba, 1800 BC–1600 BC, Sippar. 3.3 in × 3.25 in. British Museum 116624, and a terracotta antefix of Medusa, sixth century BC, Etruscan. 5 1/2 in. × 5 7/8 in. Metropolitan Museum of Art, 27.122.14.

another unchanged, but the long afterlife of the type is notable – a longevity that shows that the syntax of monstrosity is primarily a repetition of form, and only secondarily of meaning (and even then at the most basic level of monster as threat).

Humbaba's legacy is complicated. Take, for example, the astrological connection that associates Humbaba with the Pleiades. In Babylonian and Assyrian sources, such as the Neo-Assyrian carnelian seal shown in Figure 3.3, the stars are represented by the seven points above Humbaba's head and shoulder. The constellation's appearance was identified by the Babylonians with the Vernal Equinox, and in Babylonian sky-lore the Pleiades, known as MUL.MUL (the Stars), have two aspects.[43] One is positive, marking the passage of regular time, occasionally indicating the need for intercalated months and assisting the major gods. In this aspect they are agents of order, but they are also closely connected to seven demons (Sebuttu) who caused the eclipse of the Moon and are linked to the Underworld god, Nergal.[44] For the Greeks, however, the Pleiades operate with a somewhat different set of associations. Their rising in May marks the best time for harvesting, as in the Babylonian calendar, just as their setting marks the best time to plough, but their rising and setting also signal the sailing season, a concern irrelevant to those watching the skies over Babylon.[45]

Despite these differences, some elements of the Near Eastern stories beyond merely the suggestion of monstrosity do seem to make an appearance in the Greek world. In Sparta, choruses of young women performed hymns and dances in which they played the roles of stars. In Alkman's *Partheneion*, for example, the beautiful girls were identified as the Pleiades.[46] Gloria Ferrari has explored the cosmos of early Sparta and shown that these choral performances were concerned with myths of regarding 'the disintegration of established order – one in the polis, the

---

[43] On the importance of the Pleiades for marking the equinox, see Miller 1988. For the Babylonian sky-lore associated with the constellation, see Hunger and Pingree 1989. On correspondences between Babylonian constellations in the Mulapin and Greek constellations see van der Waerden 1973, p. 74. See also Barton 1994, p. 19. For Greek recognition of Babylonian astronomy see Aristotle, *de Caelo* 2.12.

[44] Verderame 2016.

[45] Pleiades marking agricultural seasons and sailing: Hes. *W&D* 383–4, 614–17, Aratus, *Phaenomena* 254–67. See Burnett 1964, Ferrari 2008: 85–8, McInerney 2015: 305–8.

[46] Alkman, *Partheneion* 60–4. That Alkman really was comparing the girls of the chorus to the stars was convincingly argued by Burnett 1964. For discussion of various attempts to elucidate the astronomical context of the poem, see Segal 1983. For similar associations between chorus and the movement of heavenly bodies, see Ferrari 2008, pp. 80–1. For Alkman's chorus as human rivals to the Pleiades, see Csapo 2008: 266–7.

other in the heavens'.⁴⁷ In other words, the Near Eastern view that cosmic and civil order are reflections of each other was transferred across to a Greek setting. Alkman's Pleiades broadly correspond to the positive aspects of the Babylonian Pleiades, and serve as agents for the confirmation of order in heaven and in Sparta. The transmission from Babylonian cosmology to a Greek setting, however unexpected, makes sense given that Jane Carter has demonstrated that there is ample evidence for Phoenician influence at the Orthia sanctuary.⁴⁸ An ivory plaque, for example, showing the culture hero Aristeas with wings recalls apotropaic figures such as the bird-headed ivory figure from Ugarit.⁴⁹ And as the older conception of cosmic order was played out in Spartan ritual, a necessary component was a monster to be vanquished, a Greek Humbaba. This would explain the presence at the sanctuary of Artemis Orthia of more than 600 grotesque terracotta masks. It has been argued that the masks from Orthia represent the origins of Greek drama, which may be true, but what can be said with certainty is that, in the Archaic period, Spartan ritual relied heavily on masks. In the performances that analogized the beauty of a chorus and the harmony of their song to the order of the cosmos, the presence of grotesques evoked the threat of monstrosity and disorder. Behind the Orthia masks can dimly be seen the figures of Gilgamesh and Humbaba.⁵⁰

The Ancient Near East supplied the Aegean world with many examples of monsters and demons but also culture heroes, all exhibiting some form of hybridity. The cultural zone, however, which we might expect to have had the most profound influence on Greek notions of hybridity was Egypt, especially given the trade relations between Egypt and Crete in the second millennium.⁵¹ In Egypt an entire cosmology was shaped around a pantheon of animal-headed (and sometimes animal-bodied) gods. However, the influence of these Egyptian theriocephalic gods is much less pronounced than we might expect. This is a paradox worth exploring more fully. Hybrids occur in Egyptian art as early as the predynastic period, when Mesopotamian influence

---

⁴⁷ Ferrari 2008: 17.   ⁴⁸ Carter 1987.
⁴⁹ Ivory plaque depicting Aristaios. Sanctuary of Orthia, Sparta. 650–600 BC. 5.08 × 2.54 cm. British Museum 1954,0910.1. Ivory figure of a griffin-headed demon. Urartu. 800–600 BC. Toprakkale, Turkey 14 × 6 × 4 cm. British Museum 118951.
⁵⁰ For Orthia as evidence of masks in Spartan ritual, see Ferrari 2008: 17. For Orthia masks and Greek drama, see Nielson 2002: 88 and Rosenberg 2015.
⁵¹ The subject of Egyptian and Cretan relations in the second millennium is a vast topic and the subject of innumerable theses, articles, books and conferences. For a very clear overview, see Cline 1999. For the influence of Egyptian hieroglyphs on Cretan Linear A, see Woudhuizen 2011.

is pronounced.[52] At Tell el-Farkha excavators have found both a griffin and a snake-woman, while excavations of the earliest dynastic sites have brought to light evidence for fantastic creatures such as the serpent-necked felines of the Narmer palette.[53] In another example, the Two Dog Palette, the non-grinding side is decorated with what David Wengrow calls 'a carefully orchestrated bedlam' consisting of animals both real and imaginary: oryx, ibex, aurochs, lions and possibly a giraffe, as well as a griffin and a serpopard (see Figure 3.4). On the lower left side is the hybrid figure of a man with an animal's head and tail playing a pipe. It is tempting to identify this figure as a shaman, and to imagine that these early dynastic scenes are snapshots of Nile culture at a time when the real and imagined worlds were still intwined. Wengrow calls attention to the restricted use of these objects and apparent changes in their use

Figure 3.4 Two dog palette. Predynastic – Early Dynastic Egypt (ca. 3300–3100 BC). 42.5 cm × 22 cm. Ashmolean Museum AN1896-1908.E.3924.

---

[52] Smith 1992 and Pittman 1996. More recently, see Wengrow 2014: 49, who emphasizes what he describes as 'an art of ambiguity where the forms of living beings mingle and interpenetrate on contact, and where meaningful relations emerge from the blending of affinities rather than the assemblage of contrasts'.

[53] Tell el-Farkha hybrids: Ciałowicz 2011.

shortly before 3,000 BC, postulating that these ceremonial objects were imbued with 'the legitimizing force of custom and social memory', useful attributes that could be harnessed by newly emerging elites.[54] These 'serpopards', though striking, soon drop out of the Egyptian repertoire, although composite griffin figures, with lion bodies and eagle heads, remain closely associated with the depiction of royal authority.[55] Over the course of the second millennium the proliferation of hybrid images of gods and hybrid beings continued, but this was closely connected to an expanding apparatus of state control. Erik Hornung has drawn attention to the role of 'hieroglyphic thinking' in the creation of hybrid figures in Egyptian iconography of the second millennium, but unlike Wengrow's emphasis on bureaucratic control of information in Mesopotamia, Hornung sees these as depictions of divine power in its most concentrated form.[56] In other words, hybrids arise in the context of centralized state power and a developed ideology of kingship and divine order. Without these conditions in the Bronze Age Aegean, the transfer of hybrids would only take place at the level of exotic objects and images of wonder. An Egyptian scarab or faience figurine outside of an Egyptian setting is a medium without a message.

Koinon and *Oikoumene*

The origins of Greek hybrids lie in sporadic episodes of adoption and adaption. Near Eastern antecedents were influential in poetry, and some connections, if not continuities, have been identified largely in the syntax of hybridity. But there is one antecedent that is qualitatively different, and this is the emergence across the Aegean and Ancient Near East in the Late Bronze Age of a body of shared artistic practices and objects often referred to as 'International Style'. This was a shared repertoire of motifs and shapes prevalent from 1400 to 1200 BC around the eastern Mediterranean and lands connected to it. International Style displayed a strong preference for hybrid forms, including, in Marian Feldman's description, 'sphinxes and griffins, fantastical vegetation in the form of volute palmettes, running spirals, and guilloche patterns'.[57] A diadem from Enkomi with alternating sphinxes and spirals is a good example (see Figure 3.5).

Although the term 'International Style' has been in use since the middle of the last century it has often been employed problematically, since it was

---

[54] Wengrow 2006: 178–82 (description of the Two Dog Palette); 185–7 (elite legitimacy).
[55] Narmer palette: Wilkinson 2000: 28. Griffins: Gerke 2014: 15–24.   [56] Hornung 2000: 20.
[57] Feldman 2006: 2.

Figure 3.5 Gold foil diadem with sphinxes and spiral patterns. Enkomi, Cyprus, 1550–1050 BC. British Museum, 1897,0401.518. © The Trustees of the British Museum.

nearly always part of an interpretive framework that assumed a pure, 'national' style (Egyptian, Mesopotamian, Hittite). Set against these original products, works that blended ingredients from different sources were often dismissed as inferior. Rejecting this approach, Feldman calls attention to the high artistry of many works fashioned in the International Style. Hybridity, she contends, is inherently neither good nor bad. In the Late Bronze Age setting of the Ancient Near East, she suggests that hybridity gained from 'the positive valuation of the material and crafting, and the association with palatial contexts'.[58] The widespread circulation of these items illuminates the function of International Style luxury goods more clearly: they are the material evidence for the existence of an eastern Mediterranean/Near Eastern World-System.[59] In this premonetized world, luxury goods served as the mediums for exchange between elites drawn from different areas and language groups. Feldman writes: 'The production, exchange, and possession of such prestigious items would have signalled in a materially permanent form the participant's acceptance and acknowledgement of reciprocal obligations as a basis for establishing and maintaining diplomatic alliances at the highest level of international rank,

---

[58] Feldman 2006: 61–2.   [59] For World-System analysis, see Hall 2014.

that of Great King.'⁶⁰ Although some motifs appeared in monumental form, such as reliefs carved on temple walls, it is noticeable that International Style objects are frequently highly portable: gold and silver jewellery, carved ivory and precious vessels made of alabaster are common, being well suited to networks of reciprocity, gift-giving and tribute that extended over hundreds of miles.

Within this World-System, hybridity matched theme to function since it allowed participants to join in a broad discourse of prestige that drew on compositional elements from different traditions. This is well illustrated by the ivory bed panels found in Ugarit, dating to the early fourteenth century BC (Figure 3.6). Many of the scenes are composed using motifs borrowed from Egyptian iconography. The female figure on the left side of panel B holds an *ankh*, while next to her the figure spearing a lion wears an Egyptian *khepresh* crown. In the third panel a victorious figure is shown smiting his enemies, a composition inspired by Egyptian prototypes but recast with a figure whose costume and headdress are Levantine. Other panels draw on Hittite motifs, such as the royal sign depicted between the horns of the goddess (A4), or carry local, Ugaritic associations, such as the depiction of twins representing the two major demographic groups: the 'men of the king' (palatial dependents) and 'the sons of Ugarit' (landholders). The effect of this mélange is to assert parity between Ugarit and the great powers around it, but the combination of these disparate elements is not random or haphazard: 'With great complexity and sophistication, the ivory panels operate on several levels as the foreign elements, in conjunction with the indigenous, are assimilated to create a nuanced iconographic and compositional work related to the royal ideology of Ugarit.'⁶¹ And just as the major compositional elements are appropriated from existing traditions and recombined for the local Ugaritic setting, the message is reinforced by the use of hybrid and exotic forms. Above the panels can be seen winged lions with horns, and to the sides lush vegetal motifs frame the composition. As elements derived from the common syntax of International Style, they mark the couch to which the ivory plaques were attached as the possession of a member of the Ugaritic and international elite: those who had exclusive access to such luxury items.

Such items circulated within a broad network of exchange and reciprocity. In this context, hybrids operated at a metaphorical level, suggesting the tension between participants who were both alike (as elites) and yet markedly different (according to external indicia such as dress, language

⁶⁰ Feldman 2006: 164.   ⁶¹ Feldman 2002: 16.

Figure 3.6 Ivory furniture panels from Ugarit. National Museum, Damascus. Side A & B. Drawings by Liz Lauter, reproduced by permission (Marian Feldman).

and local styles). For Ramses II negotiating with the Hittite queen Puduhepa, for example, the luxury goods (and women) circulating between rulers bound the partners at either end of the exchange to each other, yet they spoke different languages, dressed differently and ruled over regions hundreds of miles distant from one another.[62] Their bilateral exchanges relied upon a distinct construction of prestige consisting of the internal display and consumption of goods that were frequently generated externally. Recombining parts into creatures that did not exist in the real world

---

[62] Ramses II to Puduhepa: *KBo* 28.23: 19–29 (tr. Beckman).

and placing them in exuberant decorative frames created a shared style that equated the international with the exotic, hybrid and wondrous, a powerful claim useful to rulers and elites making the acquisition and display of foreign goods the mark of their status. This is exemplified by a Babylonian king eager for an Egyptian bride, who writes to the pharaoh: 'Send me a beautiful woman as if she were your daughter. Who is going to say, "She is no daughter of the king!"?'[63] Genuine royal status was hard to prove and less important than that she looked and sounded Egyptian. The result sought by the Babylonian king was only one of many instances of 'intermingling across international boundaries that is analogous to the artistic hybridity of the koiné'.[64] In formal terms, the International Style and the common culture milieu from which it arose did not survive the end of the Bronze Age. The major dislocation of culture that occurred with the collapse of palatial societies and long-distance gift exchange marks an undeniable break, even if marginal areas fared better and recovered more quickly.[65] Yet hybridity retained its hold on the imagination of the Greeks and hybrids continued to make their way to the surface. The long durée of hybrids provides a bridge from the World-System of the late second millennium to the new cultural landscape of the first millennium, but hybrids, above all else, are pliable, such that in the process of transmission from one setting to another a hybrid could change appearance and meaning.

Taweret and the Minoan Genius

This is key to understanding the appearance of Egyptian hybrids in the Aegean world of the late second millennium, with the formation of complex, hierarchical states on Crete. It is here that we first encounter hybrid compositions, influenced by the sustained contact between Crete and Egypt between the seventeenth and fourteenth centuries BC. The presence of Cretans on the wall painting of Egyptian tombs, the frequent references to them as *Keftiu*, the transfer of goods between the two regions and the presence of signs in Linear A deriving from Egyptian hieroglyphics all powerfully attest to the fact that Crete was integrated into the World-System of the Levant in the Middle and

---

[63] Babylonian request for an Egyptian bride: EA 1, ll. 89–92 (tr. Moran).
[64] Feldman 2006: 70.
[65] The causes and chronologies of the end of the Bronze Age around the eastern Mediterranean are all still the subject of discussion and disagreement. See Knapp and Manning 2016 for a detailed overview emphasizing scientifically derived explanations and regional variations. See Cline 2014 for discussion of documentary sources and an attempt to synthesize the data into a single, connected narrative.

Late Bronze Age. Crete was neither external nor peripheral. But Crete's place in the network of Levantine states does not mean that Egyptian composite figures were seamlessly transferred into Cretan culture. In fact, the change of setting saw Egyptian motifs redeployed in entirely new ways. This is best illustrated by the figure of Taweret, the goddess usually depicted in the Middle Kingdom as a straightforward hybrid of a human female with the head of a hippopotamus. Taweret was adopted as a figure in Cretan glyptic art and is often referred to as the Minoan Genius.[66] She was originally a wet-nurse figure and protector of children. Amulets, faience figurines and magic ivory 'knives' with depictions of Taweret are common in both the Middle and New Kingdom periods. She also assumed a significant role in pharaonic ideology: she suckled the dead pharaoh and gave him life and protection. But what does Taweret mean in a Minoan context? Or, as Judith Weingarten asks, 'When Taweret came to Crete, did she arrive devoid of concepts, a demon without ideas?'[67] Weingarten has proposed a degree of familiarity with Taweret on the part of the Cretans, but no figurines, scarabs or amulets depicting Taweret are found in Cretan settings, so there is no sign that she was invoked to protect children. The sealings which depict the hippopotamus deity/demon actually reflect a negligible understanding of Taweret's role, and suggest instead an example of a misunderstanding typical of the Middle Ground where cultures meet.[68] In the Egyptian context Taweret is depicted holding a ewer for the purpose of lustration. Her role as a protectress is connected to a gesture of cleansing. At the time when sealings depicting Taweret performing this function began to appear in Cretan settings, libation was emerging as a prominent feature of Cretan ritual. The vessels associated with libation – *rhyta* and beak-spouted ewers – were the appropriate vessels for this, and recalled Taweret's attribute. Accordingly, an Egyptian goddess or demon associated with lustration and purification was adopted into Cretan iconography to represent libation. The complicated theology associated with Taweret's protection of the pharaoh was not transmitted: outside of Egypt the image did not convey a message concerning the pharaoh's afterlife, and for this reason the image of Taweret was available for reinterpretation and reformulation. The transformation of Taweret began shortly after her

---

[66] Weingarten 1991, Weingarten 2013.   [67] Weingarten 1991: 10.
[68] On the Middle Ground, see White 1991 and Reger 2014. Kuch 2017 applies the notion of entanglement to the relationship between Egyptian Taweret and the Minoan Genius, but notions of familiarity and entanglement simply avoid the question of what exactly is signified by the signifier. See, too, Sambin 1989. The rapid bifurcation of the image in LM Crete and New Kingdom Egypt argues against a transfer of meaning.

adoption from Egypt and during MM IIB, ca. 1700 BC, the Cretan version of Taweret assumed a strange, new, hybrid appearance.

With neither hippopotami nor lions on Bronze Age Crete there were no vivid referents for Cretan artists to draw on, and the Cretan goddess was quickly divorced from the web of ideas and associations that gave her meaning in an Egyptian context. Thereafter, Taweret developed along two quite separate paths. In Egypt the straightforward hippopotamus goddess of the Middle Kingdom became a hybrid demon in the New Kingdom, acquiring female breasts, a lion's head and mane and a crocodile-like dorsal fin.[69] On Crete her transformation into the Minoan Genius was no less startling. A comparison of the genius on the large gold signet ring from Tiryns in the fifteenth century and a New Kingdom stele depicting Taweret shows how far the two creatures have diverged (see Figure 3.7). Furthermore, Egyptian Taweret always appears as a single deity or demon, but in Aegean instantiations she multiplies into a posse of attendants. In the Aegean the genius also appears in completely different settings, such as hunting and sacrificial scenes,

Figure 3.7 A. Gold signet ring from Tiryns, fifteenth century BC. National Archaeological Museum, Athens, 6208. Athens, Greece/Bridgeman Images; B. Limestone votive stela with figures of Goddesses Taweret and Mut of Isheru, 1390–1352 BC. Metropolitan Museum of Art, 47.105.4.

---

[69] Frankfort 1948: 12.

composed in ways that show the evolution of the image. As Paul Rehak observed, 'The Mycenaean use of the genius thus differs significantly from the Minoan'[70] – just as, one might add, the Minoan had differed significantly from the Egyptian.

In the second millennium the contact between Crete and Egypt resulted in surprisingly little cultural borrowing other than exotica. With the greater intensity of long-distance exchanges around the eastern Mediterranean in the first millennium we might expect this to have changed, yet paradoxically this is not so. Egyptian hybrids leave little sign of having penetrated the Greek world, or if, like the sphinx, they were taken up then they were altered in the process. Animal hybrids are prominent in two domains of Egyptian culture: depictions of anthropomorphic animal figures (whose hybridity consists of acting human while still looking like animals) and theriomorphic gods. In the case of the former, wall paintings, papyri and ostraca frequently cast animals into the role of humans: a mouse dressed in a kilt sits before a table of offerings while a cat gently fans him, or a baboon plays a harp.[71] In a satirical papyrus from Deir el-Medina, for example, a lion and a gazelle sit opposite each playing *senet*, while jackals and cats gently herd antelope and geese (see Figure 3.8).

Figure 3.8 Satirical papyrus depicting animals behaving as humans. Deir el-Medina, Egypt, 1250–1150 BC. British Museum EA10016,1. © The Trustees of the British Museum.

---

[70] Rehak 1995a: 230. On the changing roles of Taweret as Minoan Genius, see also Eder 2015: 229–30.

[71] For the seated mouse, see ostracon from the Brooklyn Museum (37.51E); for the lion and gazelle playing senet, see British Museum Papyrus (EA 10016); for the baboon with a harp, see ostracon from Medelhavsmuseet (MM 14047). Some of the scenes are reminiscent of the animals performing as humans on the Great Lyre from Ur, ca. 2600 BC.

These satirical scenes appear to contribute to the tradition of animal fables which in the Greek world would be associated with Aesop, yet the lines of transmission are opaque.[72] When the animal fable first enters Greek literature in Hesiod's famous tale of the hawk and the nightingale the immediate source is thought to be from the Near East, since similar episodes (though not exact parallels) are known from Babylonian wisdom literature.[73] An Egyptian provenance has been posited for the Greek *Batrachomyomachia* ('Battle of the Frogs and Mice') which resembles an Egyptian tale of a battle between cats and mice, but the latter is a folklore motif found across a number of ancient cultures.[74] The entire genre of the Aesopic fable has been labelled 'monstrous and chaotic', and the lesson to be learned from the *Aesopica* regarding hybridity is that there is no support for the view that Greek animal fables have a particularly Egyptian provenance.[75] Fables focused on animals have obscure origins, with no clear boundaries, and instead are themselves part of 'a wider discourse about the boundaries between humans and the rest of the animal world'.[76] If the animals of the Deir el-Medina papyrus satirize humans and their activities, there is little to suggest that this directly influenced Greek storytelling. In fact, the tradition that Aesop was originally a Thracian brought to Samos as a slave has been interpreted by some as evidence corroborating the view that animal fable entered Greek popular culture from the Near East.[77] Further complicating the idea of an Egyptian provenance for Greek animal fables is the fact that the animal fable is close to universal.[78]

It is in the expression of a cosmology that relies on animal-headed gods that the Egyptian construction of hybridity is most striking, yet here

---

[72] On the genre of fable and the difficulties of charting 'the genealogy of stories' such as the Archilochean story of the fox and the eagle, thought to derive from a Babylonian archetype, see Silva 2020.

[73] Hsd, *W&D* 202–13. See West 1997: 319–20.

[74] On Egyptian parallels to the *Batrachomyomachia*, see Morenz 1954. For the cat/mouse war, see Turin Papyrus 55001. For Near Eastern cat/mouse folklore, see Brunner-Traut 1954 and 1968: 44–6.

[75] Perry 1952: x. One can compare the inchoate origins of Greek fable with later Byzantine and Arabic traditions. In the twelfth century, Eugenios of Palermo, for example, expanded on Symeon Seth's eleventh-century translation of the Arabic *Kalīla wa-Dimna*, a collection of animal fables itself descended from the Sanskrit *Panchatantra*. The resulting work focuses on the travails of two jackal courtiers, named Stephanites and Ichnelates, at the court of the lion king. Although the lines of transmission behind this work reach from the *Mahabharata* to the court of Roger II, the various threads can be teased out in ways that highlight how indefinite by comparison the connections between Egyptian animal fable and Greek tales are. See Noble et al. 2022.

[76] Lefkowitz 2014: 7.   [77] Holzberg 2002: 15, Forsdyke 2012b: 62.

[78] Animal satires resembling the Egyptian can be identified in stories of the tengu of Tokugawa Japan (AD 1600–1868), bird-hybrid figures whose appearance and actions satirize priests and officials. See Foster 2015: 135–9.

too the relationship between Egyptian and Greek forms is complicated. Consider, for example, the cases of Anubis, the jackal-headed god, and his Greek counterpart, Hermes. Both serve the function of escorting souls to the Underworld, but, aside from vestigial wings on his sandals, there is no sign of hybridity in the Greek conception of Hermes. A comparison of the two demonstrates the degree to which the Greek god has diverged from his Egyptian counterpart. Similarly, although the eagle often serves as an emblem of Zeus, the father of the Greek gods is never depicted as eagle-headed, unlike the Egyptian sky god, Horus, who is frequently depicted as falcon-headed. Of course, this not to suggest that Egyptian culture did not leave an imprint on the Greeks, but that exchange was qualitatively very different from the Greek response to the Ancient Near East. Egyptian influence explains technical skills such as cutting marble and limestone, which the Greeks adopted from Egypt in the sixth century. The transfer of technology, however, is very different from the movement of poetic motifs, stories and images that link Gilgamesh to Herakles or Kumarbi to Kronos.[79]

This separation into clearly demarcated, opposed fields of Greek and Egyptian did not arise from natural differences. Rather, it seized upon differences and reified them, helping to create a Greek identity and an Egyptian 'Other' imagined by and for Greeks. We can see these differences operating in a well-known passage, *Histories* 2.52, in which Herodotos claims that the priests at Dodona told him that the oracle there had given instructions that the names of the gods imported from Egypt should be used by the Greeks. Unlike the organic syncretism that characterized the blending of Melqart and Herakles from Tyre to Monaco – an open-ended system that allowed Herodotos to equate Babylonian Bel with Zeus and Assyrian Mylitta with Aphrodite – the Dodona episode speaks to a deliberate juxtaposition of the entire pantheons of Egypt and Greece, in which the subject of names was part of a closed system of correspondences subject to formal deliberation.[80] But the decision to use *names* from Egypt (whether actually agreed upon or not) raised the problem of the full nature, powers and appearance of the Egyptian gods. Herodotos could claim that the Egyptians worshipped Isis and Osiris, whom they identified with Dionysos, but animal hybrids such as Taweret, the upright hippopotamus,

---

[79] Specific stone-working tools and techniques, such as the claw-tooth chisel, can be shown to have been employed in Egypt in the seventh century and to have reached the Aegean (Naxos, Paros, Delos and Athens) in the first half or second quarter of the sixth century. See Palagia and Biondi 1994 and Paga 2015: 173.
[80] On Melqart and Herakles, see Malkin 2011, Papantoniou 2013: 171, Martí-Aguilar 2017. For Bel/Zeus and Mylitta/Aphrodite, see Hdt 1.81, 88. For Dodona and the Egyptian provenance of Greek theonyms, see Lattimore 1939.

or Ammit, the crocodile/lion/hippo goddess, would have been harder to explain.[81] One strategy was to euhemerize. Egyptian statues of Zeus have a ram's head, explains Herodotos, because Zeus had skinned a ram, cut off its head and worn it as a mask when he appeared before Herakles. A second strategy was to syncretize, when resemblance made this easy: Pan's portrait is the same in Egypt as in Greece, with a goat's head and legs, explains Herodotos, and the Mendesians take their name from Pan (Mendes in Egyptian), in much the same way, he could have added, as the Athenians take their name from Athena. But if Egyptian Pan, whom any Greek would recognize, is considered one of the supreme eight gods, we hear nothing of the other seven. This is because the third strategy was simply to ignore whatever did not fit a scheme comprehensible to the Greeks.

Of course, cultural transmission cannot be controlled by a committee, and despite the attempts of Archaic poets such as Homer and Hesiod to codify the gods in ways that made them entirely Greek, Egyptian motifs did make their way into Greek myth and iconography. They did so, however, selectively, and in ways that suited Greek artists who borrowed formulaic scenes without much care for genre or context. The cup of Arkesilas, for example, a mid-sixth-century *kylix* depicting the weighing of silphium (or wool) by attendants in front of the Cyrenaean king, draws on well-established conventions of Egyptian funerary art, in particular weighing-of-the-soul scenes[82] (see Figures 3.9 and 3.10). But as Matthew Skuse has recently shown, 'The religious and supernatural elements of the weighing of the heart are largely removed, together with the most easily recognisable elements of Egyptian iconography, such as crowns or hieroglyphs.'[83] Also missing are the animal-headed gods who proliferate in such scenes. What remains alludes to Egypt, but the visual repertoire employed by the Laconian artist shows little interest in Egyptian cosmology. In fact, the Arkesilas cup is devoid of genuine Egyptian signification. The inclusion of a baboon above the scales is an Egyptian element, but more telling still is the omission of any figures resembling Anubis, Ra-Horakty, Thoth or any other hybrid figures of the Egyptian scenes. For the Laconian artist, it seems, the primate was sufficiently exotic.[84]

Egyptian cultural motifs often entered Greece *sub rosa*, as it were, so that the hybrid or composite elements that cross the barrier between

---

[81] Isis, Osiris and Dionysos: Hdt 2.42   [82] Bresson 2000: 89–94.   [83] Skuse 2018: 236.
[84] Baboons were not native to Egypt. Captured in central Africa and imported as pets, they were highly prized and may have been the subject of a captive breeding programme. See Dominy et al. 2020.

Figure 3.9 Cup of Arkesilas. Laconian black-figure *kylix*, ca. 560 BC. The king is depicted watching as either silphium or wool is weighed and loaded. Cabinet des Médailles, De Ridder 189.

Figure 3.10 Book of the Dead. The Weighing of Ani's Soul. Papyrus, ca. 1250 BC. Tomb of Ani, Thebes. British Museum, EA10470,3. © The Trustees of the British Museum. Note the presence of the baboon above the scales.

cultures are often so attenuated that the original context is entirely lost.[85] This process is well illustrated in the story of Io, the object of Zeus's desire, who was transformed into a heifer by a jealous Hera.[86] In its various Greek versions the story involves a series of discrete narratemes, such as the jealous wife (Hera) persecuting the younger woman, and the ever-popular trope of the young woman kidnapped by treacherous foreigners: in Lykophron's account Io is stolen by Phoenician sailors. In the Greek telling, Io ends up in Egypt and gives birth to a variety of children who become founders of people and nations on the edges of the Greek world: from Libye and Aigyptos to Arabos, Kilix and Phoinix. Her wanderings, described in Aeschylus' *Prometheus Bound* (707–823), amount to a mapping of the Eastern Mediterranean seen from a Greek, genealogical perspective, but the significance of Egypt to the Io story actually lies in the story's origins. As Rhys Carpenter recognized seventy years ago, Io originates as a moon goddess in a cycle of Egyptian myth located in the Nile Delta.[87] In Coptic and Egyptian before it, '*ioh*' was the word for the moon; the name would have been sounded like 'iooh' and written in Greek as Ἰώ. Her 'horns' are originally depictions of the waxing and waning moon, although they will, in time, become the tokens of her affliction. In *Hypsipyle* Euripides refers to Io's 'horn-bearing fate' (*kersaphoron atan*) (Frg 752g 30.)

Yet hardly any of these lunar associations carried over to the Greek story of Io. The Egyptian stratum of the story has disappeared. For the Greeks she is a young heifer, driven around the world by Hera. Earlier red-figure vases show her completely transformed, but in Aeschylus she describes herself as having horns and her character would have been played by an actor in a horned mask. This became the usual way of depicting her. Any suggestion of the Egyptian moon goddess is gone. Once again, the transformation of the Io story from its origins in the Delta to the Greek tale of the wandering heifer illustrates that, despite the ubiquity of composite figures in Egyptian culture, it was not from Egypt directly that the Greeks acquired their taste for *Mischwesen*. Instead, as we have seen, it was the long tradition of Near Eastern hybrids that supplied the Greeks with a bestiary of composite figures.

---

[85] Rutherford 2016 collects a number of papers that argue for an underlying familiarity with Egyptian culture on the part of the Greeks in the Classical and Hellenistic periods. In particular, see Stephens (2016) on Plato and Egyptian theology.
[86] On Greek and Egyptian Io, see McInerney 2010: 78. For a clear treatment of the different Greek versions of the myth, see Mitchell 2001.
[87] Carpenter 1950: 182–3. See also Bernal 1987: 95.

The Minotaur

So far, the adoption of Egyptian hybrids into Greek culture has emerged as fitful and piecemeal, symptomatic of the exoticization of Egypt rather than of a profound cultural encounter. And, as in the case of the rich bestiary of Near Eastern hybrids, the syntax of hybridity is once again more significant than the transfer of precise meaning or associations. In this respect, the antecedents of Greek hybrids point to the thin coherence of the Greek encounter with other cultures of the eastern Mediterranean. The particular power of a striking hybrid lies in its capacity to generate wonder and confusion, which are themselves powerful responses to whatever is alien and beyond comprehension (and classification). These are the zones where actual confrontations with other people are transformed mythopoetically into otherworldly experiences. This process is well demonstrated in an important Cretan hybrid, generated not by the Cretan experience of Egypt, but by the Mycenaean experience of Crete: the Minotaur.

Understanding the significance of the Minotaur is complicated by the fact that by the time he appears in Greek literature he is already a subject of disgust. He is one of the 'ox-headed offspring of man' in Empedokles' list of mixed-up creatures from the earliest days of creation.[88] Depictions of the creature in both red and black-figure vases usually emphasize the killing of the Minotaur by Theseus, and, like the sculpture of the Minotaur probably displayed in the early-fifth-century Theseion in Athens, these demonstrate that the Minotaur was the monster counterpart of Theseus. His principal reason for existence in an Athenian setting was to provide the monstrous foe vanquished by the founder of the democracy. Literary versions of the story of Minos, Pasiphai and the Minotaur, written down a millennium after the Bronze Age by mythographer such as Apollodoros, give his monstrosity a full family pedigree. In the best-known version of the Minotaur's origins, in Antonius Liberalis, Minos is denounced for infecting his victims with poisonous sperm, leading to the birth of monsters.[89] In this account, the Minotaur's own conception is equally squalid. Punished by Poseidon, Pasiphai is afflicted by an unnatural desire to mate with a bull. She commissions Daidalos to invent a frame in which she hides until mounted by the bull. The result of this bestial coupling is the Minotaur, a disgusting product of unnatural and monstrous desire. But it is unlikely that this object of disgust is the same as the original Minotaur, whose origins lie in

---

[88] Empedokles fr. 61= Aelian, *Nat. Anim.*   [89] Anton. Lib., *Met.* 41.

Minoan religion and bull-cult.[90] How did the demonization of the bull-headed man come about?

Towards the end of the Bronze Age, the palatial centres on Crete appear to have undergone a significant transformation. Rituals celebrating key events such as the harvest or the vendange were conducted with increasing intensity as processions and games were held in prominent theatral areas at Knossos and at the other palaces.[91] Carefully designed entry ways led to these performance areas, decorated with colourful reliefs that showed processions of libation bearers and performances of the key ritual that took place here: bull-leaping. In the religious system of Minoan Crete the cult of the bull featured prominently, due no doubt to the same mixture of power and machismo that made bulls a symbol of royal authority going back to the third millennium. Bull-cult and bull-leaping was common to the east Mediterranean world in the Late Bronze Age. Excavations within the last twenty years in Egypt at the Hyksos capital of Avaris (Tell el-Daba'a) have brought to light wall paintings dating to the sixteenth century BC showing scenes of bull-leaping. Similarly, Canaanite seals reflect an awareness of the practice, as do seals found at Alalakh in Syria dating to the seventeenth century BC, while the spectacular finds in the fifteenth-century Griffin Warrior burial at Pylos discovered in 2015 include a gold ring with a bull-leaping scene, a carnelian seal stone depicting three bulls and a bronze bull's head from the top of a wooden sceptre.[92]

Like any rituals, these performances were ephemeral, but rings produced from steatite moulds depicting bull-leaping commemorated the events. These rings were popular among members of the Minoan elite, who favoured scenes of bull-leaping as personal markers. We can infer the high status of the individuals who used these rings from the fact that identical sealings from the rings have come to light at sites all over Crete, from Khania to Zakro. Fifty-three sealings from ten so-called 'Knossos replica rings' have been found so far; of these, six depict bull-leaping.[93] The ritual was central to the ideology of Minoan society, asserting, in Livia Morgan's words, 'male prowess through ritualized bull sports'.[94] As in Egypt and the Near East, Cretan bull-cult also had a cosmological

---

[90] Burnell 1947, Ridderstad 2009.
[91] Hägg and Marinatos 1987, Gesell 1987, Soles 1995, Rehak and Younger 1998, Drieesen 2003, German 2005.
[92] Bietak 1996, especially pl. IV, Bietak et al. 2007, Brody 2002, Collon 1987: no. 708, Collon 1994 and Collon 2003, Guillaume and Blockman 2004, Davis and Stocker 2016.
[93] Betts 1967, Hallager 1996.
[94] Morgan 2018: 226. See also McInerney 2011. Shapland 2013: 204 refers to figurines showing bull-leaping as 'depiction[s] of a socially significant animal practice'.

dimension, since the most common astronomical marker known to both the Babylonians and the Aegean world was the rising of the Pleiades on the shoulder of the constellation Taurus. Traces of this star-lore can still be found as an early stratum under the later stories of Pasiphai and the wretched family of Minos. Originally, she is the daughter of the Sun god, Helios, and in some accounts the Minotaur is first known as Asterios, the Star Child.

These positive cosmological features, however, like bull-leaping itself, would be largely erased from the Greeks' memory of Minos' realm. This is because the Mycenaean conquest of Crete brought about deep changes in ritual and religious practice. Rehak and Younger, for example, have observed that in the Final Palatial period the killing of bulls became the culmination of bull-centred rituals. They speculate that this reflects Mycenaean influence, since it is in the last phase of Minoan palatial culture, around 1400 BC, that Knossos was definitely under Mycenaean control. They also point to the fact that it is at this time that the minotaur begins appearing on seals. Their tentative suggestion is that these minotaurs may represent men in masks 'appropriating the power of the bull for symbolic, even shamanistic purposes'.[95]

We can go further. The rituals associated with the late period bull-cult differed significantly from what came before. In the earlier palatial periods in which we have depictions of bull-leaping we do not see the animals being killed. But in the Final Palatial period we encounter the famous *rhyta* that surely commemorate the death of actual animals. They are portraits (see Figure 3.11). Moreover, they are too heavy to be used as drinking vessels, weighing three kilos when full, leading Nanno Marinatos to suggest that their use as a vessel to carry liquid was associated with the pouring not of wine but of blood. These vessels were ritually destroyed and buried – a second slaughter or killing of the animal.

In the context of Minoan Crete's transformation under Mycenaean control, in the fourteenth and thirteenth centuries, when the Linear B tablets from Knossos and Chania reveal that Greeks had control of the Cretan palaces, the beliefs and practices that mark Minoan religion appear to have undergone a deformation.[96] Pasiphai is transformed from the daughter of Helios into a sexual deviant, and the Star Child Asterios is recast as a bull-headed monster, a grim parody of an earlier figure of reverence. Minos too was demonized, transformed from a hieratic sun-king into a disgusting creature, ejaculating scorpions and millipedes into

---

[95] Rehak and Younger 1998.   [96] McInerney 2016.

Figure 3.11 Steatite bull's head rhyton. Knossos – Little Palace, 1450–1400 BC. Iraklion National Museum, inv. 1368. Art Resource.

his conquests. Even Talos, the magical protector of the island, was refashioned from a bull into an automaton who killed trespassers by embracing them in his burning arms.[97] The hybrid figure of the bull-man is not a Cretan version of a Near Eastern or Egyptian prototype, but an example of the active manipulation of hybridity to negotiate a highly charged cultural moment – in this case, the transformation of Minoan Crete to Mycenaean control.[98] Subsequently, in the post-palatial period even the bull's head would retain only a fraction of its former force: the glorious steatite *rhyta* of the palaces would continue to exist only as odd terracotta vessels such as the chariot *rhyton* found at Karphi. The bulls' heads here are little more than attachments, pale imitations of a once meaningful original.

Subsequently, divorced from any Bronze Age Cretan setting, the Minotaur would serve as an example of monstrosity and demonstrate how hybrids could experience an afterlife divorced from their origins. In his description of

---

[97] Rundin 2004.
[98] Wolf 2020. Interestingly, a parallel shift in religious practice centred on the bull appears to have occurred in Cyprus around the same time. Here, as metallurgy developed, votive dedications included bull figurines and the so-called Ingot God. Hadjisavvas 2003: 25 describes the phenomenon this way: 'The new image of the deity in the form of a god standing on an ingot and wearing a horned helmet appears only at sites where copper production was predominant, such as Enkomi, while the bull preserved its importance at all other settlements.'

the artworks to be seen on the Akropolis, Pausanias remarks on the depiction of Theseus fighting the Minotaur as follows (1.24):

> Opposite these I have mentioned is represented the fight which legend says Theseus fought with the so-called Bull of Minos, whether this was a man or a beast of the nature he is said to have been in the accepted story. For even in our time women have given birth to far more extraordinary monsters than this.

Although there is something monstrous about the Minotaur, Pausanias recognizes that the creature also retains a disturbing vestige of humanity, even if this is because deformity can mar a human birth. The cannibal lurking in the labyrinth is nothing less than the adult version of a monster that was once a child. In the tondo of a red-figure kylix from Vulci from ca. 340 BC, the infant minotaur sits like baby Jesus in the Virgin's lap (Figure 3.12). The kourotrophic setting cannot be ignored, as if the artist wishes to emphasize the human nature of the Minotaur, an aspect of the creature's being that normally goes unremarked, no doubt because drawing attention to its childhood raises the disturbing matter of its conception. In posing the infant in Pasiphai's lap the artist has unmonstered the Minotaur, and has instead moved him into that less scary place, the *Unheimlich*, which, as we have seen, is more unsettling than terrifying.

By the Iron Age the people of the Aegean were living at the western reaches of a *koine* that included the entire Levant, where hybridity was a firmly established part of the cultural repertoire. As a result, they

Figure 3.12 Apulian red-figure *kylix*. Pasiphai and the Minotaur. Bibliothèque nationale de France. De Ridder 1066.

encountered objects, stories, ideas and, most of all, artistic motifs that played with hybrid figures. Some of these hybrids, like the Babylonian Humbaba and Egyptian Taweret, were easily adopted and just as easily transformed, so that soon the Aegean avatars of these figures often bore only a passing resemblance to their older versions. They performed different cultural work. In the Near East monsters were the focus of heroic encounters, such as Gilgamesh's battle with nature, and supplied sky gods like Enlil with enemies to conquer in the *Chaoskampf* that expressed a cosmic struggle to establish order. In the Aegean there was some overlap with these patterns: Zeus would subdue Typhoeus in ways that repeated a basic pattern of Near Eastern cultures from Babylon to Hattusah, but Iron Age Greece was not a single state comparable to the Assyrian empire. Furthermore, while Ashurbanipal was a real king using monsters as foils for his power, Agamemnon, by contrast, was himself a poetic creation. Different conditions in Iron Age Greece would require hybrids and monsters to operate according to a different set of rules and to serve different purposes.

4 | Hybrids, Contact Zones and Margins

> Different places have different positive qualities and different negative qualities. From these arise different advantages and different disadvantages, some by nature, some by design. Natural characteristics should be noted, because they persist, while developments made by human intervention are subject to change.
>
> Strabo 2.5.17 (trans. McInerney)

Mediterranean or Aegean?

The Greeks were surrounded by hybrids, but, as we have seen, the hybrids generated from the human/animal entanglement developed in many different ways from Babylon to Cyprus. The Greek fascination with hybridity should not be taken, then, as a sign of an innate Greek genius. Rather, it reflects the adaptability of Greek culture in the face of an eastern Mediterranean network rich in cultural contact and borrowing. Recent studies have emphasized mobility and movement as key themes in Greek History, from the Archaic period onwards, and it is valuable to remember that wandering, migration and dispossession were commonplace features of the lives of individuals and even entire communities in the Greek world.[1] What sets Greece apart from the rest of the Mediterranean is the geographic setting. As Joseph Brodsky observes, 'There are places... where geography provokes history.'[2] To understand the anomaly of Aegean geography, consider its coastline. The Mediterranean littoral is 46,000 km long, of which the coastline of Greece and Aegean Turkey (occupied by Greek speakers from the tenth century BC) constitutes 19,000 km, or approximately 40 per cent. Yet, in terms of total area, this small Greek world only constitutes a fraction of the entire Mediterranean.

---

[1] Garland 2014. See also the essays edited by Mauro, Chapinal-Heras and Valdés Guía 2022.
A recent conference in Copenhagen, *Moving the Ancient Greek World* (June, 2022), featured a set of essays further developing the theme. See https://migrantsandmembership.org/2022/01/13/moving-the-ancient-greek-world/.
[2] Brodsky 1986: 395.

Figure 4.1 Relief map of the Mediterranean Basin.

For large swathes of the Mediterranean coastal world, across virtually the entire Maghreb, Spain and Mediterranean France, the prevailing conditions that influence trade, communication and cultural contact can be viewed as primarily perpendicular – that is, as phenomena occurring along two axes. One axis runs along the coast, broadly east/west, while a second axis runs perpendicular to the coast into the hinterland. Throughout most Mediterranean lands this axis is shaped by the presence of mountains, plateaux or deserts that result in rapid changes in terrain within a zone only 60 to 100 km from the coast (see Figure 4.1). Along the coastal axis ships practice cabotage, which results in the movement of goods, sometimes in stages, by various carriers from port to port. This axiality depends on the sea as a medium for communication and exchange, making the inhabitants of the Mediterranean littoral into what one scholar has termed 'netizens': citizens in a network rather than a state.[3] Goods such as metals, amber, Atlantic cod and salt come

---

[3] Cooke 1999: 298. Describing contemporary experience in the Mediterranean, Cooke claims that 'Medizens [i.e. inhabitants of the Mediterranean network] are offered the dazzling array of cultural possibilities that three continents provide, not only around the periphery but in most cases down through the earth to the earliest traces of human civilization. Medizens are at home in the shards of Phoenician, Carthaginian, Greek, Roman, Berber, Arab, European, and now US imperialist projects. Situated at the crossroads of the ancient and modern worlds as well as of multiple places in the present, they can sometimes choose between them even as they retain awareness of a history of power relations.' This is the fluidity and mutability that finds expression in Greek culture's fascination with metamorphosis and métissage.

into the Mediterranean, down from the mountains, outside from the ocean, across the desert by caravan or along river systems until, having intersected with the second, maritime axis, they are dispersed by sea across the length of the Mediterranean.

Despite these adaptions and developments, the prevailing conditions of the southern and western Mediterranean favour a very different understanding of space when compared to the Aegean, where travel over short distances involves exposure to a much greater variation of micro-environments and communication with many more interconnected communities. The geography of the Maghreb, in contrast, is simpler and communication much less convoluted than in the highly compact and interconnected world of the Aegean.[4] Consider a crude comparison: from Tunis to Tangiers one travels across the entire stretch of the southern coast of the western Mediterranean, a distance of approximately 2,150 km. By sea or by land, the distance is the same. A journey of comparable length by ship from Kerkyra (Corfu) travelling southeast along the coast of Greece (and sailing past the Corinthian Gulf) would finally reach Torone, in the Chalkidike peninsula in the Northern Aegean, having taken the sailor to every major port around the west coast of Greece and the Peloponnese, to the Gulf of Argos, the Saronic Gulf, the Euboian Gulf, up the east coast of mainland Greece, to the Thermaic Gulf and on to the Chalkidike. In other words, a journey equivalent to sailing the entire length of the western Mediterranean would not even bring a traveller in the Greek world from the Ionian Sea as far as the coast of Anatolia. Our imaginary voyage does not even include the Aegean islands, the north coast of the Aegean or the coast of Ionia; nor does it include Crete and Cyprus, two of the largest islands of the eastern Mediterranean. Yet an equivalent land-based trip from Kerkyra to Constantinople, as the crow flies, would amount to a journey of just over 500 km. In other words, compared to the attenuated geography of the western Mediterranean, the Aegean world is a highly compact space marked by a high degree of interconnectedness.

In environmental terms, Greece and the Aegean are characterized by thick and rapid change: of elevation, of climate, of zones and of coastscapes. Together they make it a space of unusual variation and intense interactions. To put this in terms that explicitly recognize the special

---

[4] There is, almost inevitably, a danger of essentializing difference and homogeneity in any diasporic discourse, making claims about 'populations' that reproduce colonial categories. See Axel 2004: 32. But, like periodicity, such categories cannot be entirely avoided if we are to write something other than a history of atoms and their interactions.

place of the Aegean region within the broader Mediterranean – the 'liquid continent' – one might say that the three fundamentals of the Mediterranean sphere – fragmentation, uncertainty and connectivity – are all experienced with far greater force and urgency in the Aegean than anywhere else in the Mediterranean world.[5] The perimeters of the Mediterranean world have been described as places of 'theoretical density', and that which holds for the Mediterranean in general applies tenfold to the Aegean.[6] It is true that, as Jonathan Hall has noted, the Greeks were only one of many actors in this Mediterranean network, but Greek speakers were intensely and repeatedly exposed to novelty, to symbols dimly understood, to languages barely comprehensible, to motifs of puzzling significance, to ways of eating, dressing, worshipping, burying and being in the world with the potential to amuse, bemuse and confuse.[7] Under these conditions, hybridity would emerge as a mechanism for expressing in-betweenness, the contingent quality of encounters with people who were similar but not the same, and of phenomena that made some sense but might also carry a threat. These are not the conditions characteristic of the imperial ideologies of states such as Sumer, Akkad or Assyria. They are, however, part of the cultural matrix in which the Greeks found themselves, characterized by the ebb and flow of people, both individuals and groups, interacting and in constant movement.[8] One particularly traumatic feature of Mediterranean connectivity was the existence of slaving-zones outside the Aegean, notably in Anatolia and Thrace.[9] Here, as the Greeks looked further afield to supply the slave markets that increasingly underpinned economic activity in the Archaic period, they encountered people sufficiently similar to be categorized as *ethne*, but foreign and, increasingly, viewed as inferior. This experience emphasized the like-yet-unlike quality that will have characterized many

---

[5] Horden and Purcell 2005: 348. Building on Horden and Purcell, Isayev 2013 reasserts Favell's injunction that we think of human mobility as the norm throughout history. This seems especially significant in understanding the Greek experience of landscape as a continuous movement between home and away.

[6] Cassano 1998: 55.   [7] Hall 2002: 92.

[8] In studies of the Mediterranean world, Braudel 1972 still looms like a colossus. More recent contributions emphasizing regional variation and interconnectivity include Horden and Purcell 2000, Abulafia 2011, Broodbank 2013, Concannon and Mazurek 2016 and Manning 2018. Strootman 2019 assembles a series of essays on the empires dispersed around the Mediterranean that also employs a network theory approach with an emphasis on polycentrism. For a network-based reading of Greek culture in the Archaic period, see Malkin 2011, and for a broader application of the network approach see the essays collected by Malkin et al. 2009. For Aegean networks, see Constantakopoulou 2007.

[9] The concept of slaving-zones and their opposite, non-slaving zones, is developed by Fynn-Paul 2009 and applied to the Aegean world by Lewis 2018.

interactions with other people and which found expression in hybrid symbols. They too expressed a tension between familiarity and strangeness. Integral to this was the maritime setting of so many Archaic Greek cultural experiences. Anna Uhlig has recently referred to the 'maritime discourse that replaces the clear boundaries of local origin with the unsettled and fluctuating world of the sea'.[10] This maritime world put the sea at the heart of early Greek culture, 'a realm of revelations and transformations, of shape-shifters and unexpected wisdom'.[11] And this cultural matrix of change is central to the diaspora experience of the Greeks. In the first half of the first millennium, Greek speakers would be one of two great diasporic waves that originated in the eastern Mediterranean from Greece and Phoenicia, which would witness the dispersal of people to the west and, to lesser degrees, to the north and south. This was a world of episodic confrontation characterized by populations constantly on the move, where every port and colony was potentially a middle ground and every encounter was a negotiation.[12] In this setting encounters were deeply fraught, and the consequences of mismanagement were potentially disastrous.

This contingent, transactional mode is nicely suggested by a famous episode described by Herodotus: the silent trade conducted by Carthaginians (4.196) on the North African Coast. They deposit goods on the shore and set a fire to signal their presence to the locals. The indigenes (ἐπιχώριοι) bring gold to the beach in exchange for the goods, which the Carthaginians either accept or leave. If the gold is accepted the exchange is complete; if not the locals leave more gold until both sides are satisfied with the transaction. At one level, this is a straightforward binary system, structured around a clear barrier: homoglots and alloglots. At the same time, however, such exchanges place the participants in relations of reciprocity. Goods on one side, such as salt, hides and possibly slaves, are exchanged for gold. The goods exchanged may be plentiful and cheap on the one side, or their value may be increased by their rarity or the distances they have travelled, making them exotic.[13] The medium that made such exchange possible was the sea.

---

[10] Uhlig 2018: 91. Uhlig's analysis of Alcaeus' maritime poems insists on moving beyond allegorical readings and takes the maritime settings as significant for the themes as well as the performance of the poems.
[11] Uhlig 2018: 64. Similar approaches have been taken by Dougherty 2001 (on the *Odyssey*) and Kowalzig 2013 (on dithyramb).
[12] Woolf 2009.
[13] For North Africa trade intersecting with the Mediterranean, see Mattingly 2003 and Mattingly 2007. Duckworth et al. 2020 have assembled evidence for the transfer of technologies across

Sea Monsters

The sea is not a fixed element that exists as the exact opposite of the land; much less is it a barrier. In Greece it is never far away, and it facilitates the movement of people, goods and ideas.[14] Odysseus reflects an awareness of this when he dismisses the land-based isolation of the Cyclops, observing that they had no ships with which to visit the cities of men. At the same time, the Greeks were also well aware of the dangers of sailing. Sirens may lure the unsuspecting onto the rocks, while Skylla devours six of Odysseus' men even as he tries to avoid Charybdis.[15] The sea was therefore ambiguous, as Menelaus' experiences attest. Nestor describes the storm that hit Menelaus' ships off Cape Malea, 'when the waves swelled to the size of mountains', yet the same storm drove him to Egypt where, in Lombardo's translation, Menelaus

> Wandered up and down that coast with his ships,
> A stranger in a strange land, amassing
> A fortune in gold and goods...
>
> Hom., *Od.* 3.333–335. (tr. Lombardo)

Menelaus' mixed fortunes reflect the fact that because the sea is ever changing, it evokes the unpredictability faced by those who sail on it, who may experience change either for better (trade and profit) or for worse (shipwreck and death). Even the wealth that sea-borne trade offered offended some conservatives, such as Plato, for whom the proximity of the sea was an invitation to corruption. In the *Laws*, his Athenian Stranger bemoans the fact that the ideal city under discussion has good harbours and ready access to the sea, since its location encourages the opposite of self-sufficiency (705a). In the same spirit, Nestor advises Telemachus, 'Don't wander long from home'. His account of Menelaus' return includes the memorable phrase 'so great is that sea and so terrible'. (358). The sea stimulates change and fosters exchange. By its nature it is dangerous and yet it makes possible experiences and encounters that are exhilarating. Death or wealth: the sea offers both.

---

a dessert network very much like the connected network of the Mediterranean described by Horden and Purcell 2005.

[14] For Mycenaean patterns of trade and interaction oriented towards the sea, see Tartaron 2013: 1–11. On the response of the Greeks to the sea, see Berg 2013 (Bronze Age) and Lindenlauf 2003 (Archaic and Classical). Both emphasize the perception of the sea as a place of threat,
a condition that conjures up the proximity of the hybrid. See also Beaulieu 2016. For the sea as a complete storyworld encompassing space, time and the experiences of individuals such as Odysseus, see Blankenborg 2020 and Ryan 2019.

[15] On Sirens, Skylla and Charybdis, see Louden 2011: 166–70.

The risks of sea travel resulted in a deep ambivalence. This is reflected not just in the mixed fortunes of Menelaus, but also in the very genealogies, some benign, some monstrous, of the mythical figures that inhabited the sea. Aside from Nereus, the Old Man of the Sea, according to Hesiod the other children of Pontos are Thaumas, Phorkys and Keto. Their offspring are among the most monstrous in the *Theogony*. Thaumas fathers the Harpies, while the incestuous marriage of Phorkys and Keto produces generation after generation of monsters, including the Graiai, the Gorgons, Echidna, Kerberos, the Lernaian Hydra, Chimaira, the Sphinx, the Nemean Lion and the snake that guards the Apples of the Hesperides. This is the sea as the source of monsters. The sea, or at least the shore and adjacent straits, is also the setting for Skylla, the hideous monster who darts from a cave to attack sailors as they try to pass through the passage below. Although fifth-century artists usually depict Skylla with a simple hybrid body – a woman from the waist up and sea-creature below, with dog-heads sprouting around her waist – Homer's detailed description suggests a far more hideous monster (see Figure 4.2).

She has twelve feet and six long necks, each with a grisly head on top, each head with three rows of teeth. Sunk waist deep in her cave, she is said to dart out and fish for dolphins, seals and even larger sea-beasts. She is described as yelping like a puppy, but Circe assures Odysseus that 'she is an evil monster that not even a god would be glad to see' (*Od.* 12.90–91). When Odysseus asks if there is a way to avoid disaster, in exasperation Circe replies:

Figure 4.2 Skylla. Terracotta plaque, Melos, 460–450 BC. Found on Aegina. British Museum GR 1867.5–8.673 (Cat. Terracotta 621). © The Trustees of the British Museum.

> She's not mortal, she's an immortal evil,
> Dread, dire, ferocious, unfightable.
> There is no defense. It's flight not fight.
>
> Hom. *Od.* 12.121–3 (tr. Lombardo)

Circe's description conveys the straightforward revulsion caused by Skylla, but there are other dimensions to the creature's monstrosity that reveal how polyvalent a hybrid may be. Drawing on North American parallels, Marianne Govers Hopman has made a strong case for seeing the dogs' heads that are frequently depicted around Skylla's groin as visual evocations of the *vagina dentata*.[16] According to this reading, Skylla's hybridity combines the (male) fear of (female) sexual rapaciousness and castration with anxieties focused on the sea. There is also a topographic dimension to the fears she embodies. Twinned with the whirlpool Charybdis, Skylla is most often connected to narrow and dangerous channels (*poroi*) of which sailors are afraid, but which could shorten a journey. The Straits of Messina between Sicily and the Italian peninsula were particularly identified as Skylla's domain. These are actual locations, places of real risk, and the analogizing of such dangerous straits to female genitalia illustrates what Hopman calls the 'wide-ranging and polymorphous semantics of the Scylla symbol'.[17] Such polysemy is one of the reasons hybrids were so valuable for giving an appearance to the rich experience of sailing the wine-dark sea. Fears and anxieties of various stripes can be layered onto the figure of the dog-serpent-woman.[18]

If Skylla personifies the dangers of the sea and sex in a monstrous physical form, by contrast Nereus, the Old Man of the Sea, is relatively benign and represents a different view of the sea. Although often depicted with a fish tail, his hybridity is contingent, changing according to circumstances. He is also sometimes presented in entirely human form, riding a hippocamp, and, like Cheiron, is shown wearing a chiton, making him culturally human, whatever his form. Hesiod's description fits a benevolent patriarch:

> they call him the old man
> because he is honest and gentle and never forgetful
> of right, but ever mindful of just and genial thought.
>
> *Theog.* 234–6 (tr. Athanasakis)

---

[16] Hopman 2012: 138–40. [17] Hopman 2012: 10.
[18] Warner 2007: 85 remarks: 'the three ordeals through which Odysseus passes dismember and scatter the female erotic body by synecdoche across the water in the path of his return home to his wife. It is as if, after the bidding of the sirens' song, the jaws of Skylla, Odysseus and his men must navigate the deep-thoated vulva-like passage of Charybdis.'

He is an oracular figure, and although he must be compelled to give up the truth, he is nevertheless an unerring guide, described as νημερτής, ('infallible', *Od.* 4.349).[19] In order, for example, to find out the exact location of the Garden of the Hesperides, Herakles must wrestle Nereus into submission – a challenge because Nereus is capable of shifting shape. In a variation of this episode, another figuration of the elusive sea-god, Proteus, is wrestled into submission by Menelaus, seeking to find which god is blocking his way home (*Od.* 4.480–90). Proteus transforms through a variety of shapes: lion, a snake, a panther, a boar; running water; a tall tree.[20] Like Nereus, Proteus must be compelled to reveal the truth, but the sea-god is never slain by the hero. The sea is never truly conquered.

The episode of Herakles wrestling with Nereus or a Triton substituting for the Old Man was popular with Attic artists in the sixth century, who visualized the challenges and dangers of the sea in compositions drawing on Archaic Greece's mania for agonistic struggle. A good example is a black-figure hydria in Boston (Figure 4.3). As they wrestle, the Triton's fish body and Herakles' limbs are entwined, and Herakles' face is obscured by the other figure's elbow, drawing attention to the lion head above him. Both characters are more and less than human. Their hybridity combines elements that make them recognizable and familiar (human faces, beards, arms) with animal parts: the ferocious lion's head and the gigantic fish tail. These animal components mark the episode as a superhuman *agon*, yet at the same time each element – fish, lion, man – is familiar and the total composition renders an elemental and superhuman struggle into something comprehensible. Although hybrids are contrafactual, here their presence actually transforms a confrontation between semi-divine beings into an episode that a viewer can grasp. This is neither allegory nor metaphor. Instead, a different process is at work here. Peter Wade has recently argued for a more precise understanding of hybridity by distinguishing between hybridity of origin, which consists of the combination of two existing forms, and hybridity of encounter, which is the result of diasporic experiences.[21] For the Greeks and their conception of the sea, the former, especially the hybrid of man and fish, metonymically signifies the latter, the uncertain movement across the water to a new territory.

---

[19] See Eur. *Or.* 360. Nereus foretells the woes of Paris and Helen (Horace, *Arm.* 1.15.) Aristotle (= Athenaeus 7.47 296 C) mentions an oracle of Neleus and his daughters on Delos. See Ninck 1921: 46.

[20] Menelaus and Proteus: Hom, *Od.* 4.365–400; Herakles and Nereus: Apollodorus, *Biblio.* 2.114; Shape shifting: Apollodoros, *Biblio.* 2. 114.

[21] The distinction between hybridity of origin and hybridity of encounter is from Wade 2005. For a useful refinement of these ideas, see Engler 2009.

Figure 4.3 Herakles and Triton wrestling. Attic black-figure hydria, attributed to the Chiusi Painter, ca. 520 BC. Museum of Fine Arts, Boston 62.1185. Photograph © 2024 Museum of Fine Arts, Boston.

Heroes like Odysseus and Herakles will lead the way, and their encounters with locals and monsters are generally more bloody than wrestling with the Old Man of the Sea. Odysseus will leave Polyphemos blind and face attack from the man-eating Laistrygonians, but it is Herakles who is best known for defeating both locals and monsters around the western Mediterranean.[22] His mission is foretold by Teiresias, according to Pindar: 'And the prophet told him and all the men what fortunes the boy would encounter: how many he would slay on land, and how many lawless monsters at sea.'[23] Near Massalia he is attacked by Alebion and Derkynis, whom he slays, before scattering the local Ligyes with boulders. On Sicily he wrestles with and kills Eryx, who had stolen one of his bulls. His victory gives him the right to Eryx's kingdom, and his descendant, the Spartan Dorieus, uses this to claim the territory of the Elymoi.[24] Alongside these

---

[22] On Greek heroes in the western Mediterranean, see D'Agostino 1996, Dougherty 2001 and McInerney 2010: 102–12.
[23] Pindar, *Nemean* 1. 62–3 (tr. Svarlien).
[24] For Alebion and Derkynis, see Apollodoros, *Bibl.* 2.5.10 and Pomponius Mela 2.5.39. For Herakles fighting the Ligyes, see Hyginus, Fab. 2.6 and Strabo 4.1.7. On Eryx and the Elymoi, see Apollodoros, *Bibl.* 2.5.10 and Pausanias 4.36.4. On Dorieus using the victory of Herakles to claim the region, see Herodotos 5.42–48. See also Visser 1982 and Munson 2006.

Figure 4.4 Perseus and Medusa Metope. Temple C, Selinus, 540–510 BC. Museo Archeologico Regionale, Palermo, Italy/Bridgeman Images.

battles with indigenes, Herakles will defeat triple-bodied Geryon in Tartessos and triple-headed Kakos in Italy. These confrontations play out according to a pattern of Indo-European myth that pits a hero against a tricephalic monster, but they have a territorial dimension as well. From an Aegean point of view, these stories explain how the West was won.[25]

The contact zone of western Sicily, where Greeks encountered Phoenicians and Sicels, is an especially fraught zone, and it provides one of the most arresting examples of a hero defeating a hybrid monster: Perseus slaying Medusa.[26] On a metope of Temple C at Selinunte, Perseus is shown grasping Medusa's hair as he beheads her (see Figure 4.4). The hero is accompanied by Athena. Medusa is in the 'Knielauf' position, her body turned at the waist, facing away, as if in flight, but she stares boldly out straight at the viewer. Like the adjoining metope of Herakles taming the mischievous Kerkopes (also displayed at Paestum), the scene succinctly encodes a message of cultural hierarchies: through the lens of Greek storytelling, Greeks are gods, goddesses and heroes. Non-Greek

---

[25] On the underlying Indo-European myth, see Lincoln 1976, who also recognizes its territorial significance (64): 'The myth is an imperialistic myth, it is true, but even imperialists need their rationalizations.'

[26] Marconi 2007: 142–50.

elements, whether monsters (Medusa), titans (Alkyoneus) or exotic animals (Kerkopes-monkeys), exist to be tamed or killed. Here, the colonial encounter is narrativized as heroic *agon*.

Nereids

From Skylla to Nereus, the sea offered a bountiful supply of the weird and the wonderful. For the Greeks, this was the ambiguity of the sea: it may contain monsters, or it may be pacific. Among its most important denizens are the daughters of Nereus, who serve as a bridge between the sea and the human domain. In fact, if monsters reinforce boundaries, the Nereids hint at the porosity of borders. Thetis and Psamathe will marry the mortals Peleus and Aiakos, Galatea is the object of Polyphemos' longing, while Amphitryte marries Poseidon: as objects of desire, these Nereids connect human, divine and monstrous realms. Furthermore, Nereus and his daughters dwell in a palace that looks very much like a large human household, and their world, though located in the depths of the sea, parallels the human realm. They are not 'other'; they are 'like', and, like their father, the Nereids are not especially fearsome.[27] They are often shown fleeing, either from Peleus as he grabs Thetis or from Herakles as he destroys their father's house.[28] Both episodes evoke domesticity rather than a cosmic dimension, and there are even hints of comedy in some depictions (Figure 4.5). The figures, for

Figure 4.5 Abduction of Thetis by Peleus. Calyx krater by the Niobid Painter, ca. 460–450 BC. Height: 48 cm; diameter: 50 cm. Boston MFA 1972.850. Photograph © 2024 Museum of Fine Arts, Boston.

---

[27] Aside from the detailed collection of illustrations in *LIMC*, see Barringer 1995. Fragments survive of Aeschylus' *Nereids*, in which it seems that the Nereids accompany their sister Thetis to deliver to Achilles his new armour. The play was part of a trilogy which drew on *Il*. 18.35–147 (the Nereids comforting Achilles) and 19.1–39 (Thetis delivering the armour). See Aeschyl. F. 150.

[28] A Boiotian black-figure dish, ca. 500–475 BC, in the Louvre (CA 2569) depicts Thetis as larger than Peleus and surrounded by snakes and a panther (?), perhaps suggesting that she shares her father's ability to change shape.

example, on the calyx krater by the Niobid painter are faintly cartoonish, running about waving tiny dolphins to show they are goddesses of the sea. Another figure brandishes a thyrsus, the symbol of fertility, that droops like a limp noodle. There is little here to frighten. This domestication of the elemental is particularly marked in the marriage of Peleus and Thetis. Their union is significant, saving Zeus from fathering a son greater than himself and resulting in the birth of Achilles, the supreme hero. The event will be witnessed by all the immortals who bring gifts for the bride, yet for all its importance the episode remains recognizably a version of a human marriage. When juxtaposed to the cosmogenic forces of the sea in *Enuma Elish* or in Hesiod, the Nereids exemplify a very different set of responses to the mythic and elemental: a tendency to collapse rather than confirm the boundaries between the human realm and the *kosmos*.

These are not dangerous sea-deities, sirens singing men to their doom.[29] Nor are they monsters with the bodies of sea-creatures. Instead they display a light hybridity, in which their human form is complemented by the proximity of non-human elements: Thetis is given the wings of Arke by Zeus, her sisters brandish dolphins and they are usually depicted as part of a marine *thiasos*, riding on the backs of sea animals: hippocamps, sea-serpents, even a cuttle fish, but most commonly dolphins.[30] Nereids, therefore, are a friendly presence, as comforting to humans at sea as the sight of dolphins leaping ahead of the ship's prow. In time, this specifically marine setting would lose its significance, and the Nereids would serve as divine escorts to characters undergoing, in Judith Barringer's words, 'a critical life transition'. It is this guise that they guide Europa, Thetis, Herakles and Theseus through the crises of marriage or death. But such narratives are, as Barringer observes, 'derived from their popular religious function as escorts or protectresses of sea travelers'.[31] This twinning of the sea as threat with the Nereids as guides, attested as early as Hesiod, suggests that crossing the Mediterranean during the great diasporic wave of the eighth and seventh centuries was profoundly challenging, both physically

---

[29] Tran 2018: 82–3 suggests a tension between the corporate identity of the Nereids reinforcing the Olympian order and 'the individual Nereid who exhibits the power to challenge and threaten that order', but none of the examples cited (Thetis, Amphitryte, Psamathe, Galatea) actually does this. Stories linking Psamathe to transformation into a seal in an (unsuccessful) attempt to escape Aiakos suggest a vestigial hybridity reminiscent of her father's power but, as Tran notes, the Nereids remain 'staunchly anthropomorphic'.

[30] *LIMC* s.v. Nereides, shows 486 scenes, in media ranging from gems to textiles. See, for example, 343 (Apulian pelike, ca. 360 BC), showing Nereids riding dolphins, hippocamps, sea-serpents and fish (tunny?); 339 (Boiotian stamnos, ca. 425 BC): hippocamps and dolphins; 454 (Apulian dinos, ca. 330 BC): dolphins and cuttlefish.

[31] Barringer 1995: 10–12.

and psychologically. The founding of new Greek communities was, in its own way, as transformative as an initiation and a rite of passage.[32]

In this respect, the names of the Nereids in Hesiod's catalogue reflect a complex nexus of associations linking the natural world with the human communities imagined by those settling new lands. Most of the names fall into three distinct groups. The first consists of names explicitly connected with the sea and can be classified as elemental: Kymothoe, Galene, Halia, Eulimene, Nesaia, Aktaia, Kymadoke and Kymatolege (Swift-Wave, Sea-Calm, Sea-Girl, Good Harbour, Island Girl, Promontory Girl, Wave-Receiver and Wave-Stiller). The second group consists of names that evoke the traveller's view of the sea, hinting at anxiety and a desire to propitiate the divinities of the sea. These include Eupompe ('Good Journey'), Pontoporeia ('Sea-Passage'), Pherousa ('Conveyer'), Lysianassa ('Lady Deliverance') and, if the traveller is lucky, at the end Eulimene ('Good Harbour'). Taken together, these first two categories of Nereid reveal the imaginative response of the Greeks to the experience of participating in colonial ventures: fear, exhilaration and the hope for an easy passage and safe arrival. There exists, however, a third class of names that reveals another anxiety: the challenge that faced them upon arrival, namely the establishment of a fair and equitable community.[33] This third group of Nereids includes Eukrante ('Good ruler'), Protomedeia ('First Counsel'), Leiagore ('Addressing the People'), Euagore ('Good Speech'), Laomedeia ('Counsel the People'), Poulynoe ('Thoughtful'), Autonoe ('Sensible'), Themisto ('Justice'), Pronoe ('Forethought') and, finally, Nemertes ('Truth'). These names unmistakably evoke the world of public assemblies and describe ethical qualities appropriate in public life, notably honest deliberative speech. The names of the Nereids express the longing for a public discourse that is sensible, just and truthful, because, like their father, the Nereids embody truthfulness.[34] A new community could not be founded without crossing the sea, the Nereids' element, so it comes as no surprise that the Nereids should stand for the dangers and uncertainties of participation in the colonial venture, but it is perhaps surprising that their

---

[32] For an overview of what is still often called Greek colonization, see McInerney 2018. For the poetic treatment of founding colonies, see Dougherty 1993a, Dougherty 1993b and Dougherty 2001.

[33] On the 'political virtues' of the Nereids, see Picard 1938: 136; Deichgräber 1965: 175–207; West 1966: 236. For outlying names and possible interpretations see McInerney 2004: 32–3.

[34] Hesiod is similarly concerned with speech and good order. See *Theog.* 83–4, where the Muses 'pour on a king's tongue sweet dew and make the words that flow from his mouth honey-sweet'. For Hesiod, Hekate sits at the side of kings in trials and grants distinction to men in assemblies. On the significance of speech in Hesiod, see Leclerc 1993.

names should suggest how the new community conceived itself.[35] Long after Hesiod, poets remained fond of exploiting the allegorical possibilities of the sea voyage.[36] As Marie-Claire Beaulieu has noted in a recent study of Pindar and Bacchylides, 'Perseus, Theseus and Jason prove themselves as heroes and political leaders through their journeys across the sea and pave the way for future political leadership in Thessaly, Athens and Cyrene.'[37] They serve as helmsmen of the ship of state, and the experience of crossing the sea foreshadows establishing a sound political community.

Along the way, the sea supplies many challenges, and these take the shape of hybrid creatures which range from the helpful to the hideous. Among the former is Triton, a fish-tailed god who, in a now familiar pattern, is sometimes shown wrestling with Herakles. (The scene, in fact, is little more than a doublet for the contest between Herakles and Nereus.) Triton is listed among the gods of the sea in Hesiod and as early as Pindar is associated with Lake Tritonis in Egypt, where the Argonauts arrive on their voyage home.[38] Apollonios offers a detailed description of the sea-god:

> The body of the god, front and back, from the crown of his head to his waist and belly, was exactly like that of the other immortals; but from the hips down he was a monster of the deep, with two long tails, each ending in a pair of curved flukes shaped like the crescent moon. With the spins of these two tails he lashed the surface of the water, and so brought Argo to the open sea, where he launched her on her way. Then he sank into the abyss, and the Argonauts cried out in wonder at the awe-inspiring sight.
> Apollon. *Argonaut.* 4.1610–19 (tr. Rieu)

This is a neat encapsulation of what distinguishes the monster from the hybrid. In the first place, before revealing his true form, Triton has appeared as a young man and encouraged Jason's men, offering to guide them home; he is a help rather than a hindrance to their return. Second, his physical transformation startles the Argonauts, but elicits astonishment

---

[35] For other examples of the impact of the diaspora on Archaic poetry, see Malkin 2000 and 2001. The first of these articles demonstrates how the *Homeric Hymn to Apollo* treats the founding of Delphi according to the tropes and norms of a colonial foundation story, while the second reads the nymphs of the *Odyssey* as mediators between the maritime and terrestrial worlds, arguing that they offer a 'proto-colonial perspective' (p. 12).

[36] Alcaeus was so addicted to it that Heracleitus complained that he went overboard in his use of the nautical allegory in his political poems, likening the evils caused by tyranny to storms on the ocean. Heracl. *Alleg. Hom.* 5 (= Alcaeus, Bgk frg 19): 'The Islander (Alcaeus) puts to sea excessively (*katakoros thalasseuei*) in his allegories.' For other nautical metaphors and similes, see Theognis 575–6, 619–20, especially 667–82 and 855–6, 1361–2 (erotic). On the metapoetic uses of sailing in Archaic poetry, see Rosen 1990.

[37] Beaulieu 2016: 59–89. [38] Hes. *Theog.* 930; Pind. *P.* IV. 20–3.

rather than revulsion. They witness his true form, and, as he propels the Argo onwards with a swish of his tail, they are reminded that the god's power is overwhelming but that his intentions are kindly. Hybridity here allows the imagination to put a face and tail to a numinous power that is beyond human control yet must be propitiated. It is fitting, therefore, that upon making landfall, Jason and his men erect altars to Poseidon and Triton.

In the Hellenistic and Imperial periods Triton figures widely in Greek and Roman poetry and mythography, and becomes a favourite figure in mosaics and on sarcophagi. Like many of the other hybrids associated with the sea, in these later periods he is not imagined to be a monster at all.[39] Rather, the anomaly of his form suggests metonymically the ambiguity of the sea, where wonder, threat and beauty go hand in hand. In this respect Triton resembles other, even more fantastic hybrids such as hippocamps (which combine a horse and a fishtail), *aigocampi* (goat–sea-creature), *leocampi* (lion–sea-creature), *taurocampi* (bull–sea-creature) and *pardalocampi* (leopard–sea-creature). Although these may have had symbolic meaning at an earlier time, such as an association in Etruscan culture with the passage of souls across the water, in Greek and Roman settings these hybrid figures seem much less freighted with meaning, and it is tempting to dismiss their supposed apotropaic function as no more than a shadow of their former power and little more than decorative.[40] This is certainly true of later instances of the hybrid sea-creature in the early Roman period. In the first or early second century AD, for example, the Apollonaris mosaic from Knossos Valley depicts Poseidon in a chariot drawn by hippocamps at the centre of the composition, framed by lozenges and rectangles containing sea centaurs (human upper torso, equine lower torso turning into serpentine fishtail) and dolphins. The composition, as Rebecca Sweetman has observed, 'does not relate to a particular myth and lacks narrative.'[41] It is unclear whether the mosaic comes from a domestic setting or a bathhouse, but even if the mosaic adorned the floor of a Roman bath the hippocamps and sea centaurs are decorative and do not convey any special meaning. Hallie Franks, however, has observed that earlier, during the Classical period, many mosaics depicting these maritime hybrids, such as the Thetis on a hippocamp from Eretria

---

[39] Apollon., *Argonaut.* 4. 1619 describes the god as τέρας αἰνὸν ἐν ὀφθαλμοῖσιν but Rieu's translation as 'awe-inspiring' is closer to the mark than 'monster'.
[40] On the Etruscan association of the sea voyage with the passage of the dead soul, see Shepard 1941 and Boosen 1986. On the apotropaic function of the maritime *thiasos* and *Grabsymbolik*, see Wrede 1976.
[41] Sweetman 2003: 527.

Figure 4.6 Thetis seated on a hippocampus, delivering a spear and the shield of Achilles newly forged by Hephaistos. Mosaic. Eretria, House of Mosaics, main andron. 400–350 BC. © Swiss School of Archaeology in Greece.

(Figure 4.6), are located in the *andrones* that were the settings for symposia. She suggests that the motifs on these floors were meant to be experienced as a metaphor for travel to distant lands.

As the wine makes its way around the room, often in vessels that depict ships riding on the wine-dark sea on the visible inside lip of the krater or cup, the symposiasts' eyes are drawn to the Nereids and hippocamps that mark the symposium's space as a kind of sea voyage. The entire area is dominated by 'griffins, lions, and Eastern Arimaspians or Ethiopians – precisely the kinds of distant, exotic landscapes, animals, and men that might be encountered on a *periplous*'.[42] It is an attractive thesis that reminds us that even as decoration the hybrid contributes to a cultural performance as significant as the symposium not because of monstrosity but because of its capacity to express excitement, and to bring safely into the daily lives of people hints of a more wondrous world beyond.

Categories, Contexts and Certainty

It is evident from these snapshots of sea-creatures from different periods that hybridity helped Greek speakers to imagine their world. At the same time, before artistic trends ossified and sea-creatures became little more

---

[42] Franks 2014: 162.

than part of the repertoire of decorative motifs, in the Archaic period hybrids signalled expanding cultural horizons. Hybrids would do powerful work shaping the encounters between Greek- and non-Greek-speaking people. One reason for this 'hybrid turn', so to speak, is that many hybrids had already entered the Aegean world in the Late Bronze Age on small and highly portable seals and their impressions.[43] These 'mute' images were easily disseminated as merchants used them to stamp their goods. Impressions might travel far afield, thus facilitating the wide dissemination of images, but they did so without clearly attached meaning or even narratives. When Near Eastern hybrid figures were adopted in the Aegean they were only loosely seen as creatures of power and were not bound by the particular associations they bore in Near Eastern settings. The griffin, for example, was the most popular hybrid to enter the Aegean canon from the Near East, but whereas it was originally a personification of evil forces, in the Aegean its predatory power was linked to its role as a protector of divine power and royal authority. Many other hybrids depicted on seals lack even these specific associations and can be thought of as generically exotic. In an exhaustive study of more than 3,300 Aegean seals, Fritz Blakolmer has concluded that the meaning of hybrid creatures was 'vague and superficial' in the sense that, '[w]hen considered in their entirety, the majority of hybrid creatures, at least essentially, appear in unspecific, exchangeable postures and contexts'[44] (see Figure 4.7).

These Minoan hybrids do not exactly replicate Egyptian or Near Eastern prototypes, but instead multiply in rich profusion, combining and recombining animal and human parts to form many new creatures. Some may have served as clan insignia, *genii locorum*, or depict rituals, but it is far more likely that most are status markers, valuable in their own right thanks to their value as exotica. The carnelian, amethyst and lapis lazuli from which seals were fabricated entered the Aegean from Yemen, the foothills of the Pamir Mountains in central Asia and the Deccan.[45] When, therefore, the occupant of the Griffin Warrior grave at Pylos was buried with gold rings, hundreds of glass beads and more than fifty seal stones, such as the exquisite combat scene carved from agate, the sheer numbers of these goods was an overwhelming display of his wealth, status and power, distinct from any precise messages encoded in the Minoan images on his gold rings.[46]

[43] For a useful introduction to seals and sealings, see Armeri et al. 2018: 1–10. For regional patterns, see the various contributions in the same volume.
[44] Blakolmer 2016: 160.   [45] Eder 2015: 223.
[46] Davis and Stocker 2016: 632. For the combat agate, see Davis and Stocker 2017.

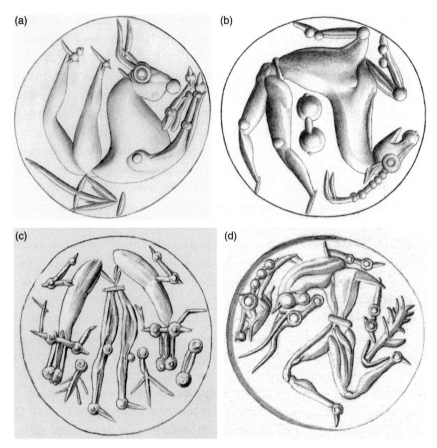

Figure 4.7 Minoan seals depicting hybrids. **a.** CMS II3 no. 67 (bull-man; Knossos); **b.** CMS V Suppl. 3 no. 113 (goat-man; Chania); **c.** CMS VI no. 301 (double-bull-man; Milatos); **d.** CMS XIII no. 84 (bull-goat-man; Knossos). Courtesy of the CMS archive, Heidelberg. **e.** CMS IX no. 165 (bird-lady, legs missing/not preserved; unknow prov.); **f.** CMS VI no. 294 (bird-lady, with legs; Crete?); Polysomatic fusion: **g.** CMS II7 no. 83 (butterfly-lion-lady; Kato Zakros impression); **h.** CMS II7 no. 145A ('bull-bird-woman'; Kato Zakros impression). Courtesy of the CMS archive, Heidelberg.

By the Iron Age, then, the people of the Aegean world were familiar with a broad array of monsters and hybrids, sometimes embedded in much older cosmogenic narratives and at other times simply free-standing images of peculiar, otherworldly creatures. Prior to the eighth century, hybrids are part of the background hum of the Mediterranean network but emerge with greater clarity as interactions intensified during the Archaic Period. Robert Garland has recently drawn attention to this intensification, identifying the movement of people around the eastern Mediterranean as a distinctive characteristic of the world of Archaic Greece. He attributes the

Categories, Contexts and Certainty 111

Figure 4.7 (cont.)

brilliance of Greek culture in part to this 'shiftlessness': 'It was also the case that the mobility of the Greeks, and the spirit of adaptability that this bred inside them, encouraged the construction of panhellenic institutions and fostered cultural homogeneity. Greece in sum was a civilization of displaced persons.'[47] In common with many who claim a special quality for Greek culture but want to avoid crude triumphalism, Garland attributes the brilliance of Greek culture to experiences external to any innate character. In similar fashion, L. H. Jeffery identified the geography of Greece as fostering 'an incandescent individualism' among the Greeks.[48]

Hybrids, however, suggest other ways of gauging how the greater intensity of commercial and cultural exchange around the Mediterranean network in the Archaic period impacted the Aegean World. An undeniable characteristic of hybrids is that they are contrafactuals, and recent work in

[47] Garland 2014: 199.   [48] Jeffery 1976: 23.

the field of cognitive neuroscience has emphasized the importance of counterfactual richness in confirming perceptual presence, or the mind's capacity to convince itself of realness.[49] In the setting of a Mediterranean network, the uncertainty and potential dangers of encounters present phenomenological challenges: how to express a consciousness of self and other, to understand the difference between like and unlike, to evaluate familiar and unfamiliar, to tell real from unreal, truth from lies – these are all dilemmas that are intensified by the thick entangled world of the Aegean and neighbouring regions. Such potentially dislocative experiences – sailing into a foreign port (hostile or friendly?), encountering a ship at sea (pirate or comrade?), visiting a rural shrine used by natives in colonized or contested territory (cooperative or resistant?) – are hedged around with doubt, anxiety and uncertainty. The hybrid straddles many of these polarities; it may be familiar but odd, comprehensible in its parts but peculiar as a whole, but paradoxically the hybrid offers the means of rebuilding the wall between phenomenal transparency, which equates representations with reality, and opacity, by which non-real representations are experienced as exactly that: unreal, and only representations. In epistemological terms, hybrids, as counterfactually rich and recognizably contrafactual, may actually confirm for the viewer and listener that their grasp of reality is sound. The ability to distinguish the hybrid from the real animal is a cognitive exercise of reassurance.

Seen in this light, the great black-figure *dinoi* by Sophilos and the Gorgon Painter, with their alternation of imaginary and real creatures, do not indicate, much less prove, that the Greeks (or Etruscans) did not distinguish between real and unreal creatures (see Figure 4.8). Quite the opposite. These vessels encourage the viewer to classify each of its images on a gradient of reality: hideous gorgons, the stuff of heroic tales; boars and lions, very much a part of the real world; and sphinxes, also unreal, but not nearly as scary as the gorgons, and not fixed within a narrative scheme. The symposia for which these vessels were intended and in which water and wine were mixed (*dinos*-whirling, rotation), might produce lightheadedness (*dinos*-vertigo). The splash of the wine in a cup is like the rhythmic beating of oars (*pitulos*), while the symposiasts drank from cups decorated with eyes to help them navigate the fog of a drinking bout, just as the ships were equipped with eyes to see through storms, but none of these vessels, with their profusion of hybrid images alongside real animals, convey any sense of threat. No monstrous powers lurk outside the

---

[49] Metzinger 2014.

Figure 4.8 Guests, including Themis, Cheiron and Hebe, arriving at the wedding of Peleus and Thetis. Detail of black-figure dinos by Sophilos, ca. 580 BC. Athens. 28 cm × 42 cm. The British Museum, 1971,1101.1. © The British Museum.

symposium. In fact, the symposium may even have been designed to evoke the experiencing of sailing the wine-dark sea transferred to the safe setting of the *andron*. Referring to one of Archilochus' sympotic songs, Anna Uhlig notes:

> Archilochus was singing about a sailor's watch, but he was singing for a sympotic audience, men who may once have been to sea, and may well have been bound to return there in the future, but who were, at least for the duration of Archilochus' song, firmly planted on dry land, enjoying their drinks in the communal institution that, perhaps more than any other, defined life in an archaic polis ... These verses would allow for a kind of vicarious sailing, ... inviting the participants in the symposium to imagine themselves aboard ship – or on the strand beside one – from the comfort of their drinking couches.[50]

The real world remains soberly distinct from fantasy.

The upsurge of Archaic hybrid images in Archaic art and poetry does not occur in a vacuum. In the west in particular, Etruscan and Phoenicians provided competitors as well as markets where Greek traders and settlers mixed with non-Greek speakers. In these contact zones, encounters were frequently bloody and violent: the Carthaginians suffered a catastrophic

---

[50] Uhlig 2018: 67. For an earlier study of the symposium--sea connection, see Slater 1976.

defeat at the hands of Gelon in 480 BC at the battle of Himera, and six years later Hieron accomplished another victory against the Etruscans.[51] Western Sicily was an especially volatile place, where Motya, Lilybaion, Panormos and Solous served as Carthaginian settlements and outposts.[52] The outright battles of the early fifth century came after two centuries of intermittent hostility. Fifty years ago, Nicholas Coldstream hinted that ethnic enmities might be traceable to the eighth and seventh centuries, observing that 'there is no Geometric battle scene where men wearing the same type of shield are fighting each other'.[53] On the Aristonothos krater from Caere, usually dated to the seventh century, the warriors are similarly equipped, but the confrontation takes place at sea and the ships can easily be identified as Greek and Etruscan (see Figure 4.9). The Greeks fight in vessels with high sterns and low prows that end in beaks or rams, decorated

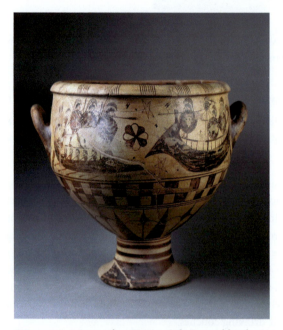

Figure 4.9 Aristonothos Krater. Side B naval battle. Second quarter of the seventh century BC. Rome, Musei Capitolini, inv. CA 172. G. Dagli Orti/© NPL – DeA Picture Library/Bridgeman Images.

---

[51] Hdt. 7.165–7; Diodorus 11.20–6; Pindar, *P.* 1.70–5: 'I entreat you, son of Cronus, grant that the battle-shouts of the Carthaginians and Etruscans stay quietly at home, now that they have seen their arrogance bring lamentation to their ships off Cumae. Such were their sufferings, when they were conquered by the leader of the Syracusans – a fate which flung their young men from their swift ships into the sea, delivering Hellas from grievous bondage' (tr. Svarlien).
[52] Funke 2010: 156.   [53] Coldstream 1974: 395. See also Ahlberg 1971.

with eyes. The Etruscan ships are quite different, with high prows more akin to the *hippoi* used by Carthaginian and other Phoenician sailors.[54] The distinction reflects an awareness of ethnic difference.

But caution is needed. Nathan Arrington notes that some of the krater's characteristics are Attic – the profiles and limbs of the figures, the large black and white rosette between the boats – but that the krater's shape and ornamental features such as the rays are locally inspired. Arrington refers to the vessel exhibiting 'heterogenous style ... bearing scenes of cross-cultural contact'.[55] The krater is signed '*Aristonothos epoiesen*' and if (although this, of course, is unproveable) the 'Noble Bastard' who made the krater is the son of Greek and Etruscan parents, then the krater's composition and manufacturing reflect an entangled history at odds with the fixed ethnic categories signalled by the ships. Instead, it hints at a more intimate story of blending and mixture: a Greek artisan in central Italy, possibly the child of a mixed union, producing a vessel that combines Attic and Etruscan elements even as it depicts the opposition of Greek and Etruscan.[56] This is the complex reality in which hybrid forms and experiences hint at messy alternatives to neat categorical distinctions.

Responding to this one-sided emphasis in modern scholarship on ethnic hostility between Greeks and non-Greeks, Corinne Bonnet offers a more nuanced scenario, breaking down the long and sometimes violent cohabitation of Phoenicians and Greeks in Sicily into smaller units: 'marriages, alliances, and exchanges, contracts, of betrayal, and of misunderstandings'. These contingent encounters help to place the Greek taste for hybrids in a context of recurring, fluid, creative tensions:

> This confrontation, day by day, in peace and in war, in the public and private spheres, in the most varied areas (business, war, culture, diplomacy, religion, technology, sailing, and so on) generated an awareness of self and other, a *social representation* characterized by a powerful tension between, on the one hand, integration, porosity, recognition, collaboration, and on the other, rejection, boundaries, separation, deprecation and indeed barbarization.[57]

---

[54] On *hippoi* in the Eastern Mediterranean, see Linder 1986. For the west and the Atlantic zone, see Mederos Martín and Escribano Cobo 2008.
[55] Arrington 2021: 79.
[56] Dougherty 2003: 56, n. 69 summarizes the explanations that have been offered for Aristonothos, including: a Greek migrant from the Cyclades first to Athens, then to Sicily and finally to Caere; a painter active in Magna Graecia but producing this krater in Caere; and a Greek potter living in Caere adapting his work to local taste.
[57] Bonnet 2014: 329.

The latter of these processes, with its emphasis on difference, produces stereotypes, such as Phoenicians who are dishonourable, untrustworthy professional traders greedy for profit. A good example is the sailor who seduces Eumaios' nurse (*Od.* 15.455–527) after arriving in a ship filled with trinkets. Having spent a year trading and filling his ship's hold, he uses a golden necklace strung with amber to distract the women of the household and the nurse runs off with him, kidnapping the infant Eumaios on the way. Yet, the *Odyssey* also hints at Bonnet's first category of collaboration. Upon his arrival on Ithaka, Odysseus fabricates a story he tells to Athena in disguise of his escape from Crete thanks to a friendly Phoenician ship. He makes a point of explaining that even though they did not land him at Pylos as promised, it was solely because of adverse winds. 'It wasn't their fault, they didn't want to cheat me,' he says. In the fictional storyworld invented by Odysseus within the storyworld of the *Odyssey*, it was possible to imagine cooperation between decent Phoenicians and stranded Greeks.[58]

Egypt, Naukratis and Samos

Odysseus' Phoenicians are a reminder that contact occurred wherever Greek speakers and non-Greek speakers interacted. In this array of interactions in the Archaic period, some stand out for their intensity: commercial activity, religious experience, warfare and the forming of new families and communities.[59] Or, to be more precise, it is the experiences of migrants, itinerant artists, traders, pirates and mercenaries that generated hybrids to give expression to the complexities of cultural encounters with non-Greeks. No two sites of such exchanges were identical, but some features of cultural interaction can be identified. In general, it is usually argued that eastern emporia such as Al Mina and Naukratis tried to limit contact between Greek and non-Greek communities, while in the west sites such as Pithekoussai and Incoronata experienced more open systems of exchange.[60] A closer look at Naukratis and Samos, however, suggests that

---

[58] On Phoenicians in the *Odyssey*, see Trahman 1952, Carpenter 1958, and for stereotypes as a discursive practice, see Skinner 2013: 116–19. For a review of attitudes towards trade, piracy and Homer's Phoenicians, see Peacock 2011. For a recent discussion of the episode involving Eumaios' nurse, see Wilson 2021.

[59] On the role of artisans in the spread of hybrid styles, see Altaweel and Squitieri 2018. For the nexus of trade, piracy and mercenary service, see Luraghi 2006, who finds compelling evidence for these practices, conducted by Greeks of the islands, beginning shortly after 750 BC.

[60] Arrington 2021: 89.

cultural contact played out on many different levels, each qualitatively distinct.

Excavations at Naukratis began shortly after Flinders Petrie's identification of a series of mounds by the village of Kom Ge'if in 1884.[61] The site is located 80 km southeast of Alexandria close to the Canopic branch of the Nile. Flinders Petrie was able to identify the location of the emporion as well as many of its most important structures: a temenos of Apollo, a temenos of the Dioskouroi, a palaestra, a scarab factory and the communal sanctuary available to all the Greeks at Naukratis, the Hellenion. His identifications were based both on excavations and the detailed descriptions of Strabo (17.1.18) and Herodotos (2.178–179). The Herodotean account in particular reflects (and perhaps overstates) the potential for emporia to be foci for ethnic tensions. The Greek historian describes the decision of the pharaoh, Amasis, to allow Greek traders to establish a foothold in the Delta but under strictly controlled conditions:

> Amasis became a philhellene, and one the ways he showed this, among the various favors he did Greeks, was to give them the city of Naucratis as a place where any Greek who came to stay in Egypt could live. Moreover, any Greeks who made voyages to the country without wishing to settle were given plots of land where they could set up altars and precincts to their gods. The largest of these precincts, as well as being the most famous and popular, is called the Hellenion, whose foundation was a joint venture undertaken by a number of Greek communities. The Ionian communities involved were Chios, Teos, Phocaea, and Clazomenae; the Dorian communities involved were Rhodes, Cnidus, Halicarnassus, and Phaselis; and the only Aeolian town involved was Mytilene. These are the cities to which the precinct belongs (they also supply the officers who are in charge of the trading-center), and any other communities which lay claim to it are making a claim to something they have no share in. However, precincts sacred to Zeus, Hera, and Apollo were built separately by Aegina, Samos, and Miletos respectively. Originally there was no other trading-center in Egypt apart from Naucratis. If anyone fetched up at any of the other mouths of the Nile, he had to swear that he had not done so deliberately, and then after making his statement under oath, bring his ship round to the Canobic mouth ... That is how important Naucratis was.
>
> Hdt 2.178–9 (tr. Waterfield)

In this account, then, the emporium at Naukratis housed a cluster of Greek communities, consisting of permanent residences and itinerant

---

[61] For a summary of Finders Petrie's excavations, see Leonard 1997: 1–36 and Leonard 1998.

visitors. The Greeks were identified by their home cities, and worshipped their Greek gods in separate sanctuaries, as well as in the joint sanctuary appropriately called the Hellenion.[62] Herodotos interprets the concession of land at Naukratis as an expression of philhellenism on the part of Amasis, but the arrangement has frequently been read as an attempt to restrict the Greek presence in Egypt. The pharaoh's concerns were legitimate: Psamtik had engaged Ionian and Karian mercenaries, 'raiders who had left home in search of rich pickings' in Herodotos' description (2.152), and paid them with land on either side of the Nile at a spot called 'The Camps' (*ta stratopeda*).[63] From here Amasis moved them to Memphis, where they served as his bodyguards. Herodotos reports seeing the slipways for their ships as well as the ruins of their first houses. In other words, from at least the seventh century the Egyptians had experienced the unsettling presence of Greek mercenaries in their midst.[64] Amasis' decision, therefore, to partition the Greek off into in a separate community was entirely understandable. For much of the last century scholarly treatments of Naukratis interpreted the archaeology of the site through the filter of this Herodotean account, resulting in a picture of clearly bounded and separate Greek and Egyptian communities.[65] Denise Demetriou has also drawn attention to the taxes paid by the Greeks, details of which are preserved on the Stele of Nektanebis, which show that the Greeks were required to make offerings to the goddess Neith.[66] Demetriou sees this as evidence of the Egyptian government asserting its sovereignty in the face of the potential threat of foreigners whose presence, nevertheless, was potentially profitable to both sides. Recent work at Naukratis, however, suggests a slightly different story. Noting the unexpectedly large amount of local Egyptian material unearthed in newly excavated parts of the site, Alan Johnston claims that this 'giv[es] the lie to the entrenched notion that Naukratis was essentially

---

[62] The bibliography on Naukratis is extensive, but good starting points for recent work are Möller 2000, Villing and Schlotzhauer 2006, and Demetriou 2012: 105–52. For more than a decade the British Museum has conducted fresh excavation and geophysical prospection under the leadership of Alexandra Villing. The results of this project and early publications are collected at: https://webarchive.nationalarchives.gov.uk/ukgwa/20190801120114/https://www.british museum.org/research/online_research_catalogues/ng/naukratis_greeks_in_egypt/bibliog raphy.asp. In addition, a succinct overview of cultural exchange at Naukratis can be found in Colburn 2018.

[63] For discussion of 'The Camps' and a possible location close to the Pelusiac mouth of the Nile, see Oren 1984.

[64] On Ionian and Karian mercenaries in Egypt, see Giangiulio 1996, Kaplan 2003 and Luraghi 2006.

[65] On Egyptian control, see Bresson 2000, Villing and Schlotzhauer 2006: 5. On Greek identity in the face of the Egyptians, see Malkin 2003 and Demetriou 2012.

[66] Demetriou 2012: 121–3.

a Greek foundation. We should see it rather as a town in which non-Egyptian traders were given an enclave and prospered, at least in part living a 'Greek' way of life but also engaging closely with their Egyptian neighbours.'[67]

It is important to recognize this intermingling of Greek and Egyptian communities as a counterpoint to an official policy of separation since the reality 'on the ground' was that encounters between Greeks and Egyptians resulted in different forms of hybridization. There were, for example, people who effectively moved between two worlds, like Wahibbreemakhet, son of Alexikles and Zenodote.[68] We do not know when his parents came to Egypt and whether their son was born there, but his sarcophagus reveals that he enjoyed very high status as the King's Seal-Bearer, known by the title of ḫtmty bjty. While he was interred at Saqqara with all the trappings of an elite – rich sarcophagus, canopic jars, shabtis and a tomb decked out with reliefs – he was also clearly identifiable as the son of Greeks. Objects offer less dramatic evidence for cultural exchange but suggest an even more complex picture than migration and assimilation. The Archaic period witnessed the production of objects that looked Egyptian but were often manufactured by and for Ionian Greeks. Such 'Aigyptiaka' were in vogue in the Aegean during the Archaic period. This is more complex than the simple export of Egyptian goods to Greek areas. Naukratis was one of the places where Egyptian and Egyptianizing goods such as beads, scarabs and faience figurines were produced for export, many finding their way to Greek sanctuaries that were connected to the trade network linking the Delta to the Aegean. Yet discussions of these objects and their significance are often conceptually imprecise and rely on vague language. Commenting on the rich cache of Egyptian figurines from the early seventh century found at the Heraion on Samos, Carol Benson remarks that '[s]carce but slowly mounting evidence from the major East Greek sanctuaries, from scattered Greek sites, and from Lydian contexts just east of Greek territories is also beginning to indicate that Egyptian influences were strongly felt in Archaic Greek centers other than Naukratis'.[69] This is true, but it is appropriate to ask precisely what is meant by 'Egyptian influences'. In fact, at the Samian Heraion, 133 of the 317 bronzes published to date are from Egypt, and they include many bronze

---

[67] Johnston 2014: 70.
[68] For Wahibbreemakhet, his identity, sarcophagus and canopic jars, see Villing 2018. For foreigners in Egypt, see Vittman 2003. On the sarcophagus his parents' names are rendered as Sentiti and Arkeskares. For their identification as Greek Zenodote and Alexikles, see Griffith 1916.
[69] Benson 2001: 12.

figurines depicting various Egyptian gods such as Mut, Neith and Hathor.[70] None are known to have been dedicated by Egyptians and instead appear to be dedications by Greeks. It is doubtful that the dedication of these Egyptian figurines is evidence of Egyptian influence, if by this we mean Egyptian cult practice or belief. Instead, Greeks who had travelled to and from Naukratis felt it appropriate to make dedications to a revered deity using precious statuettes originally designed with another deity in mind. Similar, though more modest, deposits of Aegyptiaka are attested at the Artemision at Ephesos, the sanctuary of Aphrodite in Miletos, the sanctuary of Athena at Erythrai and the sanctuaries of Hera at Perachora, Naukratis and Gravisca. Taken together, these 'Egyptianizing' goods point to a system in which the circulation of precious goods was more important than categories such as 'Greek' or 'Egyptian'. To put the matter simply, when a sailor returning from Naukratis offered thanks to his protector goddess, the protective power of Neith was indistinguishable from Hera's. The 'Egyptian influence' here amounts to little more than the place of origin of the statuette and is no more a sign of cultural exchange than an amber ring is evidence of Nordic influence on its wearer.

The vogue in Egyptian-style objects also resulted in the use of faience figurines, often depicting the Horus falcon but also other animals and humans, from 630 BC onwards. Fragments of nearly 2,000 such figurines have been found close to the Great Altar at the Heraion. Significantly, however, many of the Samian faience pieces were not up to the standards of Egyptian prototypes, and Virginia Webb suggests that the corpus of faience figurines from Samos 'is a distorted reproduction of Egyptian ritual objects, which would only have been acceptable in a foreign milieu'.[71] Furthermore, the deliberate and complete destruction of these imitation pieces hints at a very different use when compared to the original Egyptian setting, where the faience glaze marked the figurine as an evocation of the divine power of the deity depicted, usually Horus or Hathor. In fact, so attenuated is the religious power of these objects that they suggest that the encounter with Egypt did not have a significant impact on Greek religious feelings or practice. As a cultural force, Egyptian influence was weak.

The pattern of dedicating Egyptian goods at Greek sanctuaries in the late eighth and seventh centuries is repeated with respect to luxury items from Assyria and other eastern locations. North Syrian and Cypriot figurines and objects, ranging from horse bits to furniture panels as well as figurines depicting other gods, were dedicated at the Samian Heraion. Three statuettes,

[70] Ringheim 2020.   [71] Webb 2021: 270.

for example, of the Babylonian healing goddess Gula are among the more exotic dedications at the sanctuary. In evaluating the significance of these dedications John Curtis has remarked that there is no evidence for Hera being held in special esteem in the ancient Near East and, rather than interpreting this as evidence for syncretism, he concludes more modestly, 'Because some value was attached to [such figurines], they would then have been deemed worthy of dedication to Hera or other deities.'[72] The variety of objects either imported or manufactured locally with foreign protypes as models reflects an eclecticism in the dedications of the Archaic period, but the significance of that eclecticism when objects move around a network, and are reused, copied, dedicated and destroyed, can be hard to estimate. A contemporary analogy may help: Hello Kitty, the Japanese marketing phenomenon. In its Japanese setting it is an expression of a significant development in post-war Japanese aesthetics: *kawaii* (cuteness). *Kawaii*, though traceable in forms going back to the eleventh century, has found expression in many media, especially *anime* and *manga*, and has soothed economic and environmental anxieties by creating a safe alternative, an infantile storyworld.[73] In these respects it represents a serious cultural turn in Japanese life and aesthetics, with many young people identifying with an entire world of fantasy (*otaku*) in magazines, videos and, above all, through *kosupure* (cos-play).[74] But translated into a western setting, the coin-purses, note-books and backpacks emblazoned with a dot-eyed cat are stripped of these meanings. The cuteness is still there, but irony aside, it is hard to interpret Hello Kitty recontextualized to a Midwestern mall as much more than an example of successful marketing aimed at little girls.[75] This may, in fact, be the key to understanding the arrival of so many foreign and foreign-looking objects in Archaic Greek sanctuaries. It has been argued that the difference between Greece in the Late Bronze Age and in the Iron Age is marked by the transformation of rulers' houses into temples of the gods: same location, similar form, different function.[76] A similar process was at work with respect to exotic luxury items. Luxury goods in the Late Bronze Age constituted a network of gift exchange and reciprocity between elites across the eastern Mediterranean. In the seventh century and later, luxury goods once again circulated around a network, but one constituted by trade and sanctuary dedication.[77] As in the earlier

---

[72] Curtis 1994: 2.   [73] Brecher 2015.   [74] On *otaku* and *kosupure*, see Amit 2012: 174.
[75] Contra, see Lieber and Weisberg 2002: 282, reading Hello Kitty as an example of Japan's status as 'perhaps the most distinctive global alternative to American culture'.
[76] Mazarakis Ainian 1997.
[77] For changes in the way trade was conducted and earlier elite conceptions of gift exchange, see Tandy 1997.

reciprocity network, in the Archaic dedication network foreign provenance added to an object's value, not its meaning.

Many hybrid objects of the Archaic period were manufactured to meet the growing demand for foreign exotica. The result was not an Archaic revival of International Style, but rather the adaption of artistic traditions to meet new demands and supply new markets with objects that incorporated foreign elements. The results may appear eclectic, but the object's stylistic hybridity can also be taken as a sign of an openness to ignoring the strictures of established categories. A good example is the Greek statuette manufactured in an Ionian workshop depicting a woman in Egyptian-style clothing (Figure 4.10). The figurine shows a familiarity with Egyptian dress, with features such as the three decorative bands at the collar recalling the Egyptian banded collar, but there are clearly Ionian elements as well, both in the garments, including a chiton, and in the rendering of the egg-shaped head and side-curls. Benson interprets the blending of these elements 'as if a Greek artist wished to emulate an Egyptian "look" but was confused about the

Figure 4.10 Bronze statuette of a woman. Archaic. Ionian. 13.8 × 3.6 × 2.1 cm. Walters Art Museum. 54.970.

correct arrangement of Egyptian garments'.[78] This may be correct, but it is a judgement that reflects a familiar prejudice against objects that cross boundaries. It is equally possible that the Egyptian elements on display here indicate not confusion but a willingness of the Ionian craftsman to incorporate non-Ionian elements. One might even speculate that a Greek returning from Egypt with riches and a wife, like Menelaus in Herodotos' account (2.112–20), may have found an occasion to dedicate a figurine that reflected an appreciation of both cultures.

Another Greek returning from Egypt was the mercenary Pedon, who served in the army of Psamtik. Upon his return to Priene he dedicated a block statue of his patron, the pharaoh, in a sanctuary, with an inscription that recorded his (Pedon's) accomplishments: 'Pedon son of Amphinneos set me up as a votive, having brought [me] back from Egypt; and to him Psammetichos, king of Egypt, gave as prizes a golden armlet and a city on account of his valor.'[79] Even without the explanatory inscription, the statue's distinctive shape and material (basalt) would have marked it out as special, and thereby enhanced Pedon's prestige. There is also evidence that foreign styles could flow in the other direction. Klaus Parlasca examined Greek-style figurines found in Egypt, and argued that some were manufactured there as well.[80] This is certain in the case of a painted kouros from Naukratis wearing an Egyptian kilt and headgear. Naukratis may have been intended to contain the Greeks in Egypt, but the vitality of its culture is a powerful testament to hybrid vigour.

The Ionian Egyptianizing bronze statuette, the Pedon dedication and the various episodes in epic involving Odysseus and Menelaus all point to the fact that many Archaic hybrids reflect the personal experiences of men and women as they moved between different cultures and across boundaries. Items flowed around the Eastern Mediterranean as trade goods and often ended up as sanctuary dedications, and it was this very circulation of luxury items that created conditions in which hybridity flourished. Meaning and symbolism here count for less than wonder. Take, for example, the famous set of bronze repoussé reliefs excavated more than seventy years ago at Olympia. They are part of one of the largest selections of Near Eastern Bronzes found anywhere in the eastern Mediterranean, including in the regions of the Assyrian empire where they originated. In the centre of one sheet

---

[78] Benson 2001: 8.
[79] Luraghi 2006, Iancu 2017, Barbaro 2018. For the view that Pedon was 'a Hellenized Egyptian native rather than an Egyptianized Greek mercenary', see Piccolo 2019: 173.
[80] Parlasca 1975.

Figure 4.11 Bronze repoussé relief. North Syrian, ca. 710 BC. Reused to decorate a *korê* statue ca. 600 BC. Olympia Museum. D-DAI-ATH-1979/564. Photograph by Gösta Hellner.

(Figure 4.11), a figure in a woolly garment can be seen being led by two bearded men wearing odd, scaly outfits.

As Eleanor Guralnik has demonstrated, 'The men dressed in fish-skins and curly wool on the repoussé frieze relate to figures from Assyrian religious tradition.'[81] At the same time, however, Guralnik points out that most contemporary Assyrian examples depict these fish-men with fish-skin cloaks and often include a fish head and tail as well. The prototype for this figure, in fact, is the *apkallu*, a benevolent spirit in Babylonian religion (see Chapter 2). The figure of the prophetic fish-man would be later introduced to the Greeks through the writings of Berossos, who wrote a history of Babylon in Greek in the early years of the Seleucid dynasty, but no reference to, or explanation of the *apkallu* exists in Greek texts of the seventh or sixth centuries.[82] The North Syrian version that reached Olympia sometime between 700 and 600 BC was evidently fashioned by

---

[81] Guralnik 2004: 196. For other Near Eastern bronze reliefs, including a Urartian piece (from Samos?) that shows the head of a divinity wearing a horned crown, see Childs 2001.

[82] For Berossos, see Dillery 2015 and McInerney 2017.

a craftsman who, according to Guralnik, had not seen the Assyrian representations of the hybrid fish-men.

This underscores the dramatic transformations that hybrids could undergo in transmission. If the craftsman who fashioned the bronze plaque had only a dim notion of the significance of the fish-garment, it will have meant even less to the Greek speakers who first saw it when it was brought to the Peloponnese. Furthermore, when pieces of the original sheet were reworked onto the surface of a sphyrelaton *korê*, the change of context divorced the scene from any recognizable narrative. It is unlikely that it was suitable for a dedication at Olympia because it depicted a sacred tale; more probably it was seen as a luxury item, devoid of narrative meaning but valuable because of its craftsmanship, exotic appearance and distant provenance. Each stage of its movement from its time and place of origin widened the gap between its original meaning and function, until all that was left was its exotic value.

Cyprus

Moving around a network, many of the seals and statuettes of the Iron Age display hybrid features as indications of foreign origins or exotic characteristics. As a counterpoint to these mobile objects it is worth also looking at places where hybridity was a feature of daily encounters and was integrated into cultural practices and the expression of identity. While the web of connections from the Eastern Mediterranean to the Aegean was always changing, evolving, contracting and expanding, one location deserves special mention as a central node in this network: Cyprus, whose position highlights both how and why motifs of hybridity entered the Aegean. Tucked into the far eastern corner of the Mediterranean, Cyprus looks towards Ugarit and Phoenicia to the east and south, and to Rhodes and the Aegean to the west. Wind and currents facilitate the westward movement of goods, while the island's mineral resources invited the attention of settlers from both east and west. In the Middle Bronze Age, settlement patterns reflect a growing population as well as the appearance of new sites both close to the coast and with access to copper-bearing deposits in the hinterland: Enkomi, Morphou, Hala Sultan Tekke, Kourion and Palaipaphos.[83] Mycenaean vessels attest to connections with the Aegean going back to the fourteenth century, and the distinctive bird-faced

---

[83] Steele 2019: 8–9.

figurines of Late Cypriot II (1450–1200 BC) point towards close cultural relations with Syria. In addition to indigenes and those descended from the Mycenaean Greeks, Phoenician speakers began coming to the island and settling as early as 900 BC, creating the necessary conditions for rich cultural encounters.

As a place occupied by different population groups coming from east and west, Cyprus was uniquely situated to benefit from hybridity as a means of expressing the challenges of complex cultural exchange. This was certainly true even earlier in the Late Bronze Age. As outsiders came to Cyprus, drawn to the rich copper deposits, they encountered and mixed with local people, shaping a culture and an identity born of hybridization.[84] Newcomers brought with them Egyptian, Levantine and Aegean prestige goods to assert their status. In response to this flood of outside objects, languages and ethnic identities, Cypriot culture responded with an exuberant embrace of hybrid imagery, facilitating the assimilation of different exogenous populations and resulting in the expression of a broadly homogenous culture in the Iron Age.[85] In the face of the Cypriot kingdoms' subordination to outside powers, first Assyrian and later Achaemenid, hybridity served as way of negotiating the space between cultures and fashioning a true *métis* experience, particularly evident in the extramural sanctuaries of the island. In common with other middle ground encounters, each visitor to a sanctuary could bring their own perceptions to the dedications and objects that constituted the materiality of the rituals that were enacted here.[86] The Master of Animals, for example, made sense to a worshipper of Phoenician Melqart, just as it made sense to a Greek familiar with Herakles, and to just about every local farmer and herder who might seek to placate the embodied power of nature.[87] The capacity of the Master of Animals figure to cross boundaries and appeal to disparate worshippers resides, according to Derek Counts, in its ambiguity: 'The preference for this deity and the divine spheres of power, protection, and prosperity he embodied represented the collective goals of ancient

---

[84] Knapp 2015: 25. See also Voskos and Knapp 2008.   [85] Iacovou 2005.
[86] On hybridity and middle ground, see Reger 2014 and Bonnet 2014. Both are alert to the dangers of inferring ethnic identity from objects.
[87] Counts 2008: 23 concludes his study of the Master of the Lion noting that 'the relative ambiguity of hybridized, iconographical traits enabled the Master of Animals to mediate the boundaries of existing cultural differences within the context of Cypriote votive religion. The power of the Master of Animals in his ability both to control and, if necessary, conquer natural forces would certainly have appealed to farmers, shepherds, soldiers, and merchants alike.' For the widespread occurrence of the hero-between-animals motif, see Klingender 1971: 105.

Cypriotes, regardless of their particular cultural roots or social status.' Polysemy invites engagement.

In Iron Age Cyprus, where it is unlikely that the population of one ethnic group dominated all others numerically, the outside pressure from Assyrian overlords and the balance between local groups combined to favour strategies of accommodation and cooperation. One way of negotiating the complexities of ethnic and cultural diversity was to occlude identity by wearing different masks – in some cases literally. Some of the masks found on Cyprus are local versions of both demon and hero masks found throughout the Levant, brought to Cyprus by Phoenician traders and settlers. As Jane Carter has shown, these types are extraordinarily long-lived, and can be traced back to Babylon a millennium earlier.[88] On Cyprus it is usually thought that the masks served in rituals connected to the worship of Asherah or Tanit, in which the demon (ultimately going back to Humbaba) was defeated by the goddess's male consort. But it would be wrong to infer from this that the distribution of such objects is evidence for an entire cultic package, consisting of myth and ritual, that was discrete and remained unchanged. In fact, we cannot know the degree to which, if at all, the rituals associated with these masks in their Cypriot setting functioned as markers of Punic identity or exclusivity. The very spread of the grotesque demon type to Sparta, where these masks were connected to the worship of Artemis Orthia, argues the opposite. Punic in origin does not mean Punic in essence.

On Cyprus masks were also associated with animal transformation. Like the grotesque features of the demon, Cypriot animal masks dramatize the ambiguity of the hybrid, a suitable symbol and vehicle for transformation and possibly initiation. A small sixth-century limestone figurine shows a human figure in the act of donning a stag's head mask (Figure 4.12), while there are many examples in glyptic, terracotta and limestone of figures wearing a variety of animal masks: bulls' heads, rams' heads, and lions' heads as well as human heads (sometimes with horns).[89] Many of these capture the very moment when the practitioner holds the mask to his face, as if to emphasize not the composite nature of the creature but the performance of hybridity. Averett has recently suggested that these figurines represent participants in masking rituals, and proposes that these were rituals 'almost certainly enacted by those in power (priests, elites and in some cases even kings) as an expression of royal or elite authority to those

[88] Carter 1987.
[89] The bibliography on Cypriot masks is vast, but an important starting point is Belgiorno 1993. For a full catalogue and earlier bibliography, see Averett 2015.

Figure 4.12 Figure with mask. Sixth century BC, Cyprus. Limestone, 26 × 10.2 × 5.7 cm, 1.1 kg. Metropolitan Museum of Art, 74.51.2538.

in attendance'.[90] She also suggests that the masking rituals were part of the initiation into secret societies such as flourish during periods of social upheaval 'because they affirm the ideologies of those in power while at the same time weakening ties that are potentially threatening to the political structure, such as familial/clan bonds'.[91] Secret initiation is an explanation difficult to test, and perhaps even harder to reconcile with the theatricality expected if the rituals are performances of royal power. It is also unclear how the commemorative role of the masks would operate in the context of secret societies. Nevertheless, Averett's thesis points to an important feature of the mask: it effaces identity. Liane Posthumus puts it nicely: '[Masks] offer instant hybridity, converting the wearer into an animated being of uncertain nature and of monstrous appearance.'[92] There is no clear association of the masks with assertions of EteoCypriot, Phoenician or Greek identity. Instead, during the period in which this activity flourished, from CG III to CC I (absolute dates: 900–400 BC), the rituals commemorated by the theriomorphic masks on Cyprus served as a meeting space for all cultural groups, regardless of language affiliation or

[90] Averett 2015: 24. For a list of masked figures, see Averett 2018: 27–39.   [91] Averett 2015: 27.
[92] Posthumus 2011: 88.

ethnic identity. The group solidarity enacted by such rituals, secret or not, offered an alternative to sectarian divisions.

Masks make the wearer into a composite figure of the human behind the mask and whatever identity is adopted.[93] The inhabitants of Iron Age Cyprus had already long been exposed to hybrid images with Near Eastern antecedents. Hardstone seals first identified by Edith Porada as Cypriot Elaborate Style are attested on Cyprus as early as the fourteenth century BC.[94] They appear to blend Aegean and Near Eastern elements, often depicting winged figures, demons and human–animal hybrids (Figure 4.13). In older diffusionist models of cultural development such seals have been viewed as objects whose spread reflects the movement of culture from east to west, but recent studies have emphasized the eastern Mediterranean as an active network. Rather than being the passive recipient of eastern goods and ideas flowing west, Cyprus was a fertile ground of interaction, although the commercial activities connected to these seals are opaque at best. It may be that the seals marked transactions, especially connected with the trade in tin and copper that became important in the second millennium, but it is also possible that the seals were regarded as precious objects in their own right.[95]

What can be said is that the artists producing these seals for local elites developed stylistic features that mark them as distinctively Cypriot. The so-called tête-bêche style, for example, in which the seal is divided into two registers, of which the second is inverted, was a local variation on the

Figure 4.13 Hematite cylinder seal, Cyprus. Late Cypriot II, ca. fourteenth century BC. 2.8 cm. Metropolitan Museum of Art. 200827.

---

[93] Pollock 1995. [94] Porada 1948.
[95] For the commercial systems associated with seals on Crete and Cyprus, see Webb and Weingarten 2012.

established conventions of the Late Bronze Age.[96] In addition, it is now recognized that as many Elaborate Style seals are found outside the island as on Cyprus, and that the seals were not centrally produced but were created at a number of sites across the island. Even before the end of the second millennium BC, then, the presence of these seals on Cyprus attests to the fact that the island was heavily implicated in an eastern Mediterranean World-System where goods, images and ideas circulated widely. Cyprus was home to masked rituals and métis experiences. The hybrid, as a question mark over categorical difference and hard distinctions, perfectly encapsulates this. Neither purely Greek nor Syrian, Cyprus combines and synthesizes elements from both west and east. It is entirely hybrid.

Hybrid images continued to flourish in the polymorphous, image-rich world of Archaic Cyprus. At outdoor sanctuaries such as Agia Irini hundreds of figurines were displayed in wild profusion: gods, goddesses, turbaned kings, equestrians, dancers, women in childbirth.[97] But the visual environment of the Cypriot sanctuaries was also saturated with fantastic compositions: centaurs, female centaurs, minotaurs, men on horseback, men merging into bulls, not to mention the bronze cauldrons decorated with protomes not only of griffins but also of sphinx warriors. The unexpected is ever present in Cypriot art, where the fantastic and the mundane exist side by side. Take, for example, the Cypriot version of the centaur (see Figure 4.14).

Not content with merely adapting Near Eastern centaur figures (whose beards mark them as resolutely masculine), the Cypriot figurine multiplies elements from the human and the animal: a four-legged animal body is topped by a human torso, which in turn displays both male and female genitalia. Only on Cyprus is one likely to encounter hermaphroditic centaurs. Here, the composite qualities of Cypriot hybrids perfectly capture the in-betweenness of Cyprus culture, the endless negotiations between different languages and populations. The richness of Cypriot engagement with hybridity is both striking and a reminder that from the late second millennium BC Greek speakers were a part of a *koine* of Eastern Mediterranean cultures in which a repertoire of hybrid forms and figures circulated widely and freely.

---

[96] Matthews 1990: 3.

[97] For Agia Irini in particular, see Bourogiannis 2013 and Papantoniou and Bourogiannis 2018. Cypriot figurines are the subject of a number of articles, monographs and conference volumes. A good place to start is Molinari and Sisci 2016: 17–30, on bull-themed figurines.

Figure 4.14 Terracotta centaur figurine, Agia Irini, NW Cyprus. H. 43.5 cm. Museum of Mediterranean and Near Eastern Antiquities, Stockholm.

Proximity and Hybridity

In this survey of the encounter between Greek speakers and other Mediterranean and Near Eastern cultures various factors have emerged as conditioning hybridity. Despite, for example, the continuous presence in Egypt of Ionian and Karian mercenaries throughout the twenty-sixth dynasty and even a panhellenic enclave at Naukratis, the hybrids generated by this contact exhibit Egyptian characteristics as a stylistic choice. At the other end of the spectrum of hybridity, Near Eastern motifs, mythemes and especially monsters have consistently appeared, reworked in Greek settings in new forms. Poetically, the Greek engagement with Near Eastern cultures is more long-lasting and more profound than the influence of Egypt. Between both regions and the Aegean lay important islands: Crete and Cyprus. While Crete was an important node in the network that brought Egyptian goods to Greece, it is Cyprus that constituted a contact zone where the mixture of populations and cultures produced a uniquely intense degree of cultural entanglement.[98]

---

[98] For Egypt and Crete see Karetsou et al. 2000.

The most significant result of this entanglement, aside from a taste for hybrid and fantastic imagery, was a bifurcation of language and identity. It has recently been argued, for example, that Cyprus was the location for the adoption, adaption and dissemination of a Phoenician alphabet by Greek speakers. Roger Woodard identifies distinctive features of the early Greek alphabet as the result of 'a Cypriot project intended to satisfy most immediately the linguistic aperture of Cypriot Greek'.[99] Woodard postulates that it was literate Cypriot Greeks who adapted the Phoenician consonantal script to write Greek, and that distinctly Cypriot Greek syllabary spelling practices can be used to explain highly distinctive features of the early Greek alphabet, such as the presence of two symbols, *san* and *sigma*, to represent the sound [s]. He also offers a concrete proposal for the conditions under which this occurred: the military expeditions of the Assyrian king Shalmaneser III (ruled 858–824 BC) into Syria and Anatolia, when literate East Greek mercenaries adapted the Phoenician alphabet for writing down their own language.[100] As a solution to the problem of the origins of the Greek alphabet Woodard's mercenary thesis may not be definitive, as it has been pointed out that the new Greek alphabet did not become particularly widespread on Cyprus for half a millennium.[101] Nevertheless, the adoption of a Phoenician alphabet had as a necessary precondition regular contact between Greek speakers and non-Greek speakers, whether traders or mercenaries, on the edges of the Aegean world, under sufficiently stable conditions to encourage a complicated transfer of technology. If not Cyprus, then the other candidates for the adoption of the alphabet, Al Mina or Pithekoussai, still represent contact zones where the alienness of the non-Greek excited little hostility.[102]

It was on Cyprus, however, that proximity of different language groups to each other encouraged individuals to acquire the means to shift smoothly between cultures. Take, for example, the so-called Idalion bilingual, which preserves details of a statue dedication made by Baalrom, son of

[99] Woodard 2021: 95.
[100] For Greek mercenaries operating in the Near East, see Braun 1982: 22, Waldbaum 2002: 138, Raaflaub 2004: 208 and Luraghi 2006. Alcaeus' supposed reference (fr. 48) to the service of his brother Antimenidas in Nebuchadnezzar's campaign against Ashkelon in 604 BC is usually cited as evidence for Greek mercenaries in the Neo-Babylonian army, but is challenged by Fantalkin and Lytle 2016.
[101] Parker and Steele 2021: 5.
[102] For Al Mina, see Jeffery 1976: 11 (mercenaries). For Pithekoussai, see Coldstream 1990 and Coldstream 1993 (bilingual children), building on Buchner 1979 (evidence for intermarriage of Greeks and Etruscans). For Powell's explanation that the alphabet was invented to record Homer, see Powell 1991. Contra, see Thomas 2021: 58. For a review of the debate and the candidates for adoption, see Astoreca 2021: 1–8.

Abdimilk, at a sanctuary in Idalion on Cyprus.[103] The statue base is inscribed in both Phoenician and Greek, using the Cypriot syllabary. The formulae employed reveal a shared practice that permits itself to be rendered in two broadly complementary forms:

> Phoenician text (top):
> On day? of the month? in year IV of King Milkyaton King of Kition and Idalion: this is the statue which Lord Baalrom son of Abdimilk gave and raised to his Lord Reshep Mikal because he heard his voice: may he bless.
>
> Greek text (bottom):
> [In the fourth year] of King Milkyaton, reigning over Kition and Idalion, on the last (day) of the period of five intercalary days, the prince (Baalrom), son of Abdimilk, has dedicated this statuette to Apollo Amyklos, from whom he has obtained the accomplishment of his wish. To good fortune.

The dedication was evidently made by a member of the Phoenician elite from Idalion, but the practice of dedicating a statue in thanks for a god's intervention makes sense across the divide of cultures: it translates easily. In the process of translation, it is also not hard to find either exact correspondences or close approximations: the gods' epithets, Mikal and Amyklos, for example, are phonetically close. As at the other end of the Mediterranean, where Monaco takes its name from the twinning of Melqart Menouakh and Herakles Monoikos, gods' names and epithets invite aural doubling. Apollo and Reshep are not closely matched aurally, but the similarity of their functions, with both acting as gods of pestilence and healing, similarly invites syncretism.[104] Another example is from Sardinia, where a certain Kleon, slave of a corporation of salt-farmers, made a dedication, recorded in Latin, Greek and Punic, to the god who healed him: Aescolapius Merre, Asklepios Merre, Ešmun Merre.[105] The god's healing powers bridge the linguistic divide, and his epithet recurs unchanged in all three languages. In the Greek section of the Idalion dedication the dedicator's name is missing. Baalrom may have found a Greek approximation for his name, like another man who made a dedication to Reshep/Apollo at Tamassos and inscribed his name as Abdasom and Αψασωμος (Apsasomos).[106] Or he may

---

[103] Masson 1983: n. 220. For useful overview of the inscription's significance, see https://crewsproject.wordpress.com/2018/01/28/crews-display-the-idalion-bilingual/.

[104] On Melqart and Herakles, see Malkin 2011: 119–42. For the 'translation' of the epithet Menouakh to Monoikos, see Sainge 1897: 12.

[105] *CIL* 1² 2226 = *IG* XIV 608 = *KAI* 66. See Clackson 2015: 81–2.

[106] Masson 1983: n. 216. For recent discussion of the Tamassian bilingual inscriptions, see Pestarino 2020.

have found a theophoric name to convey the same meaning in both languages. Such double naming was employed by a man from Kition named Abd-Melqart and Herakleides.[107] In some circumstances, double names can arise as people code shift according to settings, but double names can also point to a genuinely bilingual culture.[108]

Fluid identities are notably on display in the Cypriot pantheon. In addition to the Idalion bilingual's Apollo and Reshep, we might add the well-known connections between Aphrodite and Astarte, as well as the very precise syncretism that equated Athena with the Phoenician goddess, Anat.[109] Sceptres dedicated to the goddess from Idalion include one inscribed in Greek (*ICS*² 18) and an identical object inscribed in Phoenician (*RES* 210) to Anat, who, like Athena, is frequently depicted in arms. The dossier of inscriptions from the sanctuary of this goddess shows that she served a worshipping community that blended Greek and Phoenician seamlessly. Around 450 BC, for example, the king of Idalion, Stasikypros, erected a bronze tablet more than thirty lines long (*ICS*² 217), detailing the community's gratitude and the gift of a land grant to a Greek doctor, Onasilos, solemnly stipulating the tablet be erected 'next to the goddess, Athena'. Around the same time, Baalmilk, king of Kition, endowed the same sanctuary with a wall and dedicated it, in a Phoenician inscription (*RES* 453), to Anat, 'because she heard his voice'. In the third century, a certain Praxidemos/Baalshillem dedicated an altar to Ptolemy in the region of Larnaka and commemorated the dedication in a bilingual inscription saluting Athena and Anat. Summing up the rich tapestry of different deities in Cyprus, Bianco and Bonnet conclude that 'Cyprus functioned as an intercultural melting pot that favored the rapprochements, interactions or superimpositions between deities from different backgrounds, in particular EteoCypriot, Greek and Phoenician'.[110]

In the Archaic period, then, prevailing conditions around the Mediterranean favoured the movement of goods and people not in a single direction from east to west, but in a continuous ebb and flow around the liquid continent. In the form of both objects and poetic motifs, hybrid monsters figured prominently in this cultural mix, but there were

---

[107] Fraser 1970. For Kition's Athenian connections, see Papanatoniou 2013: 177.

[108] On double naming in Egypt, see Calderini 1942, Clarysse 1985; on bilingualism, see Gjerstad 1979 and Yon and Childs 1997.

[109] On Aphrodite's eastern origins, see Marcovich 1996. For Anat-Athena, see Bianco and Bonnet 2016.

[110] Bianco and Bonnet 2016: 167: 'Chypre fonctionne comme un creuset interculturel qui favorise les rapprochements, interactions ou superpositions entre des divinités issues d'horizons différents, en particulier étéochypriote, grec et phénicien.'

also odd and innocuous hybrids that fell well short of the threshold of monstrosity. Far more important than the monster's scariness was the capacity of hybridity to function as a mode of cultural exchange. Dangerous natural elements, potentially hostile indigenes, alien populations, foreign military service, piracy and its twin sister, trade, all amounted to what we recognize as a network but which was experienced as a continuous confrontation with varying degrees of alterity. Hybrids, whether monstrous, luxurious or simply curious, gave this a face. In Archaic Greece this would be turned inward, instrumentalized in a variety of ways that begin with the Gorgon and the Satyr.

5 | Heads or Tails

Gorgons, Satyrs and Other Composites

> Here then for the first time baleful nature brought forth from within her dreadful pestilence. From her throat snakes rattled and hissed, their tongues flicking, as, released like a woman's hair, they slipped over her shoulders, and lashed the neck of a delighted Medusa.
>
> Lucan, *Pharsalia* 9.629–633 (tr. McInerney)

Looking at Griffins and Gorgons

From at least the eighth century BC the Greeks were enmeshed in an image-rich world populated with a great bestiary of creatures, half of which were purely imaginary. On a late seventh-century Corinthian kylix, for example, a snake-tailed demon is flanked by two roosters, while three hawks share space in the same register with sphinxes (see Figure 5.1).

The Greek imaginary of the Archaic period was populated equally by the ordinary and the extraordinary. The presence of both in the field of vase decoration is significant because hybridity carries such visual impact. Visual perception undergirds certainty. In phenomenological terms, vision is critical to shaping our perceptions of the world, on which are built our conceptions of orderliness.[1] Accordingly, hybrids are paradoxical. On the one hand, the snaky-tailed figure on the Corinthian cup in Figure 5.1 is not real in the way that the roosters facing it are real (and mundane), yet the coexistence of chickens and sphinxes constitutes a mild destabilization. Hybrids hint at other bodies and other classes, at other ways of being in the world dimly glimpsed, once known, faintly recognizable, barely remembered, all marvellous. This is best conveyed by the phrase that crops up in Archaic poetry, in which striking objects are described as *thauma idesthai* ('a wonder to behold'), reflecting a culture in which oral performances

---

[1] Merleau-Ponty 1962. The mechanisms of sensation, perception, and synthesis remain contested areas, the details of which are well beyond the scope of this study. See Noa 2004 and McClamrock 2013.

Figure 5.1 Winged snake-tailed demon in an animal frieze. Oversized Corinthian kylix, ca. 620 BC. Staatliche Antikensammlungen, Munich.

attempted synaesthetically to incorporate visuality into a full experience of amazement.[2]

Among the most visually arresting objects mentioned in epic were the twenty wheeled tripods forged by Hephaistos, capable of moving automatically through the palaces of the gods.[3] Though these were objects of fantasy, each member of Homer's audience could imagine them because the Archaic world teemed with actual objects that served as visual referents: the cauldrons and tripods that proliferated in the major sanctuaries of Greece in the eighth and seventh centuries BC. The most common decoration on these vessels was the griffin's head protome, a device that has too frequently been seen as merely decorative. However, as Nassos Papalexandrou has recently demonstrated, the griffin protome was integral to the visual impact of the cauldron, an object of wonder whose magical properties were enhanced by the hybrid creatures that adorned it.[4] There is a hint of this in Homer's description of Thetis' visit to Hephaistos. The goddess finds Hephaistos after he has finished the 'legs' of the cauldrons and as he is preparing rivets for the handles, called 'ears' (οὔατα) in Greek. Homer's description reminds us that these automata are anthropomorphic.

Even when bronze cauldrons and tripods were copied in terracotta and the details of the original attachments rendered more schematically, as in the drinking assemblage from Ficana (see Figure 5.2), the composite monstrosity of the vessels is unmistakable: the bowl and its stand present an unnerving combination of female silhouette and predatory beaks.

---

[2] Papalexandrou 2010: 36. For the relationship between wonder and ekphrasis, see Lightfoot 2021: 31–41.
[3] Hom., *Il.* 18.368–79.   [4] Papalexandrou 2016.

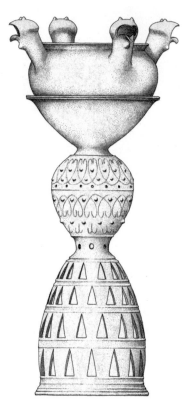

Figure 5.2 Drawing of terracotta olla with griffin protomes standing on terracotta olmos (stand). From an Orientalizing-period house in Ficana. Second half of seventh century BC. Ostia (olla) (38252) and Ostia (olmos) (38249). From Papalexandrou 2016: 270 (fig. 7). Reproduced with permission of Nassos Papalexandrou.

As sanctuary dedications and objects for elite display in both sumptuary and funerary settings, the value of these vessels as status markers was enhanced by their ability to evoke a disturbing exoticism tinged by something unnatural yet familiar. To that end, their hybridity is visually striking. They are exceptional, just as their owners aspired to be.

In fact, throughout the Iron Age and into the Archaic period these massive vessels used hybrids in various ways, both as attachments and in the very shape and size of the vessel to reinforce displays of elite status. This is nicely demonstrated by the famous gorgon amphora from Eleusis (see Figure 5.3). At 1.4 m in height, the vessel is nearly life size, giving the scenes painted on the amphora an impressive monumentality. The scene on the neck of the amphora depicting Odysseus' blinding of the Cyclops Polyphemos is justly famous as one of the earliest visual representations

Figure 5.3 Proto-Attic amphora showing Gorgon. Eleusis. Terracotta, mid-seventh century BC. Archeological Museum, Eleusis, Greece (2630). Photograph: Zdeněk Kratochvíl/Wikimedia CC BY-SA 4.0.

of a Homeric scene, attesting to the impact of oral poetry on other media as early as the mid-seventh century, but the body of the amphora is even more striking. The belly of the amphora shows two gorgons pursuing Perseus, who has slain their sister, Medusa.[5] The gorgons stride to the viewer's right, their legs alluringly revealed by their deeply slit skirts. But if their lower halves are attractive, their faces, turned directly towards the viewer and therefore engaging our gaze, are hideous. Each has a face deformed by an enormous rictus, their teeth separated like the fangs of a beast. Their eyes are widely separated and, unnaturally, their ellipsis is turned almost vertical rather than horizontal. Between them, where we expect a nose is a triangular gash that grows wider towards the top. Their grossly enlarged heads display a grimace that terrifies and a glance that petrifies.[6] Bristles sprout on their chins. From their necks and where we would expect their ears snaky creatures protrude, some of which look directly out from the scene. Others look more like lions' heads and resemble the lion depicted on the shoulder of the amphora. The monstrosity of the composition is

---

[5] The online version of the Beazley archive describes the scene as 'decapitated Gorgon "floats" behind her two sisters who flee Perseus', but the gorgons are running towards Perseus, with Athena intervening to protect the hero. For a more accurate description, see Hurwit 1977: 24.

[6] The gorgon's grimace also evokes an auditory assault, corresponding to her glare. See Steiner 2015.

compelling, and becomes even more so when one recognizes that the gorgons' heads are, in fact, modelled on cauldrons.[7]

How are we to explain this connection without imputing some kind of animate quality to the cauldron, if not a kind of mysterious agency? The cauldron is a vessel that facilitates transformations from the most basic, in cooking, to the magical, as when Medea offers to rejuvenate Pelias by putting his diced-up body parts into a cauldron that has already regenerated a slaughtered sheep.[8] Like the cauldron, the gorgon causes a magical transformation, but through her gaze. The face-on stare of the grimacing, oversized head recalls masks and depictions of demons going back to Humbaba, but the cauldron-and-tripod design that also influences the gorgon's appearance points elsewhere. Ingrid Strøm has demonstrated that cauldrons and cooking spits entered the Greek world in the eighth century and, spreading from east Greece to the mainland, quickly became a package of material goods associated with a set of ritually significant actions: sacrifice, dining and dedications.[9] These performances and the material goods associated with them rapidly established themselves as actions and objects at the centre of Greek orthopraxy, as characteristic as the killing of sheep, goats and cattle. With these as normative, the Eleusis gorgons reveal how hybrid figures of monstrosity can emerge as inversions of the normal.[10] Just as Hephaistos' automata suggest a perplexing agency hidden in a cauldron – just because it has wheels, how does it 'know' where and when to go? – so too the gorgons hint at a dark magic hidden inside the objects of orthodox practice.

All hybrids impress themselves on us in a visual encounter, but Medusa's terrifying power especially foregrounds the gaze – a motif repeated on the Eleusis amphora with its depiction on the neck of the blinding of Polyphemos.[11] This is significant, for a number of reasons. The first is that ancient notions of extromission held that sight was a physically active process according to which the eyes emitted beams.[12] The gorgon's gaze is, in terms of ancient visual theory, a hyper-real rather than unreal phenomenon. It is also rooted in modes of seeing with which we are familiar. If prey animals have broad, panoramic fields of vision that allow them to scan large areas for threats, predators have forward-facing eyes whose overlapping

---

[7] See, most recently, Steiner 2015.
[8] For both the story and visual depictions of the episode, see Mayor 2018: 33–44.
[9] Strøm 1992.
[10] For an eighth/seventh century date for the appearance of the Perseus-Gorgo myth, see Feldman 1965.
[11] On the vase's concern with visuality, see Osborne 1988 and Grethlein 2016: 89–94.
[12] For an overview of ancient theories of vision, see Squire 2016 and Bielfeldt 2016.

fields of vision capture the depth and detail that better suit hunting. Despite Vernant and Frontisi-Ducroux's suggestion that the gorgon's gaze reflects back the warrior's frenzied glare, foretelling 'impending, inevitable death', what actually lies behind the gorgon's glare is the laser-like, focused gaze of the hunter. This also reflects what Irene Winter has described as 'cathected vision', drawing on deep-rooted Near Eastern traditions of a deity's frontal stance and deep-set eyes that augment visual experience.[13] The gorgon's is a look of power, just as when Athena's eyes terrify Achilles, compelling him to stop before he slaughters Agamemnon.[14] Similarly, subordination or powerlessness is connoted by averting the eyes. Recent explorations of the power of the gaze help illuminate the gorgon's stare. For example, almost fifty years ago Laura Mulvey's investigation of the male and female gaze established that visual media usually depict a sight-world that reflects male, heterosexual pleasure.[15] Drawing on Sartre's notion of the gaze as a political act that subordinates the object of the gaze to the power of the viewer, Mulvey situated the aesthetics of representation within a framework of gender power relations. But there is also an oppositional gaze that functions as a site of potential resistance. bell hooks argues that 'Subordinates in relations of power learn experientially that there is a critical gaze, one that "looks" in order to document, one that is oppositional.'[16] In this oppositional scheme, 'don't give me that look' is an assertion of power, by adult over child or slave owner over Black person. The power to look, then, is claimed by the powerful and denied to the subordinate. The viewer brings the seen world under their power. Vision is a proxy for masculinity. If blindness in the Oidipous story serves as a symbolic castration, then equally the gorgon's stare challenges the male gaze. Medusa's power to petrify any man with her eyes is the equivalent of overwhelming a man on his own turf. The site of their contest is a battle over the gaze, as is suggested in the first instance by Perseus' need to look away, and the power over which they contend is nothing short of the primacy of the male gaze. Its principal challenger, which must be destroyed, is a monstrous, gorgeous, hideous, species-breaking, gender-bending, alluring, repulsive composite of every category that must be kept distinct, but first and foremost it is female. The irony is that as

---

[13] Death stare: Vernant and Frontisi-Ducroux 2006: 191. 'Cathected vision': Winter 2000: 38. The theme of vision, 'mis-seeing' and the deception brought about the gorgon's stare is analysed with great nuance by Harrop 2015.

[14] Hom., *Il.* 1.200: δεινώ δέ οἱ ὄσσε φάανθεν (terribly her eyes shone (describing Athena)). Also *Il.* 8.349, where Hektor's eyes in battle are compared to the eyes of the gorgon. See Feldman 1965: 487.

[15] Mulvey 1975.   [16] hooks 1992: 116.

a threat and a challenge, the gorgon makes Perseus necessary. For every monster, a hero. The power of its glare must be deflected (metaphorically, and literally when Perseus uses his shield as a mirror, a woman's tool turned against her). Her decapitation ups the ante. Perseus will look away and win; Medusa's face will forever keep looking towards us, but the power of her glare has been tamed by Perseus. Thanks to the hero's victory, the viewer is safe looking at the monster's petrifying face. Our viewing confirms that the male gaze has triumphed. In this respect it resembles another triumphant form of viewing: the *theôria*. We tend to identify this as a religious procession to visit a major sanctuary but, as Ian Rutherford has demonstrated, the *theoria* is a pilgrimage to look at the marvels of a sanctuary. Georgia Petridou recognizes what lies at the heart of this experience: 'The theôric journey to a sacred πανήγυρις [*pangeyris*] is essentially a journey to the unknown and the unfamiliar with a distinctively religious and ocularcentric dimension. *Theôria*, in short, brings an individual into contact with what is foreign and different: it is an encounter with otherness.'[17]

Pretty Woman

Approaching the gorgon is a perilous business, and there is always the danger of oversimplification. For example, in the manner typical of Archaic Greek art, perplexing variations occur: on one famous vessel Perseus slays Medusa, who also happens to be a centaur[18] (see Figure 5.4). The layers of hybridity here, in which the gorgon and the centaur overlap, result in a kind of overdetermination, as if to double down on Perseus' victory over the threat of the female. If, however, we look for a common thread connecting the Eleusis gorgons and the Medusa centaur it is surely that both demonstrate that Archaic Greek hybrids express ambivalence, exciting a contradictory set of positive and negative associations and eliciting confusion on the part of the viewer. Fifty years ago Geoffrey Lloyd established polarity and analogy as critical modes in the development of philosophical thinking.[19] Myths involving hybrids also operate in this way, except that the categories of 'similar' and 'different' by which we organize the world are, in myth, porous and fuzzy. Monsters cause terror by virtue of their alienness, but sometimes the hybrid operates in between the

---

[17] Rutherford 2000, Petridou 2013: 317.   [18] Topper 2010.
[19] Lloyd 1966. On the early poets' inductive or deductive approach to myth, see p. 421 therein.

Figure 5.4 Perseus killing Medusa. Cycladic relief pithos (neck detail). Seventh century BC, from Thebes. H: 130 cm. Paris, Musée du Louvre CA795. Photo: Freres Chuzeville. © RMN-Grand Palais. Art Resource NY.

monstrous and the recognizable, creating a confusion from the mixture of the familiar, the alluring and the safe with something threatening.

In the Medusa centaur this ambivalence is fully on display. As a woman her body is appropriately human in size and scale. As one of three sisters she also hews to the human end of the spectrum that extends from human to monstrous. The profusion of *korai* statues in the sixth century reminds us, if we need reminding, that the life-size form of a young woman is not generally perceived as a threat. But despite being one of three sisters (itself a narrateme that recurs from Aboriginal myth to Chekhov), Medusa alone is mortal while Stheno and Euryale are immortal. If humans and gods are poles apart, where is Medusa, neither one nor the other? Ambivalence is also encoded in her appearance: her lower body is human, and she wears a long modest *peplos*, so that her dress conveys a comforting femininity, but the addition of a centaur's back-half makes her as much beast as human, while the open bodice revealing her breasts replaces modesty with sexual assertiveness.[20] Her equine half and her bold appearance undercut the message of her lower half, where proper clothing conceals the most important piece of the puzzle, which is that Medusa is at least partially alluring.

---

[20] On the contrast between the gorgon's glare and the maiden's modest aversion of the eyes, see Turner 2016: 157.

At the opposite end of the spectrum of this attraction is destruction. There is no need for Freud's help to unpack the gorgon's meaning in this regard.

The gorgon's attractiveness is embedded in these early images and emerges as the principal trajectory taken by the gorgon in later periods. Representations of the gorgon undergo considerable change from the Archaic to the Hellenistic period, which led Furtwängler to classify them according to a tripartite scheme of Archaic, Middle and Beautiful (*schöne*).[21] Given that tripartite systems applied to Greek culture tend to identify the third phase with decadence, Furtwängler's scheme perhaps applies better to Klimt's gorgons than to red-figure vases, but it is clear that erotic themes of abduction, marriage and the 'taming' of young women find expression in later depictions of the gorgon.[22] Few of these later images convey the horror that we usually identify as the creature's dominant characteristic. Instead, the gorgon's fate at the hands of the hero is used to suggest the instability that surrounds the precarious transition of maiden to bride. The paradox of her allure and the dangers it poses are resolved in myth by the slaying of the gorgon, and in the real world by marriage. Like a distortion of the maidens' chorus, the three gorgons will be confronted by the young hero – a confrontation which will end in the defeat of one of them, pierced by the hero's blade.

In the case of the centaur Medusa, the blending of the gorgon with the horse also draws on the symbolic figuring of young marriageable girls as fillies ready to be broken to the bit and saddle.[23] It is the erotic possibilities of this taming that drives the change in gorgon iconography, producing the 'beautiful' gorgons of the fifth century and later. In these later, beautiful gorgons their monstrosity is only hinted at by showing them face-on to the viewer. They are often shown asleep, which has the further effect of nullifying their gaze and increasing their vulnerability. In these examples Perseus is shown looming over the woman's sleeping body, so that visually the attack on the gorgon resembles a sexual assault on a sleeping woman. These are some of the convoluted ways that a hybrid does much more

---

[21] Furtwängler 1886–90. For full discussion, see Topper 2007: 76.

[22] Furtwängler's analysis of the gorgon appeared in 1890 and may have influenced Klimt's Beethoven Frieze, which was installed in the Succession Building in Vienna in 1902. Klimt's use of the gorgoneion and his depictions of Athena have been connected to his reading of other works by Furtwängler. See Florman 1990. On the popularity of the femme fatale in fin de siècle art, see Tookey 2004. For abduction and 'beautiful' gorgons in Greek art, see Topper 2007. For a good example, see the red figure pelike, ca. 450–440 BC, attributed to Polygnotos. H. 18 13/16 in. (47.8 cm), diameter 13 ½ in. (34.3 cm), depicting Perseus attacking sleeping Medusa. Metropolitan Museum, 45.11.1.

[23] Topper 2010.

complicated work than merely serving as a monstrous embodiment of our fears. As a way of thinking through the complexities of marriage and the transformation of a young woman from maiden to bride, the gorgon does not externalize a single, unidirectional response to female sexuality but gives expression to a whole slew of fears, anxieties and undercurrents that flow back on and over each other.

Further resisting a simple reading of the gorgon as no more than a monstrous woman is the fact that these associations do not operate only at the level of symbolism or the iconography of myth. There is also evidence that the gorgon was deployed in ritual settings, where the creature evoked the threat to social order. Vanquishing the monster is both the work of the hero Perseus, but also a performance repeated as part of the initiation of boys at Mycenae and Tiryns.[24] Terracotta masks and shields depicting the gorgon and Perseus killing her reflect not just stories of Perseus' deeds but also of the re-enactments of what Susan Langdon has called 'the victory of the little Perseuses over masked female monsters'[25] (see Figure 5.5). Langdon speculates that 'killing the gorgon' marked the boys as ready to leave 'the female-dominated household and join the adolescent male community'. It is less clear that Langdon is right to connect these coming-of-age rituals to the further stages of Perseus' career. She writes: 'Having used Medusa's head to turn Polydektes to stone and prevent his mother's marriage, Perseus served as the ideal role model not only as monster-slayer but also as arranger of the community's social order.' But Perseus' role in killing Polydektes and Akrisios involves two episodes that make the hero a killer of a father (Akrisios, unintentionally) and a stepfather (Polydektes, intentionally) – roles that do not sit well with the theme of social order (although they might be reconcilable with a notion of substitution, according to which killing and replacing the father in ritual guided the young man safely from childhood to adulthood).[26]

Killing the gorgon reasserts social order, but the episode has other applications. We have already seen in Chapter 3 how Perseus beheading Medusa on a metope from Selinunte used the battle of the gaze as a metaphor for the struggle for domination between Greek and Sicel. There is one other element in the Selinunte metope that attracts attention.

[24] Jameson 1990.
[25] Langdon 2007: 175. If we knew more of the details of the rituals that employed the fearsome gorgon masks we might know whether any stupefying drugs were employed to prepare the boys for their initiations, in which case Ruck's reading of the gorgon as 'a personification of the fungal psychoactive agent' and the killing of Medusa 'a mythologized narrative of the harvest of a sacred plant' might rise to the level of plausible. See Ruck 2016: 549.
[26] Polydektes: Apollod., *Biblio.* 2.45; Akrisios: Hyginus 63–4.

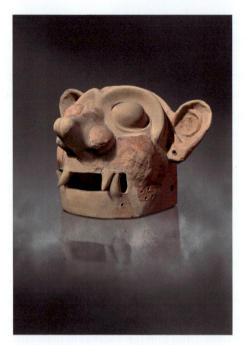

Figure 5.5 Terracotta gorgon mask, Tiryns. Late eighth–early seventh century BC. Nafplion Archaeological Museum. Inv. No. 4789. funkyfood London – Paul Williams/Alamy Stock Photo.

Cradled in her arms, Medusa holds a baby Pegasos: one of the two children she produces after lying with Poseidon. The other child of Medusa is Chrysaor, a human who mates with a goddess, Kallirhoe, and produces triple-bodied Geryon, another monstrous character.[27] Pegasos and Chrysaor are thus oddly divine twins: the one a hybrid horse that is not a monster, the other a man who is the son of one hybrid monster and father of another. Humanity and hybridity are a double-helix interwoven through the generations, not as static, diametric opposites but as generational variations on the twin themes of normality and aberration. This is foregrounded by the presence of Pegasos, a reminder that Medusa is a mother as well as a monster. His birth, springing from her severed neck as jets of blood shoot forth, falls into the class of unnatural births that include Athena (from the head of Zeus), Dionysos blasted from Semele and reborn from the thigh of Zeus, as well as the horse Arion from Demeter (sired by Poseidon Horse). The products of these unions are not monstrous, but they are abnormal. The stories of their astonishing births draw on the

[27] Clay 1993: 109.

heightened anticipation, anxieties and ambiguities that attend childbirth: will the mother produce a healthy, normal child, or something else? Each child is born covered in the blood of its mother. The uncertainty of childbirth only recedes as the child is washed, examined, and swaddled, as the realization that the baby is healthy gradually replaces the fear that it may be monstrous. At one level, an agon between human and monster, normal and abnormal, is played out every time a child is born. Yet at odds with this universalizing response to the scene on the metope is the fact that only someone who knows Pegasos' birth story is equipped to read the episode. Without knowing the fantastic story of his conception and birth, what viewer could make any sense of a grimacing monster clutching a foal as her head is cut off? Scenes depicting monster and hybrids are thus woven into the fabric of Greekness, both offering symbols of what is Greek and what is not, and providing a handy visual test for the viewer's credentials.[28]

It should be clear that gorgons exist in a dazzling variety of forms. The gorgons of Eleusis, the centaur Medusa, the masks from Tiryns, the 'Beautiful' gorgons of the fifth century and later, not to mention the apotropaic gorgoneions that multiply in profusion throughout the Archaic period cannot be reduced to a single meaning. It would be difficult, for example, to find more than a casual thematic connection between the Boiotian Medusa centaur and the bronze gorgon on the Vix krater (see Figure 5.6). Even as signifiers gorgons display a bewildering variety, from walking cauldrons to disembodied heads. So, too, what they signify varies according to context, from the maiden facing marriage to the warrior facing death, or both, as in Euripides' frequent use of gorgon references in the *Electra*, representing 'at once the victims and the killer, as well as the fear which makes them alike'.[29] What they all do have in common is that each instantiation recalls a narrative: there can be no gorgon or gorgoneion without Perseus either present or a lurking presence. And whatever the threat – monster, maiden or mare – ambivalence must be defeated. The gorgon exists to embody ambiguity of all sorts, the threat of uncertainty that must be slain. The alternative is too terrible to contemplate, as when Hypsipyle remembers the murders perpetrated by her sisters who killed their husbands: 'they slaughtered their husbands in their beds, like Gorgons!' (*Hypsip*. Frg 759a 77–8)

---

[28] A similar aesthetic sensibility characterizes Alexandrian poetry, in which understanding the allusions in Lykophron means that, more broadly, you 'get it'. On Alexandrianism, see Pontani 2014. The existence of many of these figures in Etruscan art is a complex issue that demands its own treatment, since this is its own cultural context. It would seem that the power of hybrids and monsters was broadly connected to death and sacrifice. See Warden 2012.

[29] O'Brien 1964: 39.

Figure 5.6 Gorgon head decoration on volute handle, Vix krater. Late sixth century BC. © RMN-Grand Palais (Musée du pays chatillonais-Trésor de Vix)/Mathieu Rabeau.

Scary Mormons

Medusa and her sisters are the best known but not the only examples of terrifying female monsters. Others include Lamia and Empousa, Mormo, Gello and Baubo. Collectively, these are often referred to as bogeys as they were used to scare children, who often wore amulets for protection against them.[30] A recent study by Heta Björklund succinctly defines their characteristic features and their fields of operation: 'Their common characteristics are femaleness, attacking children and pregnant women (or women in childbirth) as well as young women on the brink of marriage, partial animal form, or mixanthropy, and metamorphosis.'[31] Xenophon reports that the Spartans mocked their Mantineian allies, who fled in panic from the Athenian peltasts at the Battle of Lechaion, saying they were afraid of them 'like children afraid of Mormons' (ὥσπερ μορμόνας παιδάρια).[32]

---

[30] For the most complete treatment of these figures, see Patera 2015. Stannish and Doran 2013 offer an excellent overview of the generic versions of the demons: *lamiai, empousai* and *mormolykeiai*. For a psychoanalytical reading that links the threat of all these female figures to the declining power of the Mother Goddess, see Feldman 1965. They are depicted as witches and appear on stage in tragedy relatively frequently and in comedy relatively rarely. See Henderson 1987: 126–7. On scaring children, see Arthur 1980, Winkler 1982 and Golden 1993: 6. Socrates refers to mothers frightening their children with stories of such daimons at *Resp.* 381e. See Sansone 1997: 58. On amulets worn by children for protection, see Dasen 2003: 277–8. For demons as liminal figures, see Johnston 1999 and Doroszewska 2017. Many of the primary sources are translated in Ogden 2009.

[31] Björklund 2017: 22–3.   [32] Xen. *Hell.* 4.4.17.

The source of their childhood fears was the bogey's hideous appearance, as Erinna recalled in the *Distaff*: 'Oh, what a trembling the Bogey [Mormo] brought us then, when we were little ones! – On its head were huge ears, and it walked on all fours, and changed from one face to another!'[33] But the terror they induced tapped into deeper fears as well. The back-stories told of these female demons refer to them as women who had lost their children prior to their transformation into monsters. As a result, as Maria Patera has recently shown, they often represent an inversion of maternity. Lamia, for example, driven mad by Hera, devours the children of others and becomes herself the mother of monsters, notably Skylla. Another devourer of children is Mormo, who can adopt the shape of a horse or wolf and whose face served as a comic mask (*mormolykeion*).[34] Gello was also a tragic figure, a young woman who died before her time and who then became a killer of pregnant women and children. In each case the shape-shifter is an evil twin lurking in the shadowy borders beside the regular path from conception through childhood to adulthood. These female monsters, however, were not confined to the nursery but also turned up in other locations, notably as sex-workers. Lamia is the name of one of the most famous *hetairai* of the fourth century, and a catalogue of prostitutes' names collected by Anaxilas in the mid-fourth century included the names of various familiar female monsters: Drakaina, Chimaira, Skylla, Charybdis, Sphinx, Hydra and Echidna.[35] In addition, various writers and poets of the imperial period tell stories of blood-sucking vampires known as Lamiai and Empousai who take the form of attractive women to attack young men. In Philostratos' tale of the Corinthian *phasma* who seduces the beautiful Menippos, Apollonios explains the vampire's true nature:

> This fair bride of yours is one of those Empousai, which many folks consider to be Lamiai and Mormolykiai. They fall in love, and while they adore sex, what they really crave is human flesh, and through sex they seduce those whom they intend to devour.
> Philost., Vita Apollon. 4.25 (tr. McInerney)[36]

---

[33] Erinna, *Distaff* Fr. 1b = Pap. PSI 9, 1090, col. II, ll. 32–34 (tr. Page). Also see Plato, *Crito* 46c and *Phaedo* 77e.

[34] *Mormolykeion*: Strabo, *Geography* 1.2.8; Lucian, *Lover of Lies* 2.

[35] Lamia as prostitute's name: Aelian, *Hist. Var.* 12.17, 13.8. For the later history of Lamia, see the detailed essay by Parsons 1977. Catalogue of prostitutes: Anaxilas fr. 22 Kock. See Brown 1991: 43–4.

[36] 'ἡ χρηστὴ νύμφη μία τῶν ἐμπουσῶν ἐστιν, ἃς λαμίας τε καὶ μορμολυκίας οἱ πολλοὶ ἡγοῦνται. ἐρῶσι δ' αὗται καὶ ἀφροδισίων μέν, σαρκῶν δὲ μάλιστα ἀνθρωπείων ἐρῶσι καὶ παλεύουσι τοῖς ἀφροδισίοις, οὓς ἂν ἐθέλωσι δαίσασθαι.'

Demosthenes resorts to his combination of monstrosity and sex in his infamous character assassination of Aischines' mother, casually observing that 'Everyone knows that his worthy mother Glaukothea was called Empousa because of her willingness to give and take anything.'[37] The shape-shifting of the demon could now be analogized to aberrant female sexuality, one of the many qualities that ran counter to conventional expectations. The bad mother (more often than not, the woman who had suffered the loss of a baby) and the promiscuous woman both violated the strictly defined parameters of correct behaviour and were thus ripe for demonization.

The female demon made her appearance in one other domain where terror and monstrosity were channelled in the service of conventional social practice: mystical initiation. Eleusinian echoes recur throughout the parodos to Aristophanes' *Frogs*, where the *choreutai* are referred to as initiates (οἱ μεμυημένοι, l. 158), and resonate in the encounter in the Underworld between Xanthias and Dionysos and the shape-shifting Empousa:

XANTHIAS:	And now, by Zeus, I see a monstrous beast.
DIONYSUS:	What kind?
XANTHIAS:	O horrible! it takes all kinds of shapes, Now it's an ox, and now a mule, and now A lovely woman.
DIONYSUS:	Where is she? I'll go meet her.
XANTHIAS:	Wait, now it's not a woman, but a bitch.
DIONYSUS:	Why, this must be Empousa.
XANTHIAS:	Ah! her whole face burns like fire.
DIONYSUS:	Does she have a leg of bronze?
XANTHIAS:	By Poseidon, yes – and the other is cow dung, Be sure of it.

Aristoph., Frogs 285–95 (tr. Dillon)

Christopher Brown has argued convincingly that the appearance of Empousa here recalls an apparition of the demon which took place at an early point in the process of initiation, designed to terrify the initiates and to heighten the impact of the mystical experience.[38] This is not the only

---

[37] Dem. 18.130. 'τὴν δὲ μητέρα σεμνῶς πάνυ Γλαυκοθέαν, ἣν Ἔμπουσαν ἅπαντες ἴσασι καλουμένην, ἐκ τοῦ πάντα ποιεῖν καὶ πάσχειν.' See Süss 1910: 24.

[38] Brown 1991. Brown supports his reading with the appearance of Tisiphone the Erinyes in Lucian's *Kataplous*: 'This passage seems to imply that an apparition of this sort appeared before those undergoing initiation at Eleusis. The similarities between Lucian's text and Aristophanes' play suggest strongly that the encounter with Empousa alludes to the same cultic event' (p. 46).

instance of odd female figures at Eleusis playing a significant role in both the actions and the aitiological accounts that anticipate the initiation. When Demeter arrives at Eleusis she is disconsolate at the loss of her daughter, and it is the words and gestures that shake her out of her grief that are crucial to the Mysteries' role in affirming life and the afterlife. Iambe uses scurrilous language to make Demeter smile (*HHom.* 2.192–7), just as old women hurl abuse at the initiates as they cross the Bridge at Rhetoi. It is Baube, however, who asserts an even more peculiar power over the goddess: by lifting her dress and exposing her genitals, she forces Demeter to laugh.[39] A series of fourth-century figurines from the Demeter sanctuary at Priene appear to depict this extraordinary performance, but with an even more striking transformation. They show a pair of legs with no torso but an enlarged head where the female sexual organs should be, functioning like a female Priapus, but substituting a face to make the display of the awful power of the vagina even more startling. Maurice Olender has connected Baubo to the other female demons of the Greeks' childhood to suggest that these old women, demons and nurses 'mix shamelessness with a familiar strangeness'.[40] Here, once again, are the basic ingredients of hybridity: anomaly, disquiet and the strangely familiar. And, as with other hybrids, what seems potentially disruptive is finally folded back into the fabric of social praxis as a negative reinforcement of conventional roles.

There is a dreadful complement to these daimonic figures of the nursery and the sanctuary to be found in the household, as demonstrated by Semonides' iambic invective on women. Like the gorgon, Semonides' women are the enemy, but rather than being an exotic monster to be slain, they are everyday companions to be humiliated. They exist in various types: weasel, pig, mare and even non-animal versions, such as the woman born of the sea. Robin Osborne has argued persuasively that the function of the humiliation of women in the poem is to demonstrate and reinforce male domination. Certainly, if the poem was performed at symposia, the casual cruelty of the poem – 'You can't even shut her up if you smash out her teeth with a rock!' – will have found an audience prepared to be entertained by the poem's open misogyny, but it is also notable that the poem speaks of women as if they were actually born of other species, and so

---

[39] Clem. *Protrepticus* 20; Arnob. *Ad Nat.* 5.25.
[40] Olender 1985: 48: '[T]ous ces personnages peuvent mêler l'impudeur à l'étrangeté familière et semblent participer à un univers de bruissements et de chuchotements, consolants et perturbants' (All these figures manage to combine shamelessness with a familiar strangeness, and seem to inhabit a world of rustling and whispering, of perturbation and consolation). For a full discussion of the Baubo episode, see Suter 2015.

are, in a sense, not human at all. The mare-woman, for example, best known for avoiding any domestic chores, scorning her husband's sexual advances and wasting her time primping and preening, is also described as being born from a luxuriously maned horse (τὴν δ' ἵππος ἁβρὴ χαιτέεσσ' ἐγείνατο, l.57). From the first line, the poem emphasizes that the *nous* of woman was made separate (*choris*) by god, and when the poem identifies the animal avatars of the various types Semonides says that the woman is born 'from a pig' (*ex huos*), or 'from a fox' (*ex alopekos*), or 'from a bitch (*ek kunos*), or even 'from the sea' (*ek thalassas*). Like Pandora, Semonides' women are a separate creation whose distinctive origins not only point towards an ugly animality but also implicitly deny the woman's claim to humanity. The abjection of women in Semonides 7 is inseparable from an instrumentalized hybridity. There are many ways of degrading women, but employing hybrids to do the job was especially effective in the context of seventh-century sympotic poetry. As the wine flows and the drinkers enjoy the transformation that comes with intoxication, their imagination is released along with their inhibitions. In the imaginative space that opens up in the symposium, centaurs and satyrs will project the drinking man into the hypervirile centaur or the buffoonish satyr, while various animal–female hybrids will invite in response a misogyny as pure as undiluted wine. The fuzziness of these symposium hybrids, like drunkenness itself, is only an illusory destabilization of norms and categories. Like a hangover, the hybrid conceals a crapulous normativity.

Satyrs

The satyr is a hybrid counterpoint to the gorgon and her half-sisters, Semonides' animal women. As hypermasculine as the female figures are alluring or repulsive, satyrs are always ready for sex, even if they do not always get to consummate their desires.[41] When they fail they are left either parading around with massive erections or, in some instances, are found pleasuring themselves to the point of climaxing. A Boiotian tripod *pyxis*, for example, depicts a satyr with a tail and over-developed thighs proudly holding a gargantuan penis that is as long as his torso and as thick as his forearm.[42] He brandishes it before a woman, whose outstretched arms appear to express apprehension. The same *pyxis* shows another figure

---

[41] My treatment of satyrs draws on McInerney 2022.
[42] Athens 938: Beazley ABV 30, 4. For discussion, see Isler-Kerényi 2007: 37.

happily masturbating, while in a third scene a beardless figure reaches for another man's pubic region. These images show that, as Cornelia Isler-Kerényi has shown, in the Archaic period, dancers, revellers, symposiasts and satyrs blend into each other. She notes that the satyr 'does not belong to a mythological sphere conceptually separated from the human sphere, but to somewhere between human and mythical'.[43]

This raises a question: what exactly is the relationship of the satyr to the human? Alexandre Mitchells' 2004 essay proposes a succinct definition:

> A satyr is a hybrid mythological being, half-human and half-animal. His ears and tail are those of a horse. He is also identifiable as a satyr from a snub, squashed nose, a bald forehead, a bushy beard and an erect penis. The moral character of satyrs is nothing but a list of foibles. In literature, satyrs are cowards, drunkards and lustful creatures. The satyr is the antithesis of the hero, and is considered less than a man ... They are comic figures per se. Satyrs are found in conventional mythological scenes in the black- and red-figure techniques, ranging in date from the early sixth century until the late fifth century. Satyrs often escort Dionysos at his wedding with Ariadne. They are also often represented at vintages, or escorting Dionysos in The Return of Hephaistos. Satyrs are shown on numerous vases serving and drinking pure unmixed wine from wineskins or amphorae. Finally, satyrs pursue maenads on countless vases.[44]

Mitchell also notes that 'satyrs destabilise traditional iconography'. They were omnipresent in Classical Athenian culture not merely because of their ubiquity on vases but also because of the satyr plays that accompanied all tragic trilogies.[45] The realm of the satyr is located where divine and human activities overlap, but they also serve as a signifier of all the male behaviours that are focused on an erection: drunkenness, arousal and a variety of sexual activities. It is easy to dismiss this as little more than silly male fantasy, but vase iconography from the fifth century suggests there may be a specific connection between satyrs, Dionysos and the training of Athenian ephebes. On the Pronomos Vase, for example, the chorus members wearing *phalloi* and holding satyr masks are all unbearded, unlike the three principal actors, who are all mature, bearded men.[46] Jack Winkler has

---

[43] Isler-Kerényi 2007: 62.

[44] Mitchell 2004: 21. For other useful treatments of satyrs as embodiments of unrestrained human behaviour, see Lissarrague 1993: 220 and Smith 2007: 168. For the Return of Dionysos, see Hedreen 2004. Given the outrageous behaviour of satyrs and the frequency with which they are thwarted it is doubtful that their state of permanent arousal should be closely identified with their status as *daimones*, between men and gods, as argued by Simon 1997: 1120.

[45] On satyrs and satyr plays, see Griffith 2002 and Shaw 2014.

[46] On satyrs on the Pronomos Vase, see Lissarrague 1990a: 228–30.

proposed that members of tragic and satiric choruses were always of ephebic age.[47] If so, it is possible that in the Athenian imagination the satyr and the ephebe were twinned: hypersexual, and bordering on the ungovernable.[48] In such a reading, the dramatic festivals in which ephebes were cast as chorus members were, in Winkler's description, a 'symbolic play on themes of proper and improper civic behaviour, in which the principal component of proper male citizenship was military'.[49] Furthermore, as Mark Griffith has noted, none of the threats, assaults or ambushes that theatre-satyrs begin are ever actually brought to completion: 'they are not by nature capable of serious violence or damage to others'.[50] In the semi-religious setting of drama, then, the satyr is not just a figure of exaggerated masculinity, but is an analogue for the state of permanent sexual arousal out which the ephebe is to be guided.

Regardless of these ephebic overtones, as Robin Osborne has pointed out, satyrs usually occur in scenes that have little or no narrative point. They are simply frozen in a perpetual frenzy of sexual aggression. They do not father heroes. They do not elicit significant transformations on the part of the objects of their desire. They are just desire, full stop, and if any imagery ever existed to underscore the ludicrousness of the sexually aroused male it is the image of the satyr.[51] Building on this observation, Osborne has explored using the identification of the satyr with the Athenian male to chart changes in sexual attitudes in the fifth century. He concludes: 'The satyr's advantage, that he has no reputation to lose, was once what enabled him to do what was extraordinarily shameful; now it makes him unashamed to be ordinary, able to suggest that the exotic should be recognized in the ordinary.'[52] The satyr's power to shock has been dumbed down, as if the community's response to the riotous display of the erection is now hardly more than a shrug or a smirk, reflecting, in Martin Henig's words, 'contemporary "barrack-room" humour'.[53] Yet the satyr's virility is by no means the only visual representation of the *phallos*, and other striking images, such as that of the penis bird and the gigantic *phalloi* of the Phallophoria suggest that the erection may be a contested field of unusually complicated ideas and anxieties about the male body[54]

---

[47] Winkler 1990.

[48] Seaford 1984: 26–44 suggests that the satyrs' animality reflects an initiatory function, which would also fit with an ephebic connection.

[49] Winkler 1990: 20.   [50] Griffith 2002: 216.

[51] On satyr iconography, see Lissarrague 1990a, Hedreen 1992, Hedreen 2006: 277–83.

[52] Osborne 2018: 204.   [53] Henig 1997: 24.

[54] Boardman 1992, Barringer 2001: 93–4, Cotter 2014: 110–11. On birds as a substitute for the penis, see Wormhoudt 1950.

Figure 5.7 White-ground kyathos. Girl riding a *phallos*-bird, ca. 510 BC. Ceramic, 16 cm × 11.5 cm. Inv. F 2095. BPK, Bildagentur, Antikensammlung, Staatliche Museen zu Berlin. Photo: Johannes Laurentius, Art Resource, NY.

(see Figure 5.7). The anatomy of desire is not simple. To begin with, as Timothy McNiven has demonstrated, in Athens the ideal gentleman was characterized by a small, dainty penis, depicted flaccid. Large sexual organs were associated with foreigners and servile characters.[55]

Set against these conventions of modesty, the erection, whether displayed by a satyr or as a winged *phallos*, is either disembodied or, as it were, takes control of the male body. It signals a body at war with itself, in which *sophrosyne* and *himeros* are locked in a struggle that manifests itself anatomically. In his survey of the vases depicting the *phallos*-bird, Boardman notes that 'The idea of isolating a part of the human body and giving it independent life and motive power is uniquely applied to our creature [i.e., the *phallos*-bird]'.[56] This prompts the perhaps obvious observation that the penis is itself unique in being the only part of the male body that regularly displays independent life and motive power. Satyrs and penis-birds, easy to dismiss because they are funny and crude, give expression to a universal but rarely discussed conundrum of masculine identity: power and masculinity are emphatically manifested by an erection, but, paradoxically, a man has no control over it; as both Plato and Aristotle understood, an erection is a body part with a mind of its own.[57] In a similar vein, the massive *phallos* used to

---

[55] McNiven 1995.   [56] Boardman 1992: 237.
[57] An observation made by both Plato and Aristotle. See Pl. *Ti.* 91b and Arist. *De motu anim.* 703b.

celebrate the Phallophoria is not associated with a body, and in the fully ludic spirit of Dionysiac performance it is ridden by a giant satyr, itself a hybrid whose erection is integral to his identity.[58]

The disembodied *phallos* also raises the possibility that both it and the *phallos*-bird, so often cherished by women, are meant to suggest the dildo. Boardman generously proposed that the *phallos*-bird showed that in the Archaic period women's heterosexual appetites were acknowledged, although he perhaps gave too little weight to the vessels decorated with these images: the *kyathos* in Figure 5.7 is part of the equipment associated with a men's symposium. Equating images of parasexual activity made by and for men with female sexuality is like equating pornography with actual sex: the one is not a good indicator of the other despite the superficial similarity. In fact, nothing confirms heteronormative masculinity more than the belief that women's sexual appetites should depend on a man's penis or its substitute, the dildo. Furthermore, in a society in which sexual identities were structured in a heavily binary fashion around the act of penetration or being penetrated, the erections of satyrs and *phallos*-birds are constant reminders of the imminence of penetration, and read in terms of the performance of gender constructed on that binary they can easily be construed as a threat, a conformation of sorts of the reign of the *phallos*, but unlike the hypersexually saturated environment of modern culture, the gleeful irrationality of the satyr and the absurdity of the *phallos*-bird are also ever present reminders of the fact that male arousal is ludicrous.

Ever present, but not unchanging. The sixth century saw the merging of komastic scenes, in which the cavorting of the satyr is part dance and part drunken stumbling, with symposiastic scenes, wherein the human participants similarly drink, lurch and unleash their libido. If the symposium is one of the key cultural institutions of the sixth century, the analogizing of satyr to komasts and symposiasts points to a complicated nexus of cultural values embodied in performances of drinking and fornicating, whose relationship to the more sober public behaviour of citizens, once again characterized by *sophrosyne*, is hard to tease out: a dialectical inversion? A comic subversion? A subaltern resistance mocking aristocratic conventions? Komasts often have potbellies and are physically the opposite of the ideal athlete.[59] In the komastic setting, the images of libidinous and grotesque satyrs exist outside the world of normative sexual behaviour with its two principal foci: heterosexual encounters and paederastic episodes, orthodox sexual encounters which will end in penetration by the heterosexual man.

---

[58] Csapo 1997, pl. 3 and 4. [59] Seeburg 1971: 3.

Figure 5.8 Sexually excited satyr facing the viewer. Detail of an Athenian band (terracotta kylix) cup by the Oakeshott Painter, ca. 550 BCH. 6 7/16 in. (16.4 cm) diameter 11 3/16 in. (28.4 cm). Metropolitan Museum of Art, 17.230.5.

In contrast to these, the sexual scenes in which satyrs act are a pictorial world of frustration, voyeurism, masturbation, ejaculation and sex with objects, in a variety of situations that connect the satyrs either to sexual failure, comic deviance or absurdity (or all of these). The satyr depicted by the Oakeshott Painter, for example, stares directly out from the cup even as he grabs his engorged penis and prepares to sodomize the mule in front of him (see Figure 5.8). They chase women in vain, try to rape them in their sleep, hump each other, have sex with amphorae, prepare to have sex with animals or balance drinking cups on the tip of their penis.[60] In so doing,

---

[60] See, for example, Boeotian tripod-pyxis. Athens, National Museum 938 (satyr masturbating in front of a woman); dinos. Athens, Agora P 334 (hairy, ithyphallic satyr chasing a woman); belly lekythos. Buffalo (NY), Albright-Knox Art Gallery G 600 (hairy, ithyphallic satyr astride a mule with an erection chasing a woman; exterior of red-figure cup, attributed to Makron, ca. 490 BC. *ARV* 461.36, Boston Museum of Fine Arts 01.8072 (two satyrs attempting to rape a sleeping woman); red-figure oinochoe, unattributed, from Athens, ca. 420 BC. Boston Museum of Fine Arts 01.8085 (an erect satyr contemplates a sleeping woman while another gestures to stop); exterior of red-figure cup, attributed to the Chelis Painter, from Vulci, ca. 500 BC. *ARV* 112.1, Munich Staatliche Antikensammlungen 2589 (an aroused satyr lifts the hem of a fleeing maenad); fragment of a dinos (?) Atlantis Antiquities 1988, 55 fig. 48 (hairy satyr buggering another satyr); Attic red-figure kylix by Nikosthenes Painter. Antikensammlung Berlin (Altes Museum), Inv. 1964.4 (multiple satyrs have sex with each other and a sphinx); Nikosthenes Painter, tondo of a red-figure kylix. Kassel Staatlich Museen Alg 214 (satyr having sex with an amphora); red-figure amphora, Euthymides, ca. 520 BC (satyr penetrating an amphora); Archaic black-figure kylix, attributed to the Oakeshott Painter (satyr preparing to bugger an ithyphallic mule); red-figure cup, Ambrosios painter, ca. 500 BC (satyr balancing a kantharos on his penis). On the Euthymides amphora, see Lissarrague 2014: 78–9, and for satyrs and sex, see Lissarrague 1990b.

they participate in episodes that riotously violate conventional behaviour. A simple reading might interpret these as depictions of drunkenness and venal sex, but these are features of the visual world of the satyr, not explanations for it. The satyr is a creature inhabiting a space in Athenian culture where sexual frenzy and aberration threaten to undermine the rules of polite social intercourse. In a world of satyrs, the reassuring certainty of conventional sex roles and behaviours becomes as slippery as the greasy wineskins with which so many satyrs wrestle.[61]

Not every priapic satyr gets the girl, and the question of desire thwarted and penetration averted is an aspect of Greek sexuality that raises its head every time the satyr's gargantuan erection forces itself into our field of vision. Often, too, the ridiculousness of the erection is further emphasized by including an ithyphallic donkey or mule in the scene, analogizing the human erection to its even grosser animal counterpart. In one late Archaic Little Master Cup (Munich 7414), an aroused donkey pursues a woman as a young male onlooker watches in frustration, furiously masturbating to the point of climax. Other representations of masturbation and ejaculation suggest the same set of associations.[62] Young or old, satyrs and men ejaculating are either disgusting or ludicrous. Nor is it a coincidence that these scenes frequently depict the actor looking directly out from the scene (Figure 5.9). Frontality is uncommon in vase painting. Gorgons, dying warriors and statues exhibit themselves face on, each one category marked as outside ordinary human action, unsettling to behold.[63] Iconographically, then, the erection is not a simple assertion of male power. The truth is a good deal messier.

Metamorphosis

The presence of gorgons and satyrs in art shows that throughout the Archaic and Classical periods the imagination of the Greeks was saturated

---

[61] On satyrs wrestling with wineskins, see Lissarrague 2014: 68–76. For satyrs, masturbation scenes and drinking, see Kapparis 2018: 349.

[62] Little Master Cup. Black-figure kylix, 560–530 BC. Munich 7414. State Collection of Antiquities and Glyptothek, Munich. See, for example, cup by the Amasis Painter. Boston, Museum of Fine Arts 10.651 (pot-bellied men masturbating next to a defecating dog); aryballos by Nearchos. New York, The Metropolitan Museum of Art 26.49 (three hairy satyrs masturbating). For a discussion of these scenes and the connection between masturbation scenes and symposia, see Stafford 2011.

[63] On frontality in vase painting, see Korshak 1987. On gorgons and dying warriors, see Frontisi-Ducroux 2003. On frontality and narrative disjunction, see Mackay 2001.

Metamorphosis 159

Figure 5.9 Satyr masturbating. Attic red-figure kalpis fragment attributed to Kleophrades painter, 500–480 BC. 6.4 × 7 × 3 cm (2 $\frac{9}{16}$ × 2 $\frac{3}{4}$ × 1 $\frac{3}{16}$ in.) The J. Paul Getty Museum, Villa Collection, Malibu, California, 85.AE.188.

with creatures that pushed the boundaries of the human. They hinted at other ways of composing bodies: alluring female bodies with petrifying faces, and ridiculous male bodies with exaggerated organs and goatish ears. In each case the hybrid's peculiarity put a question mark over what it is to be a human. The hybrid also posed the question of transformation, and in some respects this was even more troubling than monstrosity. The monster simply exists as an 'other', but metamorphosis raises the possibility that the very human condition itself is unstable.

At first glance the categories of hybridity and metamorphosis seem ontologically different: a hybrid <u>is</u>, while a creature undergoing transformation <u>is becoming</u>. But the distinction is not simple. As Plato might observe, if a thing is always becoming, at what point may it be said to be?[64] One could insist that the hybrid creature, like Pegasos, is distinct from a creature undergoing a metamorphosis, like Proteus cycling through different shapes to escape capture, but the distinction between hybrid and transformed creature is often weak. On the famous *hydria* formerly in Toledo, for example, a chorus-line of the man-dolphins can be seen in the midst of their metamorphosis (see Figure 5.10). On the left, the first figure is

---

[64] On being and becoming, see Plato, *Phaedo* 78d–79a; *Symposium* 211; *Republic* 479a–b, 479d.

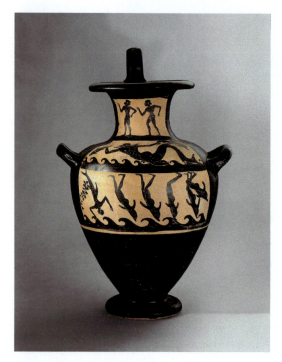

Figure 5.10 The metamorphosis of the Tyrrhenian pirates by Dionysos. Etruscan black-figure hydria, ca. 510–500 BC. Formerly in the Toledo Museum of Art, Toledo, 1982.134.

recognizably human on his top half, but then the figures begin to display the upper torsos of dolphins. They are hybrids, but only momentarily, because, as the fused legs of the fourth figure and sixth figures show, they are will soon be entirely dolphin. In the case of the dolphin-men, the complex relationship between hybridity and transformation is not only a matter of conceptual proximity, but also a question of medium. To represent the process of metamorphosis the vase painter must supply a series of snapshots, as it were, resulting in a sequence of hybrids which serve as visual markers of transformation. At least in the grammar of iconography, the hybrid product may connote the process of transformation.

Hybridity is frequently inseparable from metamorphosis.[65] In at least two important and related areas of Greek culture – theatre and religious initiation – hybrid identities resulting from metamorphosis played a key role. It is no coincidence, for example, that vase depictions of choruses

---

[65] For a sensitive treatment of the overlap of these categories, see Buxton 2009: 76–109 and Thumiger 2014: 391–3.

often show the chorus members either dressed as animals or wearing animal masks.[66] In fact, choruses dressed as animals even predate the earliest attested performances of comic plays and suggest that animal mummery was part of the prehistory of drama.[67] These 'dancing herds of animals' in Pindar's evocative phrase were a source of delight for audiences of dithyramb and its successor, comedy, unlocking the ludic potential of adopting fantastic identities only partially human. A good indicator of the popularity of such performances, in which the actors, occasionally, and choruses, frequently, wore elaborate and expensive animal costumes, is the vogue around 520–480 BC for luxurious sympotic vessels, such as skyphoi and sphykters decorated with scenes of hybrid choruses. Some of the hybrids portrayed are ranks of ostrich-men, while in other cases dolphin-riders are a fantastic mash-up of traditional hoplites and unreal dolphins cast as cavalry mounts.[68] Gwendolyn Compton-Engle has identified more than twenty such vessels.[69] Their production coincides with a critical period of Athenian history, and the vessels capture a delicate tension between the egalitarianism encoded in choruses of identical or similar figures, and the elitism of the aristocratic symposium where the vessels are displayed and used.[70] The in-betweenness of these vessels, in fact, mirrors the very same contested conditions in which both Dionysiac comedy and democracy were shaped. The vessels point to aristocrats exploring new ways of celebrating their successes as *choregoi*, converting expenditure into social capital during the fraught period around the turn of the sixth to the fifth century. Comedy as a city-sponsored competition was formally established at the City Dionysia in 487 BC, but it was not created overnight, and the appearance of these animal chorus vessels confirms the importance of these comic performances for an Athenian community facing extraordinary challenges: from within, the social upheaval accompanying the establishment of Kleisthenic democracy; from without, the threat posed by the Persian invasions. The fantasy of comedy and the imaginative stimulation supplied by hybrid figures constituted a safe place to channel uncertainty into forms of expression that were reassuringly silly.

---

[66] Sifakis 1971: 73–102.
[67] On predecessors of comedy, see Sifakis 1971, Rothwell 2007 and Farmer 2020. For animal mummery see Lawler 1952. For a good example, see the black figure belly amphora, depicting a chorus of knights with flautist, attributed to the Painter of Berlin 1686, ca. 530 BC. AVI 2209: Berlin, Antikensammlung F 1697.
[68] Red figure psykter (wine cooler), depicting hoplites riding dolphins, ca. 520–510 BC. H. 11 7/8 in. Metropolitan Museum of Art, 1989.281.69.
[69] Compton-Engle 2015: 110–13.   [70] Csapo 2003.

The possibilities of comic distancing were understood by successive comic poets: Aristophanes' *Birds* included a chorus of men wearing costumes corresponding to various species, and it is likely that the same applied to Krates' *Wild Animals* (*Theria*), Magnes' *Birds* (*Ornithes*) and Archippos' *Fishes* (*Ichthyes*).[71] In these cases the hybrid playfully undercuts regular social roles, but this represents a release rather than a subversion. In a similar vein, Eric Csapo has observed that the New Music of the late fifth century is full of nostalgia for 'Nereids, dolphins, Kouretes, maenads, satyrs, and stars – all dancing in a circle'.[72] Babette Pütz has also recently drawn attention to the mixture of Greek and animal-sounds in Aristophanes' comic choruses as a challenge 'to the traditional dichotomy between animals and humans or culture and nature'.[73] In short, the fifth-century stage offered a menagerie of fantastic creatures and hybrids, testament to the fact that Classical Greek culture embraced the notion that humans and animals shared a fundamental similarity, and the entanglement of the human and animal realms imaginatively enriched social experience.[74] Composite bodies destabilize the boundaries between categories, but the comic stage allowed and even encouraged the temporary suspension of the separation of species.[75]

The possibility of moving across the species barrier was only confusing if one expected rigid distinctions between species, but it was less troubling in a world of fluid movement between animal and human.[76] In comedy, with space for humour, exaggeration and imagination this is a liberating fluidity, as if one were trying on different identities and different constructions of humanity, but in tragedy the shadow of hybrid animality was more troubling. Theatre audiences encountered one example of the power of lurking animality in Aeschylus' *Eumenides*, and here the fluidity of the boundaries separating the human and the animal is shocking.[77] The Furies are identified not only as bloodthirsty avenging spirits but as a chorus of gorgons or

---

[71] Wilson 1977: 278; Compton-Engle 2015: 110–43. See also a black-figure chous with actors dressed as birds, ca. 510–490 BC. Attributed to the Gela Painter. British Museum 1842,0728.787.

[72] Csapo 2008: 285.   [73] Pütz 2020: 183. See also Rothwell 2020.   [74] Rothwell 2007: 101.

[75] Hughes 2010: 101 notes 'that the hybrid's "partible" body can be seen to challenge the cultural as well as the biological boundaries that separated humans and animals in the Graeco-Roman world'.

[76] Nash 1980 reports an experiment in which subjects were shown pictures of various hybrids and asked to rate them in terms of animality, unpleasantness and incongruity. An interesting datum to emerge from what is really a study of thirty American undergraduates is that the subjects tended to classify hybrids as effectively human even when they possessed animal heads by claiming that such hybrids were really humans wearing masks.

[77] On the *Eumenides* and the shifting monstrosity of the Furies, see McInerney 2021a: 26–30.

harpies. When they are roused by the Ghost of Klytaimnestra they are described by the priestess of Apollo in horrifying detail:

> Before this man an extraordinary band of women slept, seated on thrones. No! Not women, but rather Gorgons I call them; and yet I cannot compare them to forms of Gorgons either. Once before I saw some creatures in a painting, carrying off the feast of Phineus; but these are wingless (featherless?) in appearance, black, altogether disgusting; they snore with repulsive breaths, they drip from their eyes hateful drops; their attire is not fit to bring either before the statues of the gods or into the homes of men.
>
> Aesch. *Eum.* 46–59 (tr. Smyth).

They are warned by Apollo to quit his shrine lest he shoot them and force them to vomit up the gobs of blood they have swallowed. Elsewhere they are mistaken for old women or aged children, and, as with the descriptions of them as gorgon-like, they seem to have vaguely human faces that are crinkled and ugly. Based on these clues, P. G. Maxwell-Stuart argued that on stage they resembled bats.[78] Other animal similes add to the picture of their monstrosity. Klytaimnestra's ghost likens them to a pack of hunting dogs on the trail of the prey, twitching in their sleep. Upon waking they cry out that their prey has slipped through the nets, and they pursue him, using the traces of blood left by his murderous act to track him, vowing to drink his blood and to make him a bloodless victim – drained, but not ritually slaughtered like a proper sacrificial victim. They are stung by fear, as if they were horses in the traces subject to the charioteer's whip. Klytaimnestra's ghost likens them to a dragon whose strength has been sapped by sleep and care. In a particularly gruesome passage Apollo describes the Furies as attending the disembowelling of victims as if they were torturers or executioners. And yet, after all the disgust and horror that they evoke, they will be appeased and even honoured as the *Semnai Theai* (Dread Goddesses), not only in the fantastic world of the play but in the actual religious topography of Athens, where they were worshipped at an altar beneath the Akropolis.[79] Hybridity equates here to an indeterminacy expressed through constantly shifting forms. It is a means of capturing a profound religious sentiment of the Classical period: the belief that the victory of order over chaos was contingent on the continued propitiation of elemental forces.

---

[78] Maxwell-Stuart 1973: 81–4 and Heath 2005: 241.

[79] Johnston 1999: 263–73, 279–87. It was at this altar that the thread connecting the Cylonian conspirators to the image of Athena miraculously broke as they were coming down from the Akropolis (Plut., *Solon* 12).

Closely connected to bending the boundaries of species on the stage is a second locus of transformation: initiation. Little Perseuses at Tiryns, we have seen, marked their coming of age with a ritual slaying of the gorgon. Other initiatory rites, in Arkadia particularly, drew on animal transformation as part of ritual. At Phigelia, for example, Black Demeter was worshipped by devotees dressed as hybrids. Their masks allowed them try out different social identities. Particularly prominent in the Arkadian cult was werewolf transformation as a means of initiating the young into adulthood. According to Plato, at the sanctuary of Zeus on Mt Lykaion human meat was mixed with other sacrificial cuts which were then cooked together.[80] Whoever tasted the human flesh turned into a wolf. The basic plot is elaborated in Pliny and Pausanias.[81] The initiate swam across a lake and after his metamorphosis spent nine years in the wild before returning to the community, having transformed back into human form.[82] The entire ritual is structured around the wolf's savagery serving as a metaphor for the warrior's rage. How widespread such wolf-warrior secret societies were is hard to know, and too great a reliance on Indo-European parallels where evidence is slim suggests one should be cautious before seeing werewolves everywhere. Even so, wolf metaphors played an important role in Archaic culture: the duplicity of tyrants was likened to the wolf's cunning, and, at the other end of the spectrum, the wolf pack's habit of sharing meat was likened to the human value of *isonomia*. Wolves were useful for thinking about politics, and, as Elizabeth Irwin has observed in her study of Solon's wolf imagery, 'the political initiative of wolves involves a strong rhetoric of collectivity and unity, usually expressed in terms of equal division or distribution'.[83] Both the Orthagorid and Bacchiad clans modelled their claims to legitimacy on stories and rituals that drew on associations with the wolf pack: Orthagoras cast himself as the avenger sent by Apollo to

---

[80] Plato, *Rep.* 8.565d–e.   [81] Paus. 8.2.6 and Pliny, *NH* 8.81.

[82] For Pliny and Pausanias's accounts of the Arkadian ritual, see Buxton 1988: 44–7. For Arkadian lycanthropy as a form of initiation, see Burkert 1983: 89–92.

[83] Irwin 2005: 252. For the metaphor of the savage wolf as warrior, see Bouvier 2015. For wolves as tyrants, see Detienne and Svenbro 1979. For wolves sharing equally, see Timothy of Gaza 7.8. Also see Buxton 1988. On wolves as a means of exploring the problem of aggression and sexuality in pastoral, see Epstein 1995. The association of wolves with politics has not disappeared. In a study of the hunt for the last wolves on Mt Parnassos in the late 80s, Moore 1994 shows that wolves can be used metonymically for politicians and anyone else who threatens the shepherds' living. President Karamanlis thus becomes Karaman*lykos*. The killing of the wolves triggered a range of performances and displays designed to assert the masculinity and independence of the local men in the face of a dramatically changing environment lost to skiing and tourism. As Moore notes (86), 'Like the wolves, then, the shepherds of Arachova are an endangered species'.

punish the Sikyonians for having torn a certain Teletias to pieces like a pack of ravenous wolves.[84] In stories of Delphi's involvement in his rise, Orthagoras ('Straight-Talker') is known as the son of a *mageiros* (chief) Andreas, whose name recalls the men's associations of Dorian Crete, the *Andreia*, where food was shared.[85] The Bacchiads too drew on the motif of the boy torn apart, in this case Aktaion, whose killer must be driven from the land before Corinth can be cured of the plague caused by the killer's impiety. Across the Peloponnese, then, Dorian communities employed hybrids, predators and animal transformations as recurring elements in rituals of initiation and in conceptualizing commensality and male bonding. In these performances individuals underwent werewolf transformations to create new social identities, but even more, entire communities of male citizens were fashioned out of these shared experiences. Accordingly, while the first step of such initiation, like any rite of passage, entailed the breaking down of old boundaries and categories, this was neither transgressive nor permanent. The final result for the individual was an orderly transition into a new life-stage, and for the community the collective survival of the pack.

The ritual performance of metamorphosis facilitates a coherent and orderly movement through life-stages. It is temporary, but even a passing animal transformation raises some tough questions regarding consciousness and identity. Io is no longer a girl when, in the form of a heifer she is tortured by Hera and driven like a crazy creature around the world, yet she has a human form in which she complains and prophesies to Prometheus. The human remains integral to her being even if she was transformed into a young cow. Similarly, Aktaion is always shown as a stag-man hybrid when being torn apart by his dogs.[86] It is not simply that this makes him recognizable, as his horns sprout; it also clearly conveys the notion that it is the man Aktaion being punished, not just the animal whose form he takes on. Was Iphigeneia ever a deer in its entirety when transformed and saved by Artemis? Hybridity often then takes the form of an integument,

---

[84] Kunstler 1991: 197–9. Teletias was a winner in the boys' events at the Pythian Games, but was claimed by both Sikyon and neighbouring Kleonai. His name points to the setting of initiation (τελετή).

[85] Erickson 2010: 313–20 surveys the literary and archaeological evidence for what he terms 'the elusive andreion' on Crete between 700 and 500 BC. While earlier reconstructions of the institution may have been overly confident the testimony of Dosiadas (*FGrH* 458 f2), preserved in Athenaios 4.143, cannot be entirely dismissed. Commensality and an egalitarian ethos were deeply embedded in these communities. '*Andreion*' is attested in an inscription from Gortyn at the end of the seventh century (*IC* IV 4).

[86] Frontisi-Ducroux 2003: 95–143.

Figure 5.11 Bronze figurine part man, part pig, representing one of Odysseus' men undergoing transformation. Fifth century BC. Peloponnese. H: 1/2 × W: 1 7/8 × D: 3/8 in. (1.27 × 4.76 × 0.95 cm) Walter Art Museum, Baltimore. 54.1483. Creative Commons License.

a covering that connotes a form, a transformation, punishment or salvation, but not a changed consciousness. Ovid will play with this: Daphne remains the girl even as she disappears into the laurel tree. Like some hideous version of locked-in syndrome, the hybrid is sometimes trapped inside a body that does not match its being.

Nowhere is the hybrid's mismatch of consciousness and outer form clearer than in a case, that, once again, begins as a transformation. Circe's witchcraft sees Odysseus' men morphed into animals (Figure 5.11), but there are good reasons to assume that their human interior remains intact. In the famous Boston kylix they are depicted as hybrids, human bodies with theriomorphic heads. As they stand on their human legs receiving the potion from Circe they are shown pleading with her in human postures, but the words they utter are gibberish, represented by nonsense Greek[87] (see Figure 5.12). Some run from her in the full human awareness of the horror she has perpetrated on them. That they speak gibberish is important as it draws attention to their loss of humanity. When animals speak with human voices the result is much more benign. As Silva notes, 'Animal fable uses generally intuitive concepts with just the right amount of

---

[87] McInerney 2021a: 24–25, Dosoo 2021: 262–265.

Figure 5.12 Circe giving a potion to Odysseus' men: black-figure kylix, ca. 550–525 BC. Museum of Fine Arts, Boston, 99.518. Photograph © 2024 Museum of Fine Arts, Boston.

counter-intuitiveness, a pinch of the fantastic, to be salient in the sea of information though which we must sift.'[88] At the same time, the distance created by the theriomorphic shift also frees the animal fable to convey a lightly veiled critique of elite institutions. As Leslie Kurke has demonstrated, the traditions attached to Aesop give voice to a subversive message to the powers that rule Delphi.[89] An animal speaking as a human is charming; a human reduced to the animal has slipped down the chain of being.

In the post Homeric world, Plutarch will use one of these human porkers, Gryllos (Grunter), as the porcine mouthpiece for a philosophical dialogue that unsettles the human assurance of superiority by allowing the animal who can reason and speak like a human to argue for the ethical and moral superiority of the animal. Unlike the *Testamentum Porcelli*, with its 'schoolboy humour', Plutarch and Homer are exploring something much more worrisome: what if the chain of being is not secure, what if humans are not always and necessarily at the top of the ladder?[90] At the same time, if men shift their outer layers, then they may carry some aspect of their hybridity with them as an afterthought. Teiresias famously enrages Hera

---

[88] Silva 2020: 51.   [89] Kurke 2011.
[90] Champlin 1987: 175. For a succinct statement of the connection between speech and reason in Greek thinking as well as Plutarch's contribution to this in the *Gryllos* see Konstan 2011.

when he observes that, based on his own transformation, women enjoy sex nine times more than men. He has been both, having been transformed from male to female and back again, but retains experience of both, so that despite his being a man his consciousness functions as a hybrid of both sexes. This is a kind of contingent or episodic hybridity. Similarly, when Menelaus puts on the skin of a seal to conceal his approach to Proteus, he temporarily becomes a hybrid in that the outer and inner beings are an awkward mismatch, but a necessary one if the hero is to match the powers of the Old Man of the Sea who can transform into many shapes. To determine the unerring truth the hero must become a master of deception, a conundrum that corresponds to the appeal of the hybrid: it, too, is a paradox. Further up the chain of being is Herakles, a hero who outstrips the Homeric princes and approaches Olympian status: man and god, a hybrid *par excellence*, he puts on a cloak of lion-skin not, like Aktaion's deer pelt, or Io's horns, to mark his punishment (that will come with another cloak), but to advertise his strength. Other lion-wrestling heroes, like Samson and Gilgamesh, will kill their adversaries, but with the Greek taste for polarity and analogy only Herakles assumes something of the character of what he has slain. His hybridity then marks him as man-lion, even as his deeds position him as god-man.

Above the gorgon-women, cow-girls, dolphin-pirates, deer-men, horse-men, and lion-men are always finally the gods. Yet here too, hybridity lurks on the margins, hinting at a divine form that lies beyond the grasp of humans. Famously the Greek gods appear to be resolutely anthropomorphic compared to their theriomorphic Egyptian contemporaries. But this is not absolute. Here too we encounter various forms of hybridity. One is in the ability of the Greek gods to transform into animal bodies: a swan, an eagle, an owl, or an entire menagerie (Dionysos). These transformations are often regarded as temporary avatars, but this is only in the narratives that require them to function in primarily anthropomorphic fashion. Enthroned at Olympia or presiding over a council of the gods it would be hard for Zeus to appear as a shower of gold. By contrast, his appearance in the form of a swan to impregnate Leda can be read as an oddity, perhaps a holdover from some cycle of stories that renders Helen into a cosmic moon goddess, born of an egg. But in this evolutionary reading, where Zeus is only temporarily swan or eagle, and Hera is cow-eyed merely to suggest her connection with pasture animals, the animality of the god is thought of as a relic, or a symbol of some aspect of their power or the domain in which they act. Yet in many places there seems to be more at work. Arkadia, in particular, was home to various deities who did not confirm to Olympian norms. Here Eurynome, a Nereid, was represented as fish-bodied, like a mermaid.[91] Also in Arkadia Demeter transformed into a mare to escape Poseidon Stallion, unsuccessfully, and from their union come Despoina (the Mistress), and Areion (the horse).[92] This was the story told in the sanctuary of Black Demeter in Phigaleia where the goddess' statue depicted her with the head of a horse. In these stories the gods frequently slip in and out of animal form: Poseidon Hippos pursues Athena Hippia, each having transformed into horse form; Apollo is worshipped as Lykeios and Dionysos is described as bull-horned or bull faced.[93]

Hybrids also figure in the visualization of river gods such as Gela. Like Acheloos, the local river god of the northwest, Gela's hybrid form of animal and human evokes the profound imbrication of nature and the human that Brooke Holmes calls 'Natureculture.'[94] We are used to treating the broad categories of the natural and the human, referred to as *physis* and *nomos*, as polarities in Greek thought, but there are moments when the two-fold in upon each other and acquire a divine dimension as well. In the Skamander episode in *Iliad* 21, for example, the river god is choked by the corpses of men slain by Achilles, and is tormented by the burning of the trees and reeds along the riverbanks. He feels the pain of the fish and eels in his waters. Makins and Reitz-Joose have recently pointed to the complexity of his complaint: 'It is as if 'Scamander' in a sense embodies an entire riparian ecosystem, the vulnerability of which undercuts our previous understanding of him as an immortal god.'[95] Scamander, in fact, comes from a class of divine beings that belong as much to the earth as to heaven. Similarly, the bull-man river god of Gela demonstrates that the symbolism we find on Greek coins goes far beyond the literalism or simple symbolism of a rose (ῥόδον) for Rhodes or seal (φώκη) for Phokaia. The Gelan river-bull-man demonstrates that communities imbued the entire natural environment around them with agency expressed in a language of hybridity that refused to be contained by distinct categories of animal, human and divine.[96]

Hybridity in these many stories appears to be a means of fixing gods and heroes in a location comprehensible to humans, close and yet at the same time far away. And just as hybridity and metamorphosis are closely related, so too both these categories are crucial to the Greek experience of the

---

[91] On Arkadian cults see Jost 1985 and Jost 1992; for Eurynome Pausanias 8.41.6, as well as Detienne and Vernant 1991: 142. On part animal gods see Aston 2011.
[92] For Black Demeter see Pausanias 8.42.4 and Balériaux 2019, McInerney 2021a.
[93] For Athena Horse see Yalouris 1950 and Detienne 1971.
[94] Holmes 2015. See also Makins and Reitz-Joosse 2021.   [95] Makins and Reitz-Joosse 2021: 8.
[96] For the ox-bodied river god see Clarke 2004, Molinari and Sisci 2016.

divine. Herakleitos, for example, situated the divine in the fluctuations between opposites, claiming 'God is day and night, winter and summer, war and peace, surfeit and hunger; but he takes various shapes, just as fire, when it is mingled with spices, is named according to the savour of each.'[97] Plutarch explored similar contradictions, juxtaposing the eternal indestructability of Apollo with a more transient, fluid quality he identifies as the god's alter ego, Dionysos: 'As for his passage and distribution into waves and water, and earth, and stars, and nascent plants and animals, they hint at the actual change undergone as a rending and dismemberment, but name the God himself Dionysus.'[98] By situating the gods within a shifting framework of continuous change the Greeks were better able to cope with the fundamental paradox of divinity conceived anthropomorphically: it was schizophrenic. As Henk Versnel points out, the gods were both different from and yet like humans: 'Had they been only different, they would have been both inconceivable and incommunicado; had they been only and completely 'in the image of man', they would have been neither gods nor interesting.'[99] One response to this duality was to resort once again to transformation, the notion that the human could and had become divine, either as a result of a singular apotheosis, as in the case of Herakles, or in Euhemeros' conception of the human origins on Panchaia of all the Olympian gods.[100] From this vantage point the dual nature of Christ can be seen as part of a long established cultural matrix emphasizing not the hard barrier separating humans from god, but a fluid field in which humans, gods and animals each retain a shadow of the other. As humans are entangled with animals, so too are we entangled with gods.[101]

---

[97] Herakleitos Frg. 36.   [98] Plutarch, *De E apud Delph.*
[99] Versnel 2011: 389. See also Mirto 2016: 46.
[100] For Euhemos, see Montanari and Pouderon 2022.   [101] McInerney 2021a.

6 | Centaurs and Other Horses

> Then me he touch'd, and spake: 'Nessus is this,
> Who for the fair Deianira died,
> And wrought himself revenge for his own fate.
> He in the midst, that on his breast looks down,
> Is the great Chiron who Achilles nurs'd;
> That other Pholus, prone to wrath.' Around
> The foss these go by thousands, aiming shafts
> At whatsoever spirit dares emerge
> From out the blood, more than his guilt allows.
>
> Dante, *Inferno* Canto XII 67–75 (trans. Carey)

Horse-Men and Horsemen

Like gorgons and satyrs, the centaur is present throughout Greek culture, in poetry, sculpture and vase painting.[1] Conventionally, the centaur is imagined as human from the waist up, and a four-legged equine below. In this form the centaur appears throughout the Archaic and Classical periods in a variety of media: terracottas, bronzes figurines, repoussé bronze sheets and vases.[2] Examples are too numerous to include in full here, but a partial list is sufficient to demonstrate how widely known is this type: from the west pediment of the Temple of Zeus at Olympia to the Attic red-figure krater painted by the Painter of the Louvre Centauromachy, the canonical centaur is a familiar figure.[3] The centaurs on the François Vase are a good example (Figure 6.1).

---

[1] Literary sources are discussed in *BNJ* s.v. Centaurs (Walde). See also Vogel 1978. For iconography see *LIMC* VI 1, s.v. Kentauroi.

[2] Aside from the Olympia west pediment, the metopes of the Parthenon and earlier bronze figurines from the late sixth century now in the National Archaeological Museum, examples include a black-figure kylix by the Bowdoin Eye Painter in Toledo (Toledo 1963.28, Beazley 275020); a red-figure Apulian kalyx krater in the British Museum (BM F 272); a black-figure neck amphora attributed to the Paris Painter in Würzburg (L 778); and an Attic red-figure krater by the Painter of the Louvre Centauromachy (Louvre G 367; Beazley 214587).

[3] For an overview, see Padgett 2003.

Figure 6.1 The François Vase, Attic black-figure volute krater by Ergotimos, ca. 570 BC. Side A, detail: battle between the Lapiths and centaurs. Height 66cm, d. 181cm. Found in Chiusi. Florence, Museo Archeologico Inv. No. 4209. Scala/Art Resource, NY.

The creature is entirely equine up to the horse's withers. A line that marks out the powerful muscles of the horse's shoulders also clearly separates the equine segment from a human upper body and head. The centaur's wildness is evoked by his resemblance to a satyr, with his shaggy beard and equine ears. He wields a tree trunk torn straight from the ground, with fronds still attached (the next centaur to the right hurls a boulder). All of these markers distinguish him from the Lapith hoplite who turns to thrust his spear at him. The contrast is clear, the differences readily apparent to such a degree that human and centaur are well matched opposites.

Just as centaurs appear in episodes as varied as the Rape of the Lapith Women to the education of young Achilles by the centaur Cheiron, so too the explanations for their origins and their hybridity vary widely. In Homer, for example, they are no more than mountain dwelling, shaggy beasts (λαχνήεις, φῆρες) beaten by the Lapiths, and there is no explicit reference to their equine form.[4] In the late nineteenth century, when vegetation spirits were often invoked to explain the earliest strata of ancient religion, it was common to interpret the centaurs as either wildmen or even as personifications of nature's destructive power in the form of winds or torrents.[5] In these

---

[4] Homer, *Il.* 1.268 'mountain-dwelling' and 2.743 'shaggy'.

[5] Mannhardt 1876–7. For an updated discussion of the centaurs as creatures of the wilderness, see Bremmer 2012.

readings their equine form was incidental, and sometimes dismissed as little more than the elaboration of some flamboyant poetic description.[6] Such explanations, however, shed little light on the continuing popularity of centaurs, nor do they account for the recurring matter of their distinctive hybridity: throughout their history centaurs in the Greek world have been unmistakably horsey. Whatever their origins, either deriving from Mesopotamian forerunners or as the wilderness spirits of their traditional home, Mt Pelion, the centaurs draw fundamentally on the complex relationship between humans and horses.[7] This is reflected in curious accounts of how they came into existence.

By the fifth century, centaurs had acquired a complete genealogy: according to Pindar, the Lapith king Ixion became fixated on Hera. In response Zeus created a cloud, Nephele, in the form of Hera, with whom Ixion had sex. The product of this phantom union was Kentauros, who in turn coupled with the mares of Mt Pelion producing 'that strange race ... like to both parents, their mother's form below, above their sire's'.[8] These episodes of cloud sex and interspecies mating weave together various motifs, such as illicit passion, bestiality, wildness and the spirit of place, but it is the theme of sexual aggression coupled with drunkenness which is foregrounded in stories in which the centaurs play a role. Most memorably, at the wedding of Pirithous and Hippodameia, the ritual at the heart of orderly human society – marriage – devolves into chaos because of the unbridled lust of the centaurs. Their tendency, however, to violate any woman within reach is not simply a result of their weakness for wine: sexual transgression is powerfully evoked by the very manner in which their hybrid bodies came into being. They are the personification of a particular type of aberrant sexuality: the sexually hyperactive male.[9]

---

[6] Gardner 1897: 301.

[7] The Babylonian deity Pabilsaĝ, identified with the constellation Sagittarius in Babylonian skylore, is often depicted as a winged centaur shooting a bow and arrow. See *Reallexikon der Assyriologie und vorderasiatischen Archäologie*, s.v. 'Pabilsaĝ' (Krebernik) (Ebeling et al. 2005). For the associations of centaurs with Mt Pelion, see Aston 2017.

[8] Pindar, *P.* 2.21–48. Later versions: Apollodorus E1.20, Diodorus Siculus 4.69.4, Hyginus, *Fabulae* 62, Ovid, *Metamorphoses* 12.112, Cicero, *De Natura Deorum 3.20*, Philostratus the Elder 2.3.

[9] On 'centaurs' as slang for sexually hyperactive men, see Storey 1998: 90, and DuBois 1991: 31, both drawing on Aristophanes, *Cl.* 346–50. Henderson 1975: 202–3 and 219 claims the terms specifically refers to aggressive homosexual men. The association of centaurs with libido is long-lived. In 1755 in *The Centaur Not Fabulous*, Edward Young described 'men of pleasure, the licentious, and profligate' as centaurs. In both, 'the brute runs away with the man'. See Woodring 2007: 4.

Because of their form and their actions, the centaur poses a question: Can lust be curbed? But the question is not framed as an ethical dilemma or a philosophical challenge: it is given shape in a form that is a contrafactual and deployed in narrative. Telling stories about centaurs necessitates imagining a creature that embodies the triumph of appetites over reason, while taking into account the fact that no such creature ever existed. This poses a further question: is it possible to think through the primal urges of the id if one does not accept its existence? The answer is that it is possible, if those primal urges are rendered in flesh and blood (even if imaginary). One way to read this tension is as a playing out of a deep-seated oscillation in Greek culture between body and flesh. The human body, conceived in its ideal form, is a thing of beauty, self-possessed, under control and capable of perfection in the form of a beautiful statue. A *kouros*, for example, captures the moment the male body comes closest to transcendence. The flesh, by contrast, and to borrow Gerald Bruns' evocative description, is 'passive and weak, torpid and shapeless, wet and fragrant, warm and luxurious, yet for all that driven and hungry because insatiable (concupiscent)'.[10] The centaur is this tension between body and flesh realized in a single form. More than an 'Other', a creature which resembles the human but is not, the centaur is an extended meditation on humanity and animality. Its anomalous hybridity is a constant reminder that the integrity of separate categories and distinct classifications is an illusion. Given that the *scala naturae* is built on the fixity of such categories – bird, mouse, rock, flower – and that they are fundamental to Aristotle's programme, it would be going too far to suggest that for the Greeks the animal–human distinction was untenable, a position taken by some modern thinkers, but it would be fair to say that the Greek imagination allowed rich and fertile ground for playing with the fuzziness of these categories.[11] By confounding categories and certainty, stories involving the hybrid are a counterpoint to the dialectic of the philosopher and the observation of the scientist. Underlying anxieties about the boundaries between species and the forms of bodies within particular species resulted in an astonishing variety of uses for the centaur as a marker not of difference, but of indeterminacy.[12]

---

[10] Bruns 2007: 707.

[11] On the human-animal distinction in modern thought, see Ingold 1988 and Ingold 2007, as well as Calarco 2008 and Kalof and Montgomery 2011. On the fundamental significance of Aristotle's distinction between 'the inanimate' and 'the ensouled', see Agamben 2004: 14.

[12] Surprised by the confusing tracks left by his stolen cattle, Apollo (*Homeric Hymn to Hermes*, 219–26) lists the animals whose tracks are unlike those he can see, including a rough-maned centaur. As Gabriella Cursaru notes, the reference introduces the theme of indeterminacy and the in-betweenness of Hermes. See Cursaru 2015: 13: 'Pourvu que ses vaches aient pour séjour la

Anomaly begs for explanation, and not long after Pindar's odd genealogy the first rationalizing explanation for the centaurs' hybridity appears, in the work of the mythographer Palaiphatos.[13] In his account, an early version of the 'first horsemen' trope, once upon a time on Mt Pelion a herd of bulls was doing damage to the fields and crops of the locals. After Ixion offered to pay to get rid of the bulls, a group of young men from the village of Nephele took up the challenge, trained their horses as mounts and attacked the bulls. Feigning retreat, they drew the bulls (*tauroi*) on, and struck (*kenteo*) them with their javelins. It was these actions that gave rise to their name: centaurs. Etymological explanations, in fact, have never lost their appeal. Giovanni Semerano argued the etymology of *kentauroi* was based on Semitic words for family (*kintu*) and river (*harru*).[14] He also claimed that **ken-** derives from Semitic, Aramaic and Hebrew **kēn-**, meaning 'like', and that *tauros* is from Aramaic **tōrā** ('bull').[15] Neither explanation is especially persuasive, and in any case the two are mutually exclusive. A more promising approach is Henderson's observation that *kenteo* may refer to the thrusting movements of sex and that *tauros* can be used to describe the genitals. These creatures are built for sex.[16]

In the second half of his account, Palaiphatos tells of the growing arrogance of the horsemen and their feud with the Lapiths of Thessaly. Resorting to the same hit-and-run tactics as before, they would come down

prairie "pure, en dehors de tout mélange" de la Piérie, comment Apollon n'envisagerait-il la possibilité que leur vol – un acte d'intrusion au coeur d'un espace inviolable, de transgression des interdits divins et de limites infranchissables pour un mortel – ait été opéré précisément par un être hybride, donc de nature radicalement opposée, tel le Centaure dont l'anatomie mêle l'humain et l'animal, tel le δαίμων qu'il évoque, tel Hermès lui-même, être "hybride" aussi et à sa façon, comme on le verra, et, de surcroît, maître par excellence de tout ce qui relève de l'entre-deux et du passage d'un espace à l'autre et d'un monde à l'autre?' (Given that his cows reside in the "pure, untainted" meadows of Pieria, how would Apollo not consider the possibility that their theft – an incursion into the heart of an inviolable space, a transgression of divine prohibitions and impassable barriers for a mortal – was carried out precisely by a hybrid being, of a radically opposite nature, such as the Centaur whose anatomy mixes human and animal, like the δαίμων it evokes, or such as Hermes himself, a "hybrid" being too in his own way, as we will see, and, moreover, master par excellence of everything that relates to the in-between and the passage from one space to the next and from one world to another?).

[13] Palaiphatos ('Teller of Old Tales') is doubtless a pseudonym. He is usually dated to the fourth century BC. See Alganza Roldán, Barr and Hawes 2017.

[14] Semerano 1994: 137.

[15] Semerano 2005: 14. The search for an etymological explanation for *kentauros* has a long and torturous history, summarized by De Angelis 2009, whose own contribution ('Devourer of Bowels') is not convincing. See also Molinari 2022: 160. Another example of dubious etymology is the unfortunate suggestion of Vogel 1978: 32 that the centaur arose as an artistic representation of the castrated pack-animal, based on the similarity of *kentauros* to κανθήλιος, 'pack-ass'.

[16] Henderson 1975: 133.

from Pelion, hide, pillage and burn before returning to the hills. As they retreated, the cavalrymen were glimpsed by the locals, who, seeing the horses' rumps and men's backs from a distance, were responsible for the myth:

> Seeing this peculiar sight, they cried, 'The Centaurs from Nephele are overrunning us!' In fact, it was from this sight and from this cry that the unbelievable myth was created, according to which a creature both horse *and* man had come into being on the mountain from a cloud *nephele*.
>
> Palaiphatos, *Peri Apiston*, tr. McInerney

Palaiphatos' account is the first attempt to reconcile Pindaric elements such as the names of Ixion, Nephele and even *kentauros* with a rationalizing account of the centaurs as horsemen. This is an explanation for the centaur that grows out of a longer and deeper contemplation of the relationship between horse and rider.

In fact, for 300 years before Palaiphatos, artists had been manufacturing terracotta figurines that depicted the fused body of horse and man. In purely stylistic terms the composite figure of the centaur arose in part as an exaggerated expression of the intimate relationship between riders and horses. A sixth-century terracotta from Cyprus suggests this by omitting the rider's legs and posing him as if his torso emerges straight out of the back of the horse (see Figure 6.2). This fusion, while not realistic, is not hard to decipher: the physical bond between horse and rider is intense.[17] Unsurprisingly, then, arguments for explaining centaurs as 'the first cavalry' remain as popular today as they were in Antiquity.[18]

The intensity of the relationship between horse and rider results from more than proximity. It is overshadowed by the constant jostling for power between them. As in the case of the gorgon, the centaur served to embody an implicit threat and the need to master it. In this instance the danger lay in the horse's massively greater strength, which had to be tamed if the horse was to be useful. It is no coincidence that the very first horse-training manual, the Hittite text ascribed to Kikkuli, gives his title as *aššuššanni*: 'the one who pushes the horse in training to exhaustion'.[19]

---

[17] For treatments of the human–horse relationship, see Moore 2004, Johns 2006, Griffith 2006 and Lewis 2017: 27–30. For full bibliography, see the Select Bibliography in Fögen and Thomas 2017a, pp. 456–7 and 463–4.

[18] Vogel 1978: 19: 'Die Deutung der Kentauren als der ersten Reiter ist so plausibel, daß schon die antiken Mythographen auf sie kamen' (The interpretation of the centaurs as the first horsemen is so plausible that even the ancient mythographers came up with it).

[19] Raulwing 2006: 8.

Figure 6.2 Cypriot terracotta figurine depicting horse and rider, ca. 750–600 BC. Metropolitan Museum of Art. 74.51.1771.

Depictions of men breaking horses entered the repertoire of Mycenaean vase painting in the late Bronze Age and are related to the hundreds of chariot kraters produced and exported to Cyprus and the eastern Mediterranean. The chariot kraters testify to the powerful hold on the imagination exerted by horses, although there is no agreement regarding the symbolism or precise function of the vessels.[20] Magical, funerary and military associations are all possible, and the high status of the horse and chariot ensemble is certain. Similar ambiguities surround the scenes in which a horse-leader is flanked by two horses. The scene may well represent a god such as Poseidon, a local hero or an aristocrat, but even if the exact identification of the male figure is unclear the composition is an unmistakable depiction of the struggle to assert control. Susan Langdon has argued that the figure is a variant of the Master of Animals which was adapted by Mycenaean artists in places such as Kos, Rhodes, Miletos and Cyprus.[21] The circulation of people and vessels around the Aegean resulted in the motif being brought back to the Greek mainland. By the Late Geometric period the horse-leader had become one of the most popular scenes on vessels from the Argolid (Figure 6.3).

[20] Recht and Morris 2021.   [21] Langdon 1989.

Figure 6.3 Krater with male figure and horses, from Tiryns, grave XIII, ca. 730–690 BC. Nafplio Archaeological Museum. David Parker/Science Photo Library.

It is also at this time that the kings of Assyria were expressing interest in the horse-taming abilities of people within their realm. In Sargon II's *Letter to the God Aššur* (714 BC), he reports:

> The people who live in the district are without equal in all of Urartu in their knowledge of riding horses. For years they had been catching the young colts of (wild) horses, native to this wide land, and raising them for the royal army [or Urartu] … They do not saddle them, but (whether) going forward, turning to one side, or turning around, (as the tactics) of battle require, they are (never) seen to break the yoke (i.e. to become separated from their team).
> Luckenbill, *ARAB* 2.84.

The eighth century witnessed an increasing admiration for the skills of the horseman because, although horses were first domesticated in the fourth millennium (or possibly earlier), in the early first millennium riders abandoned the use of chariots in warfare and began riding horses directly.[22] This altered the role of the horse in warfare but also made possible new forms of expressing elite status in Archaic Greece. Because the ideology of *kleos* and *arete* was highly performative, elite pastimes such as hunting and racing made horsemanship and all it entailed – ownership, taming and racing – into a type of conspicuous display suitable for aristocrats.[23] It was for this reason that the speaker of Lysias 24 takes pains to explain that he rides horses because of his disability and not because of his *hybris*. Hesiod

---

[22] On domestication of horses and the shift from chariot to cavalry, see Anthony and Brown 2011.

[23] On the connection between horses and elite status, see Griffith 2006. Boardman (1998: 27) observed pithily: 'The dominant themes in Attic Late Geometric are death, horses, and warfare.' On hunting and racing, see Anderson 1961 and Bugh 1988: 14. For a recent treatment of *hippotrophia* as the mark of the good citizen, see Duplouy 2022.

may have railed against 'bribe-eating *basileis*', but for his contemporaries Homer's horse-taming heroes were models of the leaders they aspired to be. Bellerophon, for example, could not slay the Chimaira until he had bridled Pegasos with the help of either Athena Chalinitis (She who Bridles) or Poseidon.[24] It is not by accident that the closing line of the *Iliad* pays tribute to Hektor and that his epithet, 'Hippodamos' ('Horse-tamer'), should be the very last word of the poem.[25] In the constellation of aristocratic values, the rider's domination of the horse therefore served as a clear marker of elite status. There is a hint of this in a horse-taming scene on the black-figure aryballos attributed to Amasis. One onlooker holds a spear like a warrior and the horse tamer brandishes a staff over his head between two rearing horses, as if ready to strike.[26]

Whether or not the methods of training a horse are based on coercion, the rider can only sit astride a horse that has been tamed. Xenophon's treatise on horsemanship is particularly alert to the continuous struggle between horse and rider. He notes that 'spirit in a horse is precisely what anger is in a man ... so he who abstains from angering a spirited horse is least likely to rouse his anger'.[27] At a later point he advises the rider to allow the horse to relax 'when he has done something according to the rider's wishes'.[28] In Xenophon's discussion, however, the need to dominate is modified by the closeness between the human and horse, an intimacy that keeps impinging on how the one treats the other. The horse's stall should be within sight of the rider's house to prevent theft of the horse's food, just as the rider would protect his own supplies. The animal's welfare is paramount because the rider entrusts his safety to the horse in times of danger, says Xenophon. The rider must practice himself what he teaches the horse so they can help each other and be more efficient. They are a team.[29] In each of these observations Xenophon underscores an important point: a successful relationship between human and horse is based not on brutal domination, but on sympathy. It is thanks to this that the horseman can exert control, but is because of this that a human may

---

[24] Hard 2019: 221. For Athena Hippia, see Detienne 1971.
[25] Homer, *Il.* 24.804: ὣς οἵ γ' ἀμφίεπον τάφον Ἕκτορος ἱπποδάμοιο (And thus did they attend to the burial of Hector, tamer of horses). Linking this to the imminent arrival of the Trojan horse, Frank 2005/2006 notes, 'The poem's last word, *hippodamoio*, leaves the audience with the ironic foreshadowing of the inability of the Trojans without Hector to master that most fatal horse.'
[26] Black-figure terracotta aryballos, depicting horse-tamer and onlookers, ca. 550 BC. Attributed to Amasis. H. 3 1/4 in. (8.3 cm), diameter 3 1/2 in. (8.9 cm). Metropolitan Museum of Art, 62.11.11
[27] Xen., *Hipp.* 9.2.   [28] Xen., *Hipp.* 11.5.
[29] Xen., *Hipp.* 4.1 stalls, fodder and facing danger together; 8.1 exercising together. On Xenophon's feelings towards his horse, see Chandezon 2019: 67–70.

develop a close bond with the horse, as did Hadrian who erected a funeral monument to his horse, Borysthenes.[30]

Successful horsemanship relies upon a symbiosis of horse and rider. Here, the hybridity of the centaur (horse-man) provides a telling counterpoint to the rider (horseman) which in turn, somewhat paradoxically, re-establishes the boundaries between horse and human. This is illustrated by a discussion in the Xenophon's *Cyropedeia*. Cyrus' lieutenant, Chrysantas, addresses the question of whether the Persians ought to have cavalry or not. Supporting Cyrus' contention that the Persians should develop their cavalry, Chrysantas says:

> Now the creature that I have envied most is, I think, the Centaur (if any such being ever existed), able to reason with a man's intelligence and to manufacture with his hands what he needed, while he possessed the fleetness and strength of a horse so as to overtake whatever ran before him and to knock down whatever stood in his way. Well, all his advantages I combine in myself by becoming a horseman ... Indeed, my state will be better than being grown together in one piece; for, in my opinion at least, the Centaurs must have had difficulty in making use of many of the good things invented for man; and how could they have enjoyed many of the comforts natural to the horse?
>
> Xenophon, *Cyro.* 4.3.17, 19 (tr. Miller)

Chrysantas evaluates the creature in terms of its human and equine capabilities.[31] Each contributing half has its advantages, ranging from intelligence and dexterity to speed, which, if combined, result in a creature superior to its parts. But, at the same time, the aptness of the creature is compromised by its hybridity: it cannot function entirely as a human or as a horse. Chrysantas does not offer details, referring only vaguely in section 19 to the good things invented for humans (τῶν ἀνθρώποις ηὑρημένων ἀγαθῶν) and those things that are naturally pleasing to horses (πολλῶν δὲ τῶν ἵπποις πεφυκότων ἡδέων), but his remarks on the limitations of the centaur are not hard to understand. Would centaurs, for example, enjoy a human or an equine diet? Could they sail ships and engage in trade? Despite each half's strengths and abilities, the blending of the two creatures produces a hybrid that is weaker

---

[30] CIL 12.1122; Cassius Dio, *Hist.* 69.10.2. See Fögen and Thomas 2017b: 2–3 and Lewis and Llewellyn 2018: 140–1.

[31] For recent discussion of this passage, see Johnson 2005, who argues that Xenophon uses the centaur as a symbol of Cyrus' imperial Persians, an unsuccessful hybrid of Median luxury and Persian restraint. Given Cyrus' own standing as an equine hybrid – a mule, half Mede, half Persian (Herodotos 1.55.2) – Xenophon's use of a metaphor of hybridity should probably also be seen as an intertextual engagement with Herodotos.

than its parts because its entirety is made up of parts that remain, at some level, incompatible. His conclusion is that the cavalryman has all the advantages of both of his parts precisely because they remain distinct. The horseman can dismount. In this account the centaur is not an allegory for horsemanship but a weaker variation of the horseman whose fusion confirms, paradoxically, the need for a firm boundary between horse and human.

La Bête humaine

Understanding the significance of the centaur is complicated by the fact that, despite the importance of horses in Greek culture, horsemanship is not central to the place of centaurs in Greek myth. Instead, they make their appearance in episodes that emphasize their sexual appetites and their utter lack of self-control. At Olympia, for example, the west pediment of the temple of Zeus shows Apollo watching serenely over a scene of complete chaos as the centaurs, drunk on the fumes of wine, wreak havoc on the wedding feast of Peirithous and Hippodameia. Centaurs can be seen grabbing Lapith women, who resist violently even as the Lapith men punch and stab the centaurs. Despite the brutality of the scene, it has been suggested that it cannot be read as a simple allegory in which the centaurs are wholly evil. Robin Osborne has argued that on the western pediment 'we see how easily human virtues of hospitality can degenerate into uncalculating physical violence'.[32] The centaur is wild, rude and hairy, uncivilized, brutal, driven by appetites and unbridled sensuality, yet it is equally unmistakably familiar, or, as Osborne, writes, 'they carry with them the unwelcome bestiality of humanity'.[33] On the Olympia pediments the random state of preservation heightens this effect of unexpected familiarity by repeatedly presenting us with scenes of what appear at first glance to be men sexually assaulting woman. But these are not men; they are centaurs. And the blade slipping into the centaur's chest does not deliver a sacrificial

---

[32] Osborne 1994: 62.
[33] Osborne 1994: 71. The *Roman de* Troie 12.353 ff offers a description of the Sagittaire that reflects the long afterlife of these associations: 'Below the navel, the Sagittaire had the body and the semblance of a horse and no one could beat him in a race. The rest of the body, the arms, the face, were like ours, but the whole being wasn't very nice to look at. He did not need to wear clothes because he was furry all over like a beast. As for his colour, he was blacker than coal, his eyes burned in his face and lit up the darkest night. No lie, you could see him from three miles away or more. His face was so terrifying that no one who saw him could prevent himself from giving way to fear.'

thrust, or a hunter's killing shot, but a warrior's thrust at a foe in battle. Thus, the confrontation, the disruption of a civilized wedding feast, the ensuing chaos, the brawl, the assaults and the confusion we experience not as a simple triumph of human over beast or civilized over uncivilized or higher function over lower, but as a confusing tumult over which only the god towers, serene and puissant. Humans here are mired in struggle, not triumphant. We are on the same plane as the centaur. In disrupting the Lapith wedding the centaurs violate a fundamental human institution, the vulnerability of which they have exposed. This in turn demands a violent reassertion of the social and the cosmic order.

Similar anxieties regarding marriage, transgression and commensurate violence are played out in another cycle involving centaurs: the story of Deianeira, bride of Herakles. In Sophocles' *Trachiniai*, Deianeira, having been saved from marriage to the river god Acheloos (who took the form of a man-faced bull) travels to the house of her new husband, Herakles. Along the way she encounters Nessos:

> He was a centaur,
> who for a fee would hold men in his arms
> and take them through the raging waters
> of the Evenos, without oars or sails
> to help him ferry them across the stream.
> He carried me, as well, up on his shoulders,
> when I was first a bride and my father
> had sent me off to follow Herakles.
> When we reached the middle of the river,
> Nessus' carnal hands began to grope me.
> I screamed, and in an instant Zeus's son
> turned round and shot a feathered arrow
> whistling through his chest, deep into his lungs.
>
> Soph. *Trachin.* 559–568 (tr. Johnston)

A variation of the scene appears on a terracotta Melian relief plaque, on which the centaur is depicted folding his forelegs around Deianeira's waist and grabbing her wrist even as Herakles charges in with his club raised and grapples with Nessos.[34]

Herakles, as Christina Salowey has shown, is frequently associated with places that were known for waterworks, such as drains and

---

[34] Melian relief depicting Heracles killing Nessos, fifth century. From a grave in Troezen. Piraeus Museum, Athens.

canals – examples of human manipulation of the natural environment.[35] The centaur Nessos, in contrast, is associated with the Evenos river. The conflict between hero and centaur is therefore, at one level, the opposition of human culture and the natural world, another version of the familiar binary of *nomos* versus *physis*. It is also a doublet of the same conflict between Herakles and the hybrid river deity, Acheloos. Layered over this opposition of the natural and the man-made is Nessos' transgression of proper behaviour. In attempting to rape Deianeira he is clearly submitting to his animal instincts, but he is also, according the Greek conception of *hubris*, committing an act of violation against Herakles since Deianeira is part of the hero's household. The physical dimensions of the centaur's misbehaviour therefore resonate even more deeply. Situating Nessos' attack at a river maps these violations of social boundaries onto the crossing of a physical boundary. In every possible sense, then, the centaur has crossed the line. Building on the anomaly of the centaur's physical humanimality, his transgressive behaviour externalizes the threat of hypersexuality and *hubris*, demanding that it be answered with equal violence.

Varieties of violence, transgressive and corrective, are thereby encoded into the centaur, which makes the pronounced humanity of the creature so significant. The centaur operates in one field – sexual violence – and in its exact opposite; the hypersexual centaur is counterbalanced by the hypercivilized centaur: Cheiron. The difference between the two types goes back to their parentage: Cheiron is descended from Kronos and Philyra and is unrelated to the centaurs of Nephele.[36] It is also a difference marked by dress: Cheiron appears fully dressed, while the wild centaurs are always depicted naked, as if living, paradoxically, in a prelapsarian state of innocence. Tutor of Achilles and Aklepios, skilled in music and medicine, Cheiron is frequently depicted in late Archaic and Classical vases with carefully coifed hair, wearing a himation, and often holding a staff on which he carries rabbits he has caught. He is nothing less than an aristocratic *kalos k'agathos*. The rabbits are offerings for the young Achilles from his *erastes*. Cheiron displays his equine hybridity almost as an afterthought, with horse's hindquarters awkwardly sticking out of the back of his garments.

The centaur Pholos is another example of the gentlemanly centaur (see Figure 6.4). Not only is he not riotously drunken or driven by lust, he is the very model of courtesy, as in a fifth-century kylix in Basel, where he reclines in sympotic elegance with Herakles, his horse forelegs neatly

---

[35] Salowey 1994.
[36] Cheiron's parentage: Scholiast on Apollonius Rhodius 1. 554; Apollod., *Biblio*. 1. 8–9; Apollon. Rhod., *Argon*. 2. 1231–9; Hyginus, *Fab*. 138.

Figure 6.4 Herakles and Pholos reclining. Early fifth century BC. © Antikenmuseum Basel und Sammlung Ludwig BS 489.

folded beneath him in an equine equivalent of relaxation. The aroma of freshly opened wine-jugs has caught the attention of the wild centaurs entering Pholos' cave, and they point towards the pithos as Herakles serves himself. Pholos gestures towards them as he turns to Herakles, as if warning him. The symposium, as the viewer knows, will soon erupt into an orgy of violence. Recent interpretations of this and similar scenes set in caves suggest that these are instances of the 'precivilized' moment, in which an imperfect symposium signals a phase of social evolution prior to the present.[37] In this imaginative exploration of the development of culture, the staging of these scenes in the cave of Pholos draws on the duality of the centaur to suggest a tension at the heart of the symposium and elite culture more generally. As a physical body the centaur combines both human and animal, but as a social being it is capable of multiple identities that range from the purely animal (characterized by primary drives and appetites) to the perfectly human (marked by restraint, manners and learning). And, as ever, the association with wine suggests that our higher, human *sophrosyne* is only as long-lasting as our sobriety. These episodes involving the Lapith feast, Nessos and Pholos function very like parables, but the centaur figures are more than mere allegories of

---

[37] Topper 2012: 40–1; Franks 2018: 164.

libidinous drunkenness. Cheiron and Pholos are equally models of a kind of humanity to which we aspire. The figures are at once cautionary and also a way of framing this question: in the encounter with the animal, what exactly is the human?

Delineating Species

Up to this point, the centaurs we have encountered have all been of the familiar variety sometimes called hippocentaurs, but there are a great many depictions in which the centaur is human from head to toe, with equine hindquarters rather awkwardly grafted on.[38] In these depictions, the centaur more closely resembles his human opponent, though without displaying the refinement of a Cheiron or Pholos. These man-centaurs are careful to show where the human stops and the equine begins. Boeotian terracotta figurines from the eighth century on explore this quite literally (Figure 6.5).[39]

Here, the boundary between human and horse is clearly delineated by a single line of paint and the two halves of the centaur's body are differently coloured, emphasizing the creature's distinct hybridity. In vase paintings the distinction between man and beast is equally straightforward, as can be seen in a proto-Attic amphora in New York depicting Nessos holding his hands out in supplication to Herakles.[40] The centaur's figure is entirely human at the front; the equine half is a very ungainly addition that simply emerges from the man's buttocks. This way of composing the centaur is all the more remarkable given the long Near Eastern tradition of depicting centaurs and similar figures as entirely equine to the waist. The decision by Greek artists to depict the centaur as entirely human to the soles of its front feet was thus a deliberate choice. And, as with any cultural borrowing, the alteration draws attention to the new form. Divorced from a Near Eastern setting, the centaur was free to take on new meanings, emphasizing the human dimension of the struggles in which it was engaged. For the artists who preferred the human centaur to the hippocentaur, the star-lore that gave rise to Pabilsaĝ (Sagittarius) was a distant memory. Stylistically, the

---

[38] Notable examples include a black-figure amphora in the British Museum (BM 1956,1220.1), an early-sixth-century grey Tufa statue from Vulci (National Etruscan Museum prov. EX3/VU), a terracotta sarcophagus from Clazomenae (Metropolitan Museum, 21.169.1) and a Proto-Attic neck amphora attributed to the New York Nessos Painter (Metropolitan Museum, 11.210.1). For the term 'hippocentaur', see Plato, *Phaedrus* 229b.

[39] Szabo 1994.

[40] Proto-Attic Neck Amphora depicting Nessos, ca. 675–650 BC. New York Nessos Painter. H. 42 3/4 in.; diameter 22 in. Metropolitan Museum of Art 11.210.1.

Figure 6.5 Boiotian terracotta centaur, ca. 625–600 BC. Museum of Art and Archaeology. University of Missouri, Columbia. 58.20.

composition that grafts a horse's hindquarters onto a human body may seem awkward, but it was a way of imagining the centaur that remained popular. It can still be seen, for example, one hundred years later, on a black-figure *dinos* from Lakonia by the Rider Painter.[41] Once again, the scene shows Herakles wrestling with Nessos, evidence of the popularity of an episode that expressed one version of the *agon* at the heart of life in Archaic Greece: the threat to order and the need to repress it violently.

In each of these depictions it is striking that the centaur incorporates the human entirely. It is also clear that many early centaurs are, in terms of genitalia, indistinguishable from men. This is, in fact, quite common, and is evident in centaurs from places as far apart as Cyprus and Etruria, as well as the mainland.[42] Man-centaurs often seem to be designed, in fact, as if to focus our attention on the question of the hybrid creature's complex relationship to humanity. The Centauro de Royos, for example, discovered in Murcia, Spain, but of sixth-century Peloponnesian manufacture, turns his head so that if the viewer meets the centaur's gaze he sees along the length of the centaur's torso, and realizes that the figure has a horse's body but human buttocks and front legs (Figure 6.6).

---

[41] Herakles and Pholos on a Laconian dinos, ca. 560–540 by the Rider Painter. Musée du Louvre E662.
[42] Centaur of Vulci, Volcanic tuff, 590–580 BC. National Etruscan Museum; Centaur, terracotta. ca. 700 BC. Staatliche Antikensammlungen, Munich.

Delineating Species 187

Figure 6.6 Centauro de Royos, bronze, Greek. Sixth century BC, from Campo de Caravaca, Murcia. Wikimedia Commons.

The viewer is not just shown a centaur but is challenged to ask what they are seeing. The same is true of a pair of Archaic bronze statuettes, possibly cauldron attachments.[43] In both cases the centaur is striding forward so that from the front the figure appears entirely human, but viewed from the side the figure takes on a wholly different appearance. In these sixth-century figurines, the stance and twist of the body exploit the plasticity of bronze to complicate the aesthetic response of the viewer: they juxtapose the familiar with the incongruous to produce a slightly jarring, but unavoidable effect. They are mildly unsettling. There is a third class of centaur that points towards even more layers of complexity. Some Archaic centaurs appear to capture the transition from man-centaur to hippocentaur at its midpoint. In a black-figure hydria from Caere in the Louvre, both centaurs have human forelegs extending from human buttocks onto which the horse's back has been added. Their front feet, however, have been rendered like horses' hooves – a very deliberate choice emphasized by the placement of the warrior's human feet close by.[44]

Roughly contemporary with the hydria from Caere is a sarcophagus from Klazomenai, thought to have been manufactured by an Ionian artist

---

[43] Centaurs viewed side on: Bronze centaur, Laconian. Sixth century BC. Paris, Bibliothèque Nationale de France, département des monnaies, médailles et antiques bronze. 514. Bronze centaur, Athenian Akropolis, eighth–seventh century BC. National Archaeological Museum, Athens. 6680.

[44] Hydria with centauromachy, Caere, 525–500 BC. H. 43 cm. Musée du Louvre E 700.

who had fled the encroachment of Persian power.[45] On it, the artist has correctly portrayed two centaurs whose back legs display forward-bending knee joints, like horses. The front legs display human thighs and calves but end in fetlocks and horse's hooves. These images capture the centaur as if in the process of transformation from anthropic to more fully equine. The transition is unsettling. The figures are depicted in silhouette, so that one cannot pick out details, but the symmetry of the front and back legs draws the viewer's attention to the odd combination of features. The silhouette also suggests that the centaur has lost its human sexual organs. In this connection it may be relevant that these man-centaurs are most often shown battling Lapith men or Herakles, and thus operate in the setting of combat, while it is hippocentaurs who are more often shown trying to carry women off.

Shifting perception, in fact, is integral to viewing the centaur as an encounter with the self. The disquieting addition of an explicitly animal element to a human form makes this question unavoidable: what is the human? As Derrida famously observed, 'The animal looks at us and we are naked before it. Thinking perhaps begins there.'[46] Similarly, when we look upon the human centaur we see an alternative version of ourselves, distorted and troubling. A bronze sheet at Olympia demonstrates how powerful this encounter can be: the centaurs depicted are emphatically man-centaurs.[47] Instead of shaggy beards and the features of satyrs, their faces have human profiles. They sport trim beards, have Archaic hairstyles with long, elegant braids, and are wearing either caps or close-fitting helmets. They combine animal and human parts quite differently from the mostly equine hippocentaur, suggesting that humanness and wildness exist on a sliding scale. The centaur is neither mirror-image nor monster, but an anomaly whose similarity is disturbing.

An even more direct evocation of the centaur's mirror-like capacity to throw an image of the human back at the viewer is displayed by a famous bronze group in the Metropolitan Museum of Art (Figure 6.7). The composition dates to the eighth century, early in the history of Greek centaurs. A human and a centaur face each other directly. In fact, the entire piece is so strictly axial in its composition that it is possible to 'see' each figure from the point of view of the other. Within the composition the human looks

---

[45] Archaic terracotta sarcophagus rim, ca. 525–500 BC. Klazomenai. 7 1/2 × 36 1/2 × 84 in. Metropolitan Museum of Art, 21.169.1.
[46] Derrida 2008: 397.
[47] For full discussion of the bronze sheet, see Chapter 8, and Figure 8.2, as part of a treatment of the human figure Kaineus.

Figure 6.7 Bronze man and centaur. Mid-eighth century BC. Metropolitan Museum of Art, 17.190.2072.

slightly down on another figure which mirrors him. Their human bodies have the same proportions; they wear the same hats; their facial features reflect similarity to the point of being nearly identical. Within the composition like faces like, man versus man. The only significant difference is that the human is slightly taller.

Outside of the scene, however, the viewer has the opportunity to take it in panoptically by viewing the figures perpendicular to the axis running through the composition. From this external vantage point the viewer sees not a confrontation of like with like, but man versus centaur. From here the hybrid's otherness is emphatic. The horse's rear legs are massively muscled, its belly reduced to a mere bar of connective metal protruding from the human. As a result, our experience of the centaur allows us – in fact, forces us – to engage more richly, more insistently and more fully with the confrontation between the figures. The impact of the centaur can very much be read as an instance of the Uncanny (*das Unheimlich*). Freud expanded the original notion of uncanniness by noting that many literary examples involved doubling: 'These involve the idea of the "double" (the *Doppelgänger*), in all its nuances and manifestations – that is to say, the appearance of persons who have to be regarded as identical because they look alike.'[48] The same doubling occurs in the encounter with the man-horse. As the man confronts the centaur he sees another man. Only subsequently will he see what we have seen: bits of a horse. In between the familiarity of the *Doppelgänger* and the recognition of something odd and unsettling is the 'aha!' moment. It is this lightning strike of recognition and misrecognition that is so potent. All hybridity compels an unsettling dialectic of the similar and dissimilar, of something familiar yet threatening. The centaur adds nuance to the experience of this moment by forcing us to ask ourselves exactly what we are. Do we see ourselves in the centaur?

Man-Horse or Horse-Man

The rich possibilities of contemplating centaurs as at once alike and different are sometimes lost in treatments of centaur vase iconography because of a tendency to regard these variations between hippocentaurs and man-centaurs as primarily stylistic choices. The differences between types suggest an evolution from centaurs with human forelegs and equine hindquarters to creatures with wholly equine bodies from the waist down. More than a century ago, however, Paul Bauer demolished this view and showed that there was evidence for hippocentaurs as early as the Geometric period.[49] Yet Bauer's designations of Class A (junction at the withers) and Class B (human body with horse hindquarters attached) still treats the variations primarily as exercises in classification according to style. In this vein, Michael Padgett has concluded that 'After experimenting with these and other permutations, most early Greek artists settled on the two basic types of centaur – with either human or equine forelegs – both of which continued until the Early Classical period of the mid-fifth century, by which time the type with human legs had long been reserved for the "civilized" Cheiron'.[50] This interpretation is an approach rooted in connoisseurship, which, while accurate, nevertheless avoids consideration of the centaur's importance as a symbol of hypersexuality. With this in mind, one might ask what is suggested by the transformation of the centaur from a creature whose human half extends down the entire length of the body and includes human genitals, to a creature whose humanity stops at the waist and then transforms into an equine body? Centaurs are unbridled sexuality, and the threat of sexual assault is ever present. In the

---

[48] Freud 2003: 141.   [49] See Bauer 1912: 54–5.   [50] Padgett 2003: 10.

Figure 6.8 Bronze statuette of a centaur. Greek (Attic?), ca. 530 BC. 11.1 cm × 3.9 cm × 11.9 cm. Princeton University Art Museum, 1997–36. Princeton University Art Museum/Art Resource.

hippocentaur's body has bestiality been added to the threat of rape?[51] The question is more complicated than a simple matter of different genitalia: hippocentaurs are not depicted aroused. In fact, as is illustrated by the Princeton centaur, the smooth, muscular appearance at the point of fusion leaves no doubt that the creature has no human genitalia at all, and that its equine penis is retracted, the normal position for an unaroused horse (see Figure 6.8). As with the conventions of stagecraft, in which murder is kept out of sight, the threat of the centaur's lust remains latent. The centaur only suggests what the satyr displays.

Unlike satyr iconography, which is relentlessly focused on the erect phallus, both types of centaurs thus make it possible for sexual assault to remain a lurking presence in the figural imagery of Archaic Greece, operating on occasion explicitly as centaurs carry off women, at other times only raising the possibility of this. It is telling that a scene such as the one

---

[51] Modern treatments of the centaur also dwell on sexuality. In John Updike's *The Centaur* (1963), the hero, George Caldwell, moves between reality and a fantasy world in which, as Chiron, he possesses 'the massive potency of a stallion' (p. 24). A much grimmer exploration of centaur sexuality and the association with rape is to be found in Angela Carter's 1972 novel, *The Infernal Desire Machines of Doctor Hoffman*.

Figure 6.9 Drawing of a painted alabastron depicting a centaur and a woman (Cheiron and Chariklo?), ca. 625–600 BC. Rhodes Archaeological Museum 11.550.

depicted on a painted alabastron from Rhodes has variously been read as Nessos seizing Deianeira or as Cheiron saluting his bride, Chariklo (see Figure 6.9). The lines between assault and seduction are not clearly drawn here, and the possibility of the one mutating into the other are suggested by a contingent hybridity: next to the couple is a horse's head that matches the missing equine portion of the centaur figure, as if the human, civilized centaur, with his tunic and head-band, might revert to his full horse shape at any moment, perhaps once aroused.[52] The position of the woman's hand makes this likely.

The depiction of centaurs in sexually charged scenes is not restricted to heterosexual encounters. An amphora in Palermo shows a hippocentaur, with pointy ears and horse's body, reaching towards a second centaur, who is shown as a fully grown man-centaur, bearded and with human front legs. The scene is composed with gestures and postures borrowed from paederastic iconography.[53] The hippocentaur holds one hand out and reaches towards the man-centaur's genitals (see Figure 6.10). (The genitals are not depicted, with the man-centaur's hips and legs turned slightly away from

---

[52] Padgett 2003: 18 offers a slightly different reading, in which the horse's head serves as a reminder that despite having successfully wooed the nymph the old centaur still possesses a horsey character.

[53] The description in the Palermo Museum's *La Collezione Casuccini* (no photograph) merely notes 'Il Centauro selvaggio ha lineamenti brutali, orecchi ferini e un gesticolare violento con le due braccia levate' (The wild Centaur has brutal features, feral ears and gesticulates violently with both arms raised) (18). For pederastic seduction scenes employing the same gestures, see Louvre F51n2 and Martin von Wagner Museum der Universität Würzburg, L 241.

Man-Horse or Horse-Man 193

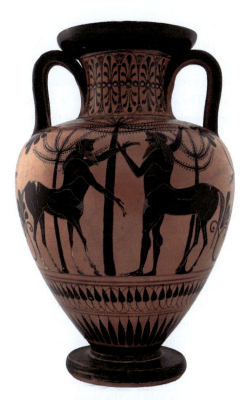

Figure 6.10 Two centaurs (Cheiron and Centaur×). Black-figure amphora, 550–500 BC, attributed to the Leagros Group. Palermo, Mus. Arch. Regionale: 1460. (Beazley 4589). Archivio fotographico del Museo Archeologico Antonino Salinas.

the viewer, but the figure's front legs guarantee that he is genitally human.) In the fifth century, 'centaur' was used as a slang expression for a sexually aggressive male. Are the Palermo centaurs mocking paederastic couples, suggesting, with about as much subtlety as Aristophanes, that such aristocratic behaviour was actually laughable?

In these various instantiations of the horse-man, the boundary between horse and human is porous. Centaurs represent various ways of exploiting that porosity. The association of centaurs with sexual assault arises from a contemplation of the sexual drives of men and is the most dramatic instance of hybridity both stimulating self-reflection and shaping an externalization of this. The result is a potent contrafactual: the man as horse. What this accomplishes is a displacement of what the centaur embodies – namely, unrestrained male lust – into the realm of storytelling in poetry, vase painting and figurines. This both trivializes the danger of assault, and, as a reminder of its ubiquity, naturalizes it. If gorgons render powerful women a monstrous threat to be neutralized and satyrs guarantee a continuous thrum of ludicrous toxic masculinity through the sixth and fifth centuries, centaurs offer a third instance of the power of hybridity: a figure of primal instincts onto which every man projects himself.

Yet this too is not straightforward. The spectre of bestiality is raised as the centaur tries to carry off the Lapith women or Deianeira, but the threat is never realized. Instead, it will be averted by the righteous violence unleashed on the centaur. It is this response that matters most, the authorization of violence made more urgent by a potential crime almost too hideous to contemplate. Changes to the centaur's form, therefore, are not merely an evolution of stylistic expression, but point to an increasing use of the centaur as signifier of threat and response. To what end? Such mixtures are quite a bit less frightening than full monsters. Instead they are examples of the uncanny, things that emphatically draw attention to themselves by playing off our expectations and intuition. Accordingly, the hybrid may be thought of as a mode of thinking, rather than a genre. The unexpected fixes our attention, and subverts, or at least unsettles, normality. In this respect the uncanny hybrid performs an important role in relation to cultural production: it destabilizes narrative. Most of the cultural forms that rely on narrative are comfortably predictable. For the Greeks this familiarity frames every Trojan War episode, every tale told on the stage, even when the poet gives an old tale a fresh gloss. Epic and tragedy rely on the reassurance of formulae. From a repertoire of stories they reshape experience into recognizably structured, orderly forms. Monsters may provide suitable antagonists in these stories, but even if some monsters are hybrids, some hybrids are not monsters. Their oddity instead marks them as hyperreal, as invitations to recognize that reality has more dimensions than are dreamt of in our philosophy.

Horses and Their Heroes

Aside from the merging of horse and human in the body of the centaur, there are other ways of exploiting the porous boundary between horses and human, most notably by imagining a breakdown of the barrier to communication that separates us. This occurs in a celebrated episode in Homer. In the *Iliad*, a poem which presses pathos to the point of tears at the most charged moments, the horses of Achilles, Xanthos and Balios, are the subject of a lengthy description in bk 16. They stand apart from the fray, lamenting for their dead driver, Patroklos. Paralysed by grief, they can neither go forward into battle nor retreat. Instead, like human mourners, they cry out (*klaion*), shed hot tears on the ground and allow their unbound hair to be defiled in the dirt. Moved by their distress, Zeus calls the horses 'Poor Wretches' (*a deilo*), using the same form of address as when he contemplates Hektor dressing himself in the armour of Achilles, unaware of his looming death. Zeus ruminates on the ways that the immortal horses have been made to share the most human of experiences: grief at the loss of a loved one. They are indistinguishable from humans in their grief.[54] Then, in an even more striking moment, Xanthos is imbued by Hera with the power to speak.[55] Achilles has rebuked the pair, telling them not to leave him to be slaughtered as they left Patroklos. Xanthos remonstrates with Achilles, explaining that is was Apollo who killed Patroklos, just as he will soon kill Achilles himself:[56]

> Mighty Achilles,
> on this occasion we will bring you safely back.
> But the day you'll die is fast approaching.
> We won't be the cause, but some mighty god
> and a strong fate. It was not our laziness
> or lack of speed which helped the Trojans
> strip that armour from Patroklos' shoulders.
> A powerful god born to Leto killed him
> among those fighting at the battle front,
> then gave Hektor glory. The two of us
> could run as quickly as the West Wind's blasts –
> men say they are the fastest thing there is –
> your fate still stays the same, to die in war,
> killed by a mortal and a god.
>
> Homer, *Il.* 19.408–417 (tr. Johnston)

What are we to make of these immortal horses, grieving for Patroklos and foretelling the imminent death of Achilles? Sarah Johnston has convincingly shown that the episodes draw on separate traditions: one in which Hera gave special horses to heroes as a mark of favour and

---

[54] The episode of Achilles' horses shows some similarities to Vedic accounts of how horses lost their wings, causing them to grieve and to complain to Shalihotra: 'Why have you cut off our wings, when we had not committed any offense? Good people do not act like this.' See Doniger 2021: 18.

[55] Hom. *Il.* 19.400–18. On the connection between Xanthos' ability to speak and Hera's intervention, see Vespa 2020: 404–5.

[56] Hom. *Il.* 19.416–17: ἀλλὰ σοὶ αὐτῷ/μόρσιμόν ἐστι θεῷ τε καὶ ἀνέρι ἶφι δαμῆναι (Yet it is your doom to fall at the hands of a god and a man).

a second in which horses were regarded as vehicles for prophesy.[57] Johnston is certainly right to conclude that Homer's audience could be expected to catch allusions to these traditions behind the episodes involving the horses of Achilles. At the same time, the way the horses of Achilles participate in the poem suggests they are more than just magical beasts. The exchange with Achilles is framed by the notice that Hera imbued Xanthos with the power of human speech when Achilles addressed the horses, and that just as quickly the Erinyes stop this when the exchange is finished. Homer's description, therefore, calls attention to the precise moment when Xanthos has been given the power of speech (*audeenta*), but this raises other questions. Has Hera given the horses the power to think as well? Or was that always there? Have they only been given the power to verbalize human thoughts, or is the mind of the horse identical to a human mind? Since we have already encountered them grieving for Patroklos, acting much like human mourners, their sudden powers of human speech seem more an unveiling of what was hidden but was there all along: the power to think. Their response to the death of Patroklos and the coming death of Achilles emphasizes not the difference between horse and human, but our affinity. Here they share human pain, and give voice to a human awareness of death both experienced and anticipated.

Another horse hybrid closely intwined in the fortunes of a hero is Pegasos, who is integral to Bellerophon's victory over the Chimaira. It is worth pursuing the history of Pegasos and the Chimaira, since as a pair they illustrate the juxtaposition of the mundane world and one in which humans interact with hybrids. The two creatures represent antithetical constructions of the hybrid. Pegasos is fathered by Poseidon, and his magnificence is enhanced by the addition of wings, although a Melian terracotta plaque of the early fifth century depicts Pegasos without wings.[58] At the other end of the spectrum is the Chimaira, offspring of Echidna. The Chimaira was a hybrid borrowed from the Ancient Near East, possibly because the Greeks identified the hybrid figures they encountered in Anatolia and further afield with apotropaic power.[59] Its composite nature is emphasized by Homer (*Il.* 6. 180–2), who describes it as 'a thing of immortal make, not human, lion-fronted and snake behind, a goat in the middle, and snorting out the breath of the terrible flame of bright fire'. It is variously depicted in vase painting, most commonly with the body of a lion, the head of a goat jutting out of its back and a serpent

---

[57] Johnston 1992.   [58] British Museum 1842,0728.1135.
[59] On the Greeks understanding certain functions of Near Eastern hybrids as apotropaic, see Childs 2003.

serving in place of a tail.⁶⁰ Hesiod's description leaves no doubt that this composite creature was conventionally monstrous:

> [Echidna] was the mother of Chimaira who breathed raging fire, a creature fearful, great, swift footed and strong, who had three heads, one of a grim-eyed lion, another of a goat, and another of a snake, a fierce dragon; in her forepart she was a lion; in her hinderpart, a dragon; and in her middle, a goat, breathing forth a fearful blast of blazing fire. Her did Pegasos and noble Bellerophon slay; but Echidna was subject in love to Orthos and brought forth the deadly Sphinx which destroyed the Kadmeans, and the Nemean lion.
>
> Hesiod, *Theogony* 319–27 (tr. Evelyn-White)

Various explanations derived from natural conditions have been suggested for the Chimaira: its name might mean 'winter air', a reference to the astrological significance of the constellation Capricorn, the Goat, whose rising foretold winter, while its fire-breathing was connected even in Antiquity to naturally occurring firepits on Mt Yanartaş in southern Turkey.⁶¹ In Homer's telling of Bellerophon's story, the hero is sent by Proitos, king of Tiryns, to Iobates, king of Lydia, with a sealed message that bids Iobates kill Bellerophon, who has been falsely accused of trying to rape Proitos' wife. Bellerophon is set the task of slaying of the Chimaira, which he accomplishes while flying over the Chimaira on Pegasos, whom he has bridled with the help of Athena. The Lycian setting points to the myth's transmission from the east through Anatolia, but on the mainland the myth took on special significance at Corinth.⁶² Bellerophon was the son of Glaukos, king of Corinth, and images of Pegasos essentially served as an emblem for the city, as the wide distribution of *pegasoi* in Greece and the western colonies attests. The city was famous for the Peirene fountain, where Pegasos set foot upon landing and where, in some accounts, Bellerophon had successfully bridled his mount. Given the local significance of Bellerophon and Pegasos, it is appropriate to ask what the Chimaira signifies in a Corinthian setting.

---

[60] On changing Greek artistic traditions regarding the Chimaira, see Schmitt 1966. Borges and Guerrero remind us that the famous bronze statue of Chimaira from Arezzo follows the Hesiodic tradition, giving the creature three heads. For a deft presentation of the Chimaira's long afterlife in the European imagination, see Warner 2007: 240–5.

[61] For astrological and meteorological explanations, see Tritsch 1957. For ancient explanations of the monster attributing the different parts of the composite – lion, goat, snake – to animals on the mountain see Servius, ad *Aen.* 6.288, 'flammisque armata Chimaera'. For Ktesias' treatment of the Lycian fires and the fire myth of Chimaira, see Lenfant 2011.

[62] On the Corinthian setting of the Bellerophon myth, see Ziskowski 2014. For the entire Bellerophon cycle, see Hard 2019.

The key to understanding Chimaira in relation to Corinthian myth lies in recognizing that the Chimaira is an allegory of Corinth's three principal neighbours in the northern Peloponnese: Nemea, Argos and Sikyon, all of which had fraught relations with Corinth in the Archaic period.[63] The three components of the Chimaira – the lion, the serpent and the goat – serve as monstrous emblems of the neighbouring communities. All three animals are closely identified with these specific places in myth. The dominant element in the chimaera's composition is the lion. Chimaera's mother, Echidna, according to Hesiod, was also the mother of the Nemean lion, making the Chimaira and Nemean Lion siblings, and if the Chimaira incorporates the lion, in geographic terms the hybrid as an emblem of the northern Peloponnese includes Nemea. The second element is the serpent attached to the lion, and a mythological reference to a snake set in the northern Peloponnese suggests the Lernaian hydra, a multiform monster killed by Herakles. The hydra is a sea-snake, and depictions of the creature on vases from the sixth and fifth centuries show that the artists imagined the monster's heads as snakes.[64] Lerna lies to the southwest of Argos on the Gulf, and was actually said by Strabo to lie in the Argeia, or Argive territory. Accordingly, two of Corinth's nearest neighbours and rivals, Nemea and Argos, could, in the language of animal allegory, have been framed as the lands of the lion and serpent. A specific Peloponnesian location is also evoked by the word for goat (*aix, aigos*). As a toponym, the term is especially associated with Corinth's western neighbour: Sikyon, where the element **aig**- occurs frequently. When the Sikyonians rejected the tribal reforms of Cleisthenes they returned to their old names – Hylleis, Dymanatai and Pamphyloi – and added a fourth, Aigialeis, after an early Sikyonian king, Aigialeus.[65] The coastal strip of the northern Peloponnese was formerly known as Aigialeia.[66] This was probably an ancient toponym since, as Yannis Lolos points out, the same toponym occurs in Linear B tablets from Pylos and Thebes.[67] Nor was the association of Aigialeia with Sikyon a relic of far-off times. Pausanias could describe features in the cultic landscape in the agora of the second century city as follows:

> When Apollo and Artemis had killed Pytho they came to Aigialeia to obtain purification. Dread coming upon them at the place now named Phobos (Fear),

---

[63] Adshead 1986, Marchand 2009.
[64] Lernaian hydra as snake headed: red-figure stamnos, Antonio Salinas Regional Archaeological Museum; Caeretan Hydria, 520–510 BC, Getty Museum 83.AE.346; Attic red-figure volute krater, 500–480 BC, Getty Museum 77.AE.11; Corinthian black-figure aryballos, ca. 600–575 BC. 4.5 × 4.5 in. Getty Museum. 92.AE.4.
[65] Hdt 5.68.   [66] Hom. *Il.* 2.575, Hdt 7.94, Strabo 8.7.1 and Paus. 7.1.1.   [67] Lolos 2011.

they turned aside to Karmanor in Crete, and the people of Aigialeia were smitten by a plague. When the seers bade them propitiate Apollo and Artemis, they sent seven boys and seven maidens as suppliants to the river Sythas. They say that the deities were persuaded by these, came to what was then the citadel, and the place that they reached first is the sanctuary of Peitho (Persuasion).'

Paus. 2.7.6 (tr. Jones)

As late as the second century AD, the notion was still current that Sikyon had a more ancient identity, Aigialeia, in much the same way that Ephyra was the ancient name of Corinth, or that Holy Pytho referred to Delphi. The persistent identification of Sikyon as Aigialeia suggests that the goat (αἴξ) was a suitable emblem for Sikyon in the same way as lions and serpents could stand for Nemea and Argos.[68]

A northern Peloponnesian provenance for the Chimaira fits well with fluctuations in local power. There are persistent legends of a period of Argive control of Sikyon. This ebbed in the late Bronze Age, when the material culture of the regions reflects a Corinthia gradually pulling away from the influence of the Argolid. Argive influence, however, increased again in the Archaic period, when Sikyon joined the Argives against Sparta in the Messenian wars. Lolos concludes that 'the emancipation of Sicyon from Argos came with the rise of tyranny and the coming of Cleisthenes to power'.[69] At much the same time that Kleisthenes was asserting Sikyon's independence, in the second quarter of the sixth century, in a move that will hardly have inspired feelings of security in neighbouring Corinth, painters such as the Boreads Painter were producing vase paintings that lumped Sicyon, Argos and Nemea into a single monster, the Chimaira, shown being defeated by the local Corinthian hero (see Figure 6.11).

At this same time, the Corinthians began minting the silver *pegasoi* that carried their emblem.[70] The battle between Bellerophon and the Chimaira, therefore, can be read as a rendering in myth of a local, regional rivalry transposed from its Lycian setting to the Peloponnese. This was expressed iconographically, employing animal and hybrid emblems as the vocabulary of that rivalry. Hybridity was something of a Sikyonian specialty. When Kleisthenes of Sikyon dropped the old Dorian tribal names of Sikyon in the

---

[68] An obvious objection to the argument that the goat was a symbol for Sikyon is the fact that the names Aigialeus and Aigialeis are more likely to have been formed from the word '*aigialos*', meaning 'beach.' False etymology, however, is revealing. When the Sikyonians adopted the tribal name Aigialeis, they explained it by reference to the eponymous king, Aigialeus, a retrojection into mythical geneaology not to the fact that they inhabited the sea-shore. The apparent semantic similarity of words for 'sea-shore' and 'goat', however coincidental, only serves to make the choice of the goat as an emblem for this coastal territory more plausible.

[69] Lolos 2011: 61.   [70] Ziskowski 2014.

Figure 6.11 Bellerophon and Pegasos slaying the Chimaira. Attributed to Boreads painter (Greek (Lakonian), active 575–550 BC). Black-figure kylix, ca. 570 BC, terracotta, 12 × 17.8 × 14 cm (4 3/4 × 7 × 5 1/2 in.), 85.AE.121.1. The J. Paul Getty Museum, Villa Collection, Malibu, California.

early sixth century, the new names he gave the tribes were Hyatai (wild boar men), Oneatai (donkey men) and Choireatai (pig men).[71] Remarkably, these names did not catch on, and not for the first time the attempt to demonize backfired; not only did the Sikyonians reassert their older Dorian names, but even more telling is the fact that in the late fifth century the Sikyonians began minting a plentiful supply of silver coins depicting the animal emblem they had adopted in response to Corinth's identification with Pegasos. The Sikyonians chose the Chimaira (see Figure 6.12).

Both states were conforming to the practice of Greek city states using images of animals as emblems, as distinctive as Aiginetan turtles and Athenian owls. Animals also figured among the *episemata*, the devices used by warriors on their shields to distinguish them in battle, and were among the most popular images on the earliest minted coins: the so-called *Wappenmünzen* (which often depicted hideous gorgon heads).[72] Given these antecedents, the Sikyonian adoption of the monster from

[71] Hdt 5.68.
[72] On shield devices, see Eurip., *Phoin.* 1090–199. In the Messenger's speech, describing the attack on Thebes by the Seven, Tydeus carries a shield emblazoned with a lion's hide, Polyneikes' shield shows 'the Potnian foals' and Adrastos' emblem is a hydra with 100 snakes. For *Wappenmünzen* emblems, especially the late series with *gorgoneion*, see Hopper 1968 and Kroll 1981. For other Archaic coins using animal symbols (including bull and dolphin), see Kagan 1988.

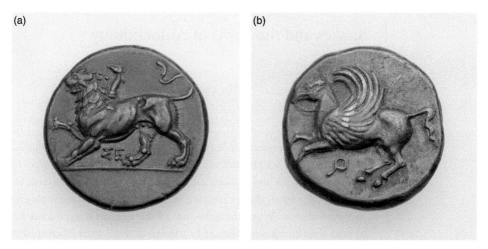

Figure 6.12 A. Silver drachma of (Sikyon) with Chimaira, 431–400 BC. Diameter: 18 mm. Weight: 5.79 gm. Museum of Fine Arts, Boston, 97 406. B. Silver stater of (Corinth) with Pegasos, 435–400 BC. Diameter: 18 mm. Weight: 8.55 gm. Museum of Fine Arts, Boston, 04 850. Photograph © 2024 Museum of Fine Arts, Boston.

a neighbour's myth-cycle as an emblem of the state is a political gesture drawing on traditions of animal symbolism that attests to an Archaic Greek culture saturated with animal metonymy. In Derrida's rich exploration of the animal/human relationship, he observed: 'The animal is there before me, there close to me, there in front of me-I who am (following) after it. And also, therefore, since it is before me, it is behind me. It surrounds me.'[73] The Greeks experienced their world in precisely this way, never entirely convinced of an absolute rupture between human and animal, but instead creating a parallel world populated by composites, where hybrids offered the possibility of different forms of being. The centaurs, Cheiron and Pegasos all invite us to shed our skin and to take on, even if only for a moment, a new humanimality.

---

[73] Derrida 2008: 380.

7 | Snakes and the Perils of Autochthony

> There is an evil creature (*dābba*) with deadly poison. It is a land animal, but mates with a sea creature called *sūriyā* in Syriac. The viper comes to the edge of the sea and makes a call to the *sūriyā*, which comes forth to him. His call arouses this sea creature, telling her that he is summoning her to mate with him. When she hears his call she emerges straight away and hastens towards him, whereupon he mounts this evil harmful creature.
>
> Characteristics of the Viper, *Kitāb Naʿt al-Hayawān* fol. 241
> (trans. Contadini)

Snakes on a Plain

While gorgons, satyrs and centaurs all retain more than a trace of humanity in their hybrid mixtures, snakes represent a somewhat different challenge when hybridized with humans. Snake-bodied men, however, are a notable feature of how the community of Archaic Athens imagined its origins. The Athenians believed that each of their earliest kings – Kekrops, Erechtheus and Erichthonios – was a man from the waist up and anguine below. This peculiarity demands attention. The snake–human hybrid is best elucidated by exploring it along three vectors: underlying human attitudes towards the snake, the antecedents in other Mediterranean cultures and the particular need in early Athens answered by imagining a composite of the human and the reptilian. The passage quoted at the start of the chapter comes from a thirteenth-century Arabic book on animals and points to a deeply embedded antipathy towards the viper; in both Jewish and Christian traditions the story of the temptation of Adam and Eve draws on an equally profound hatred of snakes. The Greek world shared these feelings: Aristoxenos recounted the story of a man who died after killing a snake with his hands even though he had not been bitten, so noxious was the reptile, and accounts of charms and herbs that repelled snakes or cured snake bite were common.[1]

---

[1] Aristoxenos, reported in Aelian 8.7. Charms and herbs against snake bite: Herakleides Kritikos, *FGrH* 369a fr. 2.3; Aelian 8.8.

Nikander of Kolophon's *Theriaka*, composed in the second century BC, devoted more than 450 lines to classifying snakes, often giving excruciating detail of the snake's deadliness. From the bite of the *chersydras*, for example, 'all the skin upon the flesh, dry, loathsome, and bloated with putrid sores, breaks out from below, disclosing a clammy wound, while innumerable and fiery are the pangs which overcome the man, and sudden swellings are raised upon his limbs, plaguing him by turns now in this quarter now in that'.[2]

Despite this familiar revulsion caused by snakes, the cultural associations of the serpent actually encompass more than just fear and loathing. Among indigenous cultures across the Australian continent, for example, traditional stories explain the creation of water holes, outcrops of rock and other features in the landscape as the result of the creator figure, Rainbow Serpent, passing through the land. In some regions the figure is benign, in others malevolent, and Rainbow Serpent also appears as both male and female, reflecting a conception of a cosmos that is in flux, renewed through ritual and dance.[3] Rainbow Serpent has a Protean quality, as illustrated by Deborah Rose's description of how the Yarralin people of Arnhem Land imagine the figure: 'Changing size and shape, it sometimes looks like an ordinary snake; sometimes it is described as having an animal head with ears, and "spines" on its back like a barramundi. The Rainbow Snake is neither precisely male nor female, mammal nor reptile, nor is it species specific.'[4] We cannot assume, therefore, that a snake–man hybrid will be viewed as inherently monstrous.

In the ancient Mediterranean it is rare to encounter snakes as ambiguous creator figures, like Rainbow Serpent, but snakes were not unknown in Aegean religion prior to the Archaic period. In the LM IIIA and B periods, at the height of the palaces' power, the Cretan elites worshipped a snake goddess, well known from the precious ivory figurines depicting a woman wearing the flounced skirt and open jacket of elite Cretan women with snakes coiled up her arms. The best known examples are from the Spring Chamber at Knossos. Commenting on these figurines, Geraldine Gesell has

---

[2] Nicander, *Ther.* 360–5 tr. A. S. F. Gow and A. F. Scholfield. Nicander's influence can be seen in the so-called Catalogue of Serpents in Lucan's *Pharsalia* 9.700–33. See Barbara 2008.
[3] Radcliffe-Brown 1926. This essay stimulated a minor industry in Rainbow Serpent studies before World War II. These covered just about every region of Australia, and were written by Radcliffe-Brown, his students and others influenced by him. Each demonstrated the extraordinary elasticity of the figure, as Radcliffe-Brown himself recognized.
[4] Rose 2000: 92. Blust 2000 suggests that the identification of the rainbow as a serpent can be traced back to the Pleistocene, and that the ubiquity of dragons in the myths and religions of at least six widely separated regions of the world is to be explained by the fact that dragons and Rainbow Serpent are identical.

concluded 'that by the time of the floruit of the Minoan civilization, the Second Palace Period, these images represent the official religion, with its rituals limited to those having access to the palace'.[5] Later figurines in the posture of the goddess with raised arms appear in shrines at a number of sites, such as Prinias, Kavousi, Gournia, Gazi and Kannia, where snake-tubes, *kalathoi* and some terracotta figurines are decorated with snakes either moulded to their interior or as exterior handles.[6] Despite the ubiquity of the snake goddess in the Late Bronze Age, however, she was a casualty of the end of the Minoan palaces and does not reappear in the Iron Age, unless the snaky tassels of Athena's *aegis* or the gorgons' serpentine hair are the faintest echoes of her worship.

Outside of Crete the Greeks will have encountered divine snakes and hybrid snake–human divinities in Egypt. The goddess Renenutet, for example, was pictured as either a cobra or a woman with the head of a cobra, and was regarded as the protector of both crops and the pharaoh.[7] In the Ptolemaic period she would be connected to Demeter. The Egyptians also associated snakes with the pharaoh's divinity, in the form of the Uraeus, and from as early as the Middle Kingdom they worshipped a snake god, Mehen, who protected both the pharaoh and ordinary folk. Mehen was associated with circumambulation and the marking of sacred space by circles.[8] His connection with circles has led to the suggestion that Mehen was the source for Ouroboros, the serpent eating its own tail, a symbol of eternity, who would appear on Greek magical amulets and gems, and eventually in alchemy. The suggestion is plausible, especially since Mehen was also associated with a circular board game that allegorized the player's movement around the board as a triumph over death, in which the player was united with Re and reborn.[9] In fact, in the Coffin Texts of the Middle Kingdom Re is frequently referred to as the Coiled One, and the snake is presented as the supreme god of creation.[10] Spells from the Greek Magical Papyri show that the figure of the snake eating its own tail would eventually be incorporated into late antique Mediterranean magical practice beyond Egypt. One spell, for example, includes instructions for the making of an amulet: 'Helios is to be engraved on a heliotrope stone as follows: a thick-bodied snake in the shape of

---

[5] Gesell 2004: 131.

[6] The precise function of 'snake-tubes' is a problem too complex to be discussed here. Gesell 1976 surveys the evidence and concludes that their precise connection to snake worship is problematic, suggesting that they were offering vessels that were placed in front of the benches on which goddess figurines stood.

[7] Flusser and Amorai-Stark 1993/1994.   [8] Roblee 2018.   [9] Piccione 1990.

[10] Van der Sluijs and Peratt 2009: 8.

a wreath should be [shown] having its tail in its mouth. Inside [the circle formed by] the snake let there be a sacred scarab.'[11] Yet despite the widespread presence of snakes and serpentiform hybrids in Egyptian religion, there is no sign that this symbolism had been incorporated into Greek magic any earlier than the third century AD.[12] Even the widespread syncretism displayed by figures such as the Alexandrian Agathos Daimon, Dionysos with a snake's body or Isis-Thermouthis with the body of a cobra is a phenomenon of the Ptolemaic period.[13] These occurred hundreds of years after the Greeks were first exposed to Egyptian culture and are not the immediate ancestors of the snake-kings of early Athens.

The same is true of another snake deity that Greeks in Egypt might have encountered: a version of Horus in the form of a giant snake, Harsomtus. A series of reliefs on the walls of a crypt below the Ptolemaic temple of Hathor depicted the snake god emerging from a lotus and resting inside an oval representing the womb of Nut.[14] The god's rebirth was celebrated each year at a New Year's festival that used the snake's sloughing off of its skin as a visual evocation of the cosmic order whose renewal relied on the god's rebirth, but here too it is not possible to identify any elements – theological, ritual or iconographic – that demonstrate a direct Egyptian influence on snake hybrids in Archaic Greek culture. There is nothing in the Archaic or Classical Aegean world, for example, that corresponds to the Meroitic depiction of Apedamak at Naqa from the late first century BC, where the indigenous lion-headed god has acquired the snaky coils and lotus blossom from Ptolemaic Harsomtus. In Meroe it is possible to demonstrate a clear derivation from an Egyptian prototype, but snake motifs deriving from Egypt are not part of the repertoire of divine creatures in Archaic Greek culture.

If divine snakes such as Mehen, Renenutet and Harsomtus leave little trace in the religion of the Archaic Aegean, there is at least evidence for fantastic Egyptian snakes entering the Greek imagination. This is thanks to Assyrian kings and Greek mercenaries. Esarhaddon invaded Egypt in 671 BC and in his own words after a journey of two days encountered 'two-headed serpents [whose attack] (spelled) death – but I trampled [upon them] and marched on'.[15] The Greek mercenaries who helped Psamtik acquire the throne probably heard accounts of these snakes, or experienced

---

[11] *PGM* 12.274–6.
[12] For a summary and critique of earlier views of Ouroboros, see Reemes 2015.
[13] Bailey 2007.   [14] Waitkus 2002: 380.
[15] Pritchard 1955: 292 (Esarhaddon's tenth campaign). West (2006: 290) suggests that 'stories of two-headed serpents might be expected to have been prominent in the reminiscences of Esarhaddon's troops, passing into camp-fire mythology to figure among the dangers with which veterans scared new recruits'.

them themselves, because by the middle of the fifth century the two-headed snake had entered the Greek bestiary.[16] In trying to put her visions of murder into words, Kassandra struggles to describe Klyaimnestra and asks, 'What odious monster shall I fitly call her? An Amphisbaina? Or a Skylla, tenanting the rocks, a pest to mariners[?]'[17] This amphisbaina, a two-headed snake, was only one example of the incredible species encountered in Egypt.[18] Herodotos reports (2.74) that there were sacred snakes in Thebes which never hurt people. They had horns and were sacred to Zeus. He also describes seeing the bones of flying snakes near the Arabian city of Buto. These snakes tried to fly to Egypt each year but were intercepted by ibises as they crossed a pass leading 'into the Egyptian plain'.[19] In another section he relates that these winged snakes guard incense trees and that their numbers are kept in check by the fact that their young devour their way out of the womb and thus kill their mothers.[20] Such *mirabilia* were part of the traditional treatment of Egypt as a land of exotica and reflect, as Jessica Lightfoot puts it, 'Herodotus' concern to create an ongoing escalation of wonder in his narrative of the earth's edges'.[21] These Egyptian rarities, however, did not become part of the Greek cultural repertoire until the occupation of Egypt in the Hellenistic period. Only then would a wide variety of Greek gods be depicted in hybrid forms. The composite figures, for example, of Isis and Dionysos on a limestone stele in the British Museum mix Egyptian and Greek elements in the eclectic fashion suited to cosmopolitan Alexandria, but in earlier periods the Greek gods are not usually depicted in such hybrid forms.[22] In fact, when one considers cosmologies steeped in snake lore and full of snake hybrids, like the Nagas and Nagini in the *Mahabharata*, many of whom help heroes, the demonization of snake hybrids in Greek myth, in the case of Typhoeus and the anguiped Titans, is all the more striking.[23]

[16] For Ionian and Karian mercenaries in the service of Psamtik, see Hdt. 2.152.
[17] Aesch., *Ag.* 1232–4, tr. Smyth. For a sensitive treatment of Kassandra's vision, see Budelman and Easterling 2010.
[18] For the amphisbaina: Aelian 9.23, Pliny, *NH* 8.85 and especially Nikander, *Ther.* 372–83 (its skin is good for chilblains).
[19] Hdt 2.75. For discussion, see Lightfoot 2021: 61–2.
[20] Hdt 3.107–9. For discussion, see Hutchinson 1958.   [21] Lightfoot 2021: 63–4.
[22] Limestone stela with snake-bodied figures of Isis and Dionysos. Egypt. First century BC–first century AD. 42cm × 39.5 cm × 13.5 cm. British Museum, EA1539.
[23] Doniger 2021: 50 notes: 'The snake mythology [of the *Mahabharata*] is dominated by Nagas – anthropomorphic above the waist, cobra from the waist down (often with a cobra hood spread over the anthropomorphic head) – and, more particularly, Naga women or Naginis. Nagas live in the underworld and often dispense valuable jewels to handsome heroes; many equestrian heroes win their princesses through the combined agency of a magic horse and a Naga or Nagini.'

When juxtaposed to other systems of myth, the ancestral snake-kings of Athens reflect a dimension of Athenian myth-making that is unusual, if not unique. Athenian snake-kings are a homegrown product.

Snake-Kings

The snake-king is earthborn.[24] The snake's connections to the earth and its ability to shed its skin made it a suitable symbol of primordial autochthony. This was not the same as divinity, and these ancestral figures were not quite gods, but they were more than ordinary humans, and, as Plutarch noted, 'the ancients associated the snake more than any other animal with heroes'.[25] This association, however, was not straightforward. At Nemea, for example, the infant Opheltes was bitten by a snake and later worshipped as the hero Archemoros (*Beginner of Woe*). The Nemean Games were held in his honour, but the child's status as a hero resists easy explanation.[26] Opheltes is bitten and dies after his nurse Hypsipyle lays him down while she fetches water for the heroes marching against Thebes. The story and its afterlife as the aetion for the Nemean Games situates Nemea in the broader cycle of the Seven Against Thebes, but accounts of his death and heroization do not dwell on the snake described by Euripides as 'living by the spring'. The connection between the snake and autochthony is much more pronounced in Athenian stories of their kings: Kekrops, Erechtheus and Erichthonios. Other, related figures, such as Kychreus, Kranaus and Pandion, were at various times either depicted with snakes or described as 'sons of the soil'. What this expression (*gegenes*) means is somewhat ambiguous, but in matters of heroic ancestry the search for exactitude can itself be a distraction. The lineage of the early snake-kings of Athens is, in fact, almost impossibly muddled. Take, for example, the fullest account of the generations of early kings of Athens found in Apollodoros' *Bibliotheca*, a first or second century AD compendium of myth that attempts to render into a coherent whole the great body of Greek legends dealing with everything from the Titans to heroes such as Sisyphos. According to Apollodoros, Kekrops was the first king of Athens (3.14.1). After him, Kranaus came to the throne (3.14.5). Yet Apollodoros also reports that

---

[24] On autochthony, see Loraux 1981, 1990, 2000 and 2002; Rosivach 1987, Saxenhouse 1992: 51–2 and 111–12; and Roy 2014. For depictions of the early kings of Athens, see Avramidou 2011.

[25] Plut., *Cleom.* 39. For the dense symbolism of the snake, see Marchetti 2017: 22.

[26] For Opheltes and child cult in general, see Pache 2004. For Opheltes as hero at Nemea, see Bravo 2018.

Kekrops was the son of Erechtheus and succeeded him to the throne after Erechtheus was destroyed by Poseidon (3.15.1–6). In this version Apollodoros names Pandion as the son who succeeded Kekrops. Pausanias offered an entirely different account of the earliest generations of Athenian kings and claimed that Aktaios, not Kekrops, was the earliest king of Athens (1.26). This tradition is attested, and challenged, as early as the fourth century: Philochoros denied the existence of Aktaios and regarded other names preceding Kekrops as fabrications.[27] Yet another tradition lies behind Herodotos' report (8.44) that the Athenians were known as Kranaoi, who subsequently changed their name to Kekropidai before finally becoming Athenians. These name changes suggest that in the version Herodotos heard in the mid-fifth century, some Athenians maintained they had been ruled by Kranaus before Kekrops. This confusion was compounded by the existence of other figures such as Erichthonios and Erisychthon – near homonyms and possibly doublets of each other (or of Erechtheus). These competing genealogies produced ludicrously complicated lineages, reflected in Pausanias' baffled response to the statues of the Eponymous Heroes in the Agora. He was aware that the monument to the Tribal Heroes included statues of Kekrops and Pandion, but he could not identify which kings of this name were represented because there were two kings named Kekrops.[28] The first Kekrops came after Aktaios, had three daughters and a son, Erysichthon, who predeceased him, and was followed by Kranaus, but Pausanias knew of a second Kekrops who was the son of Erechtheus, son of Pandion, son of Erichthonios. In effect, to make sense of the different traditions he was forced to lay out a family tree that descended from Aktaios through Kekrops to Kranaus before inverting that order from Erichthonios to Kekrops. These repetitions and variations were designed to reconcile competing traditions which existed even down to the level of the demes. Pausanias notes that 'I have already reported that many people in the demes say that they were ruled by kings even before the reign of Kekrops. Kolainos, for example, is the name of a man who was king before Kekrops.'[29]

Most of these local accounts were absorbed by the national traditions that focused on Kekrops, Erechtheus and Erichthonios, and later Theseus as the hero who united the earlier demes into a single state, but even down to the second century AD alternative traditions persisted. For example, in his story of the man who was turned into an eagle by Zeus, Antoninus Liberalis sets the scene as follows: 'There was once in Attika a certain

---

[27] Philochoros, *FGrH* 328 F 92a.   [28] Paus. 1.5.3.   [29] Paus. 1.31.5.

Periphas, of Earth-Sprung stock (*autochthon*), who lived there even before Kekrops, son of Ge had emerged.' Given this profusion of local and conflicting accounts, it is easy to understand the frustration of Strabo, who remarked, 'My account [of the history of the Athenian demes] would be a great deal longer if one were to tally up the founders of Athens beginning with Kekrops, because every source tells a different story.'[30]

What the stories have in common is that the key figures are serpentiform. Most often the genealogies begin with Kekrops.[31] He is described as 'double-formed' (διφυής), a term that drew attention to his serpent tail. Antigonos of Karystos found the term in a poem by Archelaus on marvels that claimed that snakes were born from the marrow in the spines of corpses: 'it is no wonder that the bi-formed Kekrops blossomed forth'.[32] A more awkward explanation was offered by Philochoros, who took 'double-formed' as a reference either to the length of his body or to his bilingualism, arising from the fact that he was originally Egyptian.[33] Such rationalizing may have arisen as late as the fourth century BC as Atthidographers offered competing accounts of the early history of Athens, but the snaky form of Kekrops' body was already too well established to be banished by such scholarly exegesis.[34] In Aristophanes' *Wasps* Philokleon calls on this ancestral hero, addressing him as 'Hero, Lord, Son of the Dragon (as far as the feet are concerned)'.[35] In the fifth century Kekrops was depicted with the coils of a snake for his lower body, even if, like Cheiron, his human half was modestly attired (Figure 7.1). Apollodoros' description reflects the same picture: 'Kekrops was autochthonous, and had a hybrid body of a man and a snake. He was the first king of Attica, and the land which had previously been called Akte was named Kekropia after him.'[36]

The other snake-kings of Athens are Erechtheus and Erichthonios. After Wilamowitz there was a widespread tendency to treat the two figures as a doublet.[37] This argument, however, has been challenged by more recent

---

[30] Strabo 9.1.18: πολὺ δ' ἂν πλείων εἴη λόγος, εἰ τοὺς ἀρχηγέτας τοῦ κτίσματος ἐξετάζοι τις ἀρξάμενος ἀπὸ Κέκροπος· οὐδὲ γὰρ ὁμοίως λέγουσιν ἅπαντες.

[31] For overview, see Gourmelen 2004; Scherf 2006 (*BNP* s.v. Cecrops); I. Kasper-Butz, B. Knittlmayer, I. Krauskopf, *LIMC* 6.1, 1084–91; fig.: *LIMC* 6.2, 721–3 s.v. Kekrops; Sickinger 2016 (*BNJ* 239).

[32] Antigonus of Carystus, *Collection of Marvellous Investigations* 89.   [33] *BNJ* 328 F 93.

[34] On the inadequacy of rationalizing accounts of Kekrops, see Jones in *BNJ* 328 F93. For discussion of the genealogies of the early kings, see Harding 2008: 20 and 31–2, and Fowler 2013: 119–20.

[35] Aristoph. *Vesp* 438: ὦ Κέκροψ ἥρως ἄναξ τὰ πρὸς ποδῶν Δρακοντίδη ...

[36] Apollod., *Biblioth.* 3.14.1.   [37] Wilamowitz 1893: 128; Ermatinger 1897; Dietrich 1974: 174.

Figure 7.1 Gaia, Athena and Kekrops. Melian relief, ca. 460 BC. Terracotta, height 11 cm. TC 2681. BPK, Bildagentur. Antikensammlung, Staatliche Museen zu Berlin. Photo: Johannes Laurentius/CC BY-SA 4.0.

scholars.[38] The similarities between their names gave rise to confusion between the two figures in later antiquity, but in the fifth century they appear to have been distinct. At that time, Erechtheus appears in accounts of the war with Eleusis where he fights the Thracian Eumolpos and kills him, before being destroyed by Eumolpos' father, Poseidon.[39] Erichthonios, in contrast, was primarily remembered as the child of Hephaistos and Athena and was connected to the founding of the Panathenaia.[40] Despite these convoluted and contradictory accounts, in the fifth century a master narrative of sorts began to emerge in which the three major figures were brought into alignment: Erechtheus would be associated with the Athenian control of Eleusis and fused with Poseidon, giving the god who lost to Athena an honoured place in the Athenian cult on the Akropolis in the guise of Poseidon-Erechtheus (another hybrid creation overcoming the boundary between god and hero).[41] This is

---

[38] Mikalson 1976: 141–2; Rosivach 1987: 295n4; Robertson 1985: 235–7.

[39] Erechtheus, Eumolpos and the Eleusinian War: Scholiast on Eur. *Ph.* 854; Aristides, *Or.* xiii. vol. i. pp. 190ff., ed. Dindorf, Plat. *Menex.* 239b; Isoc. 4.68, Isoc. 12.193; Dem. 60.8; Apollod. *Biblio.* 3.15.4–5. A later tradition preserved in Pausanias is slightly different: Eumolpos survives (2.14.2) and it is his son, Immarados who falls to Erechtheus.

[40] Mikalson 1976. For a useful discussion, see Parker 1988. On the myth of the birth of Erichthonios, see Frame 2009: 3.81. For the iconography of Erichthonios' birth, see Kron 1976: 55–75.

[41] Poseidon-Erechtheus: Eurip. Fr 370.90. For epigraphic evidence see *IG* I³ 873; II² 1146, 3538, 4071, and 5058. See Robertson 1985: 235–6. Frame 2009: 412. Luce 2005 argues that Erechtheus was originally an epithet of Poseidon.

reported in Euripides' lost play *Erechtheus*, which closes with Athena's instructions for the building of a shine in his honour, the Erechtheion:

> For your husband I command that a precinct be built
> in mid-city, with stone surrounds; and on account of
> his killer he shall be called August Poseidon
> surnamed Erechtheus, by the citizens in their
> sacrifices of oxen.
>
> Eur. Fr 370 ll. 88–92 (tr. Collard and Cropp)

Here the god and hero have been fused into one, and in honour of both the Athenians would adopt the name Erechtheidai.[42] In similar fashion, Kekrops would be imagined as the ancestral, earthborn king of Athens, in whose honour the Athenians would also refer to their land as Kekropia and adopt the name Kekropidai.[43] References to the Athenians as the 'sons of Kekrops' are especially common in inscriptions dealing with the cult at Eleusis, suggesting, as in the stories of Erechtheus and Eumolpos, that the incorporation of Eleusis into the burgeoning Athenian state of the Archaic period was critical to the articulation of an Athenian identity. The question of Eleusis' political integration into Attica has long been debated, but Maximilian Rönnberg has recently drawn attention to the anomalous position of Eleusis. Characterizing the area as one of dispersed settlements in the midst of which the sanctuary witnessed increasing activity in the eighth and seventh centuries, Rönnberg makes a strong case for seeing Eleusis as an independent community with its own local identity.[44] The integration of Eleusis into the Athenian state would have repercussions for how the Athenians imagined their own origins.

The fullest narrative to tease out the autochthony of the Athenians was a story that begins and ends with snake-kings: the story of the birth of Erichthonios. The story was popular in the fifth century, when it appears depicted on vases and was the subject of drama, notably Euripides' *Ion*.[45] The story is summarized in Eratosthenes' *Katasterisms* as follows:

---

[42] Pindar *Isth*. 2.19, *Pyth* 7.10, Soph. *Ai*. 201–202, Eur. *Med* 824, *Ion* 24, 1056, 1060.

[43] Kekropia: Supp. 658, El.1289, Str.9.1.20; Kekropioi: APl.4.295; Kekropidai: Hdt 8. 44, and many examples in *IG* II². See I. Eleusis 494 and 515.

[44] Rönnberg 2020: 47–51, charting the dispersed settlements in early Archaic Eleusis; Rönnberg 2021 on the place of Eleusis in the unification of Athens.

[45] Meyer 2017: 362–76; Frame 2009: 3.81. See Eur. fr. 925 Nauck. For the iconography of Erichthonios's birth, see Kron 1976: 55–75. See, for example, Adolphseck, Schloss Fasanerie Museum 77, 78 (calyx krater showing Kekrops and Athena flanking an olive tree and a kistos concealing the infant Erichthonios).

> Euripides too speaks of his [i.e., Erichthonios'] birth in this way: Hephaistos lusted for Athena and wanted to have intercourse with her, but she turned away, preferring to keep her virginity, and hid in a place in Attica which they say is named 'Hephaisteion' after him. He attacked her, expecting to subdue her, but was struck by her with her spear and released his lust, his seed being spent on the ground. From it, they say, a child was born who because of this was called Erichthonios.
>
> Eur. fr. 925 Nauck. (tr. Collard and Cropp)

In other versions Hephaistos ejaculates on her thigh and Athena, after wiping herself clean, throws away the polluted wool.[46] A child, Erichthonios, is born from the earth as a result. After the child is born Athena entrusts Erichthonios to Pandrosos, Aglauros and Herse, the daughters of Kekrops (who, like the Athenians, are 'Kekropidai').[47] Like Kekrops, Erichthonios ('He-of-the-Very-Earth') has a snake for his lower body. The Athenians' first kings, then, are a double instance of the snaky, earthborn king, recalling Freud's observation that the *Doppelgänger* is characteristic of the Uncanny. Defying the order not to look upon the child, who was given over in a closed basket to the girls for safe-keeping, Aglauros opens the vessel, sees the child's snaky lower body, is promptly driven mad and hurls herself from the Akropolis.[48] In this episode autochthony equates with madness and transgression, or what Nicole Loraux referred to as the 'Dark Side of Autochthony'. This is certainly true with regard to the death of Aglauros, whose deadly leap was identified with a cave below the east end of the Akropolis.[49] By contrast, the piety and obedience of the good sister were celebrated at the Pandrosion on the Akropolis, and in the ritual descent of the Arrhephoroi into a chasm in the rock located at the western end of the Akropolis.[50] In these ways, Athenian autochthony could be read into the topography of the Sacred Rock in the heart of the city, just as the snakes on the Akropolis served as a vivid evocation of the goddess's presence.

In contrast to these stories of madness and pollution, some associations with autochthony are benign: people who are 'earthborn' are like the rocks themselves. Indeed, in some treatments of the concept, autochthonous people are born of the very mud.[51] Furthermore, the connection to the earth can be elaborated in a number of harmless ways. The Athenians use

---

[46] Hygin. II.13; Apollod. *Biblio.* 3.14.6; Aug., *De civ. D.* 18.12. See McInerney 2019.
[47] Eurip. *Ion* 270–5.   [48] For a summary of these episodes and bibliography, see Parker 1988.
[49] On the cave of Aglauros, see Dontas 1983.
[50] On the rites of the Arrhephoroi, see Redfield 2003: 120.
[51] Nonnus 40.429; see Montiglio 2005: 73.

an olive tree 'sprung from the rock in evergreen purity' (Eurip. *Ion* 1435–6) to advertise their claims to autochthony, while iconographically lifting a rock and finding the evidence of his true parentage is central to Theseus discovering his true identity, setting in train his return to Athens.[52] But the act leading to the conception of Erichthonios was the attempted rape of Athena by her brother, Hephaistos. The serpentine form of the Athenians' first kings was thereby bound up with a claim of autochthony which was based on incest and pollution: a god trying to rape his sister and ejaculating either onto her leg or onto the ground. Autochthony thus conceived contained the seeds of disgust as much as pride. Many myths of autochthony connect earthborn status with episodes of rape, madness and punishment.[53] Poseidon will destroy autochthonous Erechtheus and bury him under the rock of the Akropolis, returning him to the earth, reversing, as Ann Burnett recognized, the scene of Erichthonios' birth.[54] Later, in another episode of the violence at the core of autochthony, the original inhabitants of Attica, the Pelasgians, must be slaughtered, the survivors expelled to Lemnos in a repetition of the recurring pattern: where there is an autochthonous founder, there is an autochthonous challenger. For every Romulus, his Remus. And just as fraternal bloodshed is built into the community's foundations, so too sexual violence also anchors lineage. Without Apollo's rape of Kreousa at the Makrai Petrai below the Akropolis and the symbolic repetition of this in Ion's marriage to her, there can be no Ionian people. These are instances of the need to re-root autochthony repeatedly.[55]

These ambiguities run through Euripides' *Ion*, in which the purity of the royal line is almost undone by rape, abandonment and murder. Kreusa is seduced by Apollo and gives birth to Ion, who is raised as a temple-slave at Delphi. Years later, meeting Ion on her visit to Delphi, she comes to believe he is the bastard son of her husband, Xouthos, and conceives a plan to kill him. The Tutor explains to Kreusa that Athena at his birth gave Erichthonios a gift of two drops of the Gorgon's blood, taken from its dying body when Athena slew the monster at the battle of Phlegra. One drop heals, the other is poison. It is this ambiguous gift that Kreusa, daughter of Erechtheus, intends to use to poison Ion. The plot is foiled through the intervention of the gods, and a reconciliation of sorts takes place, but the entire action of the play constitutes an extended meditation

---

[52] Ciardiello 2007: 179–89. [53] Loraux 2000.
[54] Burnett 1970: 147. For Erechtheus see *LIMC* 4 (1988) s.v. 'Erechtheus' (Kron).
[55] Lape 2010: 123: 'The sexual appropriation of the female body [is] necessary to transmit autochthony conceived specifically as an ancestry or bloodline.' See also Loraux 1990.

on the futility of the very concept of autochthonous purity. At every step the gods act in their own selfish interests, and mortals, acting in ignorance, cause further social upheaval, threatening the stability of the *oikos*.[56] The claim, then, that the Athenians were autochthonous was not a simple claim about a pure past, but was part of an ideology of Athenian exceptionalism.[57]

If the autochthonous past was not pure, at least the location of the snake-cult was unambiguous: it was centred on the Akropolis. Aside from the snake-myths that recur here involving Kekrops, Erechtheus, Erichthonios, the daughters of Kekrops and the tutelary snake that lived in the Erechtheion, it has recently been suggested that Athena's victory over the Giants was a triumph over snakes, celebrated in the katasterism of the constellation Drako. According to various ancient sources, the giant snake named Aster (Star) was defeated by Athena and transformed into the constellation Drako, a circumpolar constellation that never sets.[58] At the time of the Panathenaia in July/August, according to Efrosyni Boutsikas, visitors to the Akropolis would have had a clear view of the constellation around sunset, as the evening races, processions and rituals that celebrated Athena's victory were beginning. Linking observation of the stars with religious ritual, Boutsikas concludes:

> At the time of the celebrations, the celestial representation of one of these Giants – whose katasterism myth also associated him with the goddess – in the form of Draco was observed at its most important annual phase from the Akropolis. Space, time, and ritual experience seem to entwine, tuning ritual performance with the rotating cosmos. This other dimension of the festival's cognitive environment links the cosmos with the earthly location, taps memory, and strengthens Athenian identity.[59]

Sons of the Dragon

Claiming descent from snake-kings brought certain complications. The proposition that the community could trace its origins back to ancestral figures with the bodies of snakes means that either the Athenians did not understand how sex works or they treated heroic ancestry as a separate

---

[56] Abbatista 2018: 234–44.　[57] Forsdyke 2012a.
[58] Schol. ad Ar. *Knights* 566a; Arist. *Peplos* fr. 637 (Rose); schol. ad Aristid. *Or.* 1.362 (Dindorf iii, p. 323).
[59] Boutsikas 2020: 126.

construction of descent. The Greeks were familiar with the mechanics of sex, so we can be fairly confident that the literal impossibility of their descent from snake-bodied hybrids did not trouble them. In the realm of myth, as for physics, the ordinary rules of biology, clearly did not apply. In fact, Hesiod's complex genealogies had already cleared the way, putting species-specificity and the complexities of interspecies reproduction to the side in the service of evoking marvellous and monstrous lineages. But aside from magical thinking, there are two other dimensions to the Athenian construction of hybrid heroic ancestry that are notable. The first is the *Sitz im Leben* of the snake-king, the specific historical circumstances in which these stories were deployed. There is a powerful connection between the heroic figure of Erechtheus, the priesthood of the cult of Poseidon Erechtheus and the clan of the Eteoboutadai. Their name (the Real Boutadai) distinguished them from the deme of Boutadai, where they were located at the time of the Kleisthenic reforms.[60] The name also connoted an aristocratic taste for exclusivity. The clan claimed descent from Boutes, brother of Erechtheus, and continued to supply the priests of the Poseidon Erechtheus cult and priestesses of the Athena Polias cult under the democracy. Scholars have wondered at this persistence of aristocratic privilege even beyond the fourth century, but it is precisely in an egalitarian age that one can imagine a gentilician group asserting status by advancing an ancestor who was *gegenes*.[61] Basing the legitimacy of the *genos* on an autochthonous snake hybrid effectively created a back-stop: no generations could be conceived earlier than the ancestor who was earth-born. This was potentially valuable in a landscape of rivalry and competition, such as existed between and within Athenian *gene*. J. K. Davies has referred to the continuing evolution of Athenian descent groups as 'gentile bifurcation'. A good example is the well-known arbitration of the two *gene* who claimed the title of Salaminioi. Their dispute suggests that Athenian *gene* were subject to fission and fusion. The Eteoboutadai represent a reaction to these conditions, a countervailing tendency to guard their privileges jealously. From the middle of the fifth century, for two hundred years every known priestess of Athena Polias was the daughter of a man from the same deme, members of a single family descended from Drakontides of Bate, an Eteoboutad, whose name marked him as the Son of the Dragon. Like the Eumolpidai at Eleusis, the Eteoboutadai used heroic descent to claim a privileged place in the foundation myths of Athens and to translate that into aristocratic status in the contemporary world.

---

[60] Humphreys 2018: 646–7.   [61] Lambert 2019: 167–9.

A second dimension of snake ancestry merits attention. In the fullest version of the serpentiform myths Erichthonios was born of earth after Hephaistos' assault on Athena. The scene of the child's birth was a popular motif on red-figure vases of the fifth century. The involvement of Athena and Hephaistos, twin founder gods of Athens, suggests that the myth was not a local or clan-based story but was pan-Athenian. The completion of the Hephaisteion's decorative programme in the 430s and 420s points to the same conclusion. It was the Athenian state that financed the completion of the temple and the statues of Athena and Hephaistos inside the temple where the birth of Erichthonios was celebrated in reliefs on the base of the cult statues.[62] A crucial detail, however, in the story of the birth of Erichthonios is that his snaky limbs were meant to be concealed, but were seen by the daughters of Kekrops, who were driven mad by the sight. Why? Their own father is a snake hybrid, so why should the sight of a miniature version of the same hybrid send them mad? Despite the apparent silliness of the question, it points to a critical dynamic in these stories of hybrid origins. Aglauros' distress is a sign that the orderly transition from hybrid irregularity, with its overtones of monstrosity, to conventional regularity may be on the verge of breakdown. Each snaky hybrid marks the bridge from the primordial world of chaos and monsters to the establishment of a stable anthropomorphic order. In the generational movement from Kekrops to his daughters, Athens is supposed to have advanced from the liminal, hybrid state to a wholly anthropomorphic order, but with the appearance of Erichthonios and his serpentine lower half, the snake has once again raised its ugly head, suggesting the possibility of regression. How is this to be averted? As so often, with the death of a maiden: Aglauros leaps from the Sacred Rock, expiating the sin of disobeying the goddess. The story of chaos encountered and narrowly averted leads to the restoration of order. This is rendered into narrative form in this episode, which is then re-enacted in ritual. Each year on the Akropolis the Arrhephoroi will descend into a chasm on the north side of the rock and return with secret, sacred objects that are wrapped up, as was Erichthonios. In short they undergo the same test as the Kekropidai, but they will pass.[63] In the descent and return of the Arrhephoroi, ritual action through repetition and orderliness marks the banishment of chaos. Stories, then, of impiety, pollution, madness and disobedience allow ritual action to be framed as the restoration of order. In fact,

---

[62] Papaspyridi-Karusu 1954–5: 79–94.   [63] Redfield 2003: 120. See also Connelly 1996: 79.

chaotic elements of horror and madness are necessary components in the preliminary stages of aetiological myth. Without the threat of disorder there can be no (re)affirmation of order.

The Plupast

In their search for a legitimate ancestry, the Athenians faced a further predicament: time was a dimension in dynamic tension. On one side lay the present and a connected past. On the other side lay the deep past, a phenomenon sometimes referred to as the plupast.[64] In this bipolar construction of time, archon lists, chronicles, lists of the priestesses of Hera and other chronographic devices helped to shape an experience of past and present in which the gap between them collapsed. A man alive in the archonship of Kallias (412/11 BC) could read a law or a decree from the archonship of an earlier Kallias (480/79 BC) and experience a reassuring continuity. In the Olympic victor lists, an athlete could see exactly how many years had passed between Milo of Kroton's first triumph (boys' wrestling, 60th Olympiad) and his last (men's wrestling, 66th Olympiad). In this way the experience of time was elastic: no matter how far one stretched the gap between a present and past event, both present and past (and the events in those dimensions) remained connected to each other, with the present resembling the past even if it did not copy it exactly. Recognizing this, Thucydides could assert an entire philosophy of history predicated on the similitude of the present and past, since, as he saw it, the underpinning of both was human action, which would never fundamentally change since the human thing (*to anthropinon*) did not change. But before this was the past of the past, a plupast which was fundamentally different in that humans were no longer actively connected to it. It was populated by monsters and hybrids. No archon list could specify the date on which the gods defeated the Giants. In this disconnected past, gods had been immediately and tangibly present, had shared feasts with men at Mekone before the theft of fire and had created Pandora as punishment for that theft. Before the decline to the present there had been earlier ages of

---

[64] Grethlein and Krebs 2012. The distinction between events according to whether or not we are connected to them recalls grammarians' treatment of the aorist in Greek. Beetham 2002: 236, for example, concludes, 'The aorist aspect indicates *the viewpoint of a speaker or writer outside an action* not necessarily in the past, *of which the beginning and end are in view*' (italics added). The deep past was decisively over, yet the events of myth-time were also timeless, and therefore truly aorist.

gold and silver. The age of heroes partially bridged the gap, but it is notable that in the Hellenistic period when communities sought to forge stronger links to the distant past the Trojan War served as a crucial chronological marker.[65] Prior to this was the plupast. This *Urzeit* – sometimes referred to as the *spatium mythicum* to distinguish it from the time of the connected past, *spatium historicum* – was the subject of Hesiod's cosmological poetry, which imparted some order to an otherwise chaotic array of local stories. The turning point between the two can be seen in Homer. In the *Iliad* there are snippets of stories that deal with figures such as Bellerophon, but, as C. J. Mackie notes, 'Monsters ... are one feature of the heroic landscape that has disappeared from the world of Achilles.'[66]

For the Athenians, the link with the plupast was most vividly made real through cult and drama, especially those episodes that brought audiences into proximity with elemental, chthonic gods such as triple-bodied Hekate, the Semnai Theai, the Dread Goddesses (transformed from blood-sucking demons into goddesses capable of being placated) and ancestral deities who received cultic worship such as Kekrops and Erichthonios. In the stories of Athens' plupast the hybridity of the ancestral figure forcibly underscores the alienness of a deep past. That primordial time of bestial urges and monstrous bodies remains ever at odds with the normality of the present, and its presence in the present is troubling. The conventional view of the deep past, most clearly articulated by Mircea Eliade, holds that rituals repeat archetypal events which took place in mythical time, closing the gap between mythical time and the present. More recent scholarship, however, has emphasized the ambivalence felt by the Greeks towards *illud tempus* and autochthony, suggesting that ritual kept the past at a safe distance.[67] It is for this reason that the Athenian myths of autochthony cast the primordial period as one characterized by acts of violence

---

[65] On Troy as a chronological marker, see Clarke 2008: 223. Rotstein 2016: 90 notes that other chroniclers favoured the establishment of the Olympic Games or the Return of the Herakleidai to mark the beginning of computable time. In the Lindos Chronicle there are only a handful of dedications from the time before the Trojan War, such as the vessel of unknown material dedicated by the Telchines. On the Parian Marble, there are only seven entries (out of a total of at least 107) separating the Fall of Troy (945 years BP) from the first archonship (420 years BP). These seven include notices devoted to Hesiod and Homer. From the Athenocentric view of the Parian Marble not much of importance happened between the capture of Troy and the end of kingship in Athens. The list of the Antheadai, a gentilician group from Halikarnassos who served as the priests of Poseidon, covered a period of 827 years back from the time of inscription around 100 BC. See *Halikarnassos* 2, Carbon and Pirenne-Delforge 2013: 108–9, Isager 2015 and McInerney 2021b. Each of these documents illustrates the extraordinary degree to which Hellenistic communities would go in order to create a past to which they could connect.

[66] Mackie 2021: 232.

[67] Loraux 2000; Detienne 2001; Redfield 2003: 123–4; Csapo 2005: 238–44; Chlup 2008.

and pollution. The presence of serpentine hybrids in these episodes forges a connection with the past – they are our ancestors – even as monstrosity erects a barrier between primordiality and the present. And, given the presence of these snake-kings in the deep past, it is almost too good to be true that as the Athenians moved from the plupast of myth into a more recent past, their legendary lawgiver should be named Drako ('Snake'), once again emphasizing the strong connection between rulers and snakes.[68] The snake is an appropriate animal-hybrid for these founder figures since autochthony, with its emphasis on the soil and ancestry, was a principal concern of the Athenians for whom kingship was a memory rather than a contemporary reality.[69] At the same time, the peculiarity of these stories and the hybrid forms taken by the ancestors dramatically reminds us that the past is truly a foreign country.

In times of exceptional peril, such as the Persian Wars, the appearance of snake-men constitutes an activation of the mythical past for the protection of contemporary Athenians. On the Pella hydria, for example, two local snake-kings figure in scenes depicting the presence of gods and heroes on the side of the Greeks. The first is Kekrops (Figure 7.2). Jenifer Neils notes that in front of him an olive tree is sprouting, emphasizing the connection between Kekrops and the land. In a crowded composition he is accompanied by a female figure identified as the nymph of Marathon. Neils reads three registers of conflict in the vase's iconography: Athena versus Poseidon in a contest for the control of Athens, Erechtheus versus Eumolpos in the battle for control of Eleusis and an historical confrontation: Greece versus Persia, in the battles of Marathon and Salamis.[70] Visually, the Pella hydria offers a unified vision of the past in which each layer recursively connects to the others. In this way the deep past remains ever present, deploying the heroes and hybrids of myth time in the service of contemporary Athens.

The second snake-king appearing on the vase has been convincingly identified as Kychreus, a legendary king of Salamis.[71] Although he does not figure prominently in myth, stories about him were clearly modelled on

---

[68] Stroud 1968 has emphasized that no tradition speaks of Drako the Lawgiver as if he were a snake, nor am I suggesting that he was ever so envisaged. The stories of early lawgivers, however, were subject to very specific patterns of story-telling. See Szegedy-Maszak 1978. Making the Athenian Moses into 'Snake' reinforces his status as lawgiver with an authority borrowed from the earlier snake-kings. On the various words for snake in Greek, see Peter Levy's note to the Penguin translation of Paus. 8.8.5 (note 56).

[69] On the discourse on kingship, see Atack 2014. For the metaphorical appearance of snake women in Attic drama, see Abbattista 2018.

[70] Neils 2013: 609.

[71] Apollod. *Bibl.* 3.161; Diod. Sic. 4.72.4; Strabo 9.1.9; Steph. Byz. s.v. Κυχρεῖος.

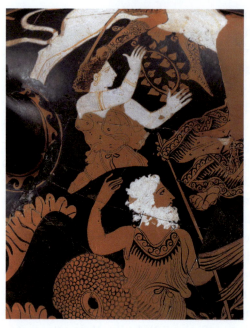

Figure 7.2 Pella hydria, ca. 400 BC. Detail: Kekrops and the nymph of Marathon. Photo S. Mavrommatis; reproduced by permission of Ioannis Akamatis.

conventions of ancestor worship that sometimes identified the hero as the slayer of a monster that terrorized the land (in Kychreus' case, a gigantic snake) and at other times combined the serpent with the king into a single hybrid.[72] As an ancestral hero he was worshipped on Salamis, where there was a sanctuary to him. Pausanias reports:

> It is said that while the Athenians were engaged in the sea-fight with the Medes, a serpent appeared among the ships, and the god announced to the Athenians that this serpent was the hero Kychreus.
>
> Paus. 1.36.1 (tr. Pritchett)[73]

On the Pella hydria he is depicted as a beardless, naked youth, not unlike the Athenian hero Theseus. He has an animal pelt loosely draped over one arm and a snake winding over the other, calling to mind Dionysos. He is depicted vigorously blowing a salpinx, suggesting the trumpet call that the Messenger in Aeschylus' *Persians* reports from the Greek camp on Salamis,

---

[72] Serpent-slaying: Diod. Sic., 4.72.4; snake-raising: Strabo 9.1.9 (citing Hesiod, *Ehoiai*).

[73] There was a shrine to Kychreus on Salamis, according to Paus. 1.36.1. Wallace 1969: 301 suggests that the resemblance of Kynosoura to a giant petrified snake (the body of Kychreus) gave rise to accounts of Kynasoura's importance in the naval battle. See also van Rookhuijzen 2021: 222.

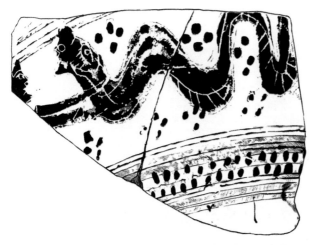

Figure 7.3 Man wrestling a human-headed snake. Black-figure vase, sixth century BC, Perachora. 421. Pl 22 L 68.

the Kychraian shore. Kekrops, Erichthonios and Kychreus, in their hybridity, each embodies the paradox of the past: it remains a disquieting presence in the present. A fragment of a sixth-century black-figure vase found in the excavations of Perachora captures this unsettling hybridity (Figure 7.3). A figure on the left reaches forward to grapple with a snake figure that has both a human and serpent's head.[74] The figures have not been identified but the drafting of the figures' heads is suggestive. The serpent seems to lie inside the human, as if to suggest a chthonic figure in which both are fused.

Bluebeard

In the sixth century one particularly graphic depiction of the snake–man loomed large in the Athenian imagination: the pedimental sculpture commonly referred to as Bluebeard (Figure 7.4). A lively debate over the last 150 years has not resolved the question of the figure's identity, but Bluebeard's prominence on the largest temple on the Akropolis for much of the sixth century attests to the character's importance.[75] The composition consists of

---

[74] Perachora pl. 22, 421.
[75] The temple on which the Bluebeard sculptural piece was located has been variously identified. I follow Paga 2015 in assigning Bluebeard to the Hekatompedon, the older temple (with limestone sculpture) that stood on the Dörpfeld Foundations, on the north side of the Akropolis. The temple and pedimental figures date to the early part of the sixth century. Around

Figure 7.4 'Bluebeard', from the Hekatompedon pediment, Akropolis, Athens. (Acr.35) limestone, ca. 575–550 BC. Album/Art Resource, NY.

three human torsos each with a man's head. Below the waist the human bodies transform into the coils of at least one massive serpent, possibly two. The creature is winged and was brightly painted.

Each of the human figures holds an elemental attribute, usually interpreted as water, fire (or an ear of wheat) and a bird. Bluebeard is sometimes identified as Typhon, the monster destroyed by Zeus' thunderbolts, but the identification is by no means secure. Euripides speaks of Herakles' victory over tripled-bodied Typhons, but there is no hint of a combat scene involving the sculpted Bluebeard, who appears to wait patiently.[76] If anything he projects a benign air, and the bird attribute he holds hardly seems like a deadly weapon. The peaceful aspect of the Bluebeard composition is further highlighted by the contrast with a battle scene depicted on the other side of the pediment, where Herakles wrestles with Triton.[77] Further complicating the identification of Bluebeard with the monster Typhon is a contemporary black-figure vase that shows Zeus hurling a thunder bolt at Typhon, snaky below the waist but with only one human torso and head.[78]

If not Typhon, then who is Bluebeard? In 1988 Bente Kiilerich presented the case for identifying Bluebeard as an early version of Geryon, the

500 BC this temple was replaced by the Old Athena Temple, which was erected on the same foundations. For the history of the discovery and reconstruction of the pieces of Bluebeard, see Mertens 2019.

[76] Tripled-bodied Typhons: Eurip. *Herakl.* 1271. For discussion of the Greek and the alternative reading of 'Geryonas', see Kiilerich 1988: 125.
[77] On Herakles and Triton, see Glynn 1981.
[78] Zeus blasting Typhon: Chalcidian hydria, 575–525 BC. Antikensammlungen 596, Munich.

triple-bodied giant whose cattle Herakles must steal for his Tenth Labour. Kiilerich cites a body of Indo-European myths in which the hero is pitted against a triple-bodied opponent. Despite these generic similarities, it is unlikely that Bluebeard can be identified as Geryon. Aside from the fact that Bluebeard is not engaged in any kind of combat, no source refers to or depicts Geryon as serpentiform. This is not a question of a gap in our sources. Throughout the sixth century Geryon was a figure popular with poets and painters. Stesichoros' *Geryoneis*, for example, is roughly contemporary with the Bluebeard sculptural group, and metopes from the Athenian Treasury at Delphi depicted Herakles' combat with the multi-bodied giant, as had many black-figure vases produced in the decades around the sculpting of Bluebeard. Geryon has a recognizable iconography, and this is reflected in all of the literary sources that refer repeatedly to Geryon's triple form. Hesiod calls Geryon 'triple-headed' and Stesichoros refers to the creature 'with six hands and six feet', while for Aeschylus he is 'triple-bodied'.[79] Similarly, vase scenes invariably show Geryon as an armed warrior with three helmets, three shields and three pairs of legs.[80] His three bodies may have been fused, marking him as a monster, but nowhere is he depicted as a snake hybrid. Kiilerich suggests that the figure is depicted with the coils of a snake because the pediment 'offered an awkward field' which was 'not an easy place to fill'.[81] This is true, but the designers of pediments were adept at solving this problem with river deities and kneeling or recumbent figures. They did not render established mythological characters unrecognizable merely to fill space.

A more popular suggestion was made by John Boardman, who placed Bluebeard in the broader context of the glorification of Peisistratos on the sixth-century Akropolis. In sculpture and on vases, many of the images of the mid-sixth century depicted the Peloponnesian hero Herakles, with whom the tyrant sought to associate himself.[82] Although Boardman was careful not to claim that Herakles was an exact allegorical representation of Peisistratos, he did suggest that the apotheosis of Herakles on sixth-century black-figure vases served to frame the return of Peisistratos to the city in 546 BC, accompanied by a woman dressed as Athena, as an analogue to the story of Herakles.[83] Herodotos' account of Peisistratos' triumphant

[79] Hes. *Theog.* 288; Stesich. *Geryoneis* Fr S87; Aeschyl. *Herakleidai* F 37.
[80] Black figure: Beazley 310309; Paris Medailles 202; Beazley 301038; Beazley 301469. Red figure: Beazley 200080. See also metope 27 from the Athenian Treasury at Delphi (Delphi Archaeological Museum n.84 bis).
[81] Kiilerich 1988: 129.   [82] Boardman 1972, Boardman 1975. See also Venit 1989.
[83] Hdt 1.59–60. For Boardman's distinction between 'political intent' and 'deliberate political propaganda', see Boardman 1989: 159.

entrance to the city certainly reads as if the episode was a piece of heavily orchestrated political theatre. Boardman made the reasonable suggestion that such contemporary political events might resonate with mythic overtones. In light of this, he further raised the possibility that Bluebeard was a fantastic representation of the Athenian body politic divided into three distinct regions.[84] In Boardman's view,

> We may attempt, then, to look for straight political symbolism in the group, possibly to serve as pendant to the Herakles and Triton group which may itself be symbolic of a Peisistratan victory. The tyrant's comparable domestic success was the enforced reconciliation of three parties in Attica, the party of the Hill (or beyond the Hill), of the Seashore and of the Plain.[85]

In this reading, the attributes held by Bluebeard would symbolize the three regions of Attica: a bird standing for the men of the Hill; water representing the men of the Seashore; wheat for the men of the Plain. Boardman's regional interpretation remains extremely plausible, even if the attributes are not unambiguous: if the second attribute is fire, not wheat, the association with men of the Plain becomes less compelling. For this and other reasons many scholars remain non-committal on the subject of Bluebeard's identity. For example, in a recent publication of the drawings and watercolours of Bluebeard produced by Émile Gilliéron (père) between 1889 and 1919, Joan Mertens notes that 'the triple-bodied figure holds symbols of the air, water, and fire, personifying potent natural forces. The subjects are not integrated into an evidently cohesive program.'[86] But the difficulty in identifying Bluebeard definitively should not lead us to conclude that the figure was chosen at random. The programme's cohesion is elusive, not illusory. There is still much to recommend Boardman's reading. Set against the regionalism that continued to exist even after Attica underwent synoecism, Bluebeard gives physical expression to the complex, convoluted entanglement of three distinct regions that were separate yet at the same time inseparable, the paradox of federation. Hans-Joachim Gehrke has interpreted the history of the Archaic period as caught in a tug of war between centripetal forces of synoecism and centrifugal forces of regionalism – a contradiction that may inform Bluebeard's hybridity.[87]

---

[84] Boardman 1972: 71–2. On the geographical zones and their designations, see Hopper 1961.
[85] Boardman 1972: 71.   [86] Mertens 2019: 17.   [87] Gehrke 1986.

Figures from the Plupast

Another way of interpreting Bluebird that complements the regional reading is to see Bluebeard as a representation of the ancestral deities who were witnesses to the origins of the Athenian community in the deep past: the Tritopatores. Their presence on the largest Athenian temple in the sixth century reminds us that contemporary Athenians were still in the process of fixing upon an historical identity. Athens had not been a major centre of Mycenaean civilization, to judge by the Homeric poems, and references to the 'strong house of Erechtheus' are more likely to reflect Athenian redactions of the epic poems that coincided, not coincidentally, with the first performances of the Panathenaia around the same time as Bluebeard was carved. The Tritopatores were the spirits of collective ancestors, whose continued existence contributed to the Athenian notion of autochthony.

Information about them is confusing. At least three Atthidographers attempted to explain who or what they were, and the variation in their accounts suggests that by the fourth century the Tritopatores were among the more obscure figures in the Athenian pantheon.[88] According to Philochoros they were 'the first to be born' (γεγονέναι πρώτους). The men of former times considered the earth and sun their parents, 'and those born of them (to be) "third fathers" (*tritoi pateres*).' According to this explanation, the '*-patores*' element in their name was due to the fact that they were the progenitors of the human race. Furthermore, it seems as if Philochoros took the prefix '*trito-*' as an indication of sequence: they were third because they were preceded by two primordial beings who had never been born. A similar family tree was reported in another work of Atthidography, the anonymous *Exegetikon*, with the additional information that the Tritopatores were named Kottos, Briareus and Gyges.[89] These names are borrowed from Hesiod's account of the Hundred-Handers who helped Zeus overcome the Titans, an episode that has nothing to do with the Tritopatores, but the error is revealing since it shows that the '*trito-*' element could be taken not as ordinal (i.e., 'third') but as cardinal (i.e., 'three' or 'triple'). This ambiguity runs through Athenian treatments of the Tritopatores. If they are 'third fathers', a natural inference would be that were understood collectively as great-grandfathers. This was appropriate in a society concerned with ancestry. As Nicholas Jones has pointed

---

[88] For sources and a useful discussion, see Nicholas Jones' commentary to Philochoros, *BNJ* 328 F182.
[89] *BNJ* 352 F1.

out, 'The "third fathers" will be great-grandfathers and thus correspond to the most recent generation of which a person in antiquity was likely to have no living memory.' As great-grandfathers they would connect the viewer to a time before the past with which the viewer was personally familiar. Instead, Bluebeard invites the viewer to tell stories and participate in the construction of a narrative shared by the community that chose the figure as adornment suitable for a temple. There is an ambiguity here. If his triple bodies signify a succession of recent generations, Bluebeard's snaky coils suggest the earthborn autochthony from a more distant past that the Athenians so prided themselves on. In this way, Bluebeard stands on the cusp of individual memory, three generations deep, and cultural memory, born of stories shared and circulated by the community. Bluebeard's hybridity marks it as a denizen of that other space: the deep past.[90] For this reason, the mythographers viewed the Tritopatores as going back not three generations but to the beginning of time and to the original act of generation. The Athenians prayed and sacrificed to the Tritopatores for fertility when they were about to marry.[91] As Renaud Gagné writes, 'The Tritopatores of ritual are textbook examples of the collective ancestors found in the cults of "kinship-based societies" throughout the world. Ambivalent figures of social continuity in death, markers of group cohesion, the Tritopatores of cult are found exactly where we expect them: in rituals of purification and procreation.'[92] Such an expression of the Athenian collectivity would be well suited to adorn an Athenian temple long before the consolidation of Athenian democracy and the emergence of Theseus as the democracy's hero. Less explicitly political than its Periclean descendant, the sixth-century Akropolis reveals an Athenian community looking not to a glorious future, but to a distant past when the kings, lawgivers and ancestors evoked autochthony through the very hybridity that made them creatures of the earth. By 500 BC, after Bluebeard was first placed in the pediment of the Hekatompedon, and perhaps in the generation after that temple and pediment were replaced, the Athenians renewed their collective worship of the Tritopatores with the construction of

---

[90] Relevant to this discussion is Vansina's well-known observation that informal generational memory rarely goes back more than three generations in oral societies. Bluebeard's triplication thus has a geographic significance (Boardman 1972) and a temporal meaning. Before the third generation comes Vansina's Floating Gap, before which lies the realm of Cultural Memory. See Vansina 1985, and for an overview of collective and cultural memory, see Assmann 2008.

[91] Phanodemos (=BNJ 325 F6). Notable in this context is the proverbial expression, Παῖς μοι Τριτογενὴς εἴη, μὴ Τριτογένεια. Schol. T Il. 9.39 offers a number of explanations for the -*trito* component but the underlying wish is unambiguous: may the child be a boy and not a girl.

[92] Gagné 2007: 3.

a shrine at the intersection of two major roads in the Kerameikos. The area was a large necropolis, and an appropriate location for a *hieron* dedicated to the ancestors.[93] These ancestral deities remained a part of local religious life. In the Marathonian Tetrapolis, the sacrificial calendar from the first half of the fourth century stipulated the sacrifice of a sheep and the presentation of a table to the Tritopatores during Skirophorion.[94]

A final piece of evidence supports identifying Bluebeard as the Tritopatores: both are manifestations of the winds. The Atthidographer Damon explicitly states that the Tritopatores were the winds, while the Orphic *Physika* claimed that the Tritopatores were doorkeepers and guardians of the winds.[95] (The *Physika* also names the Tritopatores as Amalkeides, Protokles and Protokleon, and is therefore part of the tradition that casts the Tritopatores, like Bluebeard, as three beings.) This early Orphic text has recently been dated to the fifth century and so predates the Atthidographers. More significantly, the association of the Tritopatores with the winds is not a casual meteorological association. In cosmogenic poetry wind was frequently equated with life force, so that the gods who controlled fertility were also viewed as gods who controlled the winds; 'The Tritopatores of the *Physika* are presented at once as the common mythical ancestors of mankind as well as the guardians of new life.'[96] So much for the Tritopatores as wind deities. Can Bluebeard also be identified with the winds? The suggestion was first made by Furtwängler in 1905, but the strongest case was made in 1965 by Sylvia Benton.[97] Citing Payne's observation that creatures of the air were always depicted with wings and serpent tails, she noted that Bluebeard's three heads face in different directions, odd if the demon is watching the struggle between Herakles and Triton on the other side of the pediment but appropriate if they represent the different directions of the winds. Proceeding from the view that Bluebeard was a creature of the air, she proposed that the figure holding a bird is Zephyros, the west wind, who had married Podarge, identified as a shearwater. The other winds she suggested were the northwestern wind, Skiron and the north wind, Boreas. Benton's identification of Zephyros is by far the best explanation of the bird attribute, but Hesiod (*Theogony* 380) names the three most important winds as Zephyros (west), Boreas (north) and Notos (south), and it is more likely that these are the figures personified by Bluebeard. The attributes held by the three figures fit this identification neatly. The wavy attribute identified as water is appropriate for Boreas, a northern wind that was associated with

---

[93] The shrine was three-sided. On the Tritopatreion and ancestor cult, see Antonaccio 1994: 264–5. For an up-to-date summary, see Stroszeck 2010.
[94] *SEG* 50.168 A2 32, 52.   [95] Orpheus F 318 Kern.   [96] Gagné 2007: 18.   [97] Benton 1965.

storms and winter weather, including rain, and who was described as having a serpent tail instead of feet.[98] Notos blew from the south and was associated with hot climates. Theophrastos observed there was a connection between location and the character of the wind: 'if it comes from fiery-hot locations that also have air thick and full of fire, (the wind) in fact appears to be excessive in its heat'.[99] Fire would therefore be a suitable attribute for the south wind blowing from Africa.[100]

The centaurs and snake-kings that figure so prominently in the artistic production of the Archaic period cannot be reduced to a single reading. They are not allegories waiting to be decoded, and they convey more than symbolic meaning. Instead, they are an imaginative response to a host of anxieties focused on order and disorder. As part of their grappling with these questions the Greeks recognized that the most potent threats to order are located deep within humans themselves. In an environment of intense cultural exchange with other people with their own rich traditions of monsters, the Greeks adapted and redeployed hybrid figures to give shape to fundamental questions about humanity. This was the pressing question of the classical period, but the answers were more than purely ontological. Gorgons, centaurs and snake-ancestors made different modes of existence vividly real for the Greeks. Placed on temples, painted on vases, spoken of in plays, they bridged the gap between our time and the deep, mythical past, giving it a tangible, visible form. This presence of the past in the present was a powerful component of Greek culture, rendering Greece into a mnemotope.[101]

The topography of Athens resonated with the deep past, from the Akropolis where the gods left their marks on the rock, to the buildings below, where the bones of Theseus were deposited or the oath sworn by the Amazons was recalled. The stage too provided reminders of the ties that bound Athens to its mythic past. Consider an audience's eyes as they watch

---

[98] Paus. 5.19. [99] Theophrastos, *On Winds* 21 (tr. Mayhew).

[100] Equally problematic is Kiilerich's interpretations of the attributes in Bluebeard's hands (136): 'In his hands he is holding attributes alluding to his parents. The flowing water is a symbol of his mother Kallirhoe, the beautifully flowing. The flame is a symbol of his father Chrysaor, the golden weapon. The bird is a chthonic emblem.' Such rebuses are rare in Greek sculpture. Aside from the stork that stands for the Pelargikon on the Telemachos Monument (Beschi 1967/68a: 386–97), visual puns are not well attested, with the understandable exception of instances involving the name Leon and its cognates, such as a lioness dedicated to Leiana, the mistress of Aristogeiton (Paus. 1.23.1–2) and a funerary monument of a lion dedicated to certain Leon of Sinope (Vermeule 1972: 55). Furthermore, the ingenuity of Kiilerich's reading still fails to explain why a unique, unwarlike, serpentiform Geryon would figure in the pediment of a sixth-century Athenian temple. (I thank Andrew Stewart for the references to Leon and Leiana.)

[101] On the presence of the past in the present, see Runia: 2006. On the mnemotope, see Assmann 1992: 60. The topic of cultural memory has generated a wave of recent studies. Foundational remains Halbwachs 1941. For an overview, see Schama 1995.

Aeschylus' Erinyes wake from their fitful slumber. As these bat-like creatures who thirsted for the blood of criminals begin to stir, for a moment the audience experiences the awakening of creatures from the realm of myth. Our nightmares come alive before us. Although in the audience's time these deities were venerated as the Dread Goddesses, having been transformed into the Eumenides, they never lost the bloodlust that harked back to their primeval existence.[102] Such figures reminded the Greeks that the shadow of a more savage past looms over our daily existence. By embodying the elemental, the horrific and different ways of being in the world, hybrids, monsters and the entire cast of non-human beings supplemented present realities and allowed other existences to impinge on the day-to-day world.[103]

Visualizing other, fictional realities is, of course, hardly unique to the Greeks, but primeval fears can be powerfully reanimated by current anxieties. Sci-Fi in the 1950s, especially B-grade movies and cheap magazines, gave expression to post-atomic anxiety, often in the form of irradiated monsters – *our* creations of a recent past. So too the Greeks turned to hybrids to give form and face to the primeval drives, compulsions and anxieties still lurking behind the veil of quotidian existence.[104] The transformation of the Erinyes, for example, balanced confidence in judicial institutions such as the Areopagos with the need for bloody vengeance that is never fully satisfied by a jury trial. The lurking feeling that human justice does not satisfy our thirst for retribution is hard to shake, but the transformation of the Erinyes at least gives that feeling a shape and a face. The appearance of judicial process is the Eumenides placated; the face of revenge is the implacable Erinys. By crossing the barriers between categories – past/present, primeval/quotidian, human/animal – the Greek hybrid created an imaginative space, permitting the audience to immerse themselves in a different reality. There is enormous attraction in such imaginative projection, complicating and challenging norms and expectations. In our times, for example, slasher movies appeal to male desires and anxieties focused on the female body, but paradoxically the same films also allow the audience to identify with the female victim/hero.[105] This feminine point of

---

[102] On the Erinyes as bat-like, see Maxwell-Stuart 1973. Heath 2005: 241 calls them 'vampire Erinyes'. For more discussion of the Eumenides, see McInerney 2021a: 26–9.
[103] For the Erinyes in Orphic cosmology, see Herrero de Jáuregui 2015: 613.
[104] On post-atomic anxieties in Sci-Fi, see Rabkin 2004.
[105] On slasher movies, see Clover 1987. One of Clover's observations is especially interesting from the point of view of the psychological attraction of the hybrid: 'That the slasher film speaks deeply and obsessively to male anxieties and desires seems clear – if nothing else from the maleness of the majority audience. And yet these are texts in which the categories masculine

view offers the male viewer an imaginative space at odds with the more usual male gaze, making the experience of such films more complex and engaging. Accordingly, as cultural products, Godzilla, Leatherface and Bluebeard are all inflection points in their respective cultures, signposting imaginative responses to the anxieties of the day. In the polymorphous, multilingual setting of the Greeks' engagement with the Mediterranean world, Archaic hybrids represented the taming of all that threatened, all that was monstrous, chaotic, titanic. Consigned to story, poetry and visual media, hybrids adorned every corner of Archaic culture, a constant reminder that the triumph of the current order of things human was only ever a qualified success.

    and feminine, traditionally embodied in male and female, are collapsed into one and the same character – a character who is anatomically female and one whose point of view the spectator is unambiguously invited, by the usual set of literary-structural and cinematic conventions, to share' (219–20).

8 | Hermaphrodites and Other Bodies

> Well, Dionysos, what do you think? Eros, Hermaphroditos and Priapos have the same mother, but are completely different when it comes to their appearance and their habits, no? Eros is exceptionally good looking, an archer of considerable skill and master of all. But Hermaphroditos is effeminate, only half a man, and looks pretty ambiguous. You can't tell whether he's a boy or a girl. Priapos, on the other hand, is almost too much of a man!
>
> Lucian, *Dialogues of the Gods* 273 (trans. McInerney)

Hermaphrodites and the Tyranny of Categories

Hybrids remain in the mythic imagination, exemplifying what Lévi-Strauss identified as the 'ambiguous and equivocal' character of myth, in which the tension of opposing cosmic orders is never entirely resolved.[1] This is illustrated in contrasting theogonies in Hesiod, whose Olympians must defeat the Titans but who still inhabit a cosmos in which the elemental forces of Night and Pontos bring forth hideous creatures. Each generation continues to produce monstrosities, such as the offspring of Keto and Phorkys: the Graiai, the Gorgons, Echidna (half nymph, half snake). Not only are they monstrous in form, but the ways in which they are created are also troubling. The first monster born to Echidna is Orthos (*Theogony* 309), but Hesiod reports that after being overpowered (ὑποδμηθεῖσα) by Orthos, Echidna gave birth (ἔτικτε) to the Sphinx and the Nemean Lion, making their birth the result of mother–child incest. The birth of Chimaira is equally troublesome, being the result of parthenogenesis by Hydra. These are chaotic practices that are supposed to have been left behind in the ascent of the Olympians, but rather than dismiss these as impossibilities Jenny Strauss Clay takes them as genuine anomalies that run counter to the upward trajectory of Hesiod's cosmos:

---

[1] Lévi-Strauss 1955: 440. See also Clay 2020.

But all these arguments rest on the unspoken assumption that the generation of monsters follows the patterns and norms laid out elsewhere in the *Theogony* and presupposed by its whole genealogical schema: that is that the evolution of the cosmos progresses from a relative lack of definition and differentiation to a successively higher level of differentiation and definition. It is, however, by no means clear whether, in the case of monsters, such an assumption is warranted or whether the catalogue as a whole in fact presents such a progression.[2]

As in the case of the Erinyes and the various Athenian snake-kings, Hesiod's monsters play by different rules. They are not merely a reminder of the chaos from which, following Zeus, we arose; they are the lingering presence of that chaos.

Hybrids, then, point to alternative ways of being human.[3] In Empedokles' fantastic cosmology, for example, the possibilities of how to be human are almost endless. He imagines a time of creation, when the chaos of strife gave way to the generative power of love. Out of the earth sprang up a torrent of limbs and organs: heads without necks, arms without shoulders, eyes without foreheads. The combinations of these produce a wild profusion of humans in countless different forms:

> And as these were mixed ten thousand tribes of mortals poured forth,
> Fitted together in all kinds of forms, a wonder to behold.
>
> Empedokles F 35 (D–K) (tr. Inwood)

The process of indiscriminate blending continued, producing humans with two faces and two chests. Others were oxlike with men's faces, or human-like with ox-heads.[4] For Empedokles, anticipating Darwin, the creatures that are successful combinations successfully breed, while those that are unfit to survive do not. As Gordon Campbell has pointed out, Empedokles' system is, besides Lucretius' *De Rerum Natura*, 'the only other example of a scientific non-teleological account of the origin of species extant from the ancient world'.[5] This is true, in the sense that no intelligent design is running the operation, but there is still a type of teleology at work. Aberrations are winnowed out. The human form that exists, therefore, is the

---

[2] Clay 2003: 160.
[3] Currie 2012 insists that in Hesiod's 'myth of the races' the various *gene* are neither ages, civilizations, nor generations: 'The meaning that we must accept for γένος (and γενεή) in MoR is "race", "breed" or similar.' (p. 41) He concludes, 'this is a history of discrete "mankinds"' (p. 64). See also Buxton 1999: 1–21.
[4] On Empedokles' cosmological scheme, see Campbell 2006. For discussion of F 35 and the notion that the constituent elements combine to form a superorganism, see Sedley 2016.
[5] Campbell 2006.

human at its most perfect.[6] Like Hesiod's genealogy of the gods, Empedokles' cosmology is thus ultimately constructed on a dichotomy between the human (as it is) and the many alternatives, all of which, finally, are unviable. There is, however, one hybrid body which continues to destabilize dramatically a conventional understanding of what constitutes the human: the hermaphrodite.[7] In Empedokles' cosmology the phase of monstrous creations that precede the current order includes creatures formed by the combination of male and female organs (μεμιγμένα τῆι μὲν ἀπ'ἀνδρῶν/τῆι δὲ γυναικοφυῆ. D-K61). Such hermaphrodites, in Linnea Åshede's succinct phrase, constituted 'an embodied challenge to gender binarism'.[8] At this point we are taking a step beyond the definition of hybrids as specifically human/animal combinations, but the hybridity of the male/female, as Empedokles demonstrates, is conceptually very close and similarly breaks down a categorical boundary that is normally fixed. As Brisson amply shows, in antiquity the hermaphrodite was frequently referred to as a *teras* or *paradoxon* – labels often attached also to hybrids.[9] Such anomalies existed in the animal world as well in popular thought, such as in the case of the hyena. According to popular belief, it shifted its sexual activity from male to female year by year. This was a challenge to Aristotle's attempts to produce an orderly systematization of natural phenomena. The philosopher took pains to debunk the belief that the hyena had both sets of genitals, and that it alternated between mounting and being mounted.[10] Instead, Aristotle championed a rigid view of binarism based on equally fixed embryological

---

[6] Maurice Bowra saw this vision of perfection as indicative of an identification of the human with the divine: 'The main subject of Greek art was the human body, whether it was representing divinities or men, and this is in keeping with the conception of a single world, in which gods and mortals resembled each other sufficiently to behave similarly.' See Plazy 2001: 33.

[7] When a child is born without the capacity to convert testosterone into dihydrotestosterone – a necessary precondition for virilization in utero – it appears at birth with seeming female characteristics. At puberty, however, naturally occurring testosterone initiates otherwise typical features of male development, such as testicular descent and hirsutism, as well as the fusion of the labia into a scrotum. See Herdt 1990. Such late-onset hermaphroditism has been reported in contemporary communities such as Las Salinas in the Dominican Republic and the Sambia of Papa New Guinea. In these cases, the community often perceives such individuals as members of a 'third sex' with 'ambivalent sex-role socialization'; both cultures also have specific vocabulary to explain the condition of these persons. See Fausto-Sterling 2000.

[8] Åshede 2020: 81. Von Stackelberg 2014: 395 notes that 'ἀνδρογύνος/*androgynus* and ἑρμαφρόδιτος/*hermaphroditus* are always masculine' and sees this as 'a verbal counterpoint to visual femininity'.

[9] Brisson 2002. King 2015: 254 notes that in 1575 Ambroise Paré included a discussion of the hermaphrodite in a treatise on monsters.

[10] Aristot., *GA* 757a, dismissing the idea of dual genitalia as naïve (εὐηθικῶς). See Gordon 2010: 264. Aristotle's attempts to quash popular belief were not successful. The hyena's sex-shifting was reported by Aelian, *De animal.* 1.25; Pliny, *NH* 8.105 and Timotheus of Gaza 4.1 in the fifth century AD.

theories. Whether emphasizing the importance of the right or left side of the womb, exploring the existence of male and female semen, or interpreting the role of heat and cold in determining sex, thinkers from Empedokles and Demokritos to Aristotle always began from a set of polarities that resulted in a strict gender division of male and female. Some took this binarism to extraordinary lengths: according to Aristotle, Leophanes reported that 'males who copulate with the right or left testicle tied up produce male or female offspring respectively'.[11] Such schemes are challenged by the hermaphrodite, as the images familiar from sculpture, wall painting and gems make clear. The hermaphrodite has a youthful, intersexed body with both breasts and a penis, often revealed by a carefully draped robe[12] (Figure 8.1).

Befitting this ambiguity, responses in antiquity to the hermaphrodite also fell into two camps, as Diodorus Siculus understood:

> After Priapos some mythographers give accounts of Hermaphroditos, so called because he was the off-spring of Hermes and Aphrodite. His name combines those of both his parents. Some say that he is a god who appears from time to time among men, and that when he is born his body combines that of a man and that of a woman. With respect to beauty and softness it is much like a woman, but it has the masculinity and aggression of a man, so that the natural parts of both man and woman combine in its creation. Others, however, argue that creatures of such a sort are monsters, and since they are rarely born they are omens of evil or good to come.
>
> Diod. Sic. 4.6.5 (tr. Walton)

According to Diodorus Siculus, then, for some Hermaphroditos was a god who combined feminine beauty and male strength.[13] It was a combination amounting to more than the sum of the parts, since his body, formed of both male and female parts, strikingly evokes procreation itself. Every child is a combination of its parents, so every human could be said to be a hybrid of sorts, but one in which one sex dominates and the other recedes into the shadows. Even if, as many ancient thinkers recognized, the child resembled the mother, the father or both, 'in countenance, voice and hair of their ancestors', the child's body usually displayed only one sex.[14] The hermaphrodite refuses to favour one sex over the other.

---

[11] Arist. *De Gen. Anim.* IV. 763b–765a.
[12] *LIMC* 5.1 268–85 (Ajootian). On hermaphroditism and intersexuality, see Grosz 2020: 277–8.
[13] For the tradition of the hermaphrodite as a perfect body, see King 2015: 253.
[14] Lucret., *DRN* 4.1209–26. See also Aristotle *HA* 585b32. Most ancient discussions of inherited characteristics endorsed the notion that gender was determined by the partial or total victory (ἐπικράτεια) of male seed over the female seed or the reproductive matter. See Brown 1987: 320–1.

Hermaphrodites and the Tyranny of Categories 235

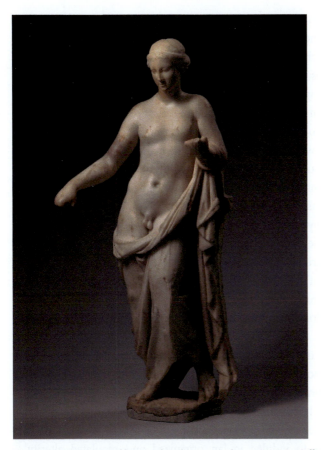

Figure 8.1 Statuette of hermaphrodite, second century BC. Hellenistic Greek. White marble. 60.3 × 30.5 × 16.5 cm (23 3/4 × 12 × 6 1/2 in.) Princeton University Art Museum. Museum purchase, Fowler McCormick, Class of 1922, Fund 2009–81.

Going beyond the boundaries of a strict gender binary, the hermaphrodite proclaims that it is both, and thereby destabilizes a cultural order constructed on binaries.[15]

If gender binarism is inextricably bound up with a conventional anthropocentric outlook, then the hermaphrodite is post-human, in the sense in which that term has recently been used – namely, to suggest the inadequacy of the view that the western male is the apex of creation and culture.[16] Yet even here the hermaphrodite presents a unique challenge. Recent critiques of the

---

[15] On the figure of the hermaphrodite in twentieth-century cultural discourse, with a focus on Tod Browning's *Freaks*, see Padva 2018. For the transgressive qualities of the hermaphrodite especially in Foucault's treatment of modern sexuality, see Leporda 2011.

[16] For discussion of this use of the term, see Fahlander 2017, Chesi and Spiegel 2020: 4–8, and Witmore 2020.

anthropocentric worldview, particularly deriving from Latour's actor–network theory and the related object-oriented ontology, see objects as agents, acting upon as much as being acted upon. These theories take humans down a peg or two, or, as Levi Bryant puts it, 'Humans are *among* beings and are beings among being, they aren't at the center of being, nor are they the necessary condition for being.'[17] But the hermaphrodite asks 'what is that being?' This is not meant facetiously. Rather, it is to suggest that this composite figure, by playing with the binary, constitutes a critique of the commonly assumed construction of the human that in its own way is as forceful as posthumanism. It permits a space for a powerfully challenging alternative to be imagined. If man is the measure of all things, what does the existence of a hermaphrodite say of that measure? All humans are produced by the union of male and female, and the hermaphrodite arises from exactly the same union, but is differently configured. Does this not suggest another way of being the product of male and female combined? The usual answer offered by ancient authors – that the hermaphrodite is a monstrous aberration – merely highlights conventional assumptions around bodies and avoids the categorical problem posed by the hybrid: these are the products of our imaginative engagement with the world beyond the limits of quotidian experience. Putting the past into the present, reconfiguring male and female, connecting us to the earth, hybrids push our imagination to new places: some dangerous, some odd, yet all rich with possibilities. Transvestism works in much the same way, if in a quieter register, allowing the performance of komasts and Dionysiac revellers to indulge in 'an organized and regulated alterity'.[18] Satyrs with chignons, maenads in satyr shorts – both undercut the neat heterosexual homogeneity of society, both in the alternative world of vase imagery and in the Anakreontic performances they depicted.

Such possibilities, as Diodorus' comments make clear, can be deeply unsettling. For those for whom culture exists to foster human perfection 'as distinguished from our animality', as Matthew Arnold put it, the blending that occurs in the body of the hermaphrodite constitutes, at best, a prophetic monstrosity.[19] In this dominant discourse binaries are the

---

[17] Bryant 2011: 130.

[18] Surtees 2014: 288. On the Anakreontic vases, see Miller 1999. On Dionysiac themes, see Frontisi-Ducroux and Lissarrague 1990. For transvestite rituals of adolescent rites of passage, see Leitao 1995.

[19] On the conflicting treatments of the hermaphrodite, encompassing appreciation and disgust, see Ajootian 1997, Brisson 2002 and Swancutt 2007. The full reference from Arnold's *Culture and Anarchy* is: 'Religion says: "The kingdom of God is within you"; and culture, in like manner, places human perfection in an internal condition, in the growth and predominance of our humanity proper, as distinguished from our animality' (Arnold 1994 [1869]: 32–3).

product of clearly defined oppositional categories: male/female, owner/slave, active/passive, civilized/barbaric. In their totality they amount to a system that only makes sense as long as the boundaries hold. Without boundaries, phenomena cannot remain discrete. Without categories, there are no distinctions. Here, then, are the two possibilities connoted by the hermaphrodite's hybridity: on the one hand, a prefiguring of integration that imagines a body free of the constraints of sex (not unlike the bodies imagined by Aristophanes in the *Symposium*); on the other, the breakdown of meaning and the subversion of culture.[20] Both readings are constructed from the hermaphrodite's binary form, which, while unusual, is nevertheless a reminder of the composite nature of all human bodies. In this sense, the hermaphrodite is an incarnation of Lévi-Strauss's reading of myth, the supreme example of one reconciling two.[21]

As holistic as this explanation may be, it fails to take account of a crucial dimension of the hermaphrodite: his cultic significance. The earliest attestation of the figure, in fact, is an early-fourth-century votive inscription from Athens: Φανώ Ἑρμαφρωδ[ί]|τωι εὐξαμένη. ('Phano in fulfilment of a vow to Hermaphroditos'.)[22] Similarly, the first literary attestation occurs in Theophrastos' *Characters* (late fourth century), in which the Superstitious Man is said to hang garlands on Hermaphroditos on the fourth and seventh days of the month. This religious dimension was never entirely effaced by either the disgust of those who were repelled by the hermaphrodite nor by those who reduced the figure to a curiosity suitable for a Roman garden.[23] The Roman hermaphrodite, in fact, is but a pale reflection of a far richer story of gender complexity, beginning with the story of the creation of Hermaphroditos in the city that claimed to be his birth place: Halikarnassos.

---

[20] Brisson 2002: 5 makes the point neatly: 'Dual sexuality may pose the problem of the origins and significance of the oppositions on which the whole of reality is organized, but at the same time it envisages the possibility of bypassing them through mediation and thereby turns out to be an integral element in metaphysics.'

[21] Lévi-Strauss 1963 [1958]. I am all too aware of the risk of treating the ancient Mediterranean as if our categories of gender, cis- and trans-, can be applied unproblematically. Yet the roles and categories labelled 'normal' or 'abnormal', 'conventional' or 'deviant', have roots, and how the ancient Mediterranean structured sex and gender roles is not entirely alien to our own discourse. I do not claim that the culture wars, so-called, of the twenty-first century occurred in Antiquity too, but our growing awareness of these points of conflict should alert us to similar tensions around bodies and gender in the ancient Mediterranean.

[22] *SEG* 40.195 bis. Although there is no evidence for a sanctuary of Hermaphroditos at this stage, the inscription is found on a small plinth on which probably stood a herm, presumably depicting the god.

[23] Swancutt 2007.

Salmakis and Hermaphroditos

The creation of Hermaphroditos is an episode well known from Ovid. In the *Metamorphoses* the Roman poet recounts the tale of a nymph, Salmacis, who falls in love with the beautiful son of Hermes and Aphrodite, named Hermaphroditus.[24] So beautiful is he that Salmacis declares her love and offers herself to him, but Hermaphroditus modestly puts her off. Salmacis retires to the bushes, but watching Hermaphroditus strip to continue bathing she is overcome by desire and leaps on him. The beautiful youth struggles to resist her, until the nymph calls on the gods to fulfil her desire:

> O Gods, so order it that from this day
> he will not part from me – nor I from him!
> Her wish was granted: their two bodies blent,
> both face and figure to a single form;
> so when a twig is grafted to a tree,
> they join together in maturity.
>
> Ovid, *Metam.* 2. 371–6 (tr. Martin)

Thus transformed into a languid half-man, Hermaphroditus in turn calls on the gods, not to release him but to inflict the same fate on any man who steps into the fountain of Salmacis. They grant his promise and the spring becomes notorious for its emasculating effect. The spring, in fact, is critical to the story, as Ovid signals at the outset when he writes 'Learn how the fountain, Salmacis, became so infamous; learn how it enervates and softens the limbs of those who chance to bathe.'[25] Ovid's story has had a long afterlife and has been a popular source for artists fascinated by the questions of female desire and sexual identity.[26] The episode, however, took on a new face when in 1995 an inscription came to light in rescue excavations in the Turkish city of Bodrum (ancient Halikarnassos). Built into the wall of a fountain house close to the shore by the southwestern entrance to the harbour, the inscription is an exchange between an interlocutor and Aphrodite, who answers the question 'What is the Pride of

---

[24] Ovid, *Meta.* 4.285–372.
[25] For other references to the waters of Salmakis, see Strabo 14.2.16 and Vitruvius 2.8.11. Brown 1927: 4, 6–9 notes that bathing in an enchanted pool is frequently associated with sex change in Hindu myth.
[26] For later depictions, see *Water Nymph Salmacis*, engraving by Philip Galle, 1587, Samuel Van Hoogstraten's oil painting of ca. 1671, Bernard Picart's etching of 1733, *The Nymph Salmacis and Hermaphroditus* by François-Joseph Navez, 1829, and Rupert Bunny's oil painting of 1919.

Halikarnassos?'[27] In response, the inscription recounts the following version of the story of Salmakis:

> And Halikarnassos settled the delightful hill beside the stream of Salmakis, sung of as dear to the immortals, and her domain includes the desirable home of the nymph, she who once received our child in her kindly arms and reared Hermaphroditos the all-excellent, he who invented marriage and was first to bind together wedded couples by his law, and she herself beneath the holy waters in the cave that she pours forth makes gentle the savage minds of men. (tr. Lloyd-Jones)

It is immediately apparent that, like Ovid, the Halikarnassian inscription is focused on the Salmakis fountain but that it treats the figure of Hermaphoditos very differently from the Roman poet's story of metamorphosis.[28] There is no suggestion in the inscription that the episode will result in freakish hybridity, and in the place of a crazed water spirit we have a loving *threpta*, who raises a wholly natural child of Hermes and Aphrodite. Furthermore, in the Halikarnassian inscription Hermaphroditos is envisaged as a culture hero: the inventor of marriage. His name therefore connotes a conventional union of male father, Hermes, and female mother, Aphrodite, without any hint of a monstrous transformation of his body. In fact, rather than subverting the gender binarism that underlies traditional codes of marriage, Halikarnassian Hermaphroditos reinforces them by mapping a social institution onto a conventional understanding of gender. There is a blending here, but it is the perfect union of a heterosexual couple in a happy marriage (ll. 15–22).[29]

It is significant that there is nothing to identify Halikarnassian Hermaphroditos as aberrant, because this Hermaphroditos represents a happy union of another sort. The community that claimed him as their own, Halikarnassos, was always known as a mixed community of Greeks and Karians, and the figure of Hermaphroditos served as a symbol of the peaceful coexistence of different communities side by side (or at least its possibility).[30]

---

[27] *Editio princeps*: Isager 1998. Other early editions include Merkelbach and Stauber 1998 and Lloyd-Jones 1999a, supplemented by Lloyd-Jones 1999b, whose translation is used here. Still more translations and commentaries are noted in *SEG* 48.1330. On the vicinity of Salmakis also see Blümel 1993: 11 and Delrieux 2013, 240. For bibliography on the inscription from 1998 to 2016, see www.sdu.dk/en/om_sdu/institutter_centre/iks/forskning/forskningsprojekter/halikarnassos/sites_and_places/salmakis-fountain.

[28] For comparison of the Ovidian and Halikarnassian stories see Isager 1998, Gagné 2006, Romano 2009, Groves 2016, Santini 2016, and McInerney 2021b.

[29] Romano 2009, Szepessy 2014.

[30] On Karian/Greek relations, see Hornblower 1982, 346–51, Virgilio 1988, 53–71 and Chrubasik 2017. Mitchell 2017 reads the Hekatomnid taste for grandiose Greek architectural forms as a means of blurring the ethnic differences of Greeks and Karians.

In the fifth century these separate communities began moving towards unification, but the *syllogos*, or assembly, that convened to decide major affairs was a still a joint meeting of two distinct ethnic groups: Halikarnassians (predominantly Greek) and Salmakitians (predominantly Karian).[31] In this bicultural environment marked by the encounter of Greek and indigenous traditions and languages, Hermaphroditos served as an allegory of cultural mixing, a phenomenon identified with the waters of Salmakis. Traces of this local story of the encounter of ethnic groups at the fountain of Salmakis can be glimpsed in Vitruvius' account of the arrival of Greek colonists from Troizen:

> Sometime after this, one of the colonists, in order to make money, set up a stall with all manner of goods near the spring because of the quality of its water. He operated the stall so well that it attracted the barbarians. At first they came down one by one, and as they collected in greater numbers, they were transformed from their rough and wild habits thanks to the pleasure of a Greek way of life and were so induced to come back. As a result, this water earned its reputation not because of the blemish of some shameless disease, but because the souls of the barbarians were softened by the sweetness of good manners.
>
> Vitruvius 2.8.12 (tr. McInerney)

In this version of Halikarnassos' local history, the waters of Salmakis were the site of a Middle Ground where Greek and Karian successfully encountered each other. Both communities continued to exist side by side for hundreds of years, and the district of Salmakis remained associated with Karian elements in the population. But not everyone bought into this vision of a happily integrated Halikarnassos. The powerful clan of the Antheadai, priests of the cult of Poseidon, remained defiantly and exclusively Greek, at least in their official genealogy. (In a list of priestholders purporting to go back more than 800 years, the only non-Greek name to occur is Maussollos.)[32] The story of Hermaphroditos at Halikarnassos lends itself to competing narratives: in one tradition his gender mixing is monstrous. This is the version known to Strabo and Vitruvius, and is most fully elaborated by Ovid. In the other account, emerging from the local discourse environment of Halikarnassos itself, he is presented as a culture hero and a model of integration. This ambiguity is a perfect example of the ambivalence surrounding hybridity in general: is it better to blend Greek and Karian

---

[31] On the *syllogos* of the Halikarnassians and Salmakitians, see *Halikarnassos* 1 (ML 32). For earlier interpretations, see Maffi 1988 and Piñol Villanueva 2013 (but Gschnitzer 1961 remains the best treatment).

[32] On the Antheadai, see Carbon and Pirenne-Delforge 2013: 108–9. For the lists of the Anthead priests of Poseidon, see Isager 2014 and 2015.

communities, allowing intermarriage, combining the Halikarnassians and the Salmakitians into a single *syllogos*, in order to create a unified community (which inscriptions refer to as *sympantes Halikarnassioi*), or does one community's survival depend on erecting walls, restricting participation and maintaining separation?[33] How one answered that question determined whether one admired or loathed Hermaphroditos.

The 'Pride of Halikarnassos' preserves a benign version of the myth, in which gender confusion is played down, so that one might be tempted to see the harsher versions like those of Strabo, Vitruvius and Ovid, in which Hermaphoditos is cast as an epicene hybrid, as a wholly Greek invention designed to demonize the indigenous Karian population. There is, however, another dimension that complicates this overly schematic breakdown but which is important to our understanding of the hermaphrodite. In southwestern Asia Minor there appears to have existed a tradition connecting divine figures with dual sexualities.[34] Aphrodite, the mother of Hermaphroditos and the addressee of the 'Pride of Halikarnassos' was represented in the region as bearded Aphrodite long before the Salmakis inscription was cut in the late second century.[35] Bearded Aphrodite's presence in southern Anatolia is part of a much older Near Eastern tradition according to which the goddess was both the Evening Star, sensual, female and associated with sexual attraction, as well as the Morning Star, cold, cruel, male and identified with war.[36] This gender duality runs through older Sumerian and Akkadian literature and cult, beginning with 'the changed *pilipili*': women who carried a broken spear as a token of masculine identity.[37] It also figured in the feminized performances of the *assinnu* (men anally penetrated in a cultic setting) and the warlike behaviour of the *kurgarrû*, thought to be cross-dressing women.[38] Both groups inverted traditional gender roles as part of cult performances in honour of Akkadian Istar and her Sumerian equivalent, Inana. As Sophus Helle has recently noted, 'Part of the awe that clung to the goddess was her power to change the sex of anyone at any time'.[39] In this tradition of gender fluidity, Anatolian Aphrodite and her worshippers blurred sexual

---

[33] *Halikarnassos* 1.41–2. Mitchell 2017: 14 has emphasized that in early Karia the number of Greek settlements was small and that 'they were always part of a hybrid Greek/non-Greek cultural mixture'.
[34] I follow here Brisson 2002: 1, who uses the expression 'dual sexuality' to refer to bodies possessing both male and female genitalia, as opposed to bisexuality.
[35] On Hermaphroditos deriving from bearded Aphrodite, see Veszy-Wagner 1963: 138. On bearded Aphrodite, see Winbladh 2012.
[36] Krappe 1945: 327.   [37] Helle 2023: 158.
[38] For *Assinu* penetrated, see Peled 2014. For cross-dressing *kurgarrû*, see Groneberg 1986: 36.
[39] Helle 2023: 158.

identities. The priests of Cypriot Aphrodite dressed as women and the priestesses dressed as men. The priestess of Athena in the Karian city of Pedasa grew a beard when the region was under threat.[40] Originally Salmakis was probably an avatar or acolyte of the bearded goddess, and the story of her fatal attraction to Hermaphroditos is likely to have come about following the arrival of the Greeks and their encounter with this cult and the stories of the Mother Goddess and her younger, male consort. This prompted a refashioning of the stories told to explain the religious practices conducted at Salmakis, the promontory opposite the headland favoured by the Greeks. For the Greeks, the addition of Hermes to a genealogy already centred on an Anatolian Aphrodite made sense since he was a god of boundaries, exchange, trickery and transformation.[41] The metamorphosis of Salmakis and Hermaphroditos serves, then, as an example of the polyvalence of myth. Drawing on established practices, it mediated the relations of different ethnic groups. A local ritual practice involving either cross-dressing or an intersexual god(dess) was subjected to *interpretatio graeca*. The result was two traditions: a positive, predominantly Karian formulation that made Hermaphroditos a divine child and culture hero, and a negative, primarily Greek formulation that made Hermaphroditos into an intersexual hybrid and monster. In the Middle Ground one man's water is another man's poison.

There is a further dimension of sexual binarism to be explored in the contact zone of Greek and Anatolian cultures. Related to the gender-crossing elements of the Aphrodite cult, in Asia Minor there existed a tradition of emasculation that entered the Graeco-Roman world through the worship of the Magna Mater (known in Phrygia as Matar and Kybele).[42] Rather than being instantiations of dual sexuality, the priests of her cult, the Galli, transformed themselves into a third sex that was marked by the absence of either set of genitals rather than the presence of both. They became notorious after the cult's arrival in Rome in 204 BC, and by the first century their flagellation and self-castration were the subject of

---

[40] Philochoros, *BNJ* 328 F 184 (= Macrob. *Sat.* 3.8.2–3.) The hybridity of Aphrodite was the subject of good deal of comment in both the Greek and Roman worlds. Aristophanes, for example, referred to 'eum Aphroditon', according to Macrobius. In the Roman world, Venus barbata was similarly biform, as Lucretius, *DRN* 4.1052–8, recognizes. For the bearded priestess of Athena, see Hdt 1.175.

[41] Decker 2019: 44: 'Hermes is a god who transgresses the borders of the cosmos and can travel between the world of the gods, the world of mortals, and the underworld; he is an excellent *summachos* for a double-speaking liminal goddess.'

[42] The literature on the Magna Mater is considerable. The cult's place in Greek religion is treated in detail by Munn 2006 and Xagorari-Gleißner 2008. For the Anatolian cult, see Roller 1999.

Catullus' poetry (63) and a lengthy description in Lucretius, *DRN* 2.600–60.[43] But, leaving aside the horrified reactions in Rome to the performances of the Galli, we have in Pausanias a version of the aitiological myth explaining the cult's distinctive practice of self-castration. As Jan Bremmer has shown, it is very likely that Pausanias reflects local tradition. He was himself from Magnesia and claimed to have recorded the local story.[44] In his version, Zeus in his sleep ejaculates upon the ground, leading to the birth of a daemonic creature named Agdistis, who possesses both male and female genitals. Afraid of him, the other gods chop off his male organ, from which spouts a mature almond tree. The daughter of the river Sangarios collects some of the almonds and immediately falls pregnant, but abandons the child after she gives birth. The child, Attis, is raised by goats, and grows up to be stunningly beautiful. When Agdistis sees him he instantly falls in love with the boy. Attis is sent to Pessinous to marry the king's daughter, but at the wedding Agdistis appears. Attis goes mad, and chops of his genitals. Agdistis remorsefully begs Zeus to preserve the body uncorrupted.

Virtually every detail of this myth has been the subject of intense scrutiny, but some aspects of Pausanias' account stand out in relation to the theme of hybridity and sexual identity. The first is that Pausanias is recording a *hieros logos*. It is designed to explain and authorize actions taken by the priests of Kybele. No matter how bloody or repellent the details of the mutilation of Agdistis or the self-castration of Attis, the entire story has to be understood as an endorsement of the actions of Kybele's priests. Whether Borgeaud is correct to explain this as an extreme form of male ritual initiation is uncertain, but the existence of a cadre of men who self-castrate does mean, as Jan Bremmer puts it, that 'the Galli belong to those transcultural groups of men who have given up their male sexuality in the service of religion, such as the American Berdaches and Indian Hijras'.[45] Yet this religious service, however serious or compelling to those involved, is still based on mutilation: in the case of Attis, motivated by despair; in the case of Agdistis, prompted by the disgust of others upon witnessing hermaphroditism. Can a horror occasioned by dual sexuality and resulting in mutilation be reconciled with a religious sensibility? The question is not rhetorical. The existence in Catholicism of self-flagellating

---

[43] Segal 1986.
[44] Paus. 7.17.5. See Hutton 2010. The version by the Athenian priest Timotheus is considerably earlier, but is preserved by a much later source, Arnobius (5.5–8), and imports details from other traditions. See Bremmer 2004.
[45] Bremmer 2004: 557, Borgeaud 1996: 78–9.

penitents shows that mortification of the flesh is as powerful an expression of religious urges as, at the opposite end of the scale, tantric sex. Both show that there are many ways of embodying religious experience, from elation and Freud's oceanic feeling to existential horror. Furthermore, the cultic performance of the Galli points towards the same deep sense of awe inspired in Hesiod's primordial genealogies by the presence of monstrous hybrids. Agdistis' dual sexuality marks him as a throwback to the chaotic mixtures of creation. Even though he is the child of Zeus, Agdistis is born parthenogenically after Zeus ejaculates in his sleep, and, like most such creatures with such an unnatural genesis, he is marked by it, in this case as a hermaphrodite. Hephaistos, born parthenogenically from Hera, is known for his deformed legs and is called Ἀμφιγυήεις (lame). Erichthonios, born of the earth after Hephaistos ejaculates on Athena's leg, is anguiform; even Athena, born from the head of Zeus, is unconventional as a woman, giving birth to no child and functioning in the heavenly community as a warrior. It is tempting to read all of these divine manifestations of abnormality as inversions of the comfortable categories on which the Greeks relied. At the same time, even if inversions serve to confirm convention, their very existence compels a greater awareness of difference. Brisson, for example, suggests that 'to think through any opposition, we must also allow for the possibility of relations between the two poles that constitute it and form an indissociable pair'.[46] At the same time, hybridity and monstrosity are more than thought exercises. Bearded, blended, bigenital or bereft of genitals, all these bodies convey the inadequacy of conventional categories. They are a disruptive presence that forever signals the existence of other classes, other forms and other bodies that, taken together, suggest other ways of being human. This is powerfully marked in the Orphic cosmology that imagined a version of the primordial god(dess), Phanes/Metis, as both male and female (*diphues*). Detienne and Vernant note that this version of the origins of the world diverges significantly from the better-known Hesiodic *Theogony*, and it is very difficult to assess how widely the Orphic explanation of the world's beginnings circulated. But it was sufficiently well known, at least, to be parodied by Aristophanes in *Birds* (693–702) and even if Orphic theology was not universal, it was striking. As Detienne and Vernant note, 'Metis is no longer a woman and subordinate to Zeus. As a bisexual being its position is higher, or, at least, beyond.'[47] This anomaly has been explored in greater detail by Brisson, whose analysis deserves to be cited fully:

[46] Brisson 2002: 149. [47] Detienne and Vernant 1991: 134.

The dual sexuality that characterizes Phanes, Eros, Protogonos, Metis, Erikepaios, Zeus, and Dionysus is simultaneous, in that it occurs before any sexual differentiation existed. It thus represents a chaos, in which, since marriage is impossible, generation is akin to schism, and in which incest, or rather auto-incest, is inevitable at every level, given that the same masculine deity is linked to the feminine part of himself in the relationships of mother, wife, and daughter.[48]

Unlike the Hesiodic *Theogony*, which broadly moved from elemental monstrous beings to anthropomorphic gods, the Orphic universe posited a distinct phase marked by an original dual sexuality followed by sexual differentiation, often resulting in generation occurring in some version of parthenogenic incest. It is the profoundly unsettling quality of this construction that makes it a suitable vehicle for conveying sacred truth to the Orphic initiate. How the gods could both resemble us and yet surmount the imperative categories that make us human only serves to underscore the mystery of divinity.

Teiresias

Aside from Hermaphroditos, Agdistis and Phanes/Metis, there is another example of gender fluidity whose experience offers a different perspective: Teiresias. His movement from male to female and back constitutes a hybridity that comments on gender identity by framing gender as contingent rather than fixed. It allows him to serve as a unique mediator between men and women and illustrates the power of hybrid contrafactuals to carve out a space for apparent alternatives to heteronormativity, although how truly subversive this is will need closer examination. There are two principal segments of the Teiresias story, and the relationship between them is opaque. The first concerns his prophetic powers. According to Apollodoros, reporting a story that he found in Philochoros, Teiresias saw the goddess Athena naked and was blinded, but when his mother, Chariklo, asked to have his sight restored she was unable to do more than 'clean his ears', allowing him to understand birdsong.[49] A similar version is told by Kallimachos (*Hymn* V. 75–130). The second episode for which he was known was a sex change that was brought about by his encounter with two snakes. A version reported by Phlegon in the second century AD distilled earlier accounts into a single story:

---

[48] Brisson 2002: 101.   [49] Apollod., *Biblio.* 3.6.7.

> Teiresias, son of Eumares, when he was in Arcadia on Mount Kyllene, observed some snakes copulating. He wounded one and changed form immediately: he went from being a man to a woman, and had sexual intercourse with a man. Apollo then prophesied to him that if he observed snakes copulating in the same way and wounded one, then he would be as he had been. Teiresias, keeping an eye out for the opportunity, brought about what had been said by the god and thus regained his previous form. When Zeus quarrelled with Hera and claimed that, during sex, women have a disproportionate share of the enjoyment of sexual pleasures compared to men, and when Hera in turn claimed the opposite, they decided to send for Teiresias, and ask him, since he had experienced sex both ways. When asked he gave his opinion, that a man has a one tenth part of the enjoyment, and a woman nine tenths. Hera, enraged, gouged out his eyes and left him blind, but Zeus granted him the mantic art, and a lifetime of seven generations.
>
> Phlegon, *BNJ* 257 F 36. 4 (tr. McInerney)[50]

In this account, very similar to the Scholiast to Homer, *Od.* 10.494, Teiresias sees the snakes copulating and is punished for hitting one by being transformed from male to female. In Phlegon Apollo offers him the means to transform back, while in the Scholiast's account he kills the male and is immediately returned to his human form. In both accounts the sex changes are like the set up for an elaborate joke, in which he is asked to decide who enjoys sex more, men or women. The question has a locker-room imbecility about it, especially when Hera punishes him for his answer. Why is she angry? Because he has revealed a secret? The full account, which moves from impiety, to punishment, to transformation, to inquiry, says nothing genuinely subversive about heterosexual attitudes.

Zeus's compensatory gift of prophesy, however, does align Teiresias' changes in sexual form with a semi-divine ability to tell the future. This appears to be at odds with the other explanation in Philochoros, Kallimachos and Apollodoros, that drew on the trope of punishment for seeing a goddess naked to explain his prophetic skills as compensation. Although the two traditions seem widely at variance, almost 100 years ago Alexander Krappe suggested that they were connected. Drawing on a variety of Hindu texts, in which both sex changes and magical serpents appear frequently, Krappe argued that a 'biography' of Teiresias could be reconstructed. In the first episode Teiresias witnesses a female snake committing adultery, wounds it, and is rewarded by the male snake with the power to understand the language of animals. Next, coming upon the goddess bathing, he is transformed into a woman, until in the third episode he is called upon by

---

[50] Armeni et al. 2014.

Zeus and Hera, gives the answer that infuriates Hera and is transformed back into a man.[51] Now, it is a fair objection that no version in Greek sources preserves the myth in this form, and that to create this Ur-myth one has to manipulate the extant versions, for example by making the snakes rather than Zeus the means by which Teiresias acquires his skill. At the same time, Krappe's reconstruction does force us to recognize themes deeply encoded in the myths of Teiresias. His movement from male to female and back again, if we stop short of making it an excuse for men to fantasize about female sexual pleasure, does place him in the unusual position of bridging the gender gap. The importance of this was that it gave expression to varieties of sexual identity, taste and performance that simply did not exist within the narrow construction of heteronormative roles.

Similar elements occur in Herodotos' account of the Skythians known as the Enareis. In bk 1.105 he reports an invasion of Syria by the Skythians and tells how they plundered the temple of Heavenly Aphrodite. As punishment, the goddess struck the violators of her temple with a woman's disease (θήλεαν νοῦσον). Furthermore, according to Herodotos, the Skythians say that people who visit Skythia may see those who have been so afflicted, who are known as 'Enareis'. Although Herodotos does not explain the term, in a later discussion of Skythian mantic practice (4.67) he refers once again to the Enareis, whom he calls *androgynoi*. The 'female disease', then, is hermaphroditism, conceived here as both a punishment and yet also as a mark of mantic skill. Herodotos reports that Aphrodite endowed them with divinatory power, which they practice with the braided bark of lime trees. As with Teiresias, then, sexual ambiguity and special access to divining the future go hand in hand.

The Hippokratic *On Airs, Water and Places* also deals with the Skythian hermaphrodites but treats their condition less as anatomical hermaphoditism and more as a social practice arising in reaction to sexual shortcomings:

> When they approach a woman but cannot have intercourse, at first they take no notice and think no more about it. But when two, three or even more attempts are made with no better success, they think that they have sinned against a god to whom they attribute the cause, and they put on women's clothes, holding that they have lost their manhood, speak like a woman and do the same work as women do.
>
> Hippocr. *Aer.* 22 (tr. Jones)

Here, the androgyny of the Skythians (in this case, called Anarieis) is interpreted as a mistaken response to a physical flaw – impotence – which is falsely attributed to divine punishment. Although the Hippocratic text

---

[51] Krappe 1928: 273.

substitutes a rational explanation for the Herodotean account, by ascribing their impotence to the amount of time they spend in the saddle, the episode reflects a similar need to recognize non-normative behaviour and to explain it as an aberration.[52]

In this respect, it is easy to exaggerate the transgressive potential of indeterminate sexual identities, whether expressed by myths of sex changes or hermaphroditism. The ancient discourse regarding gender generally falls back on biological or religious explanations, and struggles to move beyond heteronormative categories. In those instances where the question of gender is explored and the possibility of mutability is raised, the results are usually catastrophic: In *Bacchae*, Pentheus will dress as a woman to spy on the female followers of Dionysos. It does not end well. In *Trachiniai*, Herakles weeps like a girl and says as much himself, even as his flesh is consumed by flames. Medea explicitly challenges the strictures placed on women but her challenge to convention results in the death of her children and her own magical disappearance from Corinth.[53] As Grace Gillies puts it, 'Medea is so far beyond the gender binary that there is no place for her on earth.'[54]

In Lucian's *Dialogue of the Courtesans*, gender fluidity is similarly presented as a dilemma. In the eyes of one female character, Leaina, Megilla's sexual behaviours are 'excessively masculine'. She kisses Leaina with an open mouth, squeezes her breasts and becomes sexually aroused lying next to her. After Megilla removes her wig and asks Leaina, 'Have you ever seen such a good-looking young fellow?' Leiana replies that she doesn't see any young man and addresses the other with her cis-gendered name, Megilla, prompting the reply 'Don't try to make me a woman! My name is Megillos. I've been married to Demonassa here for a long time; she is my wife!'[55] The dialogue uses three avenues to explore the question further: what is Megillos/Megilla? They might be a cross-dresser, like Achilles hiding among maidens; they might be a hermaphrodite; or they might, like Teiresias, have been transformed by divine intervention and thus experience sexual desire both as male and female. Megillos/Megilla rejects each of these and emphatically asserts their own identity: 'My thoughts and my desire and everything else in me are those of a man.' Errietta Bissa reads the juxtaposition of Megilla's body and Megillos' sexual drive as an instance of gender dysphoria, and argues that none of Leiana's suggestions is endorsed by Lucian as an explanation for Megillos/Megilla's identity.[56] This is correct, but the dialogue nevertheless ends on a pessimistic note, with Leiana refusing to discuss the matter further because

---

[52] Jouanna 2012: 105, Wenghofer 2014: 527–8.
[53] For these and other examples, see Zeitlin 1985.   [54] Gillies 2017.   [55] Lucian, *DMeretr.* 5.
[56] Bissa 2013: 94. For translation and full discussion, see also Boehringer 2015.

it is, in her description, shameful (αἰσχρά). In fact, the inability of the dialogue to accomplish any kind of resolution illustrates how ancient discussions of sex and gender were poorly equipped to investigate these phenomena. At the same time, the reliance on mythical models, such as Achilles, Hermaphoditos and Teiresias, also illustrates the way in which contrafactuals made it possible to explore, even tentatively, sexual identity. This is how the hybridity of Teiresias, both man and woman, operates: it creates a space, however circumscribed, for imagining the inadequacies of conventional treatments of sexual identity.

In addition to destabilizing gender norms, Teiresias' capacity to understand the language of animals bridges the other great divide: that between humans and other species. The inclusion of the snakes in the story of Teiresias' transformation recalls, as Krappe understood, the traditions according to which a range of seers – Melampous, Kassandra and Helenos – each had their ears licked by snakes and acquired the ability to understand animals as a result.[57] Just as he breaks down the gender boundary, Teiresias breaks down the species boundary. The seer also bridges the gap between humans and gods, and finally the seer breaks down the barrier separating the present from the future.[58] In each instance, with a foot on either side of the line, Teiresias enlarges the world by creating a space for uncertainty and wonder in place of certitude.

Uncertainty and wonder are also at work in another story of sex change: Kainis and Kaineus. The episode is the subject of a well-known vignette in Ovid (*Metam.* 12.146–209), but it was popular at least as early as the Archaic period and was recounted by Akousilaos:

> Poseidon had intercourse with Kaine, the daughter of Elatos. Subsequently, as divine law did not permit her to bear children either from him or from anyone else, Poseidon made him into an invulnerable man with the greatest strength of all people then living. And whoever tried to hit him with iron or bronze was absolutely sure to lose. And he became king of the Lapiths and made war against the Centaurs. Subsequently, he set up his spear (in the agora and ordered sacrifice to be made to it. But the gods did not allow that) and when Zeus saw him doing this he threatened him and incited the Centaurs against him. And they beat him straight down under the ground and put a rock on top of him as a grave monument, and he died.
>
> Akousilaos *FGrH* 2 F 22 (tr. Bremmer)[59]

---

[57] Melampous: Schol. Ad Hom., *Od.* 11.290, Eustath. 1685, 25; Kassandra and Helenos: Schol. Ad Hom., *Il.* 7.44, Eustath. 663, 40. See Aarne 1914: 28.

[58] Brisson 2002: 126.

[59] For Akousilaos and other sources, see Bremmer 2015. In the quotation given here, the phrase in parentheses is restored. For discussion of the transformation of Kainis into Kaineus, see Laufer 1985.

Figure 8.2 Kaineus attacked by centaurs. Hammered bronze sheet, Ionian workshop, ca. 650–625 BC. Olympia Museum BE I ia.

Although impervious to iron or bronze, in the battle of the Lapiths and the centaurs Kaineus was pummelled into the earth by the centaurs under a hail of rocks and fir trees.[60] This is depicted on a bronze sheet possibly attached to a piece of furniture and dedicated at Olympia in the second half of the seventh century BC (Figure 8.2). Kaineus is in the centre, being pounded into the ground as he manages to stab one of the centaurs in the groin while grabbing the other by the genitals. Both centaurs are armed with trees freshly torn out of the ground; the root system of one can still be seen and both still have fruit, perhaps olives, on their limbs, like the trees depicted in the background. The same scene continues to appear on black-figure and red-figure vessels in the late sixth and fifth centuries.[61]

The Kaineus story may have had a significance that the Ovidian account and the subsequent Roman treatments have missed. In a recent study, Armand D'Angour suggests that the hero's name is linked to the notion of 'newness' (*kainotes*) and argues that his invincibility is connected to his

---

[60] On Kaineus as a Lapith lord battling centaurs, see Hom., *Il.* 1.261; Hes., *Asp.* 178; Pindar, frg 166; Apoll. Rhod., *Argo.* 1.58; Paus. 5.10.8; Hyginus, *Fab.* 14; Ovid, *Meta.* 12.459–65. For the transformation of Kaineus after being raped by Poseidon as Kainis, see Apollod. *Biblio.* E1.22, Ovid, *Meta.* 12.171–209, 470–3.

[61] For red-figure hippocentaurs battling Kaineus, see the stamnos attributed to the Kleophrades painter; Louvre G55 (ca. 490–480 BC).

transformation.[62] But, whereas the myth of Kainis' sex change links newness to a new sexual identity, D'Angour proposes that his *kainotes* is actually an etymological derivation from a semitic root meaning 'newly forged'. In this reading, Kaineus' name is a Hellenized version of *qāyin*, meaning spear, from the verbal root *qyn*, meaning 'to work metal'. If D'Angour's proposed etymology of Kaineus' name is correct, he is the equivalent of an iron spear personified. His name stands for the reception of 'a wide variety of metal objects perceived as "shining new"' entering the Greek world from the eastern Mediterranean between the eighth and sixth centuries BC. The man of iron, bright, shiny and new, has been born from a girl transformed. Transformation and hybridity in this way fold onto each other, each connoting a cosmos constantly slipping from one category (nature, human, animal, man, life) to another: civilized, beastly, woman, death. Behind the fixed polarities that seem to mark this world lies continuous blending, merging and transformation.

The Power to Shock

The restrictions of sexual binarism and the challenges posed by sexually anomalous beings prompts a further question regarding hybridity's place in Greek culture. Over the last generation a series of categories have entered scholarly discourse – notably transgression, the ludic, rupture, anxiety – that have extended the field of cultural studies into new and fertile fields, but they have become so commonplace that they risk becoming trite.[63] Transgression, for example, once a term of opprobrium, is now generally seen as a mark of all desirable literature – a 'condition of significance', as Robert Wilson calls it.[64] The 'ludic' can be found everywhere, from rhetoric to video games to the reception of Classics in Maori literature.[65] As critical approaches, formerly novel, gain wider acceptance, there is a danger that they will lose their bite. Similarly, equating hybridity with disruption runs the risk of saying nothing other than that hybrids challenge boundaries. It is worth asking more specific questions: who exactly, and what precisely, is

---

[62] D'Angour 2011: 74–84. Contra, see Bremmer 2015: 265.
[63] Consider, for example, the comments of Holbraad, Kapferer and Sauma (2020: 4) regarding rupture: 'However, in more recent decades it feels as if the concept of rupture has somehow fallen by the wayside for some, outmoded by a putative shift from the age of extremes of the twentieth century to a twenty-first century of multitudes and assemblies.'
[64] On transgression and the ludic, see Wilson 1986.
[65] Ludic rhetorics: Daniel-Wariya 2019; the ludic and videogames: Caracciolo 2015; ludic agendas in Maori receptions of Classics: Parry and Perris 2019.

disrupted? A thread running through most of the instances of hybridity discussed so far has been the uneven distribution of power: Greek over indigene, human over animal, man over woman, 'normal' over 'abnormal', but, as Marshall Sahlins has argued, 'Power turns out to be the secret (that is, the function) of almost any institution an anthropologist could name.'[66] In other words, without resorting to an 'invisible hand' (Sahlins again) controlling all culture, is it possible to identify the function of hybridity more precisely? The hybrid is usually treated as a phenomenon needing to be explained. Perhaps approaching the hybrid as a phenomenon which sheds light on its cultural setting offers more possibilities.

Disruption or challenge, what does the hybrid question? Put simply, fixed categories and categorical distinctions. From the Socratic cross-examinations found in Plato to Aristotle's detailed classifications of phenomena, dialectical method constitutes the backbone of classical philosophy. Claims are tested by counterclaims. Contradictions are used to expose the fallacy of a claim, or to add finesse to a philosophical position. Plato's writings furnish us with countless examples, and I offer one purely *exempli gratia*. The *Euthyphro* is a dialogue devoted to the question of piety. Euthyphro offers this entirely reasonable definition: piety is that which is pleasing to the gods. But the gods are quarrelsome, points out Socrates. Euthyphro agrees, but if there is something loved by some gods and hated by others then there must be something, by Euthyphro's definition, that is both pious and impious at the same time. As this demonstrates, Socratic *elenchus* is a technique suited to dialectical thinking. Take another well-known example: can one feel pleasure and pain at the same time? Evidently not, yet drinking and eating are pleasurable activities we undertake exactly when we feel hunger and thirst, painful experiences.[67] So, we feel pleasure and pain at the same time. Like a sculptor's blows, Socrates' questions chip away at uncertainty and imprecise thinking. What emerges from this mode of enquiry, ideally, is a holistic system that establishes first principles and processes. When, then, Aristotle investigated fundamental notions such as motion, causation, time and place, as Istvan Bodnar has noted, he integrated them 'into the framework of a single overarching enterprise describing the domain of natural entities'.[68] What has this to do with the hybrids constantly at the edge of the Greek imagination? Simply this: hybrids have no respect for the rules of the philosophers' game. If dialectical philosophy depends on

---

[66] Sahlins 2004: 145–6.
[67] The food and drink examples occur both in Gorgias 494b–496e and Republic 437b–439b. On the importance of the pleasure/pain pairing, see Erginel 2019 and Vogt 2017.
[68] Bodnar 2018.

categories and logical consistency, the hybrid represents the lurking presence of chaos, a cosmic phenomenon akin to overturning the chess board. It does not matter what the rules are if one player refuses to play by them. In this respect, the unsettling oddity of hybrids occupies a cultural space akin to humour, a recalcitrant phenomenon that presented the philosophers with a challenge to which they responded by largely ignoring it. Like hybridity, humour did not yield to neat categories and distinctions. Plato warned against it, 'for ordinarily when one abandons himself to violent laughter, his condition provokes a violent reaction'. Linking humour to scorn (not unreasonably, given the power of the iambographic tradition in Greek culture), Plato saw the objects of scorn as ridiculous: 'In laughing at them, we take delight in something evil – their self-ignorance – and that malice is morally objectionable.'[69] The building blocks of dialectic left little space for hybridity or humour in the edifice of Greek philosophy. Yet both remained major presences in the daily life of the Greeks. Scabrous, scatological humour continued to entertain them at the theatre. Hybrids continued to inhabit the landscape of their imagination, depicted on vases and temples. Like Hamlet gently reproving Horatio, the Greeks' affinity for hybrids is a reminder that there are more things in heaven and earth than are dreamt of in Plato's philosophy.

Despite this, it is hard to escape the conclusion that hybridity's capacity to astonish began to wane in the fifth and fourth centuries. Public-facing hybrids of the time, such as the centaurs on the pediments of the temple of Zeus at Olympia, for example, are not actually scary, even if the scenes are dramatic. Even satyrs, with their gargantuan erections, have become commonplace. Over the course of the fifth and fourth centuries, hybrids were, as it were, driven underground: the riotous frenzy of Archaic hybrids would be relegated to spells, where amulets depicting strange creatures yoked the shock of the hybrid to the power of magic[70] (Figure 8.3). Apotropaic amulets depicted bizarre creatures that gave a face to the supernatural. Combined with repeated, formulaic language – 'Michael', 'Raphael', 'Gabriel', 'Ouriel' are invoked in this instance, surely, in part because of the rhythmic repetition – the amulets attempt to harness cosmic powers on behalf of the individual.

---

[69] Plato, *Phileb.* 48–50.

[70] The subject of magic amulets and spells is vast and well beyond the scope of this study. For an overview of the magical texts, see Kotansky 1994. For a glimpse of the rich corpus of gems on which magical incantations are frequently accompanied by bizarre hybrids, see Michel 2001. These gems are primarily products of Late Antiquity, but the binding and cursing practices connected with this magic are well attested in the classical period; see Lamont 2015.

Figure 8.3 Cock-headed anguiped (Abrasax) amulet, jasper, first-sixth century AD, Kelsey 26054, Bonner 172. © Genevra Kornbluth.

Like the monsters in Hesiod's *Theogony*, the hybrid figure on the gem is a strange combination of body parts, as if the head of a sacrificial cock had been placed on a trophy with snakes for legs. The function of this composite is to facilitate the user's access to a realm of power in which they will triumph over a lover, business rival or neighbour. For those adrift in a world of uncertainty, the magical hybrid is part of a set of images, words and objects which work together to offer the user a degree of control.[71] The magic amulet repeats in a minor key the cosmic struggle of the *Chaoskampf*, where order and disorder contend with each other. Here, as in the earlier Near Eastern theogonies, hybridity evokes chthonic power in its mash-up of parts, while also offering the wearer an opportunity to access that power.

Meanwhile, above ground, as it were, instances of hybridity such as hermaphrodites were treated as decorations or curiosities. In the Roman copy of an earlier Hellenistic statue of a sleeping hermaphrodite, the hybrid's authentic

[71] Ameisenowa 1949 situates the phenomenon of animal headed men and gods at the junction of various antique theological systems, in particular NeoPlatonism, Cabbala and Orphism. She writes '[I]t is now clearer why the just in Paradise should assume animals' heads. I have already mentioned above the ideas current in classical times which were later recorded by Origen, according to which men assume the forms of the astral deities who rule the decades of the ecliptic when, after death, they have passed through the planetary spheres. In the light of such ideas the animal masks of Mithraic mysteries become comprehensible' (p. 17).

Figure 8.4 Sleeping hermaphrodite. Marble, second century AD, copy of an original from second century BC. Museo Nazionale-Palazzo Massimo alle Terme, Rome. Photograph: Carole Raddado CC BY-SA 2.0.

power to shock has given way to titillation. As the viewer moves around the recumbent body, the sight of a conventional body seen from behind leads to a glimpse of swelling breast and flaccid penis[72] (see Figure 8.4). There is no authentic challenge to sexual normativity here. Aside from the Galli, there would be no 'third sex' for the societies of later antiquity.

This diminishing power to shock can be seen, paradoxically, exactly in those texts which collected stories of the shocking. In the mid-first century BC, for example, while assembling his universal history, Diodorus Siculus offered a series of vignettes involving hermaphrodites, intersex individuals and people undergoing spontaneous sexual transitions. The first is an account of a young woman, Heraïs, who suddenly falls ill:[73]

> A severe tumour appeared at the base of her abdomen, and as the region became more and more swollen and high fevers supervened her physicians suspected that an ulceration had taken place at the mouth of the uterus. They applied such remedies as they thought would reduce the inflammation, but notwithstanding, on the seventh day, the surface of the tumour burst, and projecting from her groin there appeared a male genital organ with testicles attached.
>
> Diod. Sic. 32.10.3 (tr. Walton)

---

[72] For the figure of Hermaphrodite as 'a figure of unresolved duality and tension', see Trimble 2018: 26. Barrow 2018: 79–80 prefers to see the genitalia of intersex bodies like the Sleeping Hermaphroditus as 'difficult to understand' rather than ambiguous. Each of these descriptions recognizes the challenge to certitude posed by the hermaphrodite. For an overview of visual representations of the hermaphrodite in Roman art, see Groves 2016.

[73] Armeni et al. 2014.

Ashamed of her condition, Heraïs hides in her father's house until her husband takes his father-in-law to court, suing for the return of his wife. In a stunning coup de théâtre, Heraïs displays 'her masculinity to them all'. Her revelation leads to further inspection and a surgical intervention, fully described by Diodorus:

> The physicians, on being shown the evidence, concluded that her male organ had been concealed in an egg-shaped portion of the female organ, and that since a membrane had abnormally encased the organ, an aperture had formed through which excretions were discharged. In consequence they found it necessary to scarify the perforated area and induce cicatrization: having thus brought the male organ into decent shape, they gained credit for applying such treatment as the case allowed.
>
> Diod. Sic. 32.10.7 (tr. Walton)

By Diodorus' time, then, sexual anomalies had entered the realm of medical discussion. In fact, in the very next chapter Diodorus offers a detailed account of a young woman named Kallo who undergoes a similar operation:

> A tumour appeared on her genitals and because it gave rise to great pain a number of physicians were called in. None of the others would take the responsibility of treating her, but a certain apothecary, who offered to cure her, cut into the swollen area, whereupon a man's privates were protruded, namely testicles and an imperforate penis. While all the others stood amazed at the extraordinary event, the apothecary took steps to remedy the remaining deficiencies. First of all, cutting into the glans he made a passage into the urethra, and inserting a silver catheter drew off the liquid residues. Then, by scarifying the perforated area, he brought the parts together.
>
> Diod. Sic. 32.11.2–4 (tr. Walton)

Despite the casual tone of scientific objectivity that Diodorus strives for, it is notable that these episodes cannot completely avoid conventional moral and religious overtones. In the case of Heraïs, as a man she adopts her father's name, Diophantos, joins the cavalry and accompanies the king to war, while her former husband, Samiades, commits suicide. Diodorus is compelled to moralize: 'Thus she who was born a woman took on man's courage and renown, while the man proved to be less strong-minded than a woman' (32.10.9). In the case of Kallon, as Kallo is known after transitioning, Diodorus offers an addendum: 'It is stated by some that before changing to man's form she had been a priestess of Demeter, and that because she had witnessed things not to be seen by men she was brought to trial for impiety' (32.11.4). In these stories conventional morality is always lurking, but whether the episodes involve anatomy, surgery, morality or impiety, the anomalous bodies described no longer have the power to inspire awe. Instead, we catch glimpses of a fascination with freakishness as a source of entertainment. Diodorus concludes his discussion of sex changes by disclaiming such a prurient interest, and instead disingenuously invokes the edification of his readers:

> Not that the male and female natures have been united to form a truly bisexual type, for that is impossible, but that Nature, to mankind's consternation and mystification, has through the bodily parts falsely given this impression. And this is the reason why we have considered these shifts of sex worthy of record, not for the entertainment, but for the improvement of our readers. For many men, thinking such things to be portents, fall into superstition, and not merely isolated individuals, but even nations and cities.
>
> Diod. Sic. 32.12.1 (tr. Walton)

Diodorus' discussion, when contrasted with the hybrids found in magic and on amulets, points to a bifurcation of hybridity. In popular culture the awesome and the anomalous would continue to link people to other planes of the cosmos, but in literary culture paradoxes would become collector's items and the stuff of encyclopedias. Aulus Gellius' treatment of hermaphrodites is a good example. Describing his own project of collecting oddities and discussing Pliny as a source, he writes,

> The fancy took me to add to this collection of marvels a thing which Plinius Secundus, a man of high authority in his day and generation by reason of his talent and his position, recorded in the seventh book of his *Natural History*, not as something that he had heard or read, but that he knew to be true and had himself seen. The words therefore which I have quoted below are his own, taken from that book, and they certainly make us hesitate to reject or ridicule that familiar yarn of the poets of old about Caenis and Caeneus. He says that the change of women into men is not a fiction. 'We find,' says he, 'in the annals that in the consulship of Quintus Licinius Crassus and Gaius Cassius Longinus a girl at Casinum was changed into a boy in the house of her parents and by direction of the diviners was deported to a desert island. Licinius Mucianus has stated that he saw at Argos one Arescontes, whose name had been Arescusa; that she had even been married, but presently grew a beard, became a man, and had taken a wife: and that at Smyrna also he had seen a boy who had experienced the same change. I myself in Africa saw Lucius Cossutius, a citizen of Thysdrus, who had been changed into a man on his wedding day and was still living when I wrote this.' Pliny also wrote this in the same book: 'There are persons who from birth are bisexual, whom we call "hermaphrodites";

they were formerly termed *androgyni* and regarded as prodigies, but now are instruments of pleasure.'

Aulus Gellius 9.4.1 (tr. Rolfe)

Hermaphrodites are now mere physical oddities. They have become specimens or toys.[74] Furthermore, in Pliny's discussion, at least as Gellius reports it, late-onset hermaphroditism is a matter-of-fact occurrence. Aulus Gellius' dismissive reference to 'that familiar yarn of the poets of old about Caenis and Caeneus' underscores just how much vitality in Greek culture was sapped by the mythographers of the Roman age.

The difference between the earlier stories of sex change and the later catalogues of hermaphrodites is best illustrated by Phlegon of Tralles, who collected stories of wonders in the early second century AD. After recounting the story of Teiresias, Phlegon continues his discussion of sex changes:

> And in by the Maeander River there was a hermaphrodite, when was archon at Athens and when Marcus Vinicius and Titus Statilius Taurus, surnamed Corvinus, were consuls at Rome. This young girl of distinguished parents, at the age of thirteen and lovely to look upon, was sought after by many suitors. Once she had been betrothed to the man of her parents' choosing, on the day of the nuptials, she was about to leave the house when suddenly an excruciatingly violent pain seized her, and she cried out. Her family picked her up and took care of her while the pain continued deep in her belly. Her suffering went on for three days straight day and no one could find a way to relieve her suffering, since the pain diminished neither night nor day. Although the doctors in the city brought her every treatment, they were unable to find any cause for the pain. On the fourth day at around dawn, when the pain became even more intense, she cried out with a great wail. Suddenly male genitals popped out, and the girl became a man.

Phlegon, BNJ 257 F 36. 6 (tr. McInerney)

Time and place are specified with an accuracy that would please Livy, while the grim realities of the girl's pain seem more appropriate to an account in Galen than a paradoxographer. The episode might have unfolded, like other stories in Phlegon, with some prophetic utterance or otherworldly intervention – in other sections he deals with ghosts, revenants and talking heads – but here the focus remains on the factual peculiarity of a sudden, unexpected change of sex. However, the narrative simplicity of the episode, told without a moral or without any attempt to

---

[74] In fact, Gellius' report is not an accurate representation of Pliny (7.2), who speaks of a tribe called the Androgyni in North Africa but says nothing of them being 'instruments of pleasure'. One wonders if Gellius is reflecting a feature of the hermaphrodite's existence in his own day. For the expression 'instruments of pleasure' (*in deliciis*), see Holford-Strevens 2003: 103, King 2015: 256.

shape the reader's response to monstrosity or aberration, does not entirely occlude one important feature of Phlegon's compendium of hermaphrodites: they were collectibles. The fate of the girl from Antioch on the Maeander was to be paraded before Claudius, 'and because of this omen he dedicated an altar on the Capitoline to Jupiter, Averter of Evil'. Phlegon then reports a hermaphrodite named Philotis, from Smyrna, who was kept 'in the country house of Agrippina Augusta'. Phlegon can even attest to a hermaphrodite from Laodicea, in Syria, named Aitete, 'who was living with a man when her appearance changed. On becoming a man she changed her name to Aitetos ... I saw this fellow myself.' By the time of the early empire hermaphrodites were no longer seen as sacred figures. Any subversion of heteronormativity had been excised, and they were now little more than curiosities. Statues of hermaphrodites adorned wealthy Roman villa gardens, while the imperial family acquired actual hermaphrodites to add to their menageries. The different ways of comprehending the encounter with other peoples and places, other practices and other tongues, and giving this expression in magical, astonishing forms that veered between the familiar and the strange would give way in the Roman period to the most dangerous hybrid of all: the sub-human.

9 | *Adynata*, Ethnography and Paradox

> The lynx hides its urine, because when it sets it turns to stone, and can be carved, making it suitable for women's jewellery, so they say.
>
> Aelian, *De Animal.* 4.17 (trans. McInerney)

Inhuman, Non-Human and Sub-Human

If animal hybridity served to integrate mythic times with the present, it could also connect the Greeks to far-away places, inhabited by exotic animals and peculiar humans. This was a less innocent dimension of the hybrid's proximity to the human, since imagining creatures not quite human made it easier to assign them a lower rung on the *scala naturae*. In this respect the exotic, the stupefying and the paradoxical all carried with them the potential for unleashing violence directed at anything that violated the natural order of life. The origins of this pernicious link between describing the marvellous and inventing the sub-human may go back to Homer's Cyclops as well as Hesiod's monsters, but ethnography as it is conventionally understood – namely, 'the self-conscious prose study of non-Greek peoples' – formalized the practice of defining the sub-human.[1] The translation of Hanno the Carthaginian's periegetic description of the coast of West Africa marks the origins of ethnography in Greek prose. Hanno's work purports to recount the voyage of a fifth-century BC explorer whose journey takes him as far as the Gulf of Benin. This was much further into Africa than any previous writer from the Mediterranean had ventured. The date and circumstances of the composition of Hanno's *Periplous* are still vigorously debated, especially since the text we possess is presented as a Greek translation of a Punic original, and the work is incomplete, but questions of the text's original state should not distract us from recognizing a more important aspect of the work: Hanno's description of sub-Saharan Africa reads like a proto-colonial, ethnographic essay. It reflects a view of unknown and unmapped places as ripe for exploitation

---

[1] Skinner 2012: 4.

and control. The literary equivalent of this physical domination is description and classification, by which the alien and the strange are made subject to the narrative control of the author.[2] This is especially evident in Hanno's infamous description of his treatment of the Gorillai towards the end of his voyage, an episode that reads as a sadly prescient mixture of cruelty and thinly veiled racial superiority:

> In the bay there was an island similar to the first, having a lake, and in it was another island, full of wild human beings. The majority of these people were women with hairy bodies, whom our interpreters called Gorillai. Although we pursued the men we were unable to catch them, because they all escaped by climbing the cliffs and defending themselves with rocks; but we caught three women, who bit and tore their pursuers since they did not want to go with them. And so we killed them and flayed them and carried off their skins to Carthage.
>
> Hanno, *Periplous* 18. (tr. Bosak-Schroeder)

The *Periplous* makes no apology for seizing the three women, killing them and skinning them. Collecting samples is an age-old practice associated with voyages of discovery, and treating the living world as 'samples' for collection and classification is the very essence of scholarship as a tool of colonial domination.[3] But aside from our repulsion, it is important to note that the creatures skinned by the explorer are not referred to as female animals but as women. The fact that they are called 'Gorillai' should not lead us to conclude that they were regarded by Hanno or his audience as a separate species. Regardless of our use of the term 'gorilla' to refer to a particular type of primate, Hanno's use of *anthropoi, andres* and *gynaikes* reveals that he uses 'Gorillai' as an ethnonym, just as he might refer to 'Romans' or 'Greeks' or 'Libyans'. Like the Malay term 'Orangutan', meaning 'Man of the Forest', Hanno's use of 'Gorillas', 'wild men' and 'hairy women' reflects the ways in which many primates are, to use Clara Bosak-Schroeder's words, 'eerily similar to humans', even as Hanno's treatment denies that equivalence and effectively dehumanizes them.[4] They are, in fact, sub-human. They are not non-human but, as with so many hybrids, something else entirely: strange, yet at the same time disquietingly familiar. At once similar and different, their appearance is frequently unsettling

---

[2] See Romm 1992: 84 on the relationship between travel narratives and territorial conquest.

[3] On the challenge presented by Atlantic expansion from the late fifteenth century onwards, and the reliance of contemporaries on ancient ethnographic traditions, see Davies 2016.

[4] On the Malay meaning of Orangutan, see the OED. For a less neutral but more revealing rendering, 'Wildman', see Savage and Wyman 1847: 417, n. 2. On primate proximity, see Bosak-Schroeder 2020: 70.

because, as Gilbert Lascault has recognized, 'To describe an unknown creature one has to take it apart, piece by piece, and relate each piece to a creature already known. This method necessarily produces for the reader a composite monster.'[5] Many hybrids therefore carry the marks of the violence arising from our creation of categories.[6] Their appearance is also unsettling because our treatment of creatures at once alien yet familiar poses a series of questions. When Pepys saw a primate recently brought to England from Guinea his immediate reaction was 'that it [was] a monster got of a man and she-baboone'.[7] As Surekha Davies notes, Pepys faced an ontological problem: was such a creature human, animal or monster? Epistemologically, was it unique or representative of an entire species?[8] And we might add that the shock of such an encounter obfuscated the moral dilemma from which European culture averted its eyes for 400 years: must we treat those who are (un)like us as we treat ourselves? As our experiences with Koko the lowland gorilla have demonstrated, the barriers of species may be more fluid than we care to imagine. With each passing year the scepticism of those who deny the primate's ability to communicate looks more and more like a rear-guard action.[9]

Hanno's gorillas are encountered at the end of his voyage and are a good example of the placement of monsters, hybrids and exotics at the edge of civilization. Texts and maps that invite an audience to visualize new and far-off places populated them with these curiosities in order to fill the void of the unknown. They lend authority to the text, yet they also create a pernicious hierarchy in which the exotic and the fabulous not only fill the empty spaces on the map but render the people there sub-human.[10] The shadow of Caliban looms over even the most innocuous hybrids and *thaumata* of ethnography. Even before Hanno's *Periplous* the people of the Greek diaspora began transforming their ethnic encounters into tales of the marvellous.

---

[5] Lascault 1973: 220. 'Pour décrire un animal inconnu, il faut le démonter pièce a pièce et rapporter chacune d'elles à un être déja connu; cette méthode produit nécessairement pour le lecteur un monstre composite.'

[6] The fate of a more recent anomalous creature illustrates the process: when the first platypus skin was brought to Europe it was dismissed by many as a hoax. (Hall 1999: 212) Ornithorhynchus Anatinus was a paradox because the bill of a duck was not supposed to attach to a mole. Subsequent reports made the anomaly worse: it was a mammal that laid eggs, when orthodoxy held that warm-blooded creatures that lay eggs were birds and cold-blooded egg-layers were reptiles. The solution: shoot a pregnant platypus and dissect it to get at the truth. See Caldwell 1888: 464.

[7] Pepys 2000: 160.   [8] Davies 2016: 24.

[9] On scepticism regarding primates' abilities to communicate through American Sign Language, see Newmyer 2017: 117.

[10] On marvels at the margins of the known world see Redfield 1985: 100, Priestley 2014: 58 and Lightfoot 2021: 59.

Odysseus' *nostos* is dotted with meetings with remarkable creatures, from the sub-human Cyclops to the hypercivilized Phaiakians. Herakles' adventures in the West similarly involved a catalogue of beasts, monsters and indigenes to be tamed, tricked and beaten, from Atlas to Kakos. The legacy of these diasporic encounters was a taste for ethnographic description and the compiling of compendia devoted to *thaumata* and *mirabilia*.[11] The world of wonders began where Greek civilization stopped. In this sense Herodotos' fascination with Egypt and Skythia was fundamentally an account of manners relative to Greek norms. His conclusion – that custom was king – seems like a generous recognition of the relative differences that characterize different societies, but distant places, like distant times, were populated by creatures that confounded categorization. Herodotos introduces his readers to two of the most durable exotics of ancient ethnography: the Blemmyes, a headless tribe inhabiting part of Libya, and their neighbours, the Dog-Headed People (Cynocephali). Herodotos mentions them in his account of the lands west of the Triton river in Libya where the snakes are gigantic and the land teems with exotic African wildlife, such as elephants, lions and donkeys with horns. Having listed animals that an Aegean audience might have recognized, he then mentions a tribe of dog-headed men and 'headless creatures with eyes in their chests'.[12] In Herodotos the latter are simply 'acephalous', but later authors referred to them as the 'Blemmyes', a term possibly coined from the Greek *blemma* ('glance'). The search for an etymological explanation, however, risks distracting attention from the extraordinary longevity and utility of these odd creatures in literature and art.[13] Regardless of location, they gave a face to the exotic and confirmed the ethnic encounter as a meeting with the non-, and, by extension, sub-human.

Ktesias, writing around the same time as Thucydides, was determined to outdo Herodotos when it came to marvels.[14] His account of India, written after his time spent at the court of the Achaemenid king, Artaxerxes II, from 405 to 397 BC, is the real starting point for literature dominated by a fascination with the marvellous, the incredible and the exotic. For example, even though he was not the first Greek to use the term 'eunuch', he did introduce the figure of the 'perfidious eunuch', a literary type that would provide a lens for viewing the Persian kingdom from a Greek perspective for years to

---

[11] On ethnography see Skinner 2012; on collections of *thaumata* and *mirabilia* see Lightfoot 2021.
[12] Hdt 4.191.4: οἱ ἀκέφαλοι οἱ ἐν τοῖσι στήθεσι τοὺς ὀφθαλμοὺς ἔχοντες.
[13] For the identification of the Blemmyes with an Ethiopian tribe, see Theoc. 7.114, Strabo 17.1.2, Ptol. *Geog.* 4.7.10, Nonn. *D.* 17.397, OGI 201.3, 16, St.Byz. B 109.
[14] Bichler 2011 explores Ktesias' habit of correcting Herodotus and suggests his work should be read as historical fiction. Brosius 2011 reaches a similar conclusion. See also Mitchell 2021: 119–121. For Ktesias' descriptions of Indian flora and fauna, see Stoneman 2019: 100–4.

come.[15] With Ktesias begins the long tradition of reporting the wonders of far-off places. Among the wonders he records are the parrot (*bittakos*), capable of conversing like a human in Indian but also capable of learning Greek (7).[16] He also describes the *martichora*, a beast the size of a lion with a human face, three rows of teeth and stingers on its tail (15). In addition to various natural wonders such as amber and saffron, he also (re-)introduces his readers to the Cynocephali, the dog-headed men first described by Herodotos, now moved from their home in Libya to India (37–42). This peculiar episode in Ktesias captured the imagination of readers for hundreds of years and established some of the basic tropes of ethnographic reporting. As the Photian epitome of Ktesias reveals, he described the sexual manners and the longevity of the Cynocephali and noted that they were particularly just.[17] He also describes unicorns (45) and a tribe of people born without an anus who drink only milk and vomit up whatever they cannot digest (44). Other fabulous creatures in Ktesias include the Monocoli, with one leg, who 'show amazing agility by jumping' (51). They are also known as Sciapodes ('Shade-Feet'), because they lie on the ground and shade themselves with their feet. It is perhaps not surprising that as early as Aristotle there were commentators who qualified their use of Ktesias' account with such remarks as 'if we are to believe Ktesias'.[18] Yet despite this scepticism, there is another aspect to Ktesias' tales of marvellous creatures that is more deeply disquieting. Upsetting the dominant view that humans were at the top of the hierarchy of beings, characterized by the power of *logos* and often taking the shape of man at his most perfect, Ktesias presents us with animals that can speak, animals that have human features and humans whose physical shortcomings are no impediment to living a good life. As Janick Auberger puts it neatly, 'In Ktesias, on the contrary, high moral tenor conforms to physical ugliness, and one can be both a pygmy and just.'[19] Ktesias' Indian creatures suggest an India that will become, in the metageography of the Greeks, not only a place of wonders, but

---

[15] Waters 2017: 20–44. [16] Bigwood 1993.

[17] On the possibility that the Photian epitome expressed a bias towards the weird and wonderful in Ktesias, see Ruffing 2011. The paradox of people on the margins being decidedly un-Greek yet demonstrating upright morality is a trope of ethnography going back to Homer's blameless Ethiopians and fortunate Hyperboreans. As ever, the people on the edge of the map provide a mirror in which those at the centre see their anxiety. The Greek have been anxious about cultural decay, just as the Romans have fretted over their moral decline, from the earliest times. On this 'negative ethnocentric scheme', see Romm 1992: 47.

[18] Arist. *HA* 2.1 (F45da). Aristotle (*De gen. an.* 2.2) dismisses Ktesias' claim that the sperm of elephants hardens as it dries. Arrian, *Anab.* 5.4.2 (F 45 a) similarly expresses doubts about his reliability. See also Arrian, *Ind.* 3.6. Tzetzes, *Chil.* 7.738 is even more unwilling to give credence to Ktesias.

[19] Auberger 2011: 19 'Chez Ctésias au contraire, la haute teneur morale s'accommode de la laideur physique, et l'on peut être Pygmée et juste.'

a place where anomalies challenge the assurance of Platonic beauty and Aristotelian logic.[20]

Ktesias began the trend of locating exotic people and animals in India, but it was the popularity of Megasthenes' account that proved even more influential. After Alexander's return from the Indus Valley, and not long after his death, Megasthenes travelled as a diplomat from Seleukos to the court of Chandragupta at Pataliputra.[21] He stayed for an indeterminate period between 324 and 305 BC and upon his return produced an account of his time in northern India that continued to be widely read for hundreds of years.[22] In the second century AD, for example, Arrian's *Indika* took much of its material from his Hellenistic predecessor. Megasthenes' description of India included far more detail than Ktesias, and his treatment of the exotic has to be read in the overall context of his presentation of India as a complex society, in many ways not unlike the world of the eastern Mediterranean. The reader is introduced to a world of city magistracies, taxes and commerce, all of which would have looked familiar to anyone from a Greek or Macedonian background. Even the care and training of elephants could be made to parallel Greek practices, as when Megasthenes describes how the Indians nurse wounded elephants: 'They treat them in the way in which, as Homer tells us, Patroklos treated the wound of Euryplyos – they foment them with lukewarm water.'[23] And, in some respects, it was a sober ethnography. It is to Megasthenes, for example, that we owe the first lengthy description of the caste system of Indian society. For all its inaccuracies, his account of the seven castes does not include fabulous elements and avoids embellishments except to underscore the picture of Indian society as hierarchical and closed. His account left its mark on many later writers, from Diodorus and Strabo to Pliny, Aelian and Arrian, who recycled the tropes established by Megasthenes: India was a land blessed by environmental diversity with great rivers, mountains and a rich variety of flora and fauna. Powerful rulers such as Chandragupta mustered huge armies, entertained at lavish feasts, lived in large, well-organized cities, and enjoyed a sophisticated culture that had produced a venerable tradition of philosophy.[24] In many

---

[20] On metageography and the organization of space, see Lewis and Wigen 1997.
[21] Kosmin 2014: 37–53 argues that Megasthenes' account was designed to justify Seleukos' abandonment of all territories west of the Indus by painting a picture of India as unconquerable.
[22] Mitchell 2021: 121–2. For an overview of scholarship on Megasthenes, see Stoneman 2019: 129.
[23] Megasthenes fr. 38.
[24] Geography (rivers and mountains): Diod. Sic. 2.35.1–37.7: Strabo 2.1.19–20; 15.1.11–12; Arr., *Ind.* 4.2–5; diversity of crops: Strabo 15, 1, 20; superior physiognomy: Onesikritos, *BNJ* 134 F22; kings and armies: Strabo 15.1.53–5; Arr., *Ind.* 9.9–12; feasting: Athen. *Deipno.* 4.39; cities and city administration: Strabo 15.1.50–2; Arr., *Ind.* 10.2–4, 5–6; culture and philosophy: Diod. Sic.

ways India mirrored Greece, leading to points of correspondence that Megasthenes never failed to note. He claimed, for example, that despite its diverse population, all the people of India were indigenous, and that the land had never been subjected to colonization. He continues:

> The legends further inform us that in primitive times the inhabitants subsisted on such fruits as the earth yielded spontaneously, and were clothed with the skins of the beasts found in the country, as was the case with the Greeks; and that, in like manner as with them, the arts and other appliances which improve human life were gradually invented.
>
> Megasthenes, *Indika* 38 (tr. McCrindle)

The twinning of Greece and India resulted in the stories that collapsed mythical space and linked both countries: Dionysos had conquered India and Herakles had originated there.[25] The two lands thus shared some of the same gods and heroes. Myth had put India on the map.[26]

Yet, despite these similarities, India was far away and home to exotic animals and humans. The same writers who cited Megasthenes as an authority for concrete and truthful observations such as the fact that the Indians did not practice slavery were just as likely to trawl through his work for curiosities such as gold-digging ants larger than foxes, snakes with bat-wings and flying scorpions.[27] For Strabo the explanation for such marvellous details was simple – the farther east one went, the taller the tales one heard:

> It is agreed that everything beyond the Hypanis is the best, but there is no accuracy, because of ignorance and distance everything is said to be greater or more marvellous, such as the gold-mining ants and other animals and humans of peculiar form that have altered properties such as the Serres, who are said to be long-lived, surviving over 200 years.[28]
>
> Strabo 15.1.37 (tr. Roller)

2.40.1–2; Strabo 15.1.58–60, 68; Clem. Alex., *Miscell.* 1.15.72.4; Arrian, *Anab.* 7.2.2–4; castes and classes: Arr., *Ind.* 11; Strabo 15.1.39. For India as a perfect society in Greek thought, see Karttunen 1997: 77–8. See also Zambrini 2017: 235.

[25] Dionysos and Herakles in India: Diod. Sic. 2.38.3–39.4; Strabo 15, 1, 6–7. Arrian, *Ind.* 7.5–7 illustrates the mirroring nicely: 'When Dionysos did come and became the possessor of India, he founded cities, established laws in the cities, dispersed wine to the Indians just as to the Hellenes, and taught them to sow, giving them seeds, for either Triptolemos did not pass by when he was sent forth by Demeter to sow the entire earth, or it was before Triptolemos that this Dionysos came to the Indian land and gave them seeds of domesticated plants.'

[26] On the locating of an authentic Greece in India in the Second Sophistic, see Abraham 2014.

[27] No Indian slaves: Arr. *Ind.* 10; gold digging ants: Strabo 15.1.44; Arr., *Ind.* 15.4–7. Winged scorpions and winged snakes: Strabo 15.1.37; Aelian 16.41.

[28] The Hypanis river referred to here is the Beas in Punjab State, not the Bug in Ukraine. Roller (*BNJ* 715 comm. ad F21c) suggests that Serres is 'little more than a vague ethnym beyond India, perhaps silk traders known at Pataliputra who came from the north, rather than the Chinese'.

But there was more at work than armchair travellers turning India into the land of Cockaigne. Megasthenes presented India as a world that was orderly and civilized; it made sense when viewed from the vantage of Mediterranean urban culture, but his account, like that of his contemporary, Deimachos, was interspersed with stories of fabulous tribes of hybrid humans. Strabo was not impressed:

> Particularly worthy of disbelief are Deimachos and Megasthenes, for they write about the Enotokoitai ['Those Who Sleep in Their Ears'] and the Astomoi ['Those Without Mouths'] and the Arrinoi ['Those Without Noses'] as well as the Monophthalmoi ['Those With One Eye'], Makroskeles ['Those With Long Legs'], and Opisthodaktyloi ['Those With Their Toes Backward']. They have revived the Homeric tale about the battle between the cranes and pygmies who, they said, were three *spithamai* tall. There are also the gold-mining ants and Pans with wedged-shaped heads and snakes that swallow both cattle and deer with their horns.
>
> Strabo, *Geo.* 2.1.9 (= Megasthenes, *BNJ* 721 F 2) (tr. Roller)

Strabo characterizes these accounts as 'going beyond into the mythic' (ὑπερεκπίπτων δ' ἐπὶ τὸ μυθῶδες), a description which is accurate but does not explain the paradox of rendering India as both familiar and (culturally) near on the one hand but odd and (fantastically) far away on the other. In fact, these strange tribes are alien to the Indians as well. The Enotokoitai, for example, are described as wild men with feet facing backward who, once captured and brought before Chandragupta, refuse to eat and therefore perish. Chandragupta, then, like Antiochos, Caesar, and King Leopold, gives proof of his power over distant places by collecting exotica.[29] Others that are captured and brought to court come from the farthest reaches of India, near the source of the Ganges. They have no mouths, subsisting purely on the aroma of food, and so rarely survive once they are brought into military camps. The Okypodes are swifter than horses, while the rest of Megasthenes' odd tribesmen are marked by physical deformities: Enotokoitai, whose ears reach their feet, but who are strong enough to pull up trees and break a bowstring; Monommatoi, with dog ears and a single eye set in the middle of their forehead, 'the hair standing erect, and their breasts shaggy'; Amukteres, without nostrils, 'who devour everything, eat raw meat, and are short-lived, and die before old age supervenes. The upper part of the mouth protrudes far over the lower lip' (Strabo 15.1.57).

---

[29] On 'human zoos' and the display of colonized people at World Fairs and in modern royal collections, see Jonassohn 2000. For a detailed discussion of Sara Baartman, the so-called Hottentot Venus, see Qureshi 2004.

As Duane Roller correctly observes, 'All these fantastic people are typical examples of the anatomically impossible ethnic groups that inhabit the far fringes of the world.'[30] After Alexander's campaigns the world known to the Greeks had expanded dramatically, and with that expansion the weird and the wonderful were pushed ever further out and away.

At the edge of civilization physically anomalous people and tribes served as boundary markers. Such people exist on the margins wherever the ordered world of hierarchy comes to an end, in India or in Africa.[31] They are intermediaries standing between control and uncharted territory, between the known and the unknown, and this in-betweenness results in them often having two forms: a real and fantastic appearance. The Blemmyes, for example, as we have seen in Herodotos, are associated with Libya, where south of Cyrene Greek concepts of metageography populated the desert with headless tribesmen. In the Hellenistic period, as the Ptolemaic realm asserted its territorial control up the Nile Valley, Nubia and the land beyond the First Cataract became the liminal zone. This is where Theokritos places his Blemmyes, who dwell 'by the farthest pastures of Ethiopia' (πυμάτοισι παρ' Αἰθιόπεσσι νομεύοις).[32] But there is no indication that for Theokritos they are physically monstrous, and the uncertainty of earlier periods began to yield to the greater geographical certitude of writers such as Eratosthenes, who offered a matter-of-fact description of the Blemmyes as a tribe north of Meroe, subject to the Ethiopians and on the border of Egypt. Following this tradition Strabo, in the first century BC, describes them simply as nomads living in Ethiopia, not especially warlike but feared for their former habits of raiding settlements.[33] In this framework, nomads and physically anomalous people occupied parallel rungs on the scale of human communities, inferior to city-dwellers.[34] With the establishment of Roman control over Egypt and North Africa, however, the exact location of the Blemmyes would fade even as they were characterized as barely human and half animal, by Pomponius

---

[30] *BNJ* 715 F27 A and B, Commentary.

[31] For a very broad survey of the study of borders in many parts of the world, see Rieber 2003.

[32] Theok. *Id.* 7.113–14. For sources on the Blemmyes beginning with Theokritos, see Updegraff 1988: 62–7.

[33] Strabo 17.1.53.

[34] Arist. *Pol.* 1256a 40-1256b1-7 offers a famous analysis of the five 'legitimate' modes of human existence (βίος), with nomadism and agriculture at either end of the scale. The tribes of physically anomalous people appear to exist outside of the Aristotelian scheme. Strabo, in offering a rationalizing reading of the Blemmyes, brings them closest to 'real' humans by putting them at the nomadic end of the scale. For attitudes towards nomads in the Graeco-Roman world, see Shaw 1982–3: 6: 'the nomad is seen as the ultimate barbaric human type who is directly opposed to the "civilized" sedentary agriculturalist'.

Mela, and described by Pliny as having no heads, but with mouth and eyes attached to their chest.[35] The margins of the world are fuzzy, and as the Blemmyes came in and out of focus their attributes shifted from the backward to the fantastic. The gruesome, however, is finally more entertaining than the mundane, and it was the picture of headless freaks that became fixed in the imagination of the Romans and later artists. Julius Solinus, Martianus Capella, Augustine and Isidor of Seville would all keep this tradition alive.[36]

The subsequent history of these anatomically anomalous people confirms the legacy of Hellenistic and Roman ethnography: physical aberration was a convenient shorthand for the border between the familiar and the strange. At or beyond the border there was a greater risk of a sudden encounter with ugliness – the opposite of harmony, beauty and the other markers of order inherited from Plato. In 1853, in the *Aesthetics of Ugliness*, Karl Rosenkrantz defined the characteristics of ugliness as (i) Formlessness/Amorphousness; (ii) Deformation/Asymmetry; and (iii) Non-unity/Disharmony.[37] These are dominant features of the hybrid humans encountered in ethnography, regardless of the exact location of the boundary. For this reason, long before Eratosthenes and Theokritos located the Blemmyes in Libya, Ktesias had placed them in India. These people, 'who lack necks and have eyes on their shoulders' (Ktesias 51), were not the inhabitants of a particular place; they were the signifiers of a locale's marginality. In the Middle Ages, as travellers such as Marco Polo reported on lands like China and Russia, much farther away than Libya or India, the tribe of men with their heads in their chests was transferred to lands ever further beyond Ktesias' India. For example, the illustration accompanying the French translation of Marco Polo in the *Livre des Merveilles du Monde* depicts Blemmyes (along with a skiapod and a cyclops) in the kingdom of Erguiul (Liang-chou, central China).[38] As geographic networks expanded, the conventions of physical anomaly, even if generic, proved invaluable; the specific examples were simply pushed further afield. Ethnography had equipped its readers with a handy tool for

---

[35] Pomp. Mela, *De Chorogr.* 1.23 'vix iam homines magisque semiferi'; Pliny, *NH* 5.46 'Blemmyis traduntur capita abesse ore et oculis pectori adfixis'.
[36] Solinus 31.5; Mart. Cap. 6.674; Aug., *Civ.Dei* 16.8; Isidor 11.3.17.
[37] On ugliness and the opposition to order, see Rosenkrantz 1853. See also O'Donnell 2011.
[38] The illustration (BnF Fr2810 pl. 29v) is labelled 'cy dist du royaume de erguiul', but in the text Marco Polo merely describes the local people as 'fat with small noses and black hair'. The Blemmyes had acquired an iconographic afterlife of their own. For Medieval depictions of the Blemmyes and other anomalous people, see Wittkower 1957, Secomska 1975, and, more recently, Collura 2016. For the history of the French version of Marco Polo, commonly known as *Le Devisement du monde*, see Cruse 2015. For the vogue in such imagery at the court of the Valois Dukes of Burgundy, see Franke 2000.

imagining the Other as something sub-human.[39] This was the fate of the other notable hybrids of classical ethnography: the Cynocephali. Originally placed in Libya in Herodotos' account, Marco Polo identifies them as the inhabitants of Andaman, off the coast of India, and conveys his disgust: 'they are like savage beasts' (*e sono come bestie selvatiche*).[40] No matter how far travel writing took the reader, there were always sub-human hybrids waiting to show what lay beyond. In fact, even on the moon, in Lucian's description, we encounter a regiment of Dog-Faced Men and Cloud-Centaurs.[41]

A World of Wonders

Oddly shaped and misformed creatures inhabited the farthest reaches of the world, but one did not have to travel to India, Siberia or the moon to experience strange and peculiar beings. Within the Mediterranean world as well there were marvellous and strange phenomena that attracted the attention of a succession of writers who catalogued episodes of the bizarre. This was not simply a matter of compiling lists of oddities for the entertainment of Greek speakers. Paradoxical compilations, born of an impulse to capture and classify, are encyclopaedias of the unreal, and just as the birth of modernity was accompanied by the emergence of classification and natural history, so too the world-system of the Graeco-Roman Mediterranean in the wake of Alexander's conquests experienced an incredible flood of information, some accurate, some fanciful.[42] Nor was this an entirely literary

---

[39] The literature on the category of the sub-human is considerable. A useful resumé of recent work can be found in Bruneau and Kteily 2017.

[40] For depictions of the Cynocephali see *Livre des merveilles du monde* (BnF Fr2810), pl. 76v. France, ca. 1410 and Paris, Bibliothèque de l'Arsenal, ms. 5219, 133r. France, ca. 1525. Polo's full judgement: 'È sono idoli, e sono come bestie selvatiche. E tutti quelli di quest'isola ànno lo capo come di cane e denti e naso come di grandi mastini. Egli ànno molte spezie. È sono mala gente e mangiano tutti gli uomini che posson pigliare, fuori quelli di quella contrada' (They worship idols, and live just like wild beasts. And all the inhabitants of this island have a head like a dog, with the teeth and muzzle like those of a great mastiff. Their land is full of spices. They are a cruel people, and they devour any man they can catch who is from elsewhere). A sign of the instability of Polo's text is the fact that the illustration accompanying his description shows no hint of this cannibalism and depicts the Cynocephali as well-dressed merchants. On the origins of dog-headed figures as chthonic demons, see Klinger 1936. See also Mitchell 2021: 139–48. For baboons as the inspiration for the figure, see Murgatroyd 2007: 2; Holbek 2016: 1377. A particular use of the cynocephalus is the Medieval depiction of St Christopher, patron saint of travel. See Friedrich 2017.

[41] For the inhabitants of the Moon see Lucian, *Icaronenippus* 7 and 20, and all of the *True History*.

[42] On paradoxography as a literary counterpart to exploration, see Schepens and Delcroix 1996: 406. For the importance of classification, the ordering of information and the emergence of the modern, see Foucault 1974 and Withers 1996. For an explanation of a world-system, see Hall 2014. Analysing the importance attached to 'unique animals' in Hellenistic magical and scientific texts, Gordon 2010:

phenomenon. The Ptolemies, in particular, were insatiable collectors of both exotic animals and texts, matching their hegemonic ambitions with spectacular acquisitions, from leopards, panthers and giraffes displayed in the Great Procession of Ptolemy Philadelphus, to the canonical texts of the Athenian tragedians and the wisdom literature of the Jews housed in the Library of Alexandria.[43] Collecting fostered another literary development: paradoxography, a genre devoted to compiling lists of strange and bizarre episodes.[44] In the third century, Archelaus the Egyptian produced a collection entitled Peculiar Forms (Ἰδιοφυῆ) for Ptolemy, with descriptions of basilisks and the *katablepas*, whose glance could petrify.[45]

Much of the information in Archelaus and his successors, compilers such as Antigonos of Karystos, was unbelievable. That was, after all, what made the works so appealing, but it meant that writers who wanted to amaze their readers were also compelled to apologize for their work. In his *Natural History*, for example, Pliny devoted a section to *thaumata*: 'wondrous things'.[46] Pliny's decision to include descriptions of what many readers would surely dismiss as fictional was telling. His explanation underscores the onslaught of information that accompanied living in a world of wonders:

> Yet there are some that I think ought not to be omitted, and especially those of the people living more remote from the sea; some things among which I doubt not will appear portentous and incredible to many. For who ever believed in the Ethiopians before actually seeing them? or what is not deemed miraculous when first it comes into knowledge? how many things are judged impossible before they actually occur? Indeed the power and majesty of the nature of the universe at every turn lacks credence if one's mind embraces parts of it only and not the whole.... Nevertheless in most instances of these I shall not myself pledge my own faith, and shall preferably ascribe the facts to the authorities who will be quoted for all doubtful points: only do not let us be too proud to follow the Greeks, because of their far greater industry or older devotion to study.
>
> Pliny, *NH* 7.1.6–9 (tr. Rackham)

---

269 notes: 'In other words, for all its notorious irrationality, the "Magian" tradition actually relied on the appeal to an implicitly ordered and meaningful Nature.'

[43] On the Ptolemies and *thaumata*, see Fraser 1972: 515. On the Grand Procession, see Rice 1983.

[44] For collections of paradoxographical texts, see Westermann 1839 and Gianinni 1967. On the genre see Schepens and Delcroix 1996. Older critics were harsher in their estimation of the genre: Schmid and Stählin 1920–4: 237 dismissed it as 'ein Parasitengewächs am Baum den historischen und naturwissenschaftlichen Literatur.' For a more recent and nuanced treatment, see Lightfoot 2021: 42–52.

[45] For Archelaus the Egyptian, see Lightfoot 2021: 54–57.

[46] On Pliny's *Natural History* as an encyclopaedia designed to evoke imperial control, see Murphy 2004.

Pliny's reasoning appeals to the majesty of nature and the limits of human understanding, reminding us once more of the importance of the marvellous in undermining certitude. At the same time, as a genre, paradoxographic collections appealed to Greek scholarship as a guarantee of authenticity. Not all Roman readers were so generous. Aulus Gellius provides a slightly different view of paradoxography. In an autobiographical vignette rare in antiquity, he describes an occasion when strolling around Brundisium he found a bookseller offering a deal on some old, dusty Greek books full of unbelievable stories ('libri Graeci miraculorum fabularumque pleni, res inauditae, incredulae'). He explains that he used them for nuggets of recondite information to sprinkle through his own work until he grew tired of them. Disgusted at their worthlessness, since they neither adorned nor improved life, he abandoned them. Yet even Aulus Gellius was not wholly immune to the pleasure of the incredible: when he gave up his Greek books he simply decided to stick to Pliny for tales of the marvellous instead.[47] Writers both debunked tales of the bizarre yet happily indulged in perpetuating them. Lucian, with his usual perspicacity, recognized the hypocrisy at the heart of this and embraced it. He blames Homer for starting a tradition followed by others who, with 'the same intent, have written about imaginary travels and journeys of theirs, telling of huge beasts, cruel men and strange ways of living'. But, Lucian continues, he cannot blame them for lying because he saw 'that this was already a common practice even among men who profess philosophy. I did wonder, though, that they thought that they could write untruths and not get caught at it.' And then, turning the usual programmatic claim of authenticity on its head, he asserts the paradox that his history is more true because he has admitted that it contains no truth:

> But my lying is far more honest than theirs, for though I tell the truth in nothing else, I shall at least be truthful in saying that I am a liar. I think I can escape the censure of the world by my own admission that I am not telling a word of truth. Be it understood, then, that I am writing about things which I have neither seen nor had to do with nor learned from others – which, in fact, do not exist at all and, in the nature of things, cannot exist. Therefore my readers should on no account believe in them.
> Lucian, *VH* 4. (tr. Harmon)

Lucian's scepticism is not only witty and honest, but also reveals that paradoxography was driven by much more than a simple desire to entertain. Each of these writers, even the most sceptical, confirms the hold of

---

[47] Aulus Gellius, *Noct. Att.* 9.4.2. See Wittkower 1942: 166.

thaumata and *mirabilia* on Hellenistic and Roman readers. The Hellenistic novel paved the way, but paradoxography went further. With its weird animals and strange humans both on the margins and within the familiar world, it was a genre that spoke to a deep need to classify, organize and control bodies of bizarre and amazing information that challenged the bulwarks of certainty and constantly threatened to overflow the barriers of credibility. Like the conspiracy theories of QAnon, paradoxographic texts offered an alternative universe whose appeal lay in the fact that its very implausibility circumvented the regular structures of knowledge.

The works of Phlegon of Tralles represents the fullest example of a genre that collected tales of the marvellous.[48] Dating to the second century AD, Phlegon's encyclopedic writings included Olympic victor lists, chronicles and accounts of colonial foundations. What his various writings have in common is the urge to impose classificatory neatness. In addition to these, however, he compiled a miscellany of anecdotes usually known as *De Mirabilibus*: a sprawling collection of oddities ranging from sybilline oracles, lists of centenarians and woman giving birth to multiple offspring to truly astonishing vignettes: revenants, ghosts, talking heads that deliver prophesies and centaurs kept in captivity. A typical entry gives an account of gigantic bodies of twenty-three and twenty-four cubits uncovered during the digging of a canal, or reports monstrous births, such as the serving maid who gives birth to a monkey.[49] In some episodes there are hints of a political origin to the story. One lengthy episode, for example, involves the ghost of a certain Polykritos, an attested Aitolian *strategos* of the early 250s.[50] After his death his wife, a Lokrian woman, gives birth to a child with both male and female genitalia. Panic-stricken at the prodigy, the child's relatives rush to the agora to get help. An assembly is called to debate what to do with the child, whereupon the ghost of Polykritos appears. He advises the Aitolians – in somewhat menacing terms – to hand the child over to him, and when they refuse he attacks the child and devours it, all but for the head. After Polykritos disappears, the child's head continues to speak, prophesying further war and bloodshed.[51] The story may well have arisen in response to Aitolia's expansion in the mid-third century, after the incorporation of Lokris and at the time of a campaign in Akarnania, but even if the story originates in that setting, the very opacity of the episode's political message confirms that the story continued to circulate

---

[48] Phlegon of Tralles, *BNJ* 257. See Giannini 1967, Gauger 1980, Hansen 1996.
[49] Phlegon of Tralles, *BNJ* 257 F36 XIX–XXII.
[50] On Polykritos and political conditions in Aitolia at the time, see Scholten 2000: 253–6.
[51] The political point of the cephalomantic oracle has provoked different interpretations. See Scholten 2000: 89–90, Brisson 1978 and Hansen 1996: 96–8.

despite, not because of, its political significance. A second story of cephalomancy may also have had an Aitolian provenance: The Romans have defeated Antiochos III at Thermopylai and the king has fled. As the Romans set about collecting spoils on the battle field a dead Syrian cavalryman, Bouplagos, stands up and warns the Romans that their actions have offended the gods and that they will send 'a stout-hearted people' into the Romans' land to make them pay. The Romans, terrified, consult Delphi and remove themselves to Naupaktos to offer sacrifice at a shrine common to all Greeks. Here a Roman general, Publius, goes mad, climbs a tree and delivers a series of contradictory prophesies to the astonished Roman soldiers standing below. He then orders them not to interfere when a huge red wolf approaches to devour him. They obey and the wolf dutifully shreds Publius limb from limb, leaving the severed head to continue issuing warnings of impending disaster.[52] As with the story of Polykritos, the political setting is less important than the otherworldly elements which are repeated. Even if there were an Aitolian tradition of cephalomancy, this too would not be sufficient to explain the stories' long afterlife. The same can be said of other episodes in Phlegon's work drawn from well-established genres. Take, for example, the story of Philinnion, a dead girl, who appears night after night to a young man, her would-be lover, until her nightly visits are reported to her family, who interrupt them and cause the girl to return to the Underworld. Philinnion's story is an example of a revenant tale that was a feature of Greek popular literature for hundreds of years, and it has modern counterparts in both Irish folktales and German stories.[53]

Read separately and in succession, the stories of Polykritos, Bouplagos, Publius and Philinnion are so diverse that it is easy to dismiss them as a mere miscellany of the bizarre. The compilation, taken as a whole, however, is an example of a type of discourse characterized by 'situated messiness'.[54] As a totality, Phlegon's work amounts to an imaginative world full of ghosts, vampires and talking heads whose existence points to a world in flux, as if abnormality of any sort constantly threatens to disrupt order. By contrast, compilation imposes regularity: like goes with like, the same and similar elements recur, one extraordinary birth is followed by another. Thus, for example, when Phlegon turns to the disturbing business of sex transformation and hermaphroditism (treated together in the paradoxographic texts) in quick succession we are given Teiresias, Kainis/Kaineus, an unnamed hermaphrodite from Antioch, Philotis of Smyrna, Sympherousa/Sympheron

---

[52] Phlegon of Tralles, *BNJ* 257 F36 III.
[53] Phlegon of Tralles, *BNJ* 257 F36 I. For discussion of the Philinnion, see Rohde 1877: 330; Hansen 1980, Hansen 1989. The story was the inspiration for Goethe's *Die Braut von Korinth*.
[54] The expression is borrowed from Livingstone 1992: 28, who uses it in relation to geography.

of Epidauros, Aitete/Aitetos of Laodicea, and an unnamed hermaphrodite at Rome. The lists culminates in a Sibylline oracle. In the face of uncertainty the very act of compiling weird stories serves as an assertion of control, imposing a sequence on the anomalous and unsettling phenomena being collected.

Given Phlegon's taste for *mirabilia* it comes as no surprise that he has a centaur in his compendium, although this particular creature reveals that hybridity served a quite different function in the literary imagination of the Greek world in the Roman period from earlier times. Phlegon's account is as follows:

> Above Saune, a city in Arabia, a hippocentaur was discovered high up a mountain which is full of a marvellous drug. The drug is named after the city, and it is regarded as the keenest and deadliest of poisons. The king captured the hippocentaur alive and sent it with other gifts to Caesar in Egypt. It lived on meat, but was unable to endure the change of climate and died, so the prefect of Egypt had it preserved and sent to Rome. And first it was displayed in the palace, having a face more savage than a human's and hairy hands and fingers, and its lungs were connected to its forelegs and stomach. It had the hard hooves of a horse and yellowish hair, even though its skin had been blackened by the preservation process. It was not as big as some writers have recorded, but also not small. In the aforementioned city of Saune there were also said to be other hippocentaurs. If someone does not believe the one sent to Rome was real, he can investigate it. For the preserved one is kept on the property of the emperor, as I said before.
> Phlegon, *de mirab.* 11–35= *BNJ* 257 fr. 36 (tr. McInerney)

It is worth emphasizing the degree to which this account departs from the canonical versions of centaurs. There is no mention of Thessaly, the traditional homeland of the centaur in earlier Greek literature, nor any genealogy to explain its existence. Instead, the centaur is the product of a distant locale, Arabia. The exoticism of the location and the creature is reinforced by the 'marvellous drug' found there, a detail left unexplained but possibly borrowed from earlier treatments of the mountains of Thessaly.[55] There is no mention of Homer's woolly mountain beasts or Pindar's mythical marriage of Ixion and Nephele. Phlegon's centaur is not set in a narrative framework: there is no marriage of Hippodamia and Peirithous, no Battle of the Lapiths and Centaurs or any equivalent. Instead, it is a gift to Caesar. It exists as vehicle for making the spatial order of the Roman world and the hierarchy of

---

[55] Herakleides Kritikos, *BNJ* 369A F2.3 describes the 'root of arum' found on Pelion as an effective treatment for snake bite. It was taken in wine. The same chapter includes a section on a prickly plant resembling white myrtle whose berries could be used to make an ointment that made one impervious to cold.

Roman power more tangible, moving from a mountain in the desert to Egypt to Rome. Nor is there any attempt to offer a rationalizing account of how even the idea of a centaur could have come about, such as Palaiphatos' centaurs of Nephele, dimly seen through the fog as they ride away. Rather, in Phlegon we are offered tactile proof in a description that is focused on the creature's face, limbs, hooves and even internal organs. The vitality of the mythological centaur has given way to a brutal, anatomical reality, a specimen preserved in a vat of honey.[56] And, as with all fantasy creatures before CGI, anxieties about the realness of the creature swamp everything else. 'Don't believe me?', Phlegon seems to say; 'Look for yourself. It is in the emperor's cabinet of curiosities.' Stripped of its autonomous existence as a creature wholly mythical, the centaur from Saune has been captured and put to work, proof of the reach of Rome. Steven Rutledge pinpoints the connection between hybrid bodies and the articulation of power: 'The eviscerated and dismembered bodies of fantastic creatures and their bones functioned as a symbolic indicator of what Rome could do and had done to its enemies and rivals: skinned and disfigured, the Romans remade them into something Roman.'[57]

The same emphasis on physical tangibility applied to the Triton of Tanagra, a humanoid sea-creature whose remains impressed Pausanias around the same time Phlegon was examining the centaur of Saune.[58] A certain Demostratos was part of a delegation sent to investigate the Tanagran creature. According to Aelian its body was so old and decayed that its scales fell off at the slightest touch.[59] Adrienne Mayor has suggested that these creatures were probably hoaxes, fabricated by taxidermists. She offers the following explanation for this:

> Hovering between fantasy and certainty, hoaxes of all eras reflect the tensions that arise between popular belief and established science. Reports of live Centaurs and Tritons and displays of their 'remains' not only challenged the ancient philosophers' rejection of mythical hybrids but tested the limits of popular credulity. These hoaxes grew out of the estrangement of philosophical inquiry from popular knowledge, but they also reveal the age-old human longing to bring to life creatures of lost worlds.[60]

---

[56] Mayor 2011: 196.
[57] Rutledge 2012: 194–5. Similarly, given the number of descriptions of *paradoxa* that entail beheading, beatings and dismemberment, one is reminded of Derrida's insistence on the violence of the archive. See Derrida 1995.
[58] Paus. 9.20.4 describes it as a *thauma* greater than the statue in the temple of Dionysos.
[59] Aelian, *De nat. anim.* 15.18.   [60] Mayor 2011: 231.

Hoaxes, certainly, but it is difficult to see 'established science' in the Roman period posing much of an obstacle to popular belief. There may have been a growing gap between philosophical enquiry and conventional thinking, but the more pressing challenge was two-fold: for local communities to acquire prestige by claiming these monsters, and for central authorities to confirm power by asserting control of *mirabilia* at the edge of the real. When the provincial council sends a delegation to investigate and the results are reported in Rome, even a smelly, headless, decaying triton has proved its worth, linking Tanagra to the imperial capital. World Fairs tell us more about imperial powers than about the specimens on display. There the exotic animals and tableaux vivants were used to capture the exotic, tame the primitive and display it to those of superior cultures. So, too, *mirabilia* represented the reach of imperial knowledge systems to the farthest edges of the empire, and the capacity to bring this to the centre, either through collection or through encyclopedic catalogues and bestiaries.[61] In a hierarchy of imperial knowledge, the more recherché the specimen the better. The Arabian centaur illustrated the extent of the power of the empire that had acquired it. Phlegon's account comes after a list of other curiosities: a head found in Messenia three times the normal size; bodies in Dalmatia with ribs more than eleven cubits; teeth from Pontus over a foot long and brought up by earthquakes in the time of Tiberius, and transferred to Rome. From there we rapidly move on to other skeletons found in chance excavations measuring dozens if not hundreds of cubits, and then curious births: a baby born with the head of Anubis; a foetus with two heads; and a list of women who gave birth to prodigious numbers of children, one women producing twenty-four offspring in four confinements. Among these oddities, what tribute could be more fantastic than a centaur? It seems fitting that, according to Pliny (*NH* 7.35), the emperor Claudius recorded the birth of a centaur in Thessaly, and Pliny says that he himself saw another hippocentaur from Egypt which died and was preserved in honey to be shipped to the emperor (the centaur of Saune, surely). In these cases the hybrid is not a monster to scare and delight, but a vehicle for taming the exotic by bringing the far-away to the centre. If the centaurs of Nephele suggested a wildness lurking close to the surface of Greek culture, the centaur of Saune is something quite different: an emblem for what lay at the edge of empire.

---

[61] On the organization of knowledge systems and empire, see König and Whitmarsh 2007.

The Legacy of Alexander

Phlegon was only one of the compilers of *mirabilia*. His and other accounts of the marvellous remained popular, generating their own traditions in art and literature that populated the imagination of post-classical antiquity with exotic beasts and hybrids. The most significant vehicle for this was the *Alexander Romance*, which told the story of Alexander's conquest of the East. Its influence in some measure is due to the fact that it is an open text, whose many versions push the story in different directions.[62] In some Alexander is the son of Philip; in others he is the son of Darius; in yet others he is the son of the last Egyptian pharaoh, Nectanebo. But the different versions of Alexander share a fascination with the exotic and use it to shape and expand the narrative horizon of the story of Alexander into an alien world of wonders.

The transition from familiar to strange is especially marked in the Greek version of the *Romance*. Having caught up with a dying Darius and having crucified the pretender, Bessos, Alexander has completed that portion of his conquest which is set in regions with which Greeks might have had some familiarity. (He has also completed the section, we might note parenthetically, for which the historical sources offer a broadly plausible account.) Now, as the narrative moves into the unknown desert regions of Central Asia, fantasy takes over. In a series of letters written home to Olympias and Aristotle, Alexander reports on the marvels encountered on his campaign. The Macedonians come upon a forest of anaphanda trees inhabited by 36-foot tall giants: the Phytoi. These are followed by spherical wild men, and then the hairless Ochlitai, whose caves are defended by three-eyed beasts and fleas as big as frogs. The catalogue of freaks continues: for example, the Apple-Eaters, among whom the Macedonians capture a huge hairy man. Alexander orders a woman be put in the cage with him, possibly to investigate the wild man's sexual appetites, but instead he eats the captive woman. When the rest of the natives attack they are scared off by fire, as are most of the other tribes of wild folk

---

[62] On the many different versions of the Alexander Romance in different languages, see the chapters in Zuwiyya's comprehensive *A Companion to Alexander Literature in the Middle Ages* (2011). For a useful overview of the primary sources and the Latin and Greek recensions that drew on them see the chapter by Stoneman. Especially relevant to the matter of hybrids and monsters are the so-called *Letter to Aristotle about India*, in which hippotamuses are described as half men and half horses, and Pharasmanes' *On the Wonders of the East,* which included the Skiapodes and Cynocephali. Various other monsters make their appearance in the Syriac version (Monferrer-Salla), Arabic (Zuwiyya), French (Harf-Lancner), English and Scottish (Ashurst), and Italian (Morosoni).

encountered by Alexander. The three who are captured refuse to eat and die shortly after. When his three captives die, Alexander remarks that they did not have human intelligence but barked like dogs. To the audience these scenes are narrated as if they are a simple sequence of marvellous events peopled by strange creatures. Yet, as with Hanno's Gorillas and Megasthenes' Wild Men, there is a casual cruelty in Alexander's treatment of the fantastic beasts and primitive people he meets. Despite the rich fantasy of episodes such as Alexander carried aloft by griffins or descending in a bathyscope to the bottom of the sea, an unmistakable ingredient of the Alexander fantasy is its continuous emphasis on the violent mastery of everyone and everything encountered by the king. Ethnography and romance are both narratives of power, placing Alexander (youthful, successful, handsome, Graeco-Macedonian, heroic) above everyone else. For example, Alexander tricks a herd of centaurs into attacking by using untipped arrows and leading them into a ditch. The Romance attributes the success of Alexander's trick to the horse-men's inferior intellect: 'Just as their human part was incomplete, so too were their reasoning powers' (2.43). And here, too, the inhuman treatment which follows hints at a more complex cultural space inhabited by the hybrid. Having lured a number of the centaurs into the ditch Alexander dispatches some of his men to follow them, leading to the chilly comment 'and then they discovered what sort of swords the Macedonians really used – strong and murderous ones after all' (2.43). The episode concludes once again with a disastrous addition to an imperial menagerie: 'Alexander wanted to capture some of them and bring them back to our world. He brought about fifty out of the ditch. They survived for twenty-two days, but as he did not know what they fed on, they all died' (2.43). In an inversion of the themes of intelligence and captivity, the horse-man episode is followed by an encounter with a group of shy, little, light-footed men remarkable for possessing a foot like a sheep's in addition to a human foot. Once captured they plead for mercy, citing their timidity as the reason for their lonely existence. When Alexander releases them, however, they skip up the cliffs and hurl abuse at Alexander: 'Because your wits are inferior to ours, you were unable to capture us' (2.44). Outwitted by what seems to be a hybrid of a goatherd and his flock, Alexander laughs. Aside from serving as supernatural advisors or comic relief, all these creatures act as foils for the Macedonian king's performance, enhancing his accomplishments through their exoticism.

On his way east, Alexander experiences a succession of encounters with remarkable Gymnosophists and powerful Amazons whose exoticism in human form corresponds to the oddity of many of the animal hybrids. The

Gymnosophists, for example, articulate an elegant rejection of all that elite men of the Greek and Roman world regard as valuable. Their possessions are earth, daylight and the trees from which they eat. They are content drinking from the Euphrates; they have sex with their wives once per month until each wife has born two children, replacements for the father and mother. Their asceticism, unsurprisingly, includes a rejection of kingship, which they define as 'unjust power used to the disadvantage of others; insolence supported by opportunity; a golden burden' (3.6). The Amazons are larger, stronger and more beautiful than ordinary women, notable for their intelligence (3.27). The cumulative effect of these encounters – some peaceful, some bloody – is the creation of topsy-turvy world of the bizarre. In each encounter, the people and creatures Alexander meets either invert what is normal or challenge the clear-cut categories on which the normal depends. The regions off the map consist of places where regular rules do not apply. This makes the realm of the fantastic a place of opportunity, as the audience's imagination is challenged to examine every aspect of the status quo: the construction of royal authority, the power of life and death, the correct construction of gender – in short, the very nature of the social contract. As if to give that examination bite, the presence of wonder also signals that we have entered places where on occasion we can act in ways that are otherwise beyond the pale.

The potential of these hybrid creatures to challenge certainty is most pronounced in an episode that presages Alexander's impending death. Having reached Babylon, he writes another letter to Olympias describing a portent. A local woman gives birth to a creature said to resemble Skylla, its upper half human, its lower half shaped like a wild beast with the limbs and paws of a dog or lion. The first Chaldeans called upon the interpret the omen offer the reassuring reading that the human portion represents Alexander and that the animal bits are the people he has conquered. Yet, as the second interpreter correctly divines, the creature's unfortunate hybridity is a part of but not the key to the portent's meaning. The most important fact is that the human half is lifeless. This is an omen of the dead Alexander; the animal limbs are Alexander's subordinates, as savage towards men as they are ill-disposed towards him.[63] In the *Alexander Romance*, hybridity marks all manner of anomalies. It authorizes the king to indulge in violence for no good reason; it occasionally recalls him from an excess of ambition; and, finally, it offers a metaphor of the violence of his successors, his truest legacy.

---

[63] *Alex. Rom.* 3.31.

Adynata

Like many of the marvellous creatures in the *Alexander Romance*, Greek hybrids in general can lead our gaze in two directions: Medusa and Sphinx points towards threat and monstrosity, while Cheiron and Pegasos evoke wonder and awe. They allow the Greeks to give rich imaginative shape to a world of thick entanglement and contradiction, from their encounters with humans not quite like themselves to animals with whom they share powerful emotional bonds. And yet, one must not forget that hybrids do not have a material existence. Therefore, in addition to giving imagination a form, they also constitute a striking mode of figuration: hybrids force those who encounter them to engage with paradox and to grapple with the impossible. The roots of this go back to philosophical disputation in which hybrids and monsters served as allegorical tools. In the *Republic*, for example, Plato lays out a theory of appetites and morality according to which the just man indulges his worst impulses – murder, incest, temple robbery – in dreams while the unjust man plays these out in daylight. In a striking apophthegm he summarizes the unjust man, in Jowett's translation, as 'the waking reality of what we dreamed'.[64] This nightmare world of tyrannical appetites is populated by the wicked, but the monsters lurking here play a surprising role. Socrates proposes a thought experiment in which we are asked to examine the soul by imagining a creature described as *poikilos* ('variegated') and *polykephalos* ('many-headed'). Asked how one might perform such, he replies:

> 'By fashioning in our discourse a symbolic image of the soul, that the maintainer of that proposition may see precisely what it is that he was saying.' 'What sort of an image?' he said. 'One of those natures that the ancient fables tell of,' said I, 'as that of the Chimaira or Skylla or Kerberos, and the numerous other examples that are told of many forms grown together in one.' 'Yes, they do tell of them.' 'Mould, then, a single shape of a manifold and many-headed beast that has a ring of heads of tame and wild beasts and can change them and cause to spring forth from itself all such growths.'
>
> Plato, *Republic* 9.588c (tr. Shorey)

Next Socrates proposes a further stage, imagining a second, smaller creature – a lion – and a third, the smallest creature – a human.[65] All

---

[64] Plat. Rep. 9.576b (trans. Jowett): ἔστιν δέ που, οἷον ὄναρ διήλθομεν, ὃς ἂν ὕπαρ τοιοῦτος ᾖ.
[65] For bibliography on this famous passage, see Johnstone 2013. For a precise and nuanced reading, see Morgan 2012.

three he then fashions into a single creature which outwardly looks like a man, containing within it the animal and monstrous. The unjust man indulges the beast and the lion. Proper behaviour, by contrast, dictates that the human element should exercise mastery over the other two, drawing upon the lion's bravery as an ally and acting towards the creature as a farmer cultivating good crops, pruning weeds and nurturing friendly animals. (*Rep.* 9.589b) In this figuration, the hybrid supplied a vivid image of the appetites and urges that lie within us. The allegorical potential of the hybrid is uppermost here: bad appetites are literally monstrous. The ontological challenge of the hybrid, by contrast, is unimportant. Whether centaurs ever existed hardly matters for Plato, although their existence in popular culture was certainly an irritant. In the *Phaedrus* Socrates complains that myths such as the abduction of Oreithyia by Boreas lead down a rabbit hole of rationalizing explanations, all of which require a good deal of invention but which are a distraction from actual philosophy:

> But I, Phaedrus, think such explanations are very pretty in general, but are the inventions of a very clever and laborious and not altogether enviable man, for no other reason than because after this he must explain the forms of the Centaurs, and then that of the Chimaira, and there presses in upon him a whole crowd of such creatures, Gorgons and Pegasoses, and multitudes of strange, inconceivable, portentous natures. If anyone disbelieves in these, and with a rustic sort of wisdom, undertakes to explain each in accordance with probability, he will need a great deal of leisure. But I have no leisure for them at all; and the reason, my friend, is this: I am not yet able, as the Delphic inscription has it, to know myself; so it seems to me ridiculous, when I do not yet know that, to investigate irrelevant things. And so I dismiss these matters and accepting the customary belief about them, as I was saying just now, I investigate not these things, but myself, to know whether I am a monster more complicated and more furious than Typhon or a gentler and simpler creature, to whom a divine and quiet lot is given by nature.
>
> Plato, *Phaedrus* 229–30a (tr. Fowler)

Irrelevant and ridiculous, *adynata* did not merit the philosopher's attention. Yet hybrids, especially centaurs, kept popping up. As we have already seen, Xenophon, perhaps illustrating the rustic wisdom Plato referred to, explored the differences between the centaur and the horseman in a speech by Chrysantas in the *Cyropaedia*. The centaur is a model of sorts for the cavalryman (*hippeus*), but he qualifies his praise in an aside: 'if they existed' (εἰ ἐγένοντο).[66] In other words, prior to any allegorical significance they

---

[66] Xen., *Cyrop.* 4.3.17.

constituted an ontological problem: did hybrids ever exist? For Aristotle, the question of whether a centaur did or did not exist (εἰ ἔστιν ἢ μὴ ἔστι κένταυρος) was an example of a fundamental question ('without qualification') which necessarily preceded all other inquiries.[67] One could not ask 'what is the nature of god (or man)?' without first establishing that god (or man) existed. Curiously, Aristotle does not push the argument further by answering the question of whether or not the centaur existed or by exploring the significance of the implied answer (that it did not). One might ask, for example, what proof demonstrated the existence of god that did not apply to the centaur? If one cannot establish that centaurs exist, might it not follow that there is no proof for the existence of god? One wonders if using a non-existent creature to illustrate the need to establish first principles of inquiry hinted at the possibility of another, parallel, deep-seated and deeply troubling scepticism.

Questions of ontology aside, for Aristotle the centaur and hybridity were worth exploring. As a proxy for all things composite, the centaur was useful for thinking through questions of parts, wholes and classification. For example, in the *Poetics*, Aristotle addresses the question of genre. Different genres were associated with particular metres; dactylic hexameters connoted epic, iambic trimeters were used for the spoken parts of drama, and so forth. These were the parts that combined to make the whole: a tragedy, a comedy, or a hymn. But what of the medley, a hybrid of different metres that was as incongruous as a man's torso and a horse's rump? Aristotle addresses this problem in terms that again illustrate the value of thinking with hybrids:

> Similarly, if a man makes his representation by combining all the metres, as Chairemon did when he wrote his rhapsody *The Centaur*, a medley of all the metres, he too should be given the name of poet.
>
> Arist., *Poetics* 1447b (tr. Fyfe)

Chairemon's medley (*mikte rhapsodia*) mixed various metres in order to create something that defied categories and permeated the boundaries of genre. That the work in question was entitled *The Centaur* suggests that Chairemon's approach to creating a hybrid work by mixing metres was deliberate and especially fitting if, as Carl Shaw has recently argued, *The Centaur* was a satyr play.[68] Nor were Aristotle and Chairemon the only writers to use the hybrid to comment on genre boundaries. In Lucian's *Bis Accusatus*, Dialogue bemoans his fate as 'a ridiculous cross between prose and verse; a monster of incongruity;

---

[67] Aristot., *APost.* ii. 1.89b. See Bronstein 2016. [68] Shaw 2014.

a literary Centaur'.[69] Elsewhere, Lucian again uses the centaur to suggest the problem of blending genres, concluding that:

> even the combination of those two very fine creations, dialogue and comedy, is not enough for beauty of form if the blending lacks harmony and symmetry. The synthesis of two fine things can be a freak – the hippocentaur is an obvious example: you would not call this creature charming, rather a monstrosity, to go by the paintings of their drunken orgies and murders. Well then, can nothing beautiful come from the synthesis of two things of high quality, as the mixture of wine and honey is exceedingly pleasant? Yes, certainly. But I cannot maintain that this is the case with my two: I'm afraid that the beauty of each has been lost in the blending.
>
> Lucian, 'You're a Prometheus in Words' (tr. Kilburn)

But beauty is not always lost in blending. Possibly the oddest apology for mixing is found in Philostratos, who gives a brief account in the *Imagines* of female centaurs (centaurides), emphasizing the attractiveness of these hybrid creatures. In describing a scene in a painting in Naples, he evokes an idyllic picture of centaur society, wherein entire families live in the wilderness of Pelion, 'a most delightful home' where the landscape is marked by wild forests of ash, beautiful caves and springs. In this pastoral paradise the female centaurs stand out as a hybrid improved by combination, 'for the delicacy of their female form gains in strength when the horse is seen in union with it'.[70] Philostratos' rapturous description continues:

> How beautiful the Centaurides are, even where they are horses; for some grow out of white mares, others are attached to chestnut mares, and the coats of others are dappled, but they glisten like those of horses that are well cared for. There is also a white female Centaur that grows out of a black mare, and the very opposition of the colours helps to produce the united beauty of the whole.
>
> Philostratus, *Imagines* 2.3 (tr. Fairbanks)

Philostratus' enthusiasm reveals interesting tastes and assumptions. The qualification 'even where they are horses' suggests he was aware that praising the beauty of a human woman was not a problem but that waxing lyrical about the equine parts of a centaur needed a little more explanation. His justification amounts to the fact that the healthy coat of a white,

---

[69] Lucian, *Bis Accus.* 34 τὸ γὰρ πάντων ἀτοπώτατον, κρᾶσίν τινα παράδοξον κέκραμαι καὶ οὔτε πεζός εἰμι οὔτε ἐπὶ τῶν μέτρων βέβηκα, ἀλλὰ ἱπποκενταύρου δίκην σύνθετόν τι καὶ ξένον φάσμα τοῖς ἀκούουσι δοκῶ.

[70] On Centaurides, see *LIMC* VIII s.v. Kentauroi et Kentaurides (no. 326–33) (Leventopoulou).

chestnut or dappled horse is itself beautiful if the horse has been well cared for – an observation that is true, but which is still curious given that the entire creature is both imaginary and partially human. He goes on to praise a female centaur that combines a white human torso with a black mare, referring to 'the united beauty of the whole'. Yet this is a unification of exact opposites – black and white, human and animal – perhaps reflecting the growing influence of the *satura* in Roman aesthetics.

For all the oddities of Philostratos' explanation, he was not alone in appreciating centaur beauty. In the *Metamorphoses* Ovid had played with the conceit of centaur love in the story of Cyllarus and Hylonome, although in describing Cyllarus' beauty he too began with the qualification 'if hybrids such as he be granted beauty'.[71] Jeri DeBrohun has persuasively argued that Ovid is concerned here with creating 'the portrait of a double hybrid, a single figure that combines, both physically and spiritually, male and female, human and animal, *natura* and *cultus*, and even, for a brief moment, love and war'.[72] This literary use of hybridity as a metaphor for entanglement and complexity underscores the fact that by this point in the evolution of Greek and Roman culture the hybrid has completely lost its power to astonish. Hybridity has been catalogued, drawn, painted and tamed. Rather than serving as a counterpoint to the human realm, these hybrids have been fully incorporated into it. The process is encapsulated in the shifting language of the episode. Ovid begins by referring to Eurytus as 'saevorum saevissime Centaurorum' ('most savage of the savage Centaurs') as he seizes Hippodame, but by the end of the war between the Lapith and the Centaurs, the centaur Cyllarus is not a wild beast but the *maritus* of Hylanome – that is, her husband. Furthermore, in the death scene which closes the episode, Hylanome falls upon the spear that has transfixed Cyllarus, uniting the two lovers in death ('incubuit moriensque suum conplexa maritum est').[73] It is hard to imagine Hesiod describing the death of Skylla or Echidna in similarly anthropomorphic terms.

While hybrids would continue to serve the imagination of Mediterranean people as they ventured even farther afield in trade and conquest, the 'ancestral' hybrids (those rooted deep in Mediterranean culture) would look increasingly feeble by comparison. In a fourth-century AD Roman mosaic from Tunisia, for example, two *centaurides* flank Venus, holding a crown over the

---

[71] '[S]i modo naturae formam concedimus illi'; *Metamorph.* 12.394. [72] DeBrohun 2004: 447.
[73] On the erotic overtones of the language, see DeBrohun 2004: 445.

Figure 9.1 Venus crowned by two centaurides. Mosaic, fourth century AD. Elles, Tunisia. Bardo National Museum.

goddess's head (see Figure 9.1). If hybrids are shorthand for crossing boundaries, it is hard to know what type of transgression is contemplated by visualizing the crowning of Miss Mediterranean by two centauresses.

Despite the diminution of hybrids' power to shock, as impossibilities they continued to present a conundrum that could be deployed fruitfully. A passage in Diogenes Laertius shows that thinkers were keen to unlock the potential of the hybrid, not merely as an exemplum but as a category for classifying modes of perception:

> By incidence or direct contact have come our notions of sensible things; by resemblance notions whose origin is something before us, as the notion of Socrates which we get from his bust; while under notions derived from analogy come those which we get by way of enlargement, like that of Tityos or the Cyclops, or by way of diminution, like that of the Pygmy. Of notions obtained by transposition creatures with eyes on the chest would be an instance, while the centaur exemplifies those reached by composition.
>
> Diogenes Laertius 7.53 (tr. Hicks)

Here, the key to the hybrid's utility is its composite nature. It is not itself an example of a thing, but a mode of perception that operates through considering parts and their relationship to each other and the whole. We recognize things both as integral wholes and as assemblages of parts, although Diogenes Laertius' use of the hippocentaur makes the point that the *synthesis* may be somewhat different from a simple enumeration of parts: in this case, the whole may be something other than the sum of its parts.[74]

But no matter how the philosopher employs the hybrid, whether as a thought experiment, a contrafactual, a first principle or a mode of discourse, the hybrid can never shake off the persistent problem posed by its existence. The hybrid is an epistemological challenge. If it never existed, how could we even imagine such a thing? For the artist who created the mosaics of Hadrian's villa, what was the source of the image he rendered in the mosaic (Figure 9.2)? Lucretius address this question directly, using hybrids such as the centaur and the chimaira as counterintuitive examples. He begins with the reasonable assertion: 'For certainly no image of a centaur comes from one living, since there never was a living thing of his nature.'[75]

But if there was no centaur, how then is there an image of a centaur?[76] Lucretius' solution to this conundrum is a physical explanation, based on the notion that actual humans and horses give off tenuous but physically real images which collide and stick to each other. These combined images then enter the mind, which, for Lucretius, is equally fine.[77] Hybrids here are genuinely valuable as a stimulus for Lucretian thought, not as examples of objects that exist (since they do not) or even of classes of things (such as hybrids in general), but as real, composite things (images) that come about from a blending of other images (given off by real things). They are oddities with a material reality – the blended image is a thing – but whose referents (the hybrids represented by the two images) are impossible. Accordingly, while the centaur does not exist, an image combining the human and the horse does. Hence, even the impossible and non-existent centaur is a key to perception. There was, in fact, a good deal more at stake than simply explaining how we could imagine a non-existent being. As Gordon Campbell has noted, centaurs and other hybrids crossed the human/animal divide and so introduced ontological instability into a world that relied on fixity of species.[78] This was a problem for theories such as Epicureanism that assigned no place to a guiding intelligence in creation. The solution

---

[74] On the Stoic view of our ability to manipulate mental images through *phantasia*, see Sheppard 2014: 13.
[75] Lucretius, *De rerum natura* 4. 739–40 (tr. Rouse).   [76] Long 1977; Gale 1994: 91–2.
[77] This is a material process. Alganza Roldán, Barr and Hawes 2017: 193, n.18 are quite wrong to attribute this to the creativity of the human imagination, 'which creates fictitious amalgams using parts of different creatures (5.732–748)' [sic: the reference should be to bk 4, not 5].
[78] Campbell 2007.

Figure 9.2 Mosaic depicting a pair of centaurs fighting cats of prey from Hadrian's Villa, ca. 130 AD, Altes Museum, Berlin.

which Lucretius took from Empedokles was to imagine a primeval burst at the beginning of the cosmos in which all forms and combinations instantly appeared but among which only those fit to survive did. Accordingly, animal/human hybrids like centaurs, chimairas and creatures blending human and marine elements (*conecti terrestria membra marinis* [2.704], usually thought to refer to Skylla) are examples of non-existent atomic combinations.[79] This materialism anticipated Darwin by 2,000 years, and it is no coincidence that the abuse aimed at Darwin also drew on the spectre of hybridism. Caricatures that put his head on the body of an ape replay the same assumption with which we began, describing Larsen's cartoon of the Artist's Dilemma: species are fixed, and are perceived as purposefully designed so.[80] As Linnaeus put it, 'There are as many species as originally fashioned by the creator.' Lucretius' theory of blended images managed to write the creator out of creation while acknowledging the fitness of the surviving creations. A similar use of the centaur's impossibility was to classify it, as Artemidorus does, as a prodigy that cannot exist, but which has a meaning when it appears in dreams. Relying on a kind of sympathy between dream image and significance, Artemidorus claims that since it is

---

[79] Woolerton 2010: 255. See also Long 1977: 81 ('Although the earth contained many seeds at the time when living things first developed, hybrids are evidently impossible').

[80] For attacks on Darwin and his difficulty with the concept of a creator, see Kutschera 2009.

Figure 9.3 Mosaic depicting a tigress–griffin eating a lizard, Arasta Bazaar, Sultan Ahmet Mosque, Istanbul. Mosaics dated to AD 450–550 used to decorate the pavement of a peristyle courtyard in the Arasta Bazaar, within the Sultan Ahmet Mosque or Blue Mosque compound. Bridgeman.

impossible for a centaur to be born, its occurrence in dreams means that the expectations expressed in the dream will be similarly false.[81]

This response to the impossibility of the hybrid was one of its most significant legacies. From Diodorus Siculus to Galen, centaurs and other hybrids were a challenge. For the historian they challenged their power to identify origins.[82] For the doctor they challenged their understanding of biology and diet.[83] For the rhetorician they challenged their skill in refutation since their very existence was already in doubt. Later, coming from a well-established world of pagan myth, they challenged Christian apologists. From Eusebios to John Malalas, it seems that each major Christian writer felt compelled to resort to Palaiphatan-style rationalism to discredit the wonders, myths and paradoxes – one is tempted to say, the exuberance – of the pagan world of storytelling.[84] One outlet for this narrative excitement was the decorative arts, where classical hybrids continued to flourish. In a sixth-century mosaic from Jerusalem, for example, Orpheus, a centaur and

---

[81] Artemid. *Oneiro.* 2.44 and 4.47.   [82] Diod. Sic. 4.8.4; 4.26.2–3; 4.76.2–3, 19.53.4.
[83] Galen, *De usu partium* 1.1.
[84] Gibson 2012. The subject of Christian attitudes towards animals, hybrids and monsters is enormous and well beyond the scope of this study. See Gilhus 2006, especially chapters 9–12.

Pan decorate the ornate interior of buildings. Although some have argued that Orpheus was an allegory for Christ, the evidence for this is unconvincing and it is simpler to see the figures serving as decorative motifs, devoid of any special symbolism beyond a loose allegory, in Sonia Muczik's words, 'of the domestication of the bestial instincts of human beings through the power of Orpheus' music'.[85] The elites of late antiquity were not troubled by the theological challenges of pagan myth. Instead, regardless of doctrinal considerations, they relished decorating their palaces and even public spaces with vivid images of unbelievable creatures. The tigress–griffin from the Arasta Bazaar in Istanbul was a worthy adornment for an imperial capital, whether Christian or pagan (see Figure 9.3).

---

[85] Mucznik 2011: 270. Elsner 2009 and Olszewski 2011 both discuss the mosaic at length and both reject the identification of the Orpheus figure with Christ.

10 | Conclusions

> The people of Phigaleia believe that Eurynome is a title of Artemis ...
> I have not seen the statue of Eurynome, but I heard from the Phigaleans
> that it was a carved statue bound by golden chains, and that it had
> a woman's shape down as far as the buttocks, below which it was a fish.
> This fish shape may signify she is a daughter of Okeanos and lived in the
> depths of the sea with Thetis, but there is no logical reason to connect this
> shape with Artemis.
>
> Pausanias 8.41.5–6 (trans. McInerney)

Home and Away

The hybrids of Greek culture, as we have seen, arose as a form of cultural figuration parallel and sometimes opposite to normative social praxis. The roots of this, I have argued, are gnarled and intertwined. A major influence was our animal entanglement, the deeply significant phenomenon of our awareness of existing in a world teeming with other living creatures on whom our lives depend. Layered over this are the more specific circumstances of life in the eastern Mediterranean, where a particular set of polarities established the conditions of social life: near and far, familiar and strange, intelligible and unintelligible, the 'home and away' conditions of Greek life.[1] Hybrids modulated these conditions across a range of fields and in a variety of ways. In interactions with non-Greek speakers – a common experience, given the connectedness of the eastern Mediterranean – hybrids could embody the successful blending of identities of the mētis experience, expressed in bilingualism, double naming and adopting the masks of other identities. Janus-like, hybrids could also face in the opposite direction of synthesis, and put a face to an elemental monstrosity that threatened the very foundations of cosmic order. And, in between such extremes, hybrids could also evoke alternatives and other

---

[1] The expression 'home and away' is borrowed from Emily Baragwanath's study of the Pelasgian episode in Book 6 of Herodotos. It also nicely suggests the fluidity of categories more generally. See Baragwanath 2008.

possible ways of being, connoting a kind of middle ground of sexual dimorphism and the negotiation of ethnic identities.

At the same time, it is inadequate to chart the various uses of hybridity as if each is merely a charming by-product of the cultural layering of the eastern Mediterranean. The incongruities of hybridity, the shocking potential of each hybrid, and the threat of monstrosity all amount to a constant assault on the categorical certainty that was important to Greek culture, which was characterized by a coherent worldview shared by most Greek men, if not in actuality then ideally so. It is men whose enjoyment is catered for in the symposium, whose sacrifice is celebrated in the funeral oration, whose prowess is feted on vases and epinician poems. And these farmers, soldiers and sailors who penetrated every corner of the Mediterranean world were at the apex of a social hierarchy that included but had little interest in women, children and the enslaved. Whether one is reading Aristotle, watching Aeschylus or looking at red-figure vases, it is impossible to ignore the fact that Greek culture assigns most space to the male, and that women, children, the enslaved and the foreign inhabit social spaces that are severely circumscribed. It was a social order that relied heavily on classification, organization and categorization – habits and practices that became characteristic of Greek culture and served to clarify the proper order for people, animals and things. Taxonomy became central to the formal apparatus of philosophical inquiry but also operated in other spheres. It was, for example, a feature of civic life. In the courts and assemblies of the Athenian democracy, demotic (location) and patronymic (descent) labels fixed the citizen man's place in space and time.

Impermanence and Vulnerability

The place of hybrids as dislocators of certitude reminds us that classes and categories are rarely as secure in reality as in theory. Scratching the surface can reveal the deeper anxieties and tensions that were a real part of lived experience. Consider, for example, the legal case involving Apollodoros and Nikostratos, two leading Athenians of the mid-fourth century.[2] We know that they came from the upper echelons of Athenian society because both were members of the liturgical class and boasted of the largesse that they and their families had expended on Athens. On the surface, then, their dispute over the ownership of two slaves has all the hallmarks of a spat

[2] Dem. 45.

between members of the privileged elite. But there are two components of the case that hint at other dimensions to the conflict. In the first place, Apollodoros was not a citizen by birth but by adscription. His father, the banker Pasion, had been a prodigiously successful slave who was manumitted by his owners. Subsequently, he was awarded citizenship sometime between the mid-390s and the early 370s by the Athenians for his generous benefactions to the city, including the donation of 1,000 shields and 5 triremes.[3] Apollodoros was born free sometime between 395 and 393, but would not have been entered on the citizen rolls until after his father had been enfranchised. Not only, then, was Apollodoros not from old money, he was only one generation from slavery, a point that we can be sure was remarked on in court by his opponent, Nikostratos. In much the same way, Demosthenes tried to destroy Aischines' reputation by scurrilously reminding the audience of his father's supposedly servile origins, and the son's dishonest attempts to hide these.[4] In both cases, the threat of revealing slave paternity highlighted a speaker's vulnerability. There are other indications that Apollodoros' social standing remained precarious – when a dispute arose regarding the trireme he had been commanding in the northern Aegean, Apollodoros' attempts to refer the matter to his superior were laughed off with a taunt: 'The mouse is now tasting pitch, because he wanted to be an Athenian.'[5] As Jeremy Trevett notes, 'Apollodoros as a newly enfranchised citizen could not expect to have things easy.'[6] Being prominent, litigious and well-known therefore brought the rewards of status, but equally carried the risk of libel, exposure and ridicule. How secure, then, was social standing? Nor were the threats merely theatrical. In one of the more astonishing revelations of the speech against Nikostratos we learn that, having left the city to track down two runaway slaves, he was himself captured by an Aiginetan trireme and enslaved. Apollodoros supplied 300 drachmas to Nikostratos' brother to pay for his passage to Aigina, to secure Nikostratos' release, and Apollodoros refers to the marks of the shackles still visible on Nikostratos' ankles.[7] In the political theatre that was the court, the Athenian jury got to see the high and mighty brought low, the signs of their former (or recent) slave status dramatically displayed on their

---

[3] Shields and triremes: Dem. 45.85. Information about Pasion and Apollodoros is spread throughout the speeches of Demosthenes (36; 49; 59) and Isokrates (17). For full treatment, see Trevett 1992: 1–49. For debate over the date of his enfranchisement, see Trevett 1992: 20–4.

[4] At Demosthenes 19.281, delivered in 343 BC, Aischines' father is the schoolmaster Atrometos. Thirteen years later, at 18.129, he has been reduced to 'Tromes, a slave of the schoolmaster Elpias'; 18.130 recounts Aischines' supposed attempts to hide this: 'By adding two syllables he turned his father from "Tromes" into "Atrometos"'.

[5] Dem. 50.26.   [6] Trevett 1992: 13.   [7] Dem. 53.6–8.

bodies, or their slave origins rehearsed for the entertainment of the audience as speakers competed to dox each other. Status and citizenship were vulnerable. One could be exposed to ridicule, deprived of citizen privileges (*atimia*) or, worse, actually enslaved. This is clearly a part of the mental make-up of the classical world, wherein vulnerability was inescapable, and it explains why Hellenistic novels so often played with the theme of reversal. In Chariton's *Chaireas and Kallirrhoe*, for example, when the eponymous heroine's former high status is revealed after her various tribulations – assault, coma, being sold into slavery, the usual plot contrivances of the Hellenistic novel – she prefers to accept her new, servile status, saying, 'I beg you to allow me to remain silent about my fortunes. I am now what I have become: a slave and a foreigner.'[8] While Plato praised the Athenians for excluding foreigners and Aristotle argued for categorical difference between slaves and free men, the lived reality for many was that poverty, hardship and sheer bad luck made life precarious. The possibility of slipping into a different social identity was ever present. Categories were never really fixed. Oscillation and impermanence were real.

Hybrids and the Cultural Imagination

This condition of impermanence at the level of the individual's social position also existed within a world that was only weakly statist: no secret police or mechanisms of censorship or autocratic authority exerted anywhere near total control, so that phenomena such as resistance and subversion were never clearly defined or articulated. There were no manifestos and no Antifa in ancient Greece. Instead, the Greeks displaced many of the anxieties and contradictions of social and political life into an imaginative realm dominated by hybrids: the centaur giving shape to primal, cisgendered, masculine sexuality; the gorgon putting a face on men's fear of female aggression; satyrs both embodying and mocking the phallus; bat-like Erinyes avenging family bloodshed. Taken together, these hybrids are less a subversion of conformity and more a channelling of cultural energies into an alternative mode of expression. Awe, wonder, curiosity and apprehension were the creation of hybrids in action. This was instrumentalized when the boy was inducted into manhood by becoming the wolf, just as the girl was marked as marriageable by playing the bear. Popping up in every corner of the cultural imagination hybrids cumulatively suggested that

---

[8] Chariton, *Chaireas and Kallirrhoe* 2.5.5–6.

other worlds existed alongside our own. As a counterpoint to certainty, tangible materiality, and order, hybrids offered a fuller and richer engagement with the world, transforming tumult, anxiety and disorder into imaginings both wondrous and awesome.

A recent study of the Middle Ages has made a similar point regarding the vibrancy and creative possibilities of marvels in both Christian and Muslim cultures. Michelle Karnes writes;

> Marvels mark out common ground between real and invented things. Unusual by definition, they tend to be unsettling, whether or not they are real ... Their protean nature means that they can be invented and reinvented anew, inviting endless artistic adaptations. Able to inhabit different forms in different disciplines and in different places, they might elicit wonder through their very instability.[9]

In more recent times, however, the creative power of hybridity and the marvellous has often been lost on us, and not only because such creatures have been banished in the modern world to horror movies and science fiction. There is an unhappy coda in western countries, not shared by the vibrant hybrids of Asia and Africa. In the west, classical hybrids were transformed into demons, whose challenge to Christian order authorized the faithful to resort to monstrous violence: upon encountering an *Onoscelis* – a hybrid with an attractive human body and the legs of an ass – the deacon Gerontius cut off its head and threw the body into a mill.[10] Another sorry chapter had begun in the long history of figuring the other as a monster. And just as Christian homiletics and martyrology would redeploy pagan hybrids in the service of Christian eschatology, so too, at the beginning of the early modern period, cataloguing and ordering hybrids into Aristotelian taxonomies would remain a part of the enterprise of natural history. In Ambroise Paré's *Des monstres et prodiges* (1573), the author sought to classify and render into some kind of order all of Europe's monsters based on the causes of their monstrosity, which ranged from an excess of seed, to the mother's indecent posture, to the participation in their conception of Demons and the Devil.[11] This was quickly followed by Weinrich's treatise *De ortu monstrorum commentarius* (1595), Schenk von Grafenberg's *Monstrorum historia* (1609), and Bauhin's *De*

---

[9] Karnes 2022: 210.
[10] Limberis 2012: 154. For the *Onoscelis*, see the pseudepigraphical *Testament of Solomon* 4.4–7. An enormous amount of information on Mediaeval bestiaries is collected by David Badke at http://bestiary.ca/.
[11] Hoffmann 1993: 35 refers to this as a 'Borgesian taxonomy.'

hermaphroditorum monstrosorumque partuum natura (1614). The birth of the modern was midwifed by classical monsters.[12]

The hybrids of the Greek imagination reveal a world of shifting categories, and offered an alternative to the certainties of conventional thinking. Conventionality, however, applied not only to formal philosophy but also to the systems that shaped all Greek life and thought. Hybrids were produced by a discourse of alterity in which the certainties of social order were constantly challenged, though never overthrown. In fact, the presence of hybrids in the Greek imagination also suggests that current interest in post-humanism and discourses that critique anthropocentric values and worldviews were already woven into the fabric of Greek culture.[13] Since Descartes and the high-water mark of human dominion as the dominant western mode of framing the human/animal relationship, there has been a gradual tidal shift towards decentring humans and imagining a more capacious universe of various species.[14] A receding tide reveals the remains of many strange and exotic creatures, whose forms almost defy belief, but they were there all along, in the depths of our imagination.

Just as Gauguin's experiences in Tahiti crystallized a deep disgust with European culture and forced him to contemplate a different way of being in the world, so too the Greeks' engagement with a wider, more varied world provoked questions about how human existence is to be understood, and experienced, and whether the human is even at the centre of existence. Like Gauguin painting in Tahiti, the hybrid asked 'Where do we come from? What are we? Where are we going?' And, in posing questions about the variability of human existence, the people of Greece found hybrids – from gorgons and centaurs to Cynocephali and monopods – useful counterpoints to convention.

---

[12] For renaissance and early modern hermaphrodites, centaurs and other classical hybrids, see Krämer 2009.

[13] Clarke and Rossini 2017, Chesi and Speigel 2020.

[14] For an overview of speciesism in a variety of eastern and eastern religious systems, see McCance 2013: 108. On dominion as a particularly western mode of conceiving human/animal relations and Descartes, see Singer 2009: 200.

Bibliography

Aarne, A., 1914. *Der tiersprachenkundige Mann und seine neugierige Frau. Eine vergleichende Märchenstudie*, Hamina.

Abbattista, A., 2018. *Animal Metaphors and the Depiction of Female Avengers in Attic Tragedy*. Unpublished doctoral thesis, University of Roehampton. https://pure.roehampton.ac.uk/ws/portalfiles/portal/999991/Abbattista_Alessandra_Final_Thesis.pdf.

Abraham, R., 2014. 'The Geography of Culture in Philostratus' *Life of Apollonius of Tyana*', *CJ*, 109.4, pp. 465–80.

Abulafia, D., 2011. *The Great Sea. A Human History of the Mediterranean*, London.

Ackermann, A., 2012. 'Cultural Hybridity: Between Metaphor and Empiricism', in P. W. Stockhammer, ed., *Conceptualizing Cultural Hybridization: A Transdisciplinary Approach*, Berlin, pp. 4–45.

Adams, C. J., 2000. *The Sexual Politics of Meat: A Feminist–Vegetarian Critical Theory* (10th anniversary ed.), New York.

Adshead, K., 1986. *Politics of the Archaic Peloponnese: The Transition from Archaic to Classical Politics*, Dorset.

Agamben, G., 2004. *The Open. Man and Animal*, trans. K. Attell, Stanford, CA.

Ahlberg, G., 1971. *Fighting on Land and Sea in Greek Geometric Art*, Stockholm.

Ajootian, A., 1997. 'The Only Happy Couple: Hermaphrodites and Gender', in A. O. Koloski-Ostrow and C. L. Lyons, eds., *Naked Truths: Women, Sexuality, and Gender in Classical Art and Archaeology*, London, pp. 220–42.

Alganza Roldán, M., J. Barr and G. Hawes, 2017. 'The Reception History of Palaephatus 1 (On the Centaurs) in Ancient and Byzantine texts', *Polymnia*, 3, pp. 186–235.

Almog, S., 2022. *The Origins of the Law in Homer*, Berlin; Boston.

Altaweel, M. and A. Squitieri, 2018. 'Material Culture Hybridization', in *Revolutionizing a World: From Small States to Universalism in the Pre-Islamic Near East*, London, pp. 179–98.

Amandry, P., 1953, *La Colonne des Naxiens et le Portique des Athéniens.* Fouilles de Delphes, 2, 1, 4 (II. Topographie et architecture. Le sanctuaire d'Apollon) Paris.

Ameisenowa, Z., 1949. 'Animal-Headed Gods, Evangelists, Saints and Righteous Men', *Journal of the Warburg and Courtauld Institutes*, 12, pp. 21–45.

Ameri, M., S. K. Costello, G. Jamison, and S. J. Scott, eds., 2018. *Seals and Sealing in the Ancient World. Case Studies from the Near East, Egypt, the Aegean and South Asia*, Cambridge.

Amit, R., 2012. 'On the Structure of Contemporary Japanese Aesthetics', *Philosophy East and West*, 62, pp. 177–85.

Anderson, G., 2018. *The Realness of Things Past. Ancient Greece and Ontological History*, Oxford.

Anderson, J. K., 1961. *Ancient Greek Horsemanship*, Berkeley.

Andreeva, P., 2018. *Fantastic Beasts of The Eurasian Steppes: Toward a Revisionist Approach to Animal-Style Art*. University of Pennsylvania Scholarly Commons. Unpublished doctoral dissertation.

Andrewes, A., 1938. "Eunomia," *CQ*, 32, pp. 89–102,

Angier, N., 2021. 'Meet the Other Social Influencers of the Animal Kingdom', www.nytimes.com/2021/05/07/science/animals-chimps-whales-culture.html

Anthony, D. W., and D. R. Brown, 2011. 'The Secondary Products Revolution, Horse-Riding, and Mounted Warfare', *J World Prehist*, 24, pp. 131–60.

Antonaccio, C. M., 2001. 'Ethnicity and Colonization', in I. Malkin, ed., *Ancient Perceptions of Greek Ethnicity*, Cambridge, MA, pp. 113–57.

Antonaccio, C. M., 2003. 'Hybridity and the Cultures within Greek Culture', in C. Dougherty and L. Kurke, eds., *The Cultures Within Ancient Greek Culture: Contact, Conflict, Collaboration*, Cambridge, pp. 57–76.

Antonaccio, C. M., 2013. 'Networking the Middle Ground? The Greek Diaspora, Tenth to Fifth Century BC', *Archaeological Review from Cambridge*, 28, pp. 237–51.

Appert, C. M., 2016. 'On Hybridity in African Popular Music: The Case of Senegalese Hip Hop', *Ethnomusicology*, 60.2, pp. 279–99.

Armeni, A. K., V. Vasileiou, N. A. Georgopoulos, 2014. 'When Genotype Prevails: Sexual Female-to-Male Transformation in Classical Antiquity, recorded by Gaius Plinius Secundus and Phlegon', *Hormones*, 13, pp. 153–6.

Armeni, A. K., V. Vasileiou, G. Markantes, et al., 2014. 'Gender Identity Disputed in the Court of Justice: A Story of Female to Male Sexual Transformation in the Hellenistic Period, Described by Diodorus Siculus', *Hormones*, 13, pp. 579–82.

Arnold, M., 1994 (1869). *Culture and Anarchy*, ed. Samuel Lipman, New Haven.

Arrington, N., 2021. *Athens at the Margins. Pottery and People in the Early Mediterranean World*, Princeton.

Arthur, M. B., 1980. 'The Tortoise and the Mirror: Erinna *PSI* 1090', *CW*, 74.2, pp. 53–65.

Aruz, J., S. B. Graff, and Y. Rakic, eds., 2013. *Cultures in Contact: From Mesopotamia to the Mediterranean in the Second Millennium BC*, New York.

Ashe, B., 2015. *Twisted. My Dreadlock Chronicles*, Evanston, Il.

Åshede, L., 2020. 'Neutrumque et Utrumque Videntur: Reappraising the Gender Role(s) of Hermaphroditus in Ancient Art', in A. Surtees and J. Dyer, eds., *Exploring Gender Diversity in the Ancient World*, Edinburgh, pp. 81–94.

Asper, M., 2015. 'Medical Acculturation? Early Greek Texts and the Question of Near Eastern Influence', in B. Holmes and K.-D. Fischer, eds., *The Frontiers of Ancient Science: Essays in Honor of Heinrich Von Staden*, Berlin, pp. 19–46.

Assmann, J., 1992. *Das kulturelle Gedächtnis*, Munich.

Assmann, J., 2008. 'Communicative and Cultural Memory', in A. Erll & A. Nünning, eds., *Cultural Memory Studies. An International and Interdisciplinary Handbook*, Berlin, pp. 109–18.

Aston, E., 2011. *Mixanthrôpoi. Animal-Human Hybrid Deities in Greek Religion*. Liège.

Aston, E., 2014. 'Part-Animal Gods', in G. L. Campbell, ed., *The Oxford Handbook of Animals in Classical Thought and Life*, Oxford, pp. 366–83.

Aston, E., 2017. 'Centaurs and Lapiths in the Landscape of Thessaly', in G. Hawes, ed., *Myths on the Map: The Storied Landscapes of Ancient Greece*, Oxford, pp. 83–105.

Astoreca, N. E., 2021. *Early Greek Alphabetic Writing. A Linguistic Approach*, Oxford.

Ataç, M. A., 2010. *The Mythology of Kingship in Neo-Assyrian Art*, Cambridge.

Ataç, M. A., 2019. 'Reconstructing Artistic Environments', in A. C. Gunter, ed., *A Companion to Ancient Near Eastern Art*, Hoboken, NJ, pp. 525–47.

Atack, C., 2014. 'The Discourse of Kingship in Classical Athenian Thought', *Histos*, 8, pp. 329–62.

Athanasiou, A., 2003. 'Technologies of Humanness, Aporias of Biopolitics, and the Cut Body of Humanity', *Differences*, 14, pp. 125–62.

Auberger, J., 2011. 'Que reste-t-il de l'homme de science?' in J. Wiesehöfer, R. Rollinger and G. B. Lanfranchi, eds., *Ktesias' Welt/Ctesias' World*. Wiesbaden, pp. 13–20.

Aubert, M., R. Lebe, A. A. Oktaviana, et al., 2019. 'Earliest Hunting Scene in Prehistoric Art', *Nature*, 576, pp. 442–5.

Averett, E. W., 2015. 'Masks and Ritual Performance on the Island of Cyprus', *AJA*, 119.1, pp. 3–45.

Averett, E. W., 2018. 'Playing the Part: Masks and Ritual Performance in Rural Sanctuaries in Iron Age Cyprus', in A. Berlejung and J. E. Filitz, eds., *The Physicality of the Other: Masks from the Ancient Near East and the Eastern Mediterranean. Orientalische Religionen in der Antike* 27, Tübingen, pp. 305–37.

Avramidou, A., 2011. *The Codrus Painter. Iconography and Reception of Athenian Vases in the Age of Pericles*, Madison.

Axel, B. K., 2004. 'The Context of Diaspora', *Cultural Anthropology*, 19, pp. 26–60.

Ayali-Darshan, N., 2014. 'The Question of the Order of Job 26, 7–13 and the Cosmogonic Tradition of Zaphon', *Zeitschrift für die alttestamentliche Wissenschaft*, 126, pp. 402–17.

Bailey, D. M., 2007. 'A Snake-Legged Dionysos from Egypt, and Other Divine Snakes', *JEA*, 93, pp. 263–70.

Baker, S., 1993. *Picturing the Beast: Animals, Identity and Representation*, Manchester.

Bakhtin, M., 1981. *The Dialogic Imagination*. trans. C. Emerson and M. Holquist, Austin.

Balériaux, J., 2019. 'Mythical and Ritual Landscapes of Poseidon Hippios in Arcadia', *Kernos*, 32, pp. 81–100.

Ballentine, D. S., 2015. *The Conflict Myth and the Biblical Tradition*, Oxford.
Baragwanath, E., 2008. *Motivation and Narrative in Herodotus*, Oxford.
Baratay, É., 2015. 'Building an Animal History', in L. Mackenzie and S. Posthumus, eds., *French Thinking about Animals*, East Lansing, pp. 3–14.
Baratay, É., ed., 2019. *Aux sources de l'histoire animale*, Paris.
Barbara, S., 2008. 'Science, mythe et poésie dans le "Catalogue des serpents" de Lucain (*Phars.* IX, 700–733)', *Pallas* 78, *Mythes et savoirs dans les textes grecs et latins*, pp. 257–77.
Barbaro, N., 2018. 'Dedica votiva del mercenario Pedon', *Axon*, 2.1, pp. 19–30.
Barouti, K., G. K. Markantes, A. K. Armeni, V. Vasileiou, and N. A. Georgopoulos, 2017. 'The Male Bride: A Story of Sexual Female-to-Male Transformation at Marriage from the Hellenistic Period, recorded by Phlegon of Tralles', *Hormones*, 16.1, pp. 101–3.
Barringer, J. M., 1995. *Divine Escorts. Nereids in Archaic and Classical Greek Art*, Ann Arbor.
Barringer, J. M., 2001. *The Hunt in Ancient Greece*, Baltimore.
Barrow, R., 2018. *Gender, Identity and the Body in Greek and Roman Sculpture*. Cambridge.
Barton, T., 1994. *Ancient Astrology*, London.
Batto, B., 2013. 'The Combat Myth in Israelite Myth Revisited', in J. Scurlock and R. H. Beal, eds., *Creation and Chaos: A Reconsideration of Hermann Gunkel's Chaoskampf Hypothesis*, Winona Lake, IN, pp. 217–36.
Baudrillard, J., 1994. 'The Animals: Territory and Metamorphoses', in *Simulacra and Simulation*, trans. S. F. Glaser, Ann Arbor, pp. 129–41.
Bauer, P. V. C., 1912. *Centaurs in Ancient Art. The Archaic Period*, Berlin.
Beal, T. K., 2002. *Religion and its Monsters*, New York.
Beall, E. F., 1991. 'Hesiod's Prometheus and Development in Myth', *Journal of the History of Ideas*, 52.3, pp. 355–71.
Beaulieu, M.-C., 2016. *The Sea in the Greek Imagination*, Philadelphia.
Beetham, F., 2002., 'The Aorist Indicative', *G&R*, 49.2, pp. 227–36.
Bekoff, M. and J. Pierce, 2009. *Wild Justice: The Moral Lives of Animals*, Chicago.
Belgiorno, M. R., 1993. 'Maschere di bovidi e capridi nel rituale religioso egeo-cipriota', *Studi micenei ed egeo-anatolici*, 31, pp. 43–54.
Benson, C., 2001. 'A Greek Statuette in Egyptian Dress', *The Journal of the Walters Art Museum*, 59, *Focus on the Collections*, pp. 7–16.
Benton, S., 1965. 'Blue-Beard', in L. Banti, ed., *Studi in onore di Luisa Banti*, Rome, pp. 47–9.
Berg, I., 2013. 'Marine Creatures and the Sea in Bronze Age Greece: Ambiguities of Meaning', *Journal of Maritime Archaeology*, 8.1, pp. 1–27.
Berger, U., W. Hein and K. Wehrberger, 2012. 'Der Löwenmensch – wie sah er wirklich aus?' *Archäologie in Deutschland*, 1, pp. 36–7.
Bernal, M., 1987. *Black Athena: The Afroasiatic Roots of Classical Civilization, vol. 1, The Fabrication of Ancient Greece 1785–1985*, New Brunswick, NJ.

Bettini, M., 2013. *Women and Weasels. Mythologies of Birth in Ancient Greece and Rome*, Chicago.
Betts, J. H., 1967. 'New Light on Minoan Bureaucracy: A Reexamination of some Cretan Seals', *Kadmos*, 6, pp. 15–40.
Beutelspacher, T., N. Ebinger-Rist, C.-J. Kind, K. Wehrberger and S. Wolf, 2014. 'Die Rückkehr des Löwenmenschen', *Archäologie in Deutschland*, 2, pp. 8–13.
Bhabha, H., 1994. *The Location of Culture*, London.
Bianco, M. and C. Bonnet, 2016. 'Sur les traces d'Athéna chez les Phéniciens', *Pallas*, 100, *Cent chouettes pour Athéna*, pp. 155–78.
Bichler, R., 2011. 'Ktesias spielt mit Herodot', in J. Wiesehöfer, R. Rollinger and G. B. Lanfranchi, eds., *Ktesias' Welt/Ctesias' World*. Wiesbaden, pp. 21–52.
Bielfeldt, R., 2016. 'Sight and Light: Reified Gazes and Looking Artefacts in the Greek Cultural Imagination', in M. Squire, ed., *Sight and the Ancient Senses*, London, pp. 123–42.
Bietak, M., 1996. *Avaris, the Capital of the Hyksos: recent Excavations at Tell el-Dab'a*, London.
Bietak, M., N. Marinatos and C. Palyvou, 2007. *Taureador Scenes in Tell el-Dab'a (Avaris) and Knossos*, Vienna.
Bigwood, J. M., 1993. 'Ctesias' Parrot', *CQ*, 43.1, pp. 321–7.
Bissa, E., 2013. 'Man, Woman or Myth? Gender-bending in Lucian's *Dialogues of the Courtesans*', *Materiali e discussioni per l'analisi dei testi classici*, 70, pp. 79–100.
Björklund, H., 2017. 'Metamorphosis, Mixanthropy and the Child-Killing Demon in the Hellenistic and Byzantine Periods', *Acta Classica*, 60, pp. 22–49.
Black, J. A. and A. Green, 1992. *Gods, Demons and Symbols of Ancient Mesopotamia: An Illustrated Dictionary*, London.
Blakolmer, F., 2016. 'Il Buono, il Brutto, il Cattivo? Character, Symbolism and Hierarchy of Animals and Supernatural Creatures in Minoan and Mycenaean Iconography', *Cretica Antica*, 17, pp. 97–184.
Blankenborg, R., 2020. 'The Territory without a Map: The Sea as Narratological Frame and Compass in the *Odyssey*', *AOQU Epica Marina*, I.2, 9–35.
Blier, S. P., 1993. 'Art and Secret Agency: Concealment and Revelation in Artistic Expression', in M. H. Nooter, ed., *Secrecy: African Art that Conceals and Reveals*, New York, pp. 181–94.
Bliquez, L. J., 1975. 'Lions and Greek Sculptors', *CW*, 68.6, pp. 381–4.
Blümel, W., 1993. 'SGDI 5727 (Halikarnassos). Eine Revision', *Kadmos* 32, pp. 1–18.
Blust, R., 2000. 'The Origin of Dragons', *Anthropos*, 95.2, pp. 519–36.
Boardman, J., 1972. 'Herakles, Peisistratos and Sons', *RA*, 1, pp. 57–72.
Boardman, J., 1975. 'Herakles, Peisistratos and Eleusis', *JHS*, 95, pp. 1–12.
Boardman, J., 1989. 'Herakles, Peisistratos and the Unconvinced', *JHS*, 109, pp. 158–9.

Boardman, J., 1992. 'The Phallos-Bird in Archaic and Classical Greek Art', *Rev. Arch.*, 2, pp. 227–42.

Boardman, J., 1998. *Early Greek Vase Painting*. London.

Bodéüs, R., 1997. 'Les considerations aristotéliciennes sur la bestialité: traditions et perspectives nouvelles', in Cassin, B. and J.-L. Labarrière, eds., 1997. *L'Animal dans l'Antiquité*, Paris, pp. 247–58.

Bodnar, I., 2018. 'Aristotle's Natural Philosophy', in E. N. Zalta, ed., *The Stanford Encyclopedia of Philosophy* (Spring 2018 ed.), https://plato.stanford.edu/archives/spr2018/entries/aristotle-natphil/.

Bodson, L., 2000. 'Motivations for Pet-Keeping in Ancient Greece and Rome: A Preliminary Survey', in A. L. Podberscek, E. S. Paul and J. A. Serpell, eds., *Companion Animals and Us. Exploring the Relationship between People and Pets*, Cambridge, pp. 27–41.

Boehringer, S., 2015. 'Sex, Lies, and (Video)trap: The Illusion of Sexual Identity in Lucian's *Dialogues of the Courtesans* 5 (trans. R. Blondell), in R. Blondell and K. Ormand, eds., *Ancient Sex: New Essays*, Columbus, pp. 254–84.

Bonatz, D., 2019. 'Laḫmu, "The Hairy One", and the Puzzling Issue of Mythology in Middle Assyrian Glyptic Art', in P. S. Avetisyan, R. Dan and Y. H. Grekyan, eds., *Over the Mountains and Far Away: Studies in Near Eastern History and Archaeology Presented to Mirjo Salvini on the Occasion of his 80th Birthday*, Oxford, pp. 106–13.

Bonnet, C., 2014. 'Greeks and Phoenicians in the Western Mediterranean', in J. McInerney, ed., *A Companion to Ethnicity in the Ancient Mediterranean*, Oxford, pp. 327–40.

Boosen, M., 1986. *Etruskische Meeresmischwesen. Untersuchungen zur Typologie und Bedeutung* (Archaeologica 59), Rome.

Borgeaud, P., 1988. 'L'ecriture d'Attis: le récit dans l'histoire', in C. Calame, ed., *Métamorphoses du mythe en Grèce ancienne*, Geneva, pp. 87–103.

Borgeaud, P., 1996. *La Mère des dieux. De Cybèle à la Vierge Marie*. Paris.

Borgeaud, P., 2013. 'Greek and Comparatist Reflexions on Food Prohibitions', in C. Frevel and C. Nihan, eds., *Purity and the Forming of Religious Traditions in the Ancient Mediterranean*, Leiden, pp. 261–87.

Bosak-Schroeder, C., 2020. 'Making Specimens in the *Periplus* of Hanno and its Imperial Tradition', *AJP*, 140, pp. 67–100.

Bourogiannis, G., 2013. 'The Sanctuary of Ayia Irini: Looking beyond the Figurines', *Pasiphae*, 7, pp. 35–45.

Boutsikas, E., 2020. *The Cosmos in Ancient Greek Religious Experience: Sacred Space, Memory, and Cognition*, Cambridge.

Bouvier, D., 2015. 'Le héros comme un loup: usage platonicien d'une comparaison homérique', *Cahiers des études anciennes*, 52, pp. 125–47.

Braudel, F., 1972. *The Mediterranean and the Mediterranean World in the Age of Phillip II*. 2 vols, transl. Siân Reynolds, New York.

Braun, T., 2004. 'Hecataeus' Knowledge of the Western Mediterranean', in K. Lomas, ed., *Greek Identity in the Western Mediterranean: Papers in Honour of Brian Shefton*, Leiden, pp. 287–348.

Braun, T. F. R. G., 1982. 'The Greeks in the Near East', *CAH* III.3, pp. 1–31.

Bravo III, J. J., 2018. *Excavations at Nemea IV. The Shrine of Opheltes*. Oakland.

Brecher, W. P., 2015. 'Precarity, Kawaii (Cuteness), and Their Impact on Environmental Discourse in Japan', in K. Iwata-Weickgenannt and R. Rosenbaum, eds., *Visions of Precarity in Japanese Popular Culture and Literature*, New York, pp. 43–63.

Bremmer, J. N., 2004. 'Attis: A Greek God in Anatolian Pessinous and Catullan Rome', *Mnemosyne*, 57.5, pp. 534–73.

Bremmer, J. N., 2008. *Greek Religion and Culture, the Bible and the Ancient Near East*, Leiden.

Bremmer, J. N., 2012. 'Greek Demons of the Wilderness: The Case of the Centaurs', in L. Feldt, ed., *Wilderness in Mythology and Religion*, Berlin, pp. 25–54.

Bremmer, J. N., 2015. 'A Transsexual in Archaic Greece: The Case of Kaineus', in D. Boschung, A. Shapiro and F. Wascheck, eds., *Bodies in Transition. Dissolving the Boundaries of Embodied Knowledge*, Paderborn, pp. 265–86.

Bremmer, J. N., 2016. 'Shamanism in Classical Scholarship: Where are We Now?' in P. Jackson, ed., *Horizons of Shamanism: A Triangular Approach to the History and Anthropology of Ecstatic Techniques*, Stockholm, pp. 52–78.

Bremmer, J. N., 2020. 'The Theriomorphism of the Major Greek Gods', in J. Kindt, ed., *Animals in Ancient Greek Religion*, pp. 102–25.

Bresson, A., 2000. *La cité marchande*. Bordeaux.

Brisson, L., 1978. 'Aspects politiques de la bisexualité: L'histoire de Polycrite', in M. B. de Boer and T. A. Elridge, eds., *Hommages à Maarten J. Vermaseren: Édition spéciale des Études préliminaires aux Religions Orientales dans l'Empire Romain 68*, Leiden, pp. 80–122.

Brisson, L., 2002. *Sexual Ambivalence: Androgyny and Hermaphroditism in Graeco-Roman Antiquity*, Berkeley.

Brockliss, W., 2018. 'Olympian Sound in the *Theogony* and the *Catalogue of Women*: Sweet Music and Disorderly Noise', *CJ*, 113, pp. 129–49.

Brodsky, J., 1986. *Less than One. Selected Essays*, New York.

Brody, A., 2002. "From the Hills of Adonis through the Pillars of Hercules: Recent Advances in the Archaeology of Canaan and Phoenicia." *NEA*, 65, pp. 69–80.

Bronstein, D., 2016, *Aristotle on Knowledge and Learning: The Posterior Analytics*, Oxford.

Broodbank, C., 2013. *The Making of the Middle Sea: A History of the Mediterranean from the Beginning to the Emergence of the Classical World*, Oxford.

Brosius, M., 2011. 'Greeks at the Persian Court', in J. Wiesehöfer, R. Rollinger, G. B. Lanfranchi, eds., *Ktesias' Welt/Ctesias' World*, Wiesbaden, pp. 69–80.

Brown, C. G., 1991. 'Empousa, Dionysus and the Mysteries: Aristophanes, *Frogs* 285ff', *CQ*, 41.1, pp. 41–50.

Brown, J. W., 1911. *Florence, Past and Present*, New York.
Brown, N. O., 1927. 'Change of Sex as a Hindu Story Motif', *Journal of the American Oriental Society*, 47, pp. 3–24.
Brown, N. O., 1949. 'Review of *Hyakinthos* by Machteld J. Mellink', *AJA*, 53, p. 218.
Brown, R. D., 1987. *Lucretius on Love and Sex. A Commentary on* De Rerum Natura *IV, 1030-12-87*, Leiden.
Brumm, A., A. A. Oktaviana, B. Burhan, et al., 2021. 'Oldest Cave Art found in Sulawesi', *Science Advances*, 7 eabd4648, pp. 1–12.
Bruneau, E. and N. Kteily, 2017. 'The Enemy as Animal: Symmetric Dehumanization during Asymmetric Warfare', *PLoS ONE*, 12.7, https://doi.org/10.1371/journal.pone.0181422.
Brunner-Traut, E., 1954. 'Der Katzenmäusekrieg im Alten und Neuen Orient', *Zeitschrift der Deutschen Morgenländischen Gesellschaft*, 104, pp. 347–51.
Brunner-Traut, E., 1968. *Altägyptische Tiergeschichte und Fabel: Gestalt und Strahlkraft*, Darmstadt.
Bruns, G. L., 2007. 'Becoming-Animal (Some Simple Ways)', *New Literary History*, 38, pp. 702–20.
Bryant, L., 2011. *The Democracy of Objects*, Ann Arbor.
Buchner, G., 1979. 'Early Orientalizing Aspects of the Euboean Connection', in D. Ridgway and F. Ridgway, eds., *Italy before the Romans*, London, pp. 29–43.
Budelmann, F. and P. Easterling, 2010. 'Reading Minds in Greek Tragedy', *G&R*, 57.2, pp. 289–303.
Bugh, G. R., 1988. *The Horsemen of Athens*, Princeton.
Burke, P., 2016. *Hybrid Renaissance, Culture, Language, Architecture*, Budapest.
Burkert, W., 1983. *Homo Necans: The Anthropology of Ancient Greek Sacrificial Ritual and Myth*, Berkeley.
Burkert, W., 1988. 'Oriental and Greek Mythology: The Meeting of Parallels', in J. N. Bremmer, ed., *Interpretations of Greek Mythology*, Kent, pp. 10–40.
Burkert, W., 1992. *The Orientalizing Revolution: Near Eastern Influence on Greek Culture in the Early Archaic Period*, Cambridge, MA.
Burkert, W., 2004. *Babylon, Memphis, Persepolis: Eastern Contexts of Greek Culture*. Cambridge, MA.
Burnell, F. S., 1947. 'The Holy Cow', *Folklore*, 58, pp. 377–81.
Burnett, A. P., 1964. 'The Race with the Pleiades', *Classical Philology*, 59, pp. 30–4.
Burnett, A. P., 1970. *Euripides: Ion, a Translation with Commentary*, Upper Saddle River.
Buxton, R. G. A., 1994. *Imaginary Greece*, Cambridge.
Buxton, R. G. A., 1999. 'Introduction', in R. G. A. Buxton, ed., *From Myth to Reason? Studies in the Development of Greek Thought*, Oxford.
Buxton, R. G. A., 2009. *Forms of Astonishment: Greek Myths of Metamorphosis*, Oxford.
Buxton, R. G. A., 1988. 'Wolves and Werewolves in Greek thought', in J. N. Bremmer, ed., *Interpretations of Greek Mythology*, Kent, pp. 60–79.

Calarco, M., 2008. *Zoographies: The Question of the Animal from Heidegger to Derrida*. New York.
Calder, L., 2011. *Cruelty and Sentimentality: Greek Attitudes to Animals, 600–300 BC*. Studies in Classical Archaeology, 5, Oxford.
Calderini, R., 1942. 'Ricerche sul doppio nome personale nell' Egitto greco-romano II', *Aegyptus*, 22, pp. 3–5.
Caldwell, W. H., 1888. 'The embryology of Monotremata and Marsupialia. Part I', *Philosophical Transactions of the Royal Society of London B. Biological Sciences*, 178, pp. 463–86.
Campbell, G. L., 2006. *Strange Creatures: Anthropology in Antiquity*, London.
Campbell, G. L., 2007. 'Bicycles, Centaurs, and Man-Faced Ox-Creatures: Ontological Instability in Lucretius', in S. J. Heyworth, ed., *Classical Constructions: Papers in Memory of Don Fowler, Classicist and Epicurean*, Oxford, pp. 39–62.
Canfora, L., 1988, *The Vanished Library: A Wonder of the Ancient World*, Berkeley.
Caracciolo, M., 2015. 'Playing "Home": Videogame Experiences between Narrative and Ludic Interests', *Narrative*, 23.3, pp. 231–51.
Carbon, J.-M and V. Pirenne-Delforge, 2013. 'Priests and Cult Personnel in Three Hellenistic Families', in M. Horster and A. Klöckner, eds., *Cities and Priests: Cult Personnel in Asia Minor and the Aegean Islands from the Hellenistic to the Imperial Period*, Berlin and Boston, pp. 65–119.
Carpenter, R., 1950. 'Argeiphontes: A Suggestion', *AJA* 54, pp. 177–83.
Carpenter, R., 1958. 'Phoenicians in the West', *AJA*, 62.1, pp. 35–53.
Carter, J. C., 1987. 'The Masks of Orthia', *AJA*, 91.3, pp. 355–83.
Cartledge, P., 2013. *After Thermopylae: The Oath of Plataea and the End of the Graeco-Persian Wars*, Oxford.
Cassano, F., 1998. *La Pensée meridienne: Le Sud vu par lui-même*, Paris.
Cassin, B. and J.-L. Labarrière, eds., 1997. *L'Animal dans l'Antiquité*, Paris.
Cauvin, J., 1994. *Naissance des divinités, Naissance de l'agriculture. La révolution des symboles au Néolithique*, Paris.
Chaix, L., J. Dubosson and M. Honegger., 2011. 'Bucrania from the Eastern Cemetery at Kerma (Sudan) and the Practice of Cattle Horn Deformation', in J. Kabacinski, M. Chlodnicki and M. Kobusiewicz, eds., *Prehistory of Northeastern Africa: New Ideas and Discoveries*, Poznan, pp. 189–212.
Chakrabarty, D., 2009. 'The Climate of History: Four Theses', *Critical Inquiry*, 35.2, pp. 197–222.
Champlin, E., 1987. 'The Testament of the Piglet', *Phoenix*, 41.2, pp. 174–83.
Chandezon, C., 2019. 'Xenophon et l'*Anabase* des bêtes', in É. Baratay, ed., *Aux sources de l'historire animale*, Paris, pp. 61–74.
Chapman, J., 2000. *Fragmentation in Archaeology*, London.
Chapman, J., 2010. '"Deviant" Burials in the Neolithic and Chalcolithic of Central and South Eastern Europe', in K. Rebay-Salisbury, M. L. Stig Sørensen and

J. Hughes, eds., *Body Parts and Bodies Whole: Changing Relations and Meanings*, Oxford, pp. 30–45.

Chesi, G. M. and F. Spiegel, eds., 2020. *Classical Literature and Posthumanism*, London.

Childs, W. A. P., 2001. 'Early Greek Bronze Plaques in Princeton', *Record of the Art Museum, Princeton University*, 60, pp. 30–63.

Childs, W. A. P., 2003. 'The Human Animal: The Near East and Greece', in J. M. Padgett, ed., *The Centaur's Smile: The Human Animal in Early Greek Art*. New Haven, pp. 49–70.

Chlup, R., 2008. '*Illud tempus* in Greek Myth and Ritual', *Religion*, 38.4, pp. 355–65.

Chris, C., 2006. *Watching Wildlife*, Minneapolis.

Christ, C., 1996. '"A Different World": The Challenge of the Work of Marija Gimbutas to the Dominant World-View of Western Cultures', *Journal of Feminist Studies in Religion*, 12. 2, pp. 53–66.

Chrubasik, B., 2017. 'From Pre-Makkabaean Judaea to Hekatomnid Karia and Back Again', in B. Chrubasik and D. King, eds., *Hellenism and the Local Communities of the Eastern Mediterranean: 400 BCE–250 CE*, Oxford, pp. 83–110.

Ciałowicz, K. M., 2011. 'Fantastic creatures and cobras from Tell el-Farkha', *Studies in Ancient Art and Civilization*, 15, pp. 11–29.

Ciardiello, R., 2007. 'Teseo nella ceramica attica: alcune osservazioni intorno ad un libro recente', *Prospettiva* 126/127, pp. 179–89.

Clackson, J., 2015. *Language and Society in the Greek and Roman Worlds*, Cambridge.

Clare, L., O. Dietrich, J. Notroff and D. Sönmez. 2018. 'Establishing Identities in the Proto-Neolithic: "History Making" at Göbekli Tepe from the Late Tenth Millennium BCE', in I. Hodder, ed., *Religion, History, and Place in the Origin of Settled Life*, Boulder, CO, pp. 115–36.

Clark, M., 1970, 'Humour and Incongruity', *Philosophy*, 45, pp. 20–32.

Clarke, K., 2008 *Making Time for the Polis. Local History and the Polis*, Oxford.

Clarke, M., 2004. 'An Ox-Fronted River-God Sophocles, *Trachiniae* 12–13', *HSCP*, 102, pp. 97–112.

Clarysse, W., 1985. 'Greeks and Egyptians in the Ptolemaic Army and Administration', *Aegyptus*, 65, pp. 57–66.

Clay, J. S., 1993. 'The Generation of Monsters in Hesiod', *CP*, 88.2, pp. 105–16.

Clay, J. S., 2003. *Hesiod's Cosmos*, Cambridge.

Clay, J. S., 2020. 'Typhoeus or Cosmic Regression', in G. M. Chesi and F. Spiegel, eds., *Classical Literature and Posthumanism*, London, pp. 133–40.

Cline, E. H., 1999. 'The Nature of the Economic Relations of Crete with Egypt and the Near East during the Late Bronze Age', in A. Chaniotis, ed., *From Minoan Farmers to Roman Traders Sidelights on the Economy of Ancient Crete*, Stuttgart, pp. 115–38.

Cline, E. H., 2014. *1177 BC: The Year Civilization Collapsed*, Princeton.

Clover, C. J., 1987. 'Her Body, Himself: Gender in the Slasher Film', *Representations*, 20, *Special Issue: Misogyny, Misandry, and Misanthropy*, pp. 187–228.

Cohen, J. J., 1996. 'Monster Culture (Seven Theses)', in J. J. Cohen, ed., *Monster Theory. Reading Culture*, Minneapolis, pp. 3–25.

Collezione Casuccini: Ceramica attica, ceramica etrusca, ceramica falisca, 1996. Rome.

Coldstream, J. N., 1974. 'Review of Ahlberg, Fighting on Land and Sea in Greek Geometric Art', *Gnomon*, 46.4, pp. 393–7.

Coldstream, J. N., 1990. 'The Beginnings of Greek Literacy: an Archaeologist's View', *Ancient History Resources for Teachers*, 20.3, pp. 144–59.

Coldstream, J. N., 1993. 'Mixed Marriages at the Frontiers of the Early Greek World', *Oxford Journal of Archaeology*, 12.1, pp. 89–106.

Collon, D., 1987. *First Impressions, Cylinder Seals in the Ancient Near East*, Chicago.

Collon, D., 1994. 'Bull Leaping in Syria', *Ägypten und Levante*, 4, pp. 81–5.

Collon, D., 2003. 'Dance in Ancient Mesopotamia', *Near Eastern Archaeology*, 66, pp. 96–102.

Collon, D., 2005. *The Queen of the Night: British Museum Objects in Focus*, London.

Collon, D., 2007. 'The Queen under Attack: A Rejoinder', *Iraq*, 69, pp. 43–51.

Collura, A., 2016. '"Il sunt si biaus que c'en est une mervoie a voir": Zoologie e Teratologie nel *Devisement dou monde*', *Ticontre: Teoria Testo Traduzione*, 5, pp. 287–336.

Compton-Engle, G., 2015. *Costume in the Comedies of Aristophanes*, Cambridge.

Concannon, C. and L. A. Mazurek, eds., 2016. *Across the Corrupting Sea: Post-Braudelian Approaches to the Ancient Eastern Mediterranean*, Milton Park.

Connelly, J. B., 1996. 'Parthenon and Parthenoi: A Mythological Interpretation of the Parthenon Frieze', *AJA*, 100, pp. 53–80.

Constantakopoulou, C., 2007. *The Dance of the Islands: Insularity, Networks, the Athenian Empire, and the Aegean World*, Oxford.

Cooke, M., 1999. 'Mediterranean Thinking: From Netizen to Medizen', *Geographical Review*, 89, pp. 290–300.

Cotter, J., 2014. 'Φαληρίς: Coot, Plant, Phallus', *Glotta*, 90, pp. 105–13.

Counts, D., 2008. 'Master of the Lion: Representation and Hybridity in Cypriote Sanctuaries', *AJA*, 112.1, pp. 3–27.

Crielaard, J. P., 2018. 'Hybrid Go-Betweens: The Role of Individuals with Multiple Identities in Cross-Cultural Contacts in the Late Bronze Age and Iron Age Central and Eastern Mediterranean', Ł. Niesiołowski-Spanò and M. Węcowski, eds., *Change, Continuity, and Connectivity. North Eastern Mediterranean at the Turn of the Bronze Age*, Wiesbaden, pp. 196–220.

Croucher, K., 2010. 'Bodies in Pieces in the Neolithic Near East', in K. Rebay-Salisbury, M. L. Stig Sørensen and J. Hughes, eds., *Body Parts and Bodies Whole: Changing Relations and Meanings*, Oxford, pp. 6–19.

Crowley, J. L., 1989. *The Aegean and the East. An Investigation into the Transference of Artistic Motifs between the Aegean, Egypt and the Near East in the Bronze Age* (SIMA Pocket-book 51), Gothenburg.

Cruse, M., 2015. 'Marco Polo in Manuscript: The Travels of the *Devisement du monde*', *Narrative Culture*, 2.2, pp. 171–89.

Csapo, E., 1997. 'Riding the Phallus for Dionysus: Iconology, Ritual, and Gender-Role De/Construction', *Phoenix*, 51, pp. 253–95.

Csapo, E., 2003. 'The Dolphins of Dionysus', in E. Csapo and M. C. Miller, eds., *Poetry, Theory, Praxis: The Social Life of Myth, Word and Image in Ancient Greece: Essays in Honour of William J. Slater*, Oxford, pp. 69–99.

Csapo, E., 2005. *Theories of Mythology*, Malden.

Csapo, E., 2008. 'Star Choruses: Eleusis, Orphism, and New Musical Imagery and Dance', in M. Revermann and P. Wilson, eds., *Performance, Iconography, Reception: Studies in Honour of Oliver Taplin*, Oxford, pp. 262–90.

Currie, B., 2012. 'Hesiod on Human History', in J. Marincola, L. Llewellyn-Jones and C. Maciver, eds., *Greek Notions of the Past in the Archaic and Classical Eras*, Edinburgh, pp. 37–64.

Cursaru, G., 2015. 'Les traces d'un Centaure dans "l'Hymne homérique à Hermès" (*HhH*. 224–226)', *Pallas*, 97, pp. 9–29.

Curtis, J., 1994. 'Mesopotamian Bronzes from Greek Sites: The Workshops of Origin', *Iraq*, 56, pp. 1–25.

D'Agostino, B., 1996. 'The Colonial Experience in Greek Mythology', in G. Pugliese Carratelli, ed., *The Western Greeks*, Venice, pp. 214–19.

D'Angour, A., 2011. *The Greeks and the New: Novelty in Ancient Greek Imagination and Experience*, Cambridge.

Daniel-Wariya, J., 2019. 'Ludic Rhetorics: Theroies of Play in Rhetoric and Writing', in A. Alden, K. Gerdes, J. Holiday and R. Skinnell, eds., *Reinventing (with) Theory in Rhetoric and Writing Studies: Essays in Honor of Sharon Crowley*, Louisville, pp. 116–32.

Dasen, V., 2003. 'Les amulettes d'enfants dans le monde gréco-romain', *Latomus*, 62. 2, pp. 275–89.

Davies, S., 2016. *Renaissance Ethnography and the Invention of the Human: New Worlds, Maps and Monsters*, Cambridge.

Davis, J. L. and S. R. Stocker, 2016. 'The Lord of the Gold Rings: The Griffin Warrior of Pylos', *Hesperia* 85.4, pp. 627–55.

Davis, J. L. and S. R. Stocker, 2017. 'The Combat Agate from the Grave of the Griffin Warrior at Pylos', *Hesperia*, 86.4, pp. 583–605.

De Angelis, F., 2016. *Archaic and Classical Greek Sicily*, New York.

De Angelis, A., 2009. 'Tra dati linguistici e fonti letterarie: per un'etimologia del gr. κένταυρος "divoratore di viscere"', *Glotta*, 85, pp. 59–74.

DeBrohun, J. B., 2004. 'Centaurs in Love and War: Cyllarus and Hylonome in Ovid, *Metamorphoses* 12.393–428', *AJP* 125.3, pp. 417–52.

Decker, J. E., 2019. 'The Most Beautiful Thing on the Black Earth: Sappho's Alliance with Aphrodite', in H. L. Reid and T. Leyh, eds., *Looking at Beauty* to Kalon *in Western Greece: Selected Essays from the 2018 Symposium on the Heritage of Western Greece*, Sioux City, Iowa, pp. 39–50.

Deichgräber, K., 1965. *Die Musen, Nereiden und Okeaninen in Hesiods Theogonie: mit einem Nachtrag zu Natura varie ludens*, Mainz.

Deleuze, G. and F. Guattari, 1987. *A Thousand Plateaus: Capitalism and Schizophrenia*. Trans. Brian Massumi, Minneapolis.

Deleuze, G. and F. Guattari, 1994. *What Is Philosophy?* Trans. Hugh Tomlinson and Graham Burchell, New York.

Delrieux, F., 2013. 'Les ventes de biens confisqués dans la Carie des Hécatomnides. Notes d'histoire économique et monétaire', In M.-C. Ferriès and F. Delrieux, eds., *Spolier et confisquer dans les mondes grecs et romain*, Chambéry, pp. 209–65.

Demartis, G. M., 1986. *La Necropoli di Anghelu Ruju*, Sassari.

Demers, J. T., 2006. *Steal this Music: How Intellectual Property Law Affects Musical Creativity*, Athens, GA.

Demetriou, D., 2012. *Negotiating Identity in the Ancient Mediterranean*, Cambridge.

Derrida, J., 1995. 'Archive Fever: A Freudian Impression', *Diacritics*, 25.2, pp. 9–63.

Derrida, J., 1998. *Of Grammatology*. Corrected ed., trans. G. C. Spivak, Baltimore.

Derrida, J., 2008. 'The Animal That Therefore I am, (More to Follow)', *Critical Inquiry*, 28.2, pp. 369–418.

Detienne, M., 1971. 'Athena and the Mastery of the Horse', *History of Religions*, 11.2, pp. 161–84.

Detienne, M., 2001. 'The Art of Founding Autochthony: Thebes, Athens, and Old-Stock French', *Arion*, 9, pp. 46–55.

Detienne, M. and J. Svenbro, 1979. '*Les loups au festin ou la cité impossible*', in M. Detienne and J.-P. Vernant, *La cuisine du sacrifice en pays grec*, Paris, pp. 215–37.

Detienne, M. and J.-P. Vernant, 1991. *Cunning Intelligence in Greek Culture and Society*, trans. J. Lloyd, Chicago.

Di Gioia, A., 2012. 'La duplicità di Phokos e l'identità dei Focidesi', in L. Breglia, A. Moleti and M. L. Napolitano, eds., *Ethne, identità e tradizioni: la "terza" Grecia e l'Occidente*, Pisa, pp. 197–218.

Dietrich, B. C., 1974. *The Origins of Greek Religion*, Berlin.

Dietrich, O., M. Heun, J. Notroff, K. Schmidt and M. Zarnkow, 2012. 'The Role of Cult and Feasting in the Eemergence of Neolithic Communities: New Evidence from Göbekli Tepe, South-eastern Turkey', *Antiquity*, 86, pp. 674–95.

Dillery, J., 2015. *Clio's Other Sons: Berossus and Manetho*, Ann Arbor.

Diouf, M., 2008. '(Re)Imagining an African City: Performing Culture, Arts, and Citizenship in Dakar (Senegal), 1980–2000', in G. Prakash and K. M. Kruse, eds.,

The Spaces of the Modern City: Imaginaries, Politics, and Everyday Life. Princeton, pp. 346–72.

Dominy, N. J., S. Ikram, G. L. Moritz, et al., 2020. 'Mummified Baboons Reveal the Far Reach of Early Egyptian Mariners', *eLife*, 9:e60860. https://doi.org/10.7554/eLife.60860.

Doniger, W., 2021. *Winged Stallions and Wicked Mares: Horses in Indian Myth and History*, Charlottesville.

Donnellan, L., V. Nizzo and G.-J. Burgers, eds., 2016, *Conceptualizing Early Colonisation*, Brussels.

Donovan, J., 1990. 'Animal Rights and Feminist Theory', *Signs*, 15, pp. 350–75.

Dontas, G. S., 1983. 'The True Aglaurion', *Hesperia*, 52, pp. 48–63.

Doroszewska, J., 2017. 'The Liminal Space: Suburbs as a Demonic Domain in Classical Literature', *Preternature: Critical and Historical Studies on the Preternatural*, 6.1, pp. 1–30.

Dosoo, K., 2021. 'Circe's Ram: Animals in Ancient Greek Magic', in J. Kindt, ed., *Animals in Ancient Greek Religion*, London, pp. 260–88.

Dougherty, C., 1993a. 'It's Murder to Found a Colony', in C. Dougherty and L. Kurke, eds., *Cultural Poetics in Archaic Greece*, Cambridge, pp. 178–98

Dougherty, C., 1993b. *The Poetics of Colonization. From City to Text in Archaic Greece*, Oxford.

Dougherty, C., 2001. *The Raft of Odysseus: The Ethnographic Imagination of Homer's* Odyssey, Oxford.

Dougherty, C., 2003. 'The Aristonothos Krater: Competing Stories of Conflict and Collaboration', in C. Dougherty and L. Kurke, eds., *The Cultures Within Ancient Greek Culture: Contact, Conflict, Collaboration*, Cambridge, pp. 35–56.

Dougherty, C., 2019. *Travel and Home in Homer's* Odyssey *and Contemporary Literature: Critical Encounters and Nostalgic Returns*, Oxford.

Douglas, M., 1966. *Purity and Danger: An Analysis of Concepts of Pollution and Taboo*, London/New York.

Douglas, M., 1968. 'The Social Control of Cognition: Some Factors in Joke Perception', *Man*, ns 3.3, pp. 361–76.

Driessen, J., 2003. 'The Court Compounds of Minoan Crete: Royal Palaces or Ceremonial Centers?' *Athena Review*, 3, pp. 57–61.

DuBois, P., 1991. *Centaurs and Amazons: Women and the Pre-History of the Great Chain of Being*, Ann Arbor.

Duckworth, C. N., A. Cuénod, and D. J. Mattingly, eds., *Mobile Technologies in the Ancient Sahara and Beyond* (Trans-Saharan Archaeology 4), Cambridge.

Duplouy, A., 2022, 'Hippotrophia as Citizen Behaviour in Archaic Greece', in J. Bernhardt and M. Canevaro, eds., *From Homer to Solon: Continuity and Change in Archaic Greece*, Leiden, pp. 139–61.

Durkheim, E., 1912. *Formes élémentaires de la vie religieuse: Le système totémique en Australie*, Paris.

Ebeling, E., E. F. Weidner and M. P. Streck, eds., 2005. *Reallexikon der Assyriologie und vorderasiatischen Archäologie*. Oannes – Priesterverkleidung, Berlin. https://publikationen.badw.de/en/017575401.

Eder, B., 2015. 'Stone and Glass: The Ideological Transformation of Imported Materials and their Geographic Distribution in Mycenaean Greece', in B. Eder and R. Pruzsinszky, eds., *Policies of Exchange: Political Systems and Modes of Interaction in the Aegean and the Near East in the 2nd Millennium BCE, Proceedings of the International Symposium, 30th May–2nd June 2012 in Freiburg*, OREA 2, Vienna, pp. 221–42.

Elsner, J., 2009. 'Double Identity: Orpheus as David. Orpheus as Christ', *BAR*, 35.2, pp. 34–45.

Engler, S., 2009. 'Umbanda and Hybridity', *Numen*, 56.5, pp. 545–77.

Epstein, S. J., 1995. 'Longus' Werewolves', *CP*, 90.1, pp. 58–73.

Erginel, M. M., 2019. 'Plato on Pleasures Mixed with Pains: An Asymmetrical Account', *Oxford Studies in Ancient Philosophy*, 56, pp. 73–122.

Erickson, B. L., 2010. *Crete in Transition: Pottery Styles and Island History in the Archaic and Classical Periods. Hesperia Supplements*, vol. 45. Princeton.

Ermatinger, E., 1897. *Die attische Autochthonensage bis auf Euripides*, Berlin.

Etheredge, L. S., ed., 2011. *Iraq. Middle East: Region in Transition*, Chicago.

Evans-Pritchard, E. E., 1940. *The Nuer*, Oxford.

Fahlander, F., 2009. 'Third Space Encounters: Hybridity, Mimicry and Interstitial Practice', in F. Fahlander and P. Cornell, eds., *Encounters, Materialities, Confrontations: Archaeologies of Social Space and Interaction*, Newcastle, pp. 15–41.

Fahlander, F., 2017. 'Ontology Matters in Archaeology and Anthropology: People, Things, and Posthumanism', in J. D. Englehardt and I. A. Rieger, eds., *These 'Thin Partitions'. Bridging the Growing Divide between Cultural Anthropology and Archaeology*, Boulder, pp. 69–87.

Fantalkin, A. and E. Lytle, 2016. 'Alcaeus and Antimenidas: Reassessing the Evidence for Greek Mercenaries in the Neo-Babylonian Army', *Klio*, 98.1, pp. 90–117.

Farmer, M., 2020. 'Choral Disrobing in Aristophanes', *Illinois Classical Studies*, 45.2, pp. 424–46.

Fausto-Sterling, A., 2000. *Sexing the Body: Gender Politics and the Construction of Sexuality*, New York.

Feldman, M. H., 2002. 'Luxurious Forms: Redefining a Mediterranean "International Style", 1400–1200 BCE', *The Art Bulletin*, 84.1, pp. 6–29.

Feldman, M. H., 2006. *Diplomacy by Design. Luxury Arts and an "International Style" in the Ancient Near East, 1400–1200 BC*, Chicago.

Feldman, T., 1965. 'Gorgo and the Origins of Fear', *Arion*, 4.3, pp. 484–94.

Ferrari, G., 2008. *Alcman and the Cosmos of Sparta*, Chicago.

Florman, L., 1990. 'Gustav Klimt and the Precedent of Ancient Greece', *The Art Bulletin*, 72.2, pp. 310–26.

Flusser, D. and S. Amorai-Stark, 1993/4. 'The Goddess Thermuthis, Moses, and Artapanus', *Jewish Studies Quarterly*, 1.3, pp. 217–33.

Fögen, T., 2006. 'Animals in Graeco-Roman Antiquity and Beyond: A Select Bibliography', *Telemachos*. https://web.archive.org/web/20180411020221/http://www.telemachos.hu-berlin.de/esterni/Tierbibliographie_Foegen.pdf.

Fögen, T. and E. Thomas, eds., 2017a. *Interactions Between Animals and Humans in Graeco-Roman Antiquity*, Berlin.

Fögen, T. and E. Thomas, 2017b. 'Introduction', in T. Fögen and E. Thomas, *Interactions Between Animals and Humans in Graeco-Roman Antiquity*, Berlin, pp. 1–18.

Fornari, G., 2021. *Dionysus, Christ, and the Death of God, Volume 1: The Great Mediations of the Classical World*, East Lansing.

Forsdyke, S., 2012a. '"Born from the Earth": The Political Uses of an Athenian Myth', *JANER*, 12, pp. 119–41.

Forsdyke, S., 2012b. *Slaves Tell Tales and Other Episodes in the Politics of Popular Culture in Ancient Greece*, Princeton.

Forsyth, N., 1987. *Satan and the Combat Myth*, Princeton.

Foster, M. D., 2015. *The Book of Yōkai. Mysterious Creatures of Japanese Folklore*, Oakland.

Foucault, M., 1974. *The Order of Things. An Archaeology of the Human Sciences*, London.

Foucault, M., 2003. *Abnormal: Lectures at the Collège de France 1974–75*. Trans. G. Burchell, London.

Fowke, J., 1995. *Kundi Dan: Dan Leahy's Life Among the Highlanders of Papua New Guinea*, Brisbane.

Fowler, R. L., 1998. 'Genealogical Thinking, Hesiod's *Catalogue*, and the Creation of the Hellenes', *PCPS*, 44, pp. 1–19.

Fowler, R. L., 2013. *Early Greek Mythography* 2, Oxford.

Foxhall, L., K. Michelaki, and P. Lazrus, 2007. 'The Changing Landscapes of Bova Marina, Calabria', in M. Fitzjohn, ed., *Uplands of Ancient Sicily and Calabria: The Archaeology of Landscape Revisited*, London, pp. 19–34.

Frame, D., 2009. *Hippota Nestor*, Hellenic Studies Series 37, Washington, DC.

Franchi, E., 2017. 'Genealogies and Politics: Phocus on the Road', *Klio*, 2, pp. 1–25.

Franco, C., 2014. *Shameless. The Canine and the Feminine in Ancient Greece*, trans. M. Fox, Berkeley.

Frank, R. and G. Stollberg, 2004. 'Conceptualizing Hybridization. On the Diffusion of Asian Medical Knowledge to Germany', *International Sociology*, 19.1, pp. 71–88.

Franke, B., 2000. 'Alexander der Große und die Herzöge von Burgund', *Marburger Jahrbuch für Kunstwissenschaft*, 27, pp. 121–69.

Frankfort, H., 1946. *Before Philosophy: The Intellectual Adventure of Ancient Man*, Chicago.

Frankfort, H., 1948. *Ancient Egyptian Religion: An Interpretation*, New York.

Franko, G. F., 2005/2006. 'The Trojan Horse at the Close of the *Iliad*', *CJ*, 101.2, pp. 121–3.

Franks, H. M., 2014. 'Traveling, in Theory: Movement as Metaphor in the Ancient Greek Andron', *The Art Bulletin*, 96.2, pp. 156–69.

Franks, H. M., 2018. *The World Underfoot. Mosaics and Metaphor in the Greek Symposium*, Oxford.

Fraser, P. M., 1970. 'Greek-Phoenician Bilingual Inscriptions from Rhodes', *ABSA*, 65, pp. 31–6.

Fraser, P. M., 1972. *Ptolemaic Alexandria* I, Oxford.

Freud, S., 1930. *Civilization and Its Discontents*. In *The Standard Edition of the Complete Psychological Works of Sigmund Freud*, Volume XXI, London.

Freud, S., 2003. *The Uncanny*. Trans. D. McLintock, London.

Frey-Anthes, H., 2007. 'Mischwesen', www.bibelwissenschaft.de/stichwort/27841/.

Friedrich, J., 2017. 'Saint Christopher's Canine Hybrid Body and its Cultural Autocannibalism', *Preternature: Critical and Historical Studies on the Preternatural*, 6. 2, pp. 189–211.

Frontisi-Ducroux, F., 2003. *L'homme-cerf et la femme-araignée: Figures grecques de la metamorphose*, Paris.

Frontisi-Ducroux, F. and F. Lissarrague, 1990. 'From Ambiguity to Ambivalence: A Dionysiac Excursion through the "Anakreontic" Vases', in D. M. Halperin, J. J. Winkler, and F. I. Zeitlin, eds., *Before Sexuality: The Construction of Erotic Experience in the Ancient Greek World*, Princeton, pp. 211–56.

Funke, P., 2010. 'Western Greece (Magna Graecia)', In K. H. Kinzl, ed., *A Companion to the Classical Greek World*, Chichester, pp. 153–73.

Furtwängler, A., 1886–90. 'Gorgones und Gorgo', in W. H. Roscher, ed., *Ausführliches Lexikon der griechischen und römischen Mythologie* 1.2, Leipzig, pp. 1695–728.

Fynn-Paul, J., 2009. 'Empire, Monotheism and Slavery in the Greater Mediterranean Region from Antiquity to the Early Modern Era', *Past and Present*, 205, pp. 3–40.

Gagarin, M., 1986. *Early Greek Law*, Berkeley, CA.

Gagné, R., 2006. 'What Is the Pride of Halikarnassos?' *Class. Antiq.*, 25, pp. 1–33.

Gagné, R., 2007. 'Winds and Ancestors: The *Physika* of Orpheus', *HSCP*, 103, pp. 1–23.

Gale, M. R., 1994. *Myth and Poetry in Lucretius*, Cambridge.

Gane, C., 2012. *Composite Beings in Neo-Babylonian Art*. Unpublished doctoral dissertation. UC Berkeley Electronic Theses and Dissertations, Berkeley. https://escholarship.org/uc/item/3p25f7wk.

Gardner, E., 1897. 'Caeneus and the Centaurs: A Vase at Harrow', *JHS*, 17, pp. 294–305.

Garland, R., 2014. *Wandering Greeks: The Ancient Greek Diaspora from the Age of Homer to the Death of Alexander the Great*, Princeton.

Gauger, J. D., 1980. 'Phlegon von Tralleis, mirab. III: Zu einem Dokument geistigen Widerstandes gegen Rom', *Chiron* 10, pp. 225–61.

Gauvreau, A., D. Lepofsky, M. Rutherford and M. Reid, 2017. '"Everything revolves around the herring": The Heiltsuk–Herring Relationship Through Time', *Ecology and Society* 22(2).10. https://doi.org/10.5751/ES-09201-220210.

Gehrke, H.-J., 1986. *Jenseits von Athen und Sparta: Das dritte Griechenland und seine Staatenwelt*, Munich.

Geller, M. J., 2016. *Healing Magic and Evil Demons. Canonical Udug-hul Incantations.* With the assistance of Luděk Vacín, Berlin.

Gerke, S., 2014. *Der altägyptische Greif: Von der Vielfalt eines 'Fabeltiers'*, Hamburg.

German, S., 2005. *Performance, Power and the Art of the Aegean Bronze Age*. BAR International Series 1347, Oxford.

Gesell, G., 1976. 'The Minoan Snake Tube: A Survey and Catalogue', *AJA*, 80.3, pp. 247–59.

Gesell, G. C., 1987. 'Minoan Palace and Public Cult', in R. Hägg and N. Marinatos, eds., *Function of the Minoan Palaces*, Stockholm, pp. 123–8.

Gesell, G., 2004. 'From Knossos to Kavousi: The Popularizing of the Minoan Palace Goddess', *Hesperia Supplements*, Vol. 33, ΧΑΡΙΣ: *Essays in Honor of Sara A. Immerwahr*, Princeton, pp. 131–50.

Giangiulio, M., 1996. 'Avventurieri, mercanti, coloni, mercenari. Mobilità umana e circolazione di risorse nel Mediterraneo antico', in S. Settis, ed., *I Greci. Storia Cultura Arte Società. Una storia greca. Formazione* II.1, Turin, pp. 497–525.

Giannini, A., ed., 1965. *Paradoxographorum Graecorum Reliquiae*, Milan.

Gibson, C. A., 2012. 'Palaephatus and the Progymnasmata', *ByzZ*, 105, pp. 85–92.

Gifford, P. and P. Antonello, 2015. 'Rethinking the Neolithic Revolution: Symbolism and Sacrifice at Göbekli Tepe', in P. Gifford and P. Antonello, eds., *How We Became Human: Mimetic Theory and the Science of Evolutionary Origins*, Ann Arbor, pp. 261–88.

Gilhus, I. S., 2006. *Animals, Gods and Humans. Changing Attitudes to Animals in Greek, Roman and Early Christian Ideas*, Abingdon.

Gill, M. A. V., 1963. 'The Minoan Dragon', *BICS*, 10, pp. 2–6.

Gillies, G., 2017. 'The Body in Question. Looking At Non-Binary Gender in the Greek and Roman World', *Eidolon*, Nov. 9, 2017. https://medium.com/eidolon/the-body-in-question-d28045d23714.

Gilmore, D. D., 2003. *Monsters, Evil Beings, Mythical Beasts and All Manner of Imaginary Terrors*, Philadelphia.

Gimbutas, M., 1989. *The Language of the Goddess: Unearthing the Hidden Symbols of Western Civilization*, San Francisco.

Girard, R., 2015. 'Animal Scapegoating at Çatalhöyük', in P. Antonello and P. Gifford, eds., *How We Became Human: Mimetic Theory and the Science of Evolutionary Origins*, Ann Arbor, pp. 217–31.

Gjerstad, E., 1979. 'The Phoenician Colonization and Expansion in Cyprus', *Report of the Department of Antiquities, Cyprus*, pp. 230–54.

Glynn, R., 1981. 'Herakles, Nereus and Triton: A Study of Iconography in Sixth Century Athens', *AJA* 85.2, pp. 121–32.

Golden, M., 1993. *Children and Childhood in Classical Athens*, Baltimore.

Golder, H., 2011. 'The Greek Invention of the Human', *Arion*, 18.3, pp. 1–19.

Gönster, Y., 2015. 'The Silphion Plant in Cyrenaica: An Indicator for Intercultural Relationships?', in E. Kistler, B. Öhlinger, M. Mohr and M. Hoernes, eds., *Networking and the Formation of Elites in the Archaic Western Mediterranean World: Proceedings of the International Conference in Innsbruck, 20th 23rd March 2012*, Wiesbaden, pp. 169–84.

Gordon, R., 2010. 'Magian Lessons in Natural History: Unique Animals in Graeco-Roman Natural Magic', in J. Dijkstra, J. Kroesen, and Y. Kuiper, eds., *Myths, Martyrs, and Modernity: Studies in the History of Religions in Honour of Jan N. Bremmer*, Leiden, pp. 249–69.

Gourmelen, L., 2004. *Kékrops, le roi-serpent: Imaginaire athénien, représentations de l'humain et de l'animalité en Grèce ancienne*, Paris.

Grethlein, J., 2016. 'Sight and Reflexivity: Theorizing Vision in Greek Vase Painting', in M. Squire, ed., *Sight and the Ancient Senses*, London, pp. 85–106.

Grethlein, J. and C. B. Krebs, 2012. 'The Historian's Plupast: Introductory Remarks on its Forms and Functions', in J. Grethlein and C. B. Krebs, eds., *Time and Narrative in Ancient Historiography: The 'Plupast' from Herodotus to Appian*, Cambridge; New York, pp. 1–16.

Griffith, F. L., 1916. 'Review of *Beschreibung der Aegyptischen Sammlung des Niederländischen Reichsmuseums der Altertümer in Leiden*', *JEA* 3, 142–3.

Griffith, M., 2002. 'Slaves of Dionysos: Satyrs, Audience, and the Ends of the *Oresteia*', *Class. Antiq.*, 21.2, pp. 195–258.

Griffith, M., 2006. 'Horsepower and Donkeywork: Equids and the Ancient Greek Imagination', *CP*, 101, pp. 185–246, 307–58.

Groneberg, B., 1986. 'Die sumerisch-akkadische Inanna/Ištar: Hermaphroditos?' *Die Welt des Orients*, 17, pp. 25–46.

Grosman, L., N. D. Munro and A. Belfer-Cohen, 2008. 'A 12,000-year-old Shaman Burial from the Southern Levant (Israel)', *PNAS*, 105 (46) 17665–9.

Grosz, E., 1995. 'Animal Sex: Libido as Desire and Death', in E. Grosz and E. Probyn, eds., *Sexy Bodies: The Strange Carnalities of Feminism*, London, pp. 278–99.

Grosz, E., 2020. 'Intolerable Ambiguity: Freaks as/at the Limit', in J. A. Weinstock, ed., *The Monster Theory Reader*, Minneapolis, pp. 272–85.

Groves, R., 2016. 'From Statue to Story: Ovid's Metamorphosis of Hermaphroditus', *CW*, 109.3, pp. 321–56.

Grube, G., 2020. 'An Image Description Method to Access Palaeolithic Art: Discovering a Visual Narrative of Gender Relations in the Pictorial Material of Chauvet Cave', in T. Meaden and H. Bender, eds., *Anthropomorphic Images in Rock Art Paintings and Rock Carvings*, Oxford, pp. 33–48.

Gschnitzer, F., 1961. 'Zur Geschichte der griechischen Staatenverbindungen: Halikarnassos und Salmakis (Syll.3 45)', *RhM*, 104.3, pp. 237–41.
Guillaume, P. and N. Blockman, 2004. '"By my god, I bull leap" (Psalm 18.30/2 Samuel 22.30),' *lectio difficilior*, 2, pp. 1–8.
Gunkel, H., 1895. *Schöpfung und Chaos in Urzeit und Endzeit. Eine religionsgeschichtliche Untersuchung über Gen 1 und Ap Joh 12*, Göttingen.
Guralnik, E., 2004. 'A Group of Near Eastern Bronzes from Olympia', *AJA*, 108, pp. 187–222.
Hadjisavvas, S., 2003. 'Cyprus discovers the world', in S. Hadjisavvas, ed., *From Ishtar to Aphrodite: 3200 Years of Cypriot Hellenism*, New York, pp. 21–5.
Hägg, R. and N. Marinatos, eds., 1987. *The Function of the Minoan Palaces: Proceedings of the Fourth International Symposium at the Swedish Institute in Athens, 10–16 June, 1984*, Göteborg.
Halbwachs, M., 1941. *La topographie légendaire des évangiles en terre sainte. Étude de mémoire collective*, Paris.
Hall, B. K., 1999. 'The Paradoxical Platypus', *BioScience*, 49.3, pp. 211–18.
Hall, J. M., 2002. *Hellenicity: Between Ethnicity and Culture*, Chicago.
Hall, T. D., 2014. 'Ethnicity and World-Systems Analysis', in J. McInerney, ed., *A Companion to Ethnicity in the Ancient Mediterranean*, Chichester, pp. 50–65.
Hallager, E., 1996. *The Minoan Roundel and Other Sealed Documents in the Neopalatial Linear A Administration*, Liège.
Hansen, W. F., 1980. 'An Ancient Greek Ghost Story', in N. Burlakoff and C. Lindahl, eds., *Folklore on Two Continents: Essays in Honor of Linda Dégh*, Bloomington, IN, pp. 71–7.
Hansen, W. F., 1989. 'Contextualizing the Story of Philinnion', *Midwestern Folklore*, 15, pp. 101–8.
Hansen, W. F., 1996. *Phlegon of Tralles' Book of Marvels*, Exeter.
Harari, M., 2004. 'A Short History of Pygmies in Greece and Italy', in K. Lomas, ed., *Greek Identity in the Western Mediterranean: Papers in Honour of Brian Shefton*, Leiden, pp. 163–90.
Hard, R., 2019. 'The Early Mythical History of Argos', in R. Hard (ed.), *The Routledge Handbook of Greek Mythology, Based on H. J. Rose's A Handbook of Greek Mythology*, London, pp. 210–34.
Harding, P., 2008. *The Story of Athens*, London.
Harris, E. M., 2013. *The Rule of Law in Democratic Athens*, Oxford.
Harrop, S., 2015. 'Grounded, Heracles and the Gorgon's Gaze', *Arion*, 23.1, pp. 169–86.
Haubold, J., 2013. *Greece and Mesopotamia: Dialogues in Literature*, Cambridge.
Hawes, G., 2014a. *Rationalizing Myth in Antiquity*, Oxford.
Hawes, G., 2014b. 'Story Time at the Library: Palaephatus and the Emergence of a Hyperliterate Mythology', in R. Scodel, ed., *Between Orality and Literacy: Communication and Adaptation in Antiquity*, Leiden, pp. 125–47.

Hawhee, D., 2017. *Rhetoric in Tooth and Claw. Animals, Language, Sensation*, Chicago.

Heath, J., 2005. *The Talking Greeks: Speech, Animals, and the Other in Homer, Aeschylus, and Plato*, Cambridge.

Hedreen, G., 2004. 'The Return of Hephaistos, Dionysiac Processional Ritual, and the Creation of a Visual Narrative', *JHS*, 124, pp. 38–64.

Hedreen, G., 2006. '"I Let Go My Force Just Touching Her Hair": Male Sexuality in Athenian Vase-Paintings of Silens and Iambic Poetry', *Class. Antiq.*, 25, pp. 277–325.

Hedreen, G., 1992. *Silens in Attic Black-Figure Vase-Painting: Myth and Performance*, Ann Arbor.

Heidegger, M., 1995. *The Fundamental Concepts of Metaphysics: World, Finitude, Solitude*, Trans. W. McNeill and N. Walker, Bloomington.

Heil, F., 2018. 'The Roles of Ritual Practice in Prehistoric Cyprus', in V. Müller, M. Luciani, M. Ritter and M. Guidetti, eds., *Proceedings of the 10th International Congress on the Archaeology of the Ancient Near East, Volume 1*, Wiesbaden, pp. 247–58.

Helle, S., 2023. 'The Honeyed Mouth', in *The Complete Poems of Enheduana*, New Haven, pp. 134–61.

Helmer, D., L. Gourichon and D. Stordeur, 2004. 'À l'aube de la domestication animale. Imaginaire et symbolisme animal dans les premières sociétés néolithiques du nord du proche-Orient', *Anthropozoologica* 39, pp. 143–63.

Henderson, J., 1975. *The Maculate Muse: Obscene Language in Attic Comedy*, New Haven and London.

Henderson, J., 1987. 'Older Women in Attic Old Comedy', *TAPA*, 117, pp. 105–29.

Henig, M., 1997. '"Et in Arcadia Ego": Satyrs and Maenads in the Ancient World and Beyond', *Studies in the History of Art*, 54, *Symposium Papers XXXII: Engraved Gems: Survivals and Revivals*, pp. 22–31.

Herdt, G., 1990. 'Mistaken Identity: 5–Alpha Reductase Hermaphroditism and Biological Reductionism in Sexual Identity Reconsidered', *American Anthropologist*, 92, pp. 433–46.

Herrero de Jáuregui, M., 2015, 'The Construction of Inner Religious Space in Wandering Religion of Classical Greece', *Numen*, 62.5/6, pp. 596–626.

Hodder, I., 2006. *The Leopard's Tale: Revealing the Mysteries of Çatalhöyük*, London.

Hodder, I. and L. Meskell, 2011. 'A "Curious and Sometimes a Trifle Macabre Artistry": Some Aspects of Symbolism in Neolithic Turkey', *Current Anthropology*, 52.2, pp. 235–63.

Hodos, T., 1999. 'Intermarriage in the Western Greek Colonies', *Oxford Journal of Archaeology*, 18, pp. 61–78.

Hoffmann, G., 1993. 'Monsters and Modal Logic among French Naturalists of the Renaissance', *South Central Review*, 10.2, *Reason, Reasoning, and Literature in the Renaissance*, pp. 32–48.

Holbek, B., 2016. 'Hundsköpfige', in K. Ranke, ed., *Enzyklopädie des Märchens. Handwörterbuch zur historischen und vergleichenden Erzählforschung*, Berlin, col. 1372–80.

Holbraad, M., B. Kapferer and J. F. Sauma, 2020. 'Introduction: Critical Ruptures', in M. Holbraad, B. Kapferer and J. F. Sauma, eds., *Anthropolgies of Discontinuity in Times of Turmoil*, Chicago, pp. 1–26.

Holford-Strevens, L., 2003. *Aulus Gellius: An Antonine Scholar and His Achievement*. 2nd ed. Oxford.

Holmes, B., 2015. 'Situating Scamander: "Natureculture" in the *Iliad*', *Ramus* 44.1/2, pp. 29–51.

Hölscher, T., 2009. 'Architectural Sculpture: Messages? Programs? Towards Rehabilitating the Notion of "Decoration"', in P. Schultz and R. van den Hoff, eds., *Structure, Image, Ornament: Architectural Sculpture in the Greek World*, Oxford, pp. 54–67.

Holzberg, N., 2002. *The Ancient Fable. An Introduction*, Bloomington.

Honigman, S., 2014. *Tales of High Priests and Taxes: The Books of the Maccabees and the Judean Rebellion against Antiochos IV*, Berkeley.

hooks, b., 1992. *Black Looks: Race and Representation*, Boston.

Hopkins, C., 1934. 'Assyrian Elements in the Perseus-Gorgon Story', *AJA*, 38, pp. 341–58.

Hopman, M. G., 2012. *Scylla: Myth, Metaphor, Paradox*, Cambridge.

Hopper, R. J., 1961. '"Plain", "Shore," and "Hill" in Early Athens', *BSA*, 56, pp. 189–219.

Hopper, R. J., 1968, 'Observations on the *Wappenmünzen*', in C. M. Kraay and G. K. Jenkins, eds., *Essays in Greek Coinage Presented to Stanley Robinson*, Oxford, pp. 16–39.

Horden, P., and N. Purcell, 2000. *The Corrupting Sea: A Study of Mediterranean History*, Oxford.

Horden, P., and N. Purcell, 2005. 'Four Years of Corruption: A Response to Critics', in W. V. Harris, ed., *Rethinking the Mediterranean*, Oxford, pp. 348–75.

Hornblower. S., 1982. *Mausolos*, Oxford.

Hornung, E., 2000. 'Komposite Gottheiten in der ägyptischen Ikonographie', in C. Uehlinger, ed., *Images as Media: Sources for the Cultural History of the Near East and the Eastern Mediterranean (1st Millennium BCE)*, Fribourg, pp. 1–20.

Hughes, J., 2010. 'Dissecting the Classical Hybrid', in K. Rebay-Salisbury, M. L. Stig Sørensen and J. Hughes, eds., *Body Parts and Bodies Whole: Changing Relations and Meanings*, Oxford, pp. 101–10.

Hume, L., 2004. 'Accessing the Eternal: Dreaming "the Dreaming" and Ceremonial Performance', *Zygon* 39, pp. 237–58.

Humphreys, S. C., 2018. *Kinship in Ancient Athens: An Anthropological Analysis*, Oxford.

Hunger, H. and D. Pingree, 1989. *MULAPIN: An Astronomical Compendium in Cuneiform*. Horn.

Hurwit, J. M., 1977. 'Image and Frame in Greek Art', *AJA*, 81.1, pp. 1–30.
Hurwit, J. M, 2006. 'Lizards, Lions, and the Uncanny in Early Greek Art', *Hesperia*, 75.1, pp. 121–36.
Hutchinson, R. W., 1958. 'The Flying Snakes of Arabia', *CQ*, 8.1–2, pp. 100–1.
Hutnyk, J., 2005. 'Hybridity', *Ethnic and Racial Studies*, 28:1, pp. 79–102.
Hutton, W., 2010. 'Pausanias and the Mysteries of Hellas', *TAPA* 140, pp. 423–59.
Iacovou, M., 2005. 'Cyprus at the Dawn of the first Millennium BC: Cultural Homogenization versus the Tyranny of Ethnic Identifications', in J. Clarke, ed., *Archaeological Perspectives on the Transmission and Transformation of Culture in the Eastern Mediterranean*. Levant Supplementary Series 2, Oxford, pp. 125–34.
Iancu, L., 2017. 'A Golden Bracelet and a City as a Prize for Valor', in *Aegean Mercenaries and a New Theoretical Model for the Archaic Eastern Mediterranean*. Anthesteria 6, pp. 49–61.
Iasager, S., 2014. 'New Inscriptions in the Bodrum Museum. A Hellenistic Foundation from the area of Mylasa', *Opuscula*, 7, pp. 185–92.
Ingold, T., ed., 1988. *What Is an Animal?* London.
Ingold, T., 2007. *Lines: A Brief History.* London.
Irwin, E., 2005. *Solon and Early Greek Poetry*, Cambridge.
Isaac, B., J. Ziegler and M. Eliav-Feldon, eds., 2009. *The Origins of Racism in the West*, Cambridge.
Isager, S., 1998. 'The Pride of Halikarnassos. Editio Princeps of an Inscription from Salmakis', *ZPE*, 123, pp. 1–23.
Isager, S., 2015. 'On a List of Priests. From the Son of Poseidon to Members of the Elite in Late Hellenistic Halikarnassos', in J. Fejfer, M. Moltesen and A. Rathje, eds., *Tradition: Transmission of Culture in the Ancient World. Acta Hyperborea 14*, Copenhagen, pp. 131–48.
Isayev, E., 2013. 'Mediterranean Ancient Migrations, 2000–1 BCE', in I. Ness, ed., *The Encyclopedia of Global Human Migration*, Hoboken, NJ, pp. 1—5.
Isler-Kerényi, C., 2007. *Dionysos in Archaic Greece: An Understanding through Images*, Leiden.
Jameson, M. H., 1990. 'Perseus, the Hero of Mykenai', in R. Hägg and G. C. Nordquist, eds., *Celebrations of Death and Divinity in the Bronze Age Argolid*, Stockholm, pp. 213–22.
Jeffery, L. H., 1976. *Archaic Greece. The City-States, c. 700–500 BC*, London.
Jiménez, A., 2011. 'Pure Hybridism: Late Iron Age Sculpture in Southern Iberia', *World Archaeology*, 43.1, pp. 102–23.
Johns, C., 2006. *Horses: History, Myth, Art*, Cambridge, MA.
Johnson, D. M., 2005. 'Persians as Centaurs in Xenophon's *Cyropaedia*', *TAPA*, 135, 177–207.
Johnston, A., 2014. 'The Naukratis Project: Petrie, Greeks and Egyptians', *Archaeology International*, 17, pp. 69–73.

Johnston, S. I., 1992. 'Xanthus, Hera and the Erinyes (*Iliad* 19.400–418)', *TAPA*, 1992, pp. 85–98.

Johnston, S. I., 1999. *Restless Dead: Encounters Between the Living and the Dead in Ancient Greece*, Berkeley.

Johnstone, M., 2013. 'Plato's Depiction of the "Democratic Man"', *Phronesis*, 58.2, pp. 139–59.

Jonassohn, K., 2000. 'On A Neglected Aspect of Western Racism', *Montreal Institute for Genocide and Human Rights Studies, Occasional Paper Series*, pp. 1–4.

Jost, M., 1985. *Sanctuaires et culte d'Arcadie*, Paris.

Jost, M., 1992. 'Mystery Cults in Arcadia', in M. Cosmopoulos, ed., *Greek Mysteries. The Archaeology of Ancient Greek Secret Cults*, London, pp. 143–68.

Jouanna, J., 2012. 'Hippocrates and the Sacred', in *Greek Medicine from Hippocrates to Galen. Selected Papers*, Leiden, pp. 97–118.

Kagan, J., 1988. 'Some Bovine Curiosities', *Museum Notes (American Numismatic Society)*, 33, pp. 37–44.

Kalof, L., A. Fitzgerald, J. Lerner and J. Temeles, 2004. 'Animal Studies: A Bibliography', *Human Ecology Review*, 11.1, pp. 75–99.

Kalof, L. and G. M. Montgomery, eds., 2011. *Making Animal Meaning*. East Lansing, MI.

Kapchan, D. A. and P. T. Strong, 1999. 'Theorizing the Hybrid', *Journal of American Folklore*, 112, pp. 239–53.

Kaplan, P., 2003. 'Cross-Cultural Contacts among Mercenary Communities in Saite and Persian Egypt', *MHR* 18.1, pp. 1–31.

Kapparis, K., 2018. *Prostitution in the Ancient Greek World*, Berlin.

Karetsou, A., M. Andreadaki-Vlazaki and N. Papadakis, eds., 2000. ΚΡΗΤΗ – ΑΙΓΥΠΤΟΣ. Πολιτισμικοί δεσμοί τριών χιλιετιών, Herakleion.

Karnes, M., 2022. *Medieval Marvels and Fictions in the Latin West and Islamic World*, Chicago.

Karttunen, K., 1997. *India and the Hellenistic World*, Helsinki.

Kearns, E., 1989. *The Heroes of Attica*. BICS Supplement 57, London.

Keusch, G. T., M. Pappaioanou, M. C. Gonzalez, K. A. Scott and P. Tsai, 'Drivers of Zoonotic Diseases', in National Research Council, ed., *Sustaining Global Surveillance and Response to Emerging Zoonotic Diseases*, Washington, DC, pp. 77–114.

Kiilerich, B., 1988. 'Bluebeard – A Snake-tailed Geryon?' *Opuscula Atheniensia*, 17.8, pp. 123–36.

Kilroy-Ewbank, L., 2015. 'Transformation Masks', in *Smarthistory*, August 9, 2015, https://smarthistory.org/transformation-masks/.

Kindt, J., 2017. 'Capturing the Ancient Animal: Human/Animal Studies and the Classics', *JHS*, 137, pp. 213–25.

Kindt, J., ed., 2021. *Animals in Ancient Greek Religion*, London.

King, H., 2015. 'Between Male and Female in Ancient Medicine', in D. Boschung, A. Shapiro and F. Wascheck, eds., *Bodies in Transition. Dissolving the Boundaries of Embodied Knowledge*, Paderborn, pp. 249–64.

Kitto, M. R. and M. Tabish, 2004. 'Aquaculture and Food Security in Iraq', *Aquaculture Asia*, 9.1, pp. 31–3.

Klingender, F., 1971. *Animals in Art and Thought to the End of the Middle Ages*, Cambridge, MA.

Klinger, W., 1936. 'Hundsköpfige Gestalten in der antiken und neuzeitlichen Überlieferung', *Bull. International de l'Acad. Polonaise des sciences. Cl. d'hist. et de phil.*, pp. 119–23.

Knapp, A. B., 2015, 'Prehistoric Cyprus: A 'Crossroads' of Interaction?', in A. Lichtenberger and C. von Rüden, eds., *Multiple Mediterranean Realities: Current Approaches to Spaces, Resources, and Connectivities*, Paderborn, pp. 17–30.

Knapp, A. B. and S. W. Manning, 2016. 'Crisis in Context: The End of the Late Bronze Age in the Eastern Mediterranean', *AJA*, 120.1, pp. 99–149.

Knoepflmacher, U. C., 2008. 'Editor's Preface: Hybrid Forms and Cultural Anxiety', *Studies in English Literature, 1500–1900*, 48.4, *The Nineteenth Century*, pp. 745–54.

Knox, B., 1993. *The Oldest Dead White European Males and Other Reflections on the Classics*, New York.

Knox, M., 1979. 'Polyphemos and his Near Eastern Relations', *JHS*, 99, pp. 164–5.

König, J. and T. Whitmarsh, 2007. 'Introduction: Ordering Knowledge', in J. König and T. Whitmarsh, eds., *Ordering Knowledge in the Roman Empire*, Cambridge, pp. 3–40.

Konstan, D., 2011. 'A Pig Convicts Itself of Unreason: The Implicit Argument of Plutarch's *Gryllus*', in N. Almazova, O. Budaragine, S. Egorova, et al., eds., *Variante Loquella: Alexandro Gavrilov Septuagenario*, Petropoli, pp. 371–85.

Konstan, D., 2013. 'Between Appetite and Emotion, or Why can't Animals have *Erôs*?', in E. Sanders, C. Thumiger, C. Carey and N. J. Lowe, eds., *Erôs in Ancient Greece*, Oxford, pp. 13–26.

Korhonen, T. and E. Ruonakoski, 2017. *Human and Animal in Ancient Greece: Empathy and Encounter in Classical Literature*, London.

Korshak, Y., 1987. *Frontal Faces in Attic Vase-Painting of the Archaic Period*, Chicago.

Kosmin, P. J., 2014. *The Land of the Elephant Kings. Space, Territory, and Ideology in the Seleucid Empire*, Cambridge, MA.

Kotansky, R., 1994. *Greek Magical Amulets: The Inscribed Gold, Silver, Copper, and Bronze Lamellae, part 1. Published Texts of Known Provenance, Text and Commentary, Papyrologica Coloniensia* 22.1, Opladen.

Kowalzig, B., 2013. 'Dancing Dolphins on the Wine-Dark Sea: Dithyramb and Social Change in the Archaic Mediterranean', in B. Kowalzig and P. Wilson, eds., *Dithyramb in Context*, Oxford, pp. 31–58.

Krämer, F., 2009. 'The Persistent Image of an Unusual Centaur: A Biography of Aldrovandi's Two-legged Centaur Woodcut', *Nuncius*, 24.2, pp. 313–40.
Kraidy, M., 2017. 'Hybridity', in J. Gray and L. Ouellette, eds., *Keywords for Media Studies*, New York, pp. 90–4.
Krappe, A. H., 1928. 'Teiresias and the Snakes', *AJP*, 49.3, pp. 267–75.
Krappe, A. H., 1945. 'The Bearded Venus', *Folklore*, 56.4, pp. 325–35.
Krentz, P. M., 2007. 'The Oath of Marathon, not Plataia?' *Hesperia* 76, pp. 731–42.
Kristeva, J., 1982. *Powers of Horror: An Essay on Abjection*, New York.
Kroll, J. H., 1981. 'From *Wappenmünzen* to Gorgoneia to Owls', *ANSMN*, 26, pp. 1–32, pls. 1–2.
Kron, U., 1976. *Die zehn attischen Phylenheroen: Mitteilungen des Deutschen Archäologischen Instituts, Athenische Abteilung*. Beiheft 5, Berlin.
Kuch, N., 2017. 'Entangled Itineraries A Transformation of Taweret into the "Minoan Genius"?', *Distant Worlds*, 3, pp. 45–66.
Kunstler, B., 1991. 'The Werewolf Figure and Its Adoption into the Greek Political Vocabulary', *CW*, 84.3, pp. 189–205.
Kuper, A., 2005. *The Reinvention of Primitive Society: Transformations of a Myth*, 2nd ed., London.
Kurke, L., 2011. *Aesopic Conversations: Popular Tradition, Cultural Dialogue, and the Invention of Greek Prose*, Princeton.
Kurtz, D. C. and J. Boardman, 1971. *Greek Burial Customs*, Ithaca, NY.
Kutschera, U., 2009. 'Darwin's Philosophical Imperative and the Furor Theologicus', *Evo Edu Outreach*, 2, pp. 688–94.
Kuzniar, A., 2011. 'Where is the Animal after Post-Humanism?: Sue Cole and the Art of Quivering Life', *The New Centennial Review*, 11.2, pp. 17–40.
Kvanvig, H., 1988. *Roots of Apocalyptic: The Mesopotamian Background of the Enoch Figure and the Son of Man*, Neukirchen-Vluyn.
Lada-Richards, I., 1998. '"Foul Monster or Good Saviour?" Reflections on Ritual Liminality', in C. Atherton, ed., *Monsters and Monstrosity in Greek and Roman Culture*, Bari, pp. 41–82.
Lambert, S. D., 2019. 'The Priesthoods of the Eteoboutadai', in Z. Archibald and J. Haywood, eds., *The Power of Individual and Community in Ancient Athens and Beyond: Essays in honour of John K. Davies*, Swansea, pp. 163–76.
Lamont, J. L., 2015. 'A New Commercial Curse Tablet from Classical Athens', *ZPE*, 196, pp. 159–74.
Lane Fox, R., 2008. *Travelling Heroes: Greeks and their Myths in the Epic Age of Homer*, London.
Lang, A., 1911. *Method in the Study of Totemism*, Glasgow.
Lang, M., 2013. 'Book Two: Mesopotamian Early History and the Flood Story', in J. Haubold, G. B. Lanfranchi, R. Rollinger and J. Steele, eds., *The World of Berossos: Proceedings of the 4th International Colloquium on the Ancient Near East Between Classical and Ancient Oriental Traditions*, Wiesbaden, pp. 47–60.

Langdon, S., 2007. 'The Awkward Age: Art and Maturation in Early Greece', in A. Cohen and J. B. Rutter, eds., *Constructions of Childhood in Ancient Greece and Italy. Hesperia Supplements*, vol. 41, Princeton, pp. 173–91.

Langdon, S., 1989. 'The Return of the Horse-Leader', *AJA*, 93.2, pp. 185–201.

Lape, S., 2010. *Race and Citizen Identity in the Classical Athenian Democracy*, Cambridge.

Leporda, C. L. 2011. 'To Be or Not to Be a Monster'. In P. L. Yoder and P. M. Kreuter, eds., *The Horrid Looking Glass: Reflections on Monstrosity*, Oxford, pp. 83–100.

Lascault, G., 1973. *Les monstres dans l'art occidental: Un problème esthétique*, Paris.

Lattimore, R., 1939. 'Herodotus and the Names of Egyptian Gods', *CP*, 34.4, pp. 357–65.

Laufer, E., 1985. 'Kaineus: Studien zur Ikonographie', *RdA* Suppl. 1, Rome.

Lawler, J. B., 1952. 'Dancing Herds of Animals', *CJ*, 47.8, pp. 317–24.

Leach, E., 1964. 'Anthropological Aspects of Language: Animal Categories and Verbal Abuse.', in E. H. Lenneberg, ed., *New Directions in the Study of Language*, Cambridge, MA, pp. 23–63.

Leclerc, M.-C., 1993. *La parole chez Hésiode: À la recherche de l'harmonie perdue. Collection d'Études anciennnes* 121. Paris.

Lefkowitz, J. B., 2014. 'Aesop and Animal Fable', in G. L. Campbell, ed., *The Oxford Handbook of Animals in Classical Thought and Life*, Oxford, pp. 1–23.

Leick, G., 2001. *Mesopotamia: The Invention of the City*, London.

Leitao, D. D., 1995. 'The Perils of Leukippos: Initiatory Transvestism and Male Gender Ideology in the Ekdusia at Phaistos', *Class. Antiq.*, 14.1, pp. 130–63.

Lenfant, D., 2011. 'Le feu immortel de Phasélis et le prétendu volcan Chimère: les textes, le mythe et le terrain', in J. Wiesehöfer, R. Rollinger and G. B. Lanfranchi, eds., *Ktesias' Welt/Ctesias' World*. Wiesbaden, pp. 225–46.

Leonard, Jr, A., 1997. *Ancient Naukratis: Excavations at a Greek Emporium in Egypt. Part I: The Excavations at Kom Ge'if*, Cambridge, MA.

Leonard, Jr, A., 1998, *Ancient Naukratis: Excavations at a Greek Emporium in Egypt. Part II: The Excavations at Kom Hadid*, Cambridge, MA.

Leporda, C. L., 2011. 'To Be or Not to Be a Monster', in P. L. Yoder and P. M. Kreuter, eds., *The Horrid Looking Glass: Reflections on Monstrosity*, Oxford, pp. 83–100.

Lévi-Strauss, C., 1955. 'The Structural Study of Myth', *Journal of American Folklore*, 68, pp. 428–44.

Lewis, D. M., 2018. *Greek Slave Systems in their Eastern Mediterranean Context, c. 800–146 BC*, Oxford.

Lewis, M. W and K. E. Wigen, 1997. *The Myth of Continents: A Critique of Metageography*. Berkeley.

Lewis, S., 2017. 'A Lifetime Together? Temporal Perspectives on Animal-Human Interactions', in T. Fögen and E. Thomas, *Interactions Between Animals and Humans in Graeco-Roman Antiquity*, Berlin, pp. 19–38.

Lewis, S. and L. Llewellyn-Jones, eds., 2018. *The Culture of Animals in Antiquity. A Sourcebook with Commentaries*, London.

Lewis, T. J., 1996. 'CT 13.33-34 and Ezekiel 32: Lion-Dragon Myths', *Journal of the American Oriental Society*, 116, pp. 28-47

Lewis, T. J., 2020. *The Origin and Character of God: Ancient Israelite Religion through the Lens of Divinity*, Oxford.

Lieber, R. J. and R. E. Weisberg, 2002. 'Globalization, Culture, and Identities in Crisis', *International Journal of Politics, Culture, and Society*, 16.2, pp. 273–96.

Lightfoot, J., 2021. *Wonder and the Marvellous from Homer to the Hellenistic World*, Cambridge.

Limberis, V., 2012. 'Bishops Behaving Badly: Helladius Challenges Gregory of Nazianzus and Gregory of Nyssa', in C. Beeley, ed., *Gregory of Nazianzus, Theology, History, Church: Essays in Honor of Frederick Norris*. CUAP Studies in Early Christianity, Washington, DC, pp. 159–77.

Lincoln, B., 1976. 'The Indo-European Cattle-Raiding Myth', *History of Religions*, 16, pp. 42–65.

Lindenlauf, A., 2003. 'The Sea as a Place of No Return in Ancient Greece', *World Archaeology*, 35, pp. 416–33.

Linder, E., 1986. 'The Khorsabad Wall Relief: A Mediterranean Seascape or River Transport of Timbers?', *Journal of the American Oriental Society*, 106.2, pp. 273–81.

Lissarrague, F., 1990a. 'Why Satyrs are good to represent', in J. J. Winkler and F. I. Zeitlin, eds., *Nothing to Do with Dionysos?* Princeton, pp. 228–36.

Lissarrague, F., 1990b. 'The Sexual Life of Satyrs', in D. M. Halperin, J. J. Winkler, and F. Zeitlin, eds., *Before Sexuality*, Princeton, 53–81.

Lissarrague, F., 1993. 'On the Wildness of Satyrs', in T. H. Carpenter and C. Faraone, eds., *Masks of Dionysos*, Ithaca, NY, pp. 207–20.

Lissarrague, F., 1997. 'L'homme, le singe et le satyre', in B. Cassin and J.-L. Labarrière, eds., *L'Animal dans l'Antiquité*, Paris, pp. 454–72.

Lissarrague, F., 2014. *The Aesthetics of the Greek Banquet: Images of Wine and Ritual*, Princeton.

Livingstone, D. N., 1992. *The Geographical Tradition: Episodes in the History of a Contested Enterprise*, Oxford.

Lloyd, G. E. R., 1966. *Polarity and Analogy: Two Types of Argumentation in Early Greek Thought*, Cambridge.

Lloyd, G. E. R., 1997. 'Les animaux de l'Antiquité étaient bons à penser: quelques points de comparaison entre Aristote et Huainanzi', in Cassin, B. and J.-L. Labarrière, eds., 1997. *L'Animal dans l'Antiquité*, Paris, pp. 545–62.

Lloyd, G. E. R., 2007. 'Pneuma between Body and Soul', *JRAI*, 13, pp. 135–46.

Lloyd-Jones, H., 1999a. 'The Pride of Halikarnassos', *ZPE* 124, pp. 1–14.

Lloyd-Jones, H., 1999b: 'The Pride of Halikarnassos (*ZPE* 124, 1999, 1–14): Corrigenda and Addenda', *ZPE* 127, pp. 63–5.

Lolos, Y. A., 2011. *Land of Sikyon: Archaeology and History of a Greek City-State*. Hesperia supplements, 39, Princeton.

Lomas, K., ed., 2004, *Greek Identity in the Western Mediterranean*. Mnemosyne, Suppl. 246, Leiden.

Lombardi, M., 2012. 'Chaos e Ade in Hes. *Th*.720-819', *Hermes*, 140.1, pp. 1–24.

Lombardini, J., 2013. '*Isonomia* and the Public Sphere in Democratic Athens', *History of Political Thought*, 34, pp. 393–420.

Lommel, A. and D. Mowaljarlai, 1994. 'Shamanism in Northwest Australia', *Oceania*, 64.4, pp. 277–87.

Long, A. A., 1977. 'Chance and Natural Law in Epicureanism', *Phronesis*, 22.1, pp. 63–88.

Lonsdale, S. H., 1979. 'Attitudes towards Animals in Ancient Greece', *G&R*, 26.2, pp. 146–59.

López-Ruiz, C., 2010. *When the Gods Were Born: Greek Cosmogonies and the Near East*, Cambridge, MA.

López-Ruiz, C., ed., 2017. *Gods, Heroes and Monsters*, 2nd ed., New York.

Loraux, N., 1981. *Les enfants d'Athéna: Idées athéniennes sur la citoyenneté et la division des sexes*, Paris.

Loraux, N., 1990. 'Kreousa the Autochthon: A Study of Euripides' *Ion*', in J. J. Winkler and F. I. Zeitlin, eds., *Nothing to Do with Dionysos?* Princeton, pp. 168–206.

Loraux, N., 2000. *Born of the Earth: Myth and Politics in Athens*, Ithaca.

Loraux, N., 2002. *The Divided City: On Memory and Forgetting in Ancient Athens*, New York.

Louden, B., 2011. *Homer's* Odyssey *and the Near East*, Cambridge.

Lowenthal, D., 2005. 'Why Sanctions Seldom Work: Reflections on Cultural Property Internationalism', *International Journal of Cultural Property*, 12, pp. 393–423.

Luce J. M., 2005. 'Erechthée, Thésée, les Tyrannoctones et les espaces publics athéniens', in E. Greco, ed., *Teseo e Romolo: Le origini di Atene e Roma a confronto: Atti Convegno Internazionale di Studi*. Scuola Archeologica Italiana di Atene, Athens, pp. 143–64.

Luckenbill, D. D., 1926. *Ancient Records of Assyria and Babylonia*. Chicago.

Lucretius, 1986. *De Rerum Natura. Prolegomena, Text and Critical Apparatus, Translation, Commentary*. III vol. Edited by C. Bailey, Oxford.

Lupack, S., 2022. 'The Mycenaeans and Ecstatic Ritual Experience', in D. L. Stein, S. K. Costello and K. P. Foster, eds., *The Routledge Companion to Ecstatic Experience in the Ancient World*, Abingdon, pp. 284–95.

Luraghi, N., 2006. 'Traders, Pirates, Warriors: The Proto-History of Greek Mercenary Soldiers in the Eastern Mediterranean', *Phoenix*, 60.1/2, pp. 21–47.

M'Baye, B., 2019. 'Afropolitan Sexual and Gender Identities in Colonial Senegal', *Humanities*, 8, pp. 1–16.

McCabe, D. F., 1991. *Halicarnassus Inscriptions: Texts and Lists*, Princeton.

McCance, D., 2013. *Critical Animal Studies*, Albany.

McClamrock, R., 2013. 'Visual Consciousness and the Phenomenology of Perception', *Metaphilosophy*, 44.1/2, pp. 63–8.

McDonald, K. and J. Clackson, 2020. 'The Language of Mobile Craftsmen in the Western Mediterranean', in J. Clackson, K. McDonald, L. Tagliapietra, N. Zair and P. James, eds., *Migration, Mobility and Language Contact in and Around the Ancient Mediterranean*, Cambridge, pp. 75–97.

McGovern, P. E., 2009. *Uncorking the Past: The Quest for Wine, Beer, and Other Alcoholic Beverages*, Berkeley.

McInerney, J., 1997 (1999). 'Parnassus, Delphi, and the Thyiades', *GRBS*, 38.3, 263–83.

McInerney, J., 2004. 'Nereids, Colonies and the Origins of *Isegoria*', in R. M. Rosen and I. Sluiter, eds., *Free Speech in Classical Antiquity*, Leiden, pp. 21–40.

McInerney, J., 2010. *The Cattle of the Sun: Cows and Culture in the World of the Ancient Greeks*, Princeton.

McInerney, J., 2011. 'Bulls and Bull-leaping in the Minoan World', *Expedition*, 53.3, pp. 6–13.

McInerney, J., 2015. 'There Will be Blood: The Cult of Artemis Tauropolos at Halai Araphenides', in K. Daly and L. A. Riccardi, eds., *Cities Called Athens: Studies Honoring John McK. Camp II*. Bucknell, pp. 289–320.

McInerney, J., 2016. 'Of Monsters and Men: The Minotaur and the Mycenaeans', in F. Coimbra, ed., *The Horse and The Bull in Prehistory and History*, Genoa, pp. 199–210.

McInerney, J., 2017. 'Fish or Man, Babylonian or Greek: Oannes between Cultures', in T. Fögen and E. V. Thompsen, eds., *Interactions between Animals and Humans in Graeco-Roman Antiquity*, Berlin, pp. 253–73.

McInerney, J., 2018. 'Greek Colonisation', in D. Clayman, ed., *Oxford Bibliographies in Classics*, New York, pp. 1–26.

McInerney, J., 2019. 'The Location of the Hephaisteion', *TAPA* 149.2, pp. 219–60.

McInerney, J., 2021a. 'The "Entanglement" of Gods, Humans, and Animals in Ancient Greek Religion', in J. Kindt, ed., *Animals in Ancient Greek Religion*, London, pp. 17–40.

McInerney, J., 2021b. 'Salmakis and the Priests of Halikarnassos', *KLIO*, 103.1, pp. 1–31.

McInerney, J., 2022. 'Hephaistos among the Satyrs: Semen, Ejaculation and Autochthony in Greek Culture', in A. Seraphim, G. Kazantzidis and K. Demetriou, eds., *Sex and the Ancient City: Sex and Sexual Practices in Greco-Roman antiquity*, Berlin, pp. 285–304.

Mackay, E. A., 2001. 'The Frontal Face and "You": Narrative Disjunction in Early Greek Poetry and Painting', *Acta Classica* 44, pp. 5–34.

Mackie, C. J., 2021. 'War in a Landscape: The Dardanelles from Homer to Gallipoli', in B. Reitz-Joose, M. W. Makins and C. J. Mackie, eds., *Landscapes of War in Greek and Roman Literature*, London, pp. 229–40.

McMahon, L., 2019. *Animal Worlds: Film, Philosophy and Time*, Edinburgh.
McNiven, T. J., 1995. 'The Unheroic Penis. Otherness Exposed', *Source: Notes in the History of Art*, Vol. 15, No. 1, Special Issue: *Representations of the "Other" in Athenian Art, c. 510–400 BC*, pp. 10–16.
McWilliams, S., 2013. 'Hybridity in Herodotos', *Political Research Quarterly*, 66.4, pp. 745–55.
Maffi, A., 1988. *L'iscrizione di Ligdamis*, Trieste.
Maher, L. A., J. T. Stock, S. Finney, et al., 2011. 'A Unique Human-Fox Burial from a Pre-Natufian Cemetery in the Levant (Jordan)', *PLoS ONE* 6(1), pp. 1–10.
Makins, M. W. and B. Reitz-Joosse, 2021. 'Introduction', in M. W. Makins, B. Reitz-Joosse and C. J. Mackie, eds., *Landscapes of War in Greek and Roman Literature*, London, pp. 1–22.
Malkin, I., 2000. 'La fondation d'une colonie Apollonienne: Delphes et *l'Hymne homérique à Apollon*', *BCH Suppl.* 36, pp. 68–77.
Malkin, I., 2001. 'The *Odyssey* and the Nymphs', *Gaia* 5, pp. 11–27.
Malkin, I., 2003. 'Pan-Hellenism and the Greeks of Naukratis', in M. Reddé, ed., *La naissance de la ville dans l'antiquité*, Paris, pp. 91–5.
Malkin, I., 2011. *A Small Greek World: Networks in the Ancient Mediterranean*, Oxford.
Malkin, I., 2016. 'Migration and Colonization: Turbulence, Continuity, and the Practice of Mediterranean Space (11th–5th centuries BCE)', in M. Dabag, N. Jaspert and A. Lichtenberger, eds., *Mittelmeerstudien*, Paderborn, pp. 285–308.
Malkin, I., C. Constantakopoulou and K. Panagopoulou, eds., 2009. *Greek and Roman Networks in the Mediterranean*, London.
Mannhardt, W., 1876-7. *Wald- und Feldkulte*, 2 vols. Berlin.
Manning, J. G., 2018. *The Open Sea: The Economic Life of the Ancient Mediterranean World from the Iron Age to the Rise of Rome*, Princeton.
Marchand, J. C., 2009. 'Kleonai, the Corinth-Argos Road, and the "Axis of History"', *Hesperia* 78.1, pp. 107–63.
Marchetti, L., 2017. 'Alla ricerca di un segno: Dal Tannîn al Drákōn: Alcune riflessioni sull'avvento dei "draghi" nell'immaginario zoologico-biblico della "Settanta"', in S. Cresti and I. Gagliardi, eds., *Leggerezze sostenibili: Saggi d'affetto e di Medioevo per Anna Benvenuti*, Florence, pp. 113–34.
Marconi, C., 2007. *Temple Decoration and Cultural Identity in the Archaic Greek World: The Metopes of Selinus*, New York.
Marcovich, M., 1996. 'From Ishtar to Aphrodite', *The Journal of Aesthetic Education*, 30.2, Special Issue: *Distinguished Humanities Lectures* II (Summer, 1996), pp. 43–59.
Markoe, G. E., 1989. 'The "Lion Attack" in Archaic Greek Art: Heroic Triumph', *Class. Antiq.*, 8.1, pp. 86–115.
Martí-Aguilar, M. A., 2017. 'The Network of Melqart: Tyre, Gadir, Carthage and the Founding God', in T. Ñaco del Hoyo and F. López Sánchez, eds., *War,*

Warlords, and Interstate Relations in the Ancient Mediterranean, Leiden, pp. 113–50.

Masson, O., 1983. *Les inscriptions chypriotes syllabiques: Recueil critique et commenté*. 2nd ed. Paris.

Matthews, D., 1992. 'The Random Pegasus: Loss of Meaning in Middle Assyrian Seals', *Cambridge Archaeological Journal*, 2.2, pp. 191–210.

Matthews, D. M., 1990. *Principles of Composition in Near Eastern Glyptic of the Later Second Millennium BC*. Freiburg.

Mattingly, D. J., ed., 2003. *The Archaeology of Fazzan: Volume 1. Synthesis*, London.

Mattingly, D. J., ed., 2007. *The Archaeology of Fazzan: Volume 2. Site Gazetteer, Pottery and Other Survey Finds*, London.

Mauro, C. M., D. Chapinal-Heras and M. Valdés Guía, eds., 2022, *People on the Move Across the Greek World*, Seville.

Maxwell-Stuart, P. G., 1973. 'The Appearance of Aeschylus' Erinyes', *G&R*, 20, pp. 81–4.

Mayor, A., 2011. *The First Fossil Hunters: Dinosaurs, Mammoths, and Myth in Greek and Roman Times*, Princeton.

Mayor, A., 2018. *Gods and Robots: Myths, Machines, and Ancient Dreams of Technology*, Princeton.

Mazarakis-Ainian, A., 1997. *From Rulers' Dwellings to Temples: Architecture, Religion and Society in Early Iron Age Greece (1100–700 BC)*, Jonsered.

Mbembe, A., 2007. 'Afropolitanism', in N. Simon and L. Durán, eds., *Africa Remix: Contemporary Art of a Continent*, Johannesburg, pp. 26–9.

Mederos, A. and G. Escribano, 2008. 'Caballos de Poseidón: Barcos de juncos y *hippoi* en el sur de la Península ibérica y el litoral atlántico norteafricano', *Saguntum*, 40, pp. 63–78.

Mehregan, I. and J. W. Kadereit, 2009. 'The role of hybridization in the evolution of Cousinia s.str. (Asteraceae, Cardueae)', *Willdenowia*, 39, pp. 35–47.

Merkelbach, R. and J. Stauber, 1998. *Steinepigramme aus dem griechischen Osten, I: Die Westküste Kleinasiens von Knidos bis Ilion*, Stuttgart.

Merleau-Ponty, M., 1962. *The Phenomenology of Perception*, trans. Colin Smith, London.

Mertens, J. R., 2019. 'Watercolors of the Acropolis: Émile Gilliéron in Athens', *The Metropolitan Museum of Art Bulletin*, Spring 2019.

Metzinger, T. H., 2014. 'How does the Brain encode Epistemic Reliability? Perceptual Presence, Phenomenal Transparency, and Counterfactual Richness', *Cognitive Neuroscience*, 5.2, pp. 122–4.

Meyer, M., 2017. *Athena, Göttin von Athen: Kult und Mythos auf der Akropolis bis in klassische Zeit*, Vienna.

Michel, S., 2001. *Die Magischen Gemmen im Britischen Museum*, London.

Mikalson, J. D., 1976. 'Erechtheus and the Panathenaia', *AJP*, 97.2, pp. 141–53.

Miller, M. C., 1999. 'Reexamining Transvestism in Archaic and Classical Athens: The Zewadski Stamnos', *AJA*, 103.2, pp. 223–53.

Miller, R. A., 1988. 'Pleiades perceived: MUL.MUL to Subaru', *Journal of the American Oriental Society*, 108, pp. 1–25.

Miralles, C., 1993. 'le Spose di Zeus e l'Origine del Mondo nella *Teogonia* di Esiodo', in M. Bettini, ed., *Maschile/Femminile: Genere e Ruoli nelle Culture antiche*, Rome, pp. 17–44.

Mirto, M. S., 2016. '"Rightly does Aphrodite's Name begin with *aphrosune*": Gods and Men between Wisdom and Folly', in P. Kyriakou and A. Rengakos, eds., *Wisdom and Folly in Euripides*. Berlin, pp. 45–64.

Mitchell, A. G., 2004. 'Humour in Greek Vase Painting', *Revue Archéologique*, 1, pp. 3–32.

Mitchell, F., 2021. *Monsters in Greek Literature: Aberrant Bodies in Ancient Greek Cosmogony, Ethnography, and Biology*, Abingdon.

Mitchell, L. G., 2001. 'Euboean Io', *CQ*, 51.2, pp. 339–52.

Mitchell, S., 2017. 'The Greek Impact in Asia Minor, 400–250 BCE', in B. Chrubasik and D. King, eds., *Hellenism and the Local Communities of the Eastern Mediterranean: 400–250 CE*, Oxford, pp. 13–28.

Mithen, S., 2009, 'Out of the Mind: Material Culture and the Supernatural', in C. Renfrew and I. Morley, eds., *Becoming Human: Innovation in Prehistoric Material and Spiritual Culture*, Cambridge, pp. 122–34.

Molinari, N. J., 2022. *Acheloios, Thales, and the Origin of Philosophy: A Response to the Neo-Marxians*, Oxford.

Molinari, N. J. and N. Sisci, 2016. 'The Westward Migrations of Man-Faced Bull Iconography', in *Potamikon: Sinews of Acheloios: A Comprehensive Catalog of the Bronze Coinage of the Man-Faced Bull, with Essays on Origin and Identity*, Oxford, pp. 17–30.

Möller, A., 2000. *Naukratis: Trade in Archaic Greece*, Oxford.

Montanari, S. and B. Pouderon, 2022. *Évhémère de Messène: Inscription sacrée. Fragments*, 23, Paris.

Montiglio, S., 2005. *Wandering in Ancient Greek Culture*, Chicago.

Moore, M., 2000. 'Ships on a "Wine-Dark Sea" in the Age of Homer', *Metropolitan Museum Journal*, 35, pp. 13–38.

Moore, M., 2004. 'Horse Care as Depicted on Greek Vases before 400 BC', *Metropolitan Museum Journal*, 39, pp. 35–67.

Moore, R. S., 1994. 'Metaphors of Encroachment: Hunting for Wolves on a Central Greek Mountain', *Anthropological Quarterly*, 67.2, pp. 81–8.

Morenz, S., 1954. 'Ägyptische Tierkriege und die Batrachomyomachie', *Neue Beträge zur Klassischen Altertumswissenschaft: Festschrift zum 60. Geburtstag von Bernhard Schweitzer*, Stuttgart, pp. 87–94.

Morgan, K., 2012. 'Theriomorphism and the Composite Soul in Plato', in C. Collobert, P. Destrée and F. J. Gonzalez, eds., *Plato and Myth. Studies in the Use and Status of Platonic Myths*, Leiden, pp. 323–42.

Morgan, L., 2018. 'Play, Ritual and Transformation: Sports, Animals and Manhood in Egyptian and Aegean Art', in C. Renfrew, I. Morley and M. Boyd, eds., *Ritual, Play and Belief, in Evolution and Early Human Societies*, Cambridge, pp. 211–36.

Morris, C. and A. Peatfield, 2022. 'Bodies in Ecstasy: Shamanic Elements in Minoan Religion', in D. L. Stein, S. K. Costello and K. P. Foster, eds., *The Routledge Companion to Ecstatic Experience in the Ancient World*, Abingdon, pp. 264–83.

Morrissette, J. J., 2014. 'Zombies, International Relations, and the Production of Danger: Critical Security Studies versus the Living Dead', *Studies in Popular Culture*, 36.2, pp. 1–27.

Mucznik, S., 2011. 'Musicians and Musical Instruments in Roman and Early Byzantine Mosaics of the Land of Israel: Sources, Precursors and Significance', *Gerión*, 29.1, pp. 265–86.

Mulvey, L., 1975. 'Visual Pleasure and Narrative Cinema', *Screen*, 16.3, pp. 6–18.

Munn, M. H., 2006. *The Mother of the Gods, Athens, and the Tyranny of Asia: A Study of Sovereignty in Ancient Religion*, Berkeley.

Munson, R. V., 2006. 'An Alternate World: Herodotus and Italy', in C. Dewald and J. Marincola, eds., *The Cambridge Companion to Herodotus*, Cambridge, pp. 257–73.

Murgatroyd, P., 2007. *Mythical Monsters in Classical Literature*, London.

Murphy, T., 2004. *Pliny the Elder's Natural History: The Empire in the Encyclopedia*, Oxford.

Nash, H., 1980. 'Human/Animal Body Imagery: Judgment of Mythological Hybrid (Part-Human, Part-Animal) Figures', *Journal of General Psychology*, 103, pp. 49–108.

Nash, H. and H. Pieszko, 1982. 'The Multidimensional Structure of Mythological Hybrid (Part-Human, Part-Animal) Figures', *The Journal of General Psychology*, 106.1, pp. 35–55.

Nederveen Pieterse, J., 1994. 'Globalization as Hybridisation', *International Sociology*, 9, pp. 161–84.

Neils, J., 2013. 'Salpinx, Snake, and Salamis. The Political Geography of the Pella Hydria', *Hesperia*, 82, pp. 595–613.

Newmyer, S. T., 2014. 'Being the One and Becoming the Other: Animals in Ancient Philosophical Schools', in G. L. Campbell, ed., *The Oxford Handbook of Animals in Classical Thought and Life*, Oxford, pp. 507–35.

Newmyer, S. T., 2017. *The Animal and the Human in Ancient and Modern Thought. The 'Man Alone of Animals' Concept*, Abington.

Nichols, A., 2011. *Ctesias on India: Translation and Commentary*, London.

Nielsen, I., 2002. *Cultic Theatres and Ritual Drama*, Aarhus.

Ninck, M., 1921. *Die Bedeutung des Wassers im Kult und Leben der Alten: Eine symbolgeschichtliche Untersuchung*. Philologus Suppl. 14.2, Leipzig.

Noble, A., A. Alexakis and R. P. H. Greenfield, eds., 2022. *Animal Fables of the Courtly Mediterranean: The Eugenian Recension of* Stephanites and Ichnelates, Cambridge, MA.

Noe, A., 2004. *Action in Perception*, Cambridge.
O'Brien, M. J., 1964. 'Orestes and the Gorgon: Euripides' *Electra*', *AJP*, 85.1, pp. 13–39.
O'Donnell, C., 2011. 'Fugly', *Log*, 22, *The Absurd*, pp. 90–100.
Oberhuber, K., 1974. 'Der Kyklop Polyphem in altorientalistischer Sicht', *Innsbrucker Beiträge zur Sprachwissenschaft*, 12, pp. 147–53.
Ogden, D., 2009. *Magic, Witchcraft, and Ghosts in the Greek and Roman Worlds: A Sourcebook* (2nd ed.), Oxford.
Olender, M., 1985. 'Aspects de Baubô: Textes et contexts antiques', *Revue de l'histoire des religions*, 202.1, pp. 3–55.
Oliver, D. L., 1989. *Native Cultures of the Pacific Islands*, Honolulu.
Olszewski, M. T., 2011. 'The Orpheus Funerary Mosaic from Jerusalem in the Archaeological Museum at Istanbul', in M. Şahin, ed., *Mosaics of Turkey and Parallel Developments in the Rest of the Ancient and Medieval World: Questions of Iconography, Style and Technique from the Beginnings of Mosaic until the Late Byzantine Era*, Istanbul, pp. 655–64.
Oppenheim, A. L., 1964. *Ancient Mesopotamia: Portrait of a Dead Civilization*, Chicago.
Oren, E. D., 1984., 'Migdol: A New Fortress on the Edge of the Eastern Nile Delta', *Bulletin of the American Schools of Oriental Research*, 256, pp. 7–44.
Osborne, R. G., 1988. 'Death Revisited; Death Revised. The Death of the Artist in Archaic and Classical Greece', *Art History*, 11.1, pp. 1–16.
Osborne, R. G., 1994. 'Framing the Centaur: Reading Fifth-Century Architectural Sculpture', in S. Goldhill and R. Osborne, eds., *Art and Text in Ancient Greek Culture* (Cambridge Studies in New Art History and Criticism), Cambridge, pp. 52–84
Osborne, R., 1998. 'Early Greek Colonization? The Nature of Greek settlement in the West', in N. Fisher and H. van Wees, eds., *Archaic Greece: New Approaches and New Evidence*, London, pp. 251–69.
Osborne, R., 2001. 'The Use of Abuse: Semonides 7', *PCPS*, 47, pp. 47–64.
Osborne, R., 2018. *The Transformation of Athens: Painted Pottery and the Creation of Classical Greece*, Princeton.
Ostwald, M., 2009. *Language and History in Ancient Greek Culture*, Philadelphia.
Özdoğan, A., 1999. 'Çayönü', in M. Özdoğan and N. Başgelen, eds., *Neolithic in Turkey*, Istanbul, pp. 35–63.
Özdoğan, M. and A. Özdoğan, 1998. 'Buildings of Cult and The Cult of Buildings', in G. Arsebük, M. Mellink and W. Schirmer, eds., *Light on Top of the Black Hill*, Istanbul, pp. 581–93.
Pache, C. O., 2004. *Baby and Child Heroes in Ancient Greece*, Chicago.
Padgett, J. M., 2003. 'Horse Men: Centaurs and Satyrs in Early Greek Art', in J. M. Padgett, ed., *The Centaur's Smile: The Human Animal in Early Greek Art*. New Haven, pp. 3–48.

Paga, J., 2015. 'The Claw-Tooth Chisel and the Hekatompedon Problem', *MDAI. Ath.Abt.*, (2012–13) 127–8, pp. 169–204.

Palagia, O. and R. S. Bianchi, 1994, 'Who Invented the Claw Chisel?' *Oxford Journal of Archaeology* 13.2, pp. 185–97.

Palaiologou, H., 1995. '"Minoan Dragons" on a Sealstone from Mycenae', *BICS* Suppl. 63, pp. 195–9.

Papadopoulos, J. K., 1997. 'Phantom Euboeans', *Journal of Mediterranean Archaeology*, 10.2, pp. 191–219.

Papalexandrou, N., 2010. 'Are there Hybrid Visual Cultures?' *Ars Orientalis*, 38, pp. 31–50.

Papalexandrou, N., 2016. 'From Lake Van to the Guadalquivir: Monsters and Vision in the Pre-Classical Mediterranean', in J. Aruz and M. Seymour, eds., *Assyria to Iberia. Art and Culture in the Iron Age*, New York, pp. 263–72.

Papantoniou, G., 2013. 'Cypriot Autonomous Polities at the Crossroads of Empire: The Imprint of a Transformed Islandscape in the Classical and Hellenistic Periods', *BASOR*, 370, pp. 169–205.

Papantoniou, G. and G. Bourogiannis, 2018. 'The Cypriot Extra-Urban Sanctuary as a Central Place: The Case of Agia Irini', *Land*, 7, 139, pp. 1–27.

Papaspyridi-Karusu, S., 1954–5. 'Alkamenes und das Hephaisteion', *Ath. Mitt.*, 69/70, pp. 67–94.

Parker, R., 1988. 'Myths of Early Athens', in J. N. Bremmer, ed., *Interpretations of Greek Mythology*, London, pp. 187–214.

Parker, R. and P. M. Steele, 2021. 'Introduction', in R. Parker and P. M. Steele, eds., *The Early Greek Alphabets: Origin, Diffusion, Uses*, Oxford, pp. 1–18.

Parlasca, K., 1975. 'Zur archaisch-griechischen Kleinplastik aus Ägypten', *Wandlungen. Studien zur antiken und neueren Kunst*, Ernst Homann-Wedeking gewidmet, Waldsassen-Bayern, pp. 57–61.

Parsons, C. O., 1977. 'The Refining of Lamia', *The Wordsworth Circle*, Spring, 8.2, pp. 183–92.

Patera, M., 2015. *Figures grecques de l'épouvante de l'antiquité au present: Peurs enfantines et adultes*, Leiden.

Pavda, G., 2018. 'Joseph/Josephine's Angst: Sensational Hermaphroditism in Tod Browning's *Freaks*', *Social Semiotics*, 28.1, pp. 108–24.

Pawlett, W., 2016. *Georges Bataille: The Sacred and Society*, Abingdon.

Peacock, M., 2011. 'Rehabilitating Homer's Phoenicians: On Some Ancient and Modern Prejudices against Trade', *Ancient Society*, 41, pp. 1–29.

Peled, I., 2014. '*assinnu* and *kurgarrû* Revisited', *Journal of Near Eastern Studies*, 73.2, pp. 283–97.

Pepys, S., 2000. *The Diary of Samuel Pepys: A New and Complete Transcription*, ed. Robert Latham and William Matthews, 2 vols., London.

Perry, B. E., 1952. *Aesopica*, Urbana.

Perry, H. and S. Perris, 2019. 'Classical Reception in New Zealand Literature', *Journal of New Zealand Literature*, 37.1, pp. 159–86.

Pestarino, B., 2020. 'A Cypriot City-Kingdom for Sale: Looking for Political Implications in Two Tamassian Bilingual Inscriptions', *Kadmos* 59, pp. 63–76.

Peters, J. and K. Schmidt, 2004. 'Animals in the Symbolic World of Pre-Pottery Neolithic Göbekli Tepe, South-Eastern Turkey: A Preliminary Assessment', *Anthropozoologica* 39.1, pp. 179–218.

Petit, T., 2011. *Oedipe et le Chérubin: Les Sphinx levantins, cypriotes et grecs comme gardiens d'Immortalité*, Fribourg.

Petit, T., 2013. 'The Sphinx on the Roof: The Meaning of the Greek Temple Acroteria', *ABSA*, 108, pp. 201–34.

Petit, T., 2019. 'Les sphinx sur le Vase François et l'Olpè Chigi: L'héroïsation des élites', *Mélanges de l'Ecole française de Rome*, 131.2 (posted online 22 April 2020).

Petridou, G., 2013. '"Blessed Is He, Who Has Seen": The Power of Ritual Viewing and Ritual Framing in Eleusis', *Helios*, 40.1–2, pp. 309–41.

Picard, C., 1938. 'Néreides et Sirènes: Observations sur le folklore hellénique de la mer', *Etudes d'archéologie grecque, annales de l'ecole des hautes études de Gand* 2, Gand, pp. 127–53.

Piccione, P. A., 1990. 'Mehen, Mysteries, and Resurrection from the Coiled Serpent', *Journal of the American Research Center in Egypt*, 27, pp. 43–52.

Piccolo, A., 2019. 'Pedon, Son of Amphinnes. A Game of Donors?' *Aegyptus* 99, pp. 163–80.

Pierotti, R., 2020. 'Learning about Extraordinary Beings', *Ethnobiology Letters*, 11.2, special issue: Avian Voices, pp. 44–51.

Piñol Villanueva, A., 2013. 'Halicarnaso y Salmacis: Historia de una communidad greco-caria', in R.-A. Santiago Álvarez and M. Oller Guzmán, eds., *Faventia Supplementa, II: Contacto de poblaciones y extranjería en el mundo griego antiguo: Estudio de fuentes*, Bellaterra, pp. 169–85.

Pittmann, H., 1996. 'Constructing Context. The Gebel el-Arak Knife. Greater Mesopotamia and Egyptian Interaction in the Late Fourth Millennium BCE', in J. S. Cooper and G. M. Schwartz, eds., *The Study of the Ancient Near East in the Twenty-First Century*, Winona Lake, pp. 9–32.

Plazy, G., 2001. *The History of Art in Pictures: Western Art from Prehistory to the Present*, New York.

Pollock, D., 1995. 'Masks and the Semiotics of Identity', *The Journal of the Royal Anthropological Institute*, 1.3, pp. 581–97.

Pommerening, T., 2010. 'βούτυρος *"Flaschenkürbis"* und κουροτόκος im Corpus Hippocraticum, *De sterilibus* 214: Entlehnung und Lehnübersetzung aus dem Ägyptischen', *Glotta*, 86, pp. 40–54.

Pongratz-Leisten, B. and K. Sonik, eds., 2015. *The Materiality of Divine Agency*, Berlin.

Pontani, F., 2014. 'Your First Commitments Tangible Again: Alexandrianism as an Aesthetic Category?' in R. Hunter, A. Rengakos and E. Sistakou, eds., *Hellenistic*

Studies at a Crossroads: Exploring Texts, Contexts and Metatexts, Berlin, pp. 157–84.

Porada, E., 1948. 'The Cylinder Seals of the Late Cypriote Bronze Age', *AJA*, 52.1, pp. 178–98.

Porada, E., 1980. 'The Iconography of Death in Mesopotamia in the Early Second Millennium BC', in B. Alster, ed., *Death in Mesopotamia: Papers Read at the XXVIe Rencontre Assyriologique Internationale. Mesopotamia, Copenhagen Studies in Assyriology*. 8, Copenhagen, pp. 259–70.

Posèq, A. W. G., 2001. 'Ingres' Oedipal "Oedipus and the Sphinx"', *Notes in the History of Art*, 21.1, pp. 24–32.

Posthumus, L., 2011. *Hybrid Monsters in the Classical World*. Unpublished MPhil thesis, University of Stellenbosch. https://scholar.sun.ac.za/items/55af013c-7239-42c8-8cd0-003bb05161a8.

Powell, B. B., 1991, *Homer and the Origin of the Greek Alphabet*, Cambridge.

Priestley, J., 2014. *Herodotus and Hellenistic Culture: Literary Studies in the Reception of the Histories*, Oxford.

Pritchard, J. B., 1955. *Ancient Near Eastern Texts Relating to the Old Testament with Supplement*, Princeton.

Propp, V., 1927. *Morphology of the Folktale*, trans. Laurence Scott, 2nd ed. (1968), Austin.

Puchelt, W., 2018. 'Studien zur Geschichte und Sprache des traditionellen Schattentheaters im Mittelmeerraum', *Mediterranean Language Review*, 25, pp. 97–178.

Pütz, B., 2020. 'Straight from the Horse's Mouth: Speaking Animals in Aristophanes' Comedy', in H. Schmalzgruber, ed., *Speaking Animals in Ancient Literature*, Heidelberg, pp. 159–89.

Qureshi, S., 2004. 'Displaying Sara Baartman, the "Hottentot Venus"', *Hist. Sci.*, 62, pp. 233–57.

Raaflaub, K. A., 2004. 'Archaic Greek Aristocrats as Carriers of Cultural Interaction', in R. Rollinger and C. Ulf, eds., *Commerce and Monetary Systems in the Ancient World. Means of Transmission and Cultural Interaction*, Stuttgart, pp. 197–217.

Rabkin, E. S., 2004. 'Science Fiction and the Future of Criticism', *PMLA*, 119.3, Special Topic: Science Fiction and Literary Studies: The Next Millennium, pp. 457–73.

Radcliffe-Brown, A. R., 1926. 'The Rainbow-Serpent Myth of Australia', *The Journal of the Royal Anthropological Institute of Great Britain and Ireland*, 56, pp. 19–25.

Raulwing, P., 2006. 'The Kikkuli Text (CTH 284): Some Interdisciplinary Remarks on Hittite Training Texts for Chariot Horses in the Second Half of the 2nd Millennium BC', in A. Gardiesen, ed., *Les Équidés dans le monde méditerranéen antique: Actes du colloque organisé par l'École française d'Athènes, le Centre Camille Jullian, et l'UMR 5140 du CNRS, Athènes, 26–28 Novembre 2003*. Lattes:

Éd. de l'Association pour le développement de l'archéologie en Languedoc-Rousillon, pp. 61–75.

Recht, L. and C. E. Morris, 2021. 'Chariot Kraters and Horse–Human Relations in Late Bronze Age Greece and Cyprus', *ABSA*, 116, pp. 95–132.

Redfield, J., 1985. 'Herodotus the Tourist', *CP*, 90, pp. 97–118.

Redfield, J., 2003. *The Locrian Maidens: Love and Death in Greek Italy*, Princeton, NJ.

Reemes, D. M., 2015. *The Egyptian Ouroboros: An Iconological and Theological Study*, UCLA. Unpublished doctoral dissertation. https://escholarship.org/uc/item/6c0153p7.

Regan, T., 1983. *The Case for Animal Rights*, London.

Reger, G., 2014. 'Ethnic Identities, Borderlands, and Hybridity', in J. McInerney, ed., *A Companion to Ethnicity in the Ancient Mediterranean*, Oxford, pp. 112–26.

Rehak, P., 1995a. 'The "Genius" in Late Bronze Age Glyptic: The Later Evolution of an Aegean Cult Figure', *Corpus der Minoischen und Mykenischen Siegel*, 5, pp. 215–31.

Rehak, P., 1995b. 'The Use and Destruction of Minoan Stone Bull's Head Rhyta', in R. Laffineur and W.-D. Niemeier, eds., *Politeia: Society and State in the Aegean Bronze Age*, Liège, pp. 435–59.

Rehak, P. and J. G. Younger, 1998. 'Review of Aegean Prehistory VII: Neopalatial, Final Palatial, and Postpalatial Crete', *AJA*, 102, pp. 91–173.

Rhodes, P. J. and R. Osborne, 2003. *Greek Historical Inscriptions: 404–323 BC*, Oxford.

Rice E. E., 1983. *The Grand Procession of Ptolemy Philadelphus*. Oxford.

Richardson, S., 1999. 'Libya Domestica: Libyan Trade and Society on the Eve of the Invasions of Egypt', *Journal of the American Research Center in Egypt*, 36, pp. 149–64.

Ridderstad, M., 2009. 'Evidence of Minoan Astronomy and Calendrical Practices', http://arxiv.org/ftp/arxiv/papers/0910/0910.4801.pdf.

Rieber, A. J., 2003. 'Changing Concepts and Constructions of Frontiers: A Comparative Historical Approach', *Ab Imperio*, 1, pp. 23–46.

Ringheim, H. L., 2020. 'Hera and the Sea. Decoding Dedications at the Samian Heraion', *Studia Hercynia*, 22.1, pp. 11–25.

Robertson, N., 1985. 'The Origin of the Panathenaea', *Rh.M.*, 128, pp. 231–95.

Robertson, V. L. D., 2013. 'The Beast Within: Anthrozoomorphic Identity and Alternative Spirituality in the Online Therianthropy Movement', *Nova Religio*, 16.3, pp. 7–30.

Roblee, M., 2018. 'Performing Circles in Ancient Egypt from Mehen to Ouroboros', *Preternature: Critical and Historical Studies on the Preternatural*, 7.2, pp. 133–53.

Rohde, E., 1877. *Der Griechische Roman und seine Vorläufer*, Leipzig.

Roller, L., 1999. *In Search of God the Mother: The Cult of Anatolian Cybele*, Berkeley.

Romano, A. J., 2009. 'The Invention of Marriage: Hermaphroditus and Salmacis at Halicarnassus and in Ovid', *CQ* ns. 59.2, pp. 543–61.

Romm, J., 1992. *Edges of the Earth in Ancient Thought: Geography, Exploration, and Fiction*, Princeton, NJ.

Rönnberg, M., 2020. 'Überlegungen zu Eleusis in geometrischer und früharchaischer Zeit. Mit einem Anhang zu eleusinischen 'Stempelidolen' in Tübingen', *BABESCH*, 95, pp. 47–68.

Rönnberg, M., 2021. *Athen und Attika vom 11. bis zum frühen 6. Jh. v. Chr.: Siedlungsgeschichte, politische Institutionalisierungs- und gesellschaftliche Formierungsprozesse*. Rahden.

Root, M. C., 2002. 'Animals in the Art of Ancient Iran', in B. J. Collins, ed., *A History of the Animal World in the Ancient Near East*, Leiden, pp. 169–211.

Rose, D. B., 2000. *Dingo Makes Us Human. Life and Land in an Australian Aboriginal Culture*. Cambridge.

Rosen, R. M., 1990. 'Poetry and Sailing in Hesiod's Works and Days', *CA*, 9.1, pp. 99–113.

Rosenberg, J. L., 2015. 'The Masks of Orthia: Form, Function and the Origins of Theatre', *ABSA*, 110.1, pp. 247–61.

Rosenstein, N., 2012. *Rome and the Mediterranean 290 to 146 BC: The Imperial Republic*, Edinburgh.

Rosivach, V. J., 1987. 'Autochthony and the Athenians', *CQ*, 37, pp. 294–306.

Rothwell, K. S., 2007. *Nature, Culture and the Origins of Greek Comedy: A Study of Animal Choruses*, Cambridge.

Rothwell, K. S., 2020. 'The Animal Voices of Greek Comic Choruses', in H. Schmalzgruber, ed., *Speaking Animals in Ancient Literature*, Heidelberg, pp. 189–296

Rotstein, A., 2016. *Literary History in the Parian Marble*, Cambridge, MA.

Rousseau, J.-J., 1927. *Reveries of the Solitary Walker*, trans. J. G. Fletcher, New York.

Roy, J., 2014. 'Autochthony in Ancient Greece', in J. McInerney, ed., *A Companion to Ethnicity in the Ancient Mediterranean*, Oxford, pp. 241–55.

Rozenkrantz, K., 1853. *Ästhetik des Häßlichen*, Königsberg.

Ruck, C. A. P., 2016. 'The Wolves of War. Evidence of an Ancient Cult of Warrior Lykanthropy', *NeuroQuantology*, 14.3, pp. 544–66.

Ruffing, K., 2011. 'Ktesias' Indienbilder', in J. Wiesehöfer, R. Rollinger, G. B. Lanfranchi, eds., *Ktesias' Welt/Ctesias' World*. Wiesbaden, pp. 351–66.

Rundin, J. S., 2004. 'Pozo Moro, Child Sacrifice, and the Greek Legendary Tradition', *Journal of Biblical Literature*, 123, pp. 425–47.

Runia, E., 2006. 'Presence', *History and Theory*, 45, pp. 1–29.

Rutherford, I., ed., 2016. *Graeco-Egyptian Interactions: Literature, Translation, and Culture, 500 BC–AD 300*, Oxford.

Rutherford, I., 2000. 'Theoria and Darśan: Pilgrimage and Vision in Greece and India', *CQ*, 50.1, pp. 133–46.

Rutledge, S., 2012. *Ancient Rome as a Museum: Power, Identity, and the Culture of Collecting*, Oxford.

Ryan, D., 2015. *Animal Theory. A Critical Introduction*, Edinburgh.

Ryan, M.-L., 2019. 'From Possible Worlds to Storyworlds: On the Worldness of Narrative Representation', in A. Bell and M.-L. Ryan, eds., *Possible Worlds Theory and Contemporary Narratology*, Lincoln, pp. 62–87.

Sagiv, I., 2018. *Representations of Animals on Greek and Roman Engraved Gems: Meanings and Interpretations*, Oxford.

Sahlins, K., 2004. *Apologies to Thucydides. Understanding History as Culture and Vice Versa*, Chicago.

Sainge, G., 1897. *Monaco: Ses Origins et son Histoire*. Paris.

Sallares, R., 1991. *The Ecology of the Ancient Greek World*, Ithaca.

Salowey, C., 1994. 'Herakles and the Waterworks in the Peloponnesos: Mycenaean Dams, Classical Fountains, and Roman Aqueducts', in K. Sheedy, ed., *Archaeology in the Peloponnese: New Excavations and Research*. Oxford, pp. 77–94.

Sambin, C., 1989. 'Génie Minoen et Génie Égyptien. Un emprunt raisonné', *Bulletin de Correspondance Hellénique*, 113.1, pp. 77–96.

Sanders, G. D. R., 2010. 'The Sacred Spring: Landscape and Traditions', in S. Friesen, D. Schowalter, and J. Walters, eds., *Corinth in Context*, Leiden, pp. 365–89.

Sansone, D., 1997. 'Hermippus, Fragment 22 Wehrli', *ICS*, 22, pp. 51–64.

Santini, M., 2016. 'A Multi-Ethnic City shapes its Past: The "Pride of Halikarnassos" and the memory of Salmakis', *Ann Sc Norm Sup Pisa, Cl. Lett. E Filos. Quaderni*, 8.1, pp. 3–35.

Sapir, J. D., 1977. 'Fecal Animals: An Example of Complementary Totemism', *Man*, 12.1, pp. 1–21.

Savage, T. S. and J. Wyman, 1847. 'Notice of the External Characters and Habits of Troglodytes Gorilla, a New Species of Orang from the Gaboon River', *Boston Journal of Natural History*, 5.4, pp. 417–42.

Saxenhouse, A. W., 1992. *Fear of Diversity. The Birth of Political Science in Ancient Greek Thought*, Chicago.

Schama, S., 1995. *Landscape and Memory*, London.

Schepens, G. and K. Delcroix, 1996. 'Ancient Paradoxography: Origin, Evolution, Production and Reception', in O. Pecere and A. Stramaglia, eds., *La letteratura di consumo nel mondo greco-latino*. Atti del convegno internazionale, Cassino, 14–17 settembre 1994, Cassino, pp. 375–460.

Schmalzer, S., 2015. *Red Revolution, Green Revolution: Scientific Farming in Socialist China*, Berlin.

Schmid, W. and O. Stählin, 1920–4, *Griechische Literaturgeschichte*, Munich.

Schmidt, K., 2010. 'Göbekli Tepe – The Stone Age Sanctuaries: New Results of Ongoing Excavations with a Special Focus on Sculptures and High Reliefs', *Documenta Praehistorica*, 37, pp. 239–56.

Schmitt, M. L., 1966. 'Bellerophon and the Chimaera in Archaic Greek Art', *AJA*, 70, pp. 341–7.

Scholten, J. B., 2000. *The Politics of Plunder: Aitolians and Their Koinon in the Early Hellenistic Era, 279-217 BC*, Berkeley.

Seaford, R., 1984. *Euripides, 'Cyclops'*, Oxford.

Sealey, R., 1987. *The Athenian Republic: Democracy or the Rule of Law*. University Park.

Secomska, K., 1975. 'The Miniature Cycle in the Sandomierz Pantheon and the Medieval Iconography of Alexander's Indian Campaign', *Journal of the Warburg and Courtauld Institutes*, 38, pp. 53–71.

Sedley, D., 2016. 'Empedoclean Superorganisms', *Rhizomata*, 4.1, pp. 111–25.

Seeberg, A., 1971, *Corinthian Komos Vases*. London.

Segal, C., 1983. 'Sirius and the Pleiades in Alcman's Louvre Partheneion', *Mnemosyne*, 36, pp. 260–75.

Segal, C., 1986. 'War, Death and Savagery in Lucretius: The Beasts of Battle in 5.1308-49', *Ramus*, 15, pp. 1–34.

Semerano, G., 1994. *Le Origini della Cultura Europea: Dizionario etimologico: Basi semitiche delle lingue indoeuropee*, vol. II, Florence.

Semerano, G., 2005. *L'infinito: Un equivoco millenario: Le antiche civiltà del Vicino Oriente e le origini del pensiero Greco*, Milan.

Shapland, A., 2013, 'Jumping to Conclusions: Bull-Leaping in Minoan Crete', *Society & Animals*, 21, pp. 194–207.

Shaw, B. D., 1982-3. '"Eaters of Flesh, Drinkes of Milk." The Ancient Mediterranean Ideology of the Pastoral Nomad', *Ancient Society*, 13/14, pp. 5–31.

Shaw, C., 2014. *Satyric Play: The Evolution of Greek Comedy and Satyr Drama*, Oxford.

Shepard, K., 1941. *The Fish-Tailed Monster in Greek and Etruscan Art*, New York.

Shepherd, G., 2005. 'Dead Men Tell No Tales: Ethnic Diversity in Sicilian Colonies and the Evidence of the Cemeteries', *Oxford Journal of Archaeology*, 24, pp. 115–36.

Shepherd, G., 2009. 'Greek "Colonisation" in Sicily and the West: Some Problems of Evidence and Interpretation 25 years on', *Pallas: Revue d'études antiques*, 79, pp. 15–25.

Shepherd, G., 2011. 'Hybridity and Hierarchy: Cultural Identity and Social Mobility in Archaic Sicily', in M. Gleba and H. W. Horsnæs, eds., *Communicating Identity in Italic Iron Age Communities*, Oxford, pp. 113–29.

Sheppard, A., 2014. *The Poetics of Phantasia: Imagination in Ancient Aesthetics*, London.

Shipman, P., 2015. 'When Is a Wolf not a Wolf?', in *The Invaders: How Humans and their Dogs Drove Neanderthals to Extinction*, Cambridge, MA, pp. 214–25.

Sifakis, G. M., 1971. *Parabasis and Animal Choruses*, London.

Sillitoe, P., 2003. *Managing Animals in New Guinea: Preying the Game in the Highlands*, London.

Silva, I., 2020. 'Is a Praying Fox a Humanized Animal or a Human in an Animal Body? A Cognitive Reading of Archilochus' Fox and Eagle Epode (*frr.* 172–181 W)', in H. Schmalzgruber, ed., *Speaking Animals in Ancient Literature*, Heidelberg, pp. 23–54.

Simadiraki-Grimshaw, A., 2010. 'Minoan Animal–Human Hybridity', in D. B. Counts, ed., *The Master of Animals in Old World Iconography*, Budapest, pp. 93–106.

Simon, E., 1997. 'Silenoi', *LIMC* 8, 1108–33.

Singer, P., 1989. 'All Animals are Equal', in T. Regan and P. Singer, eds., *Animal Rights and Human Obligations*. Englewood Cliffs, NJ, pp. 148–62.

Singer, P., 2009. *Animal Liberation*. 4th ed., New York.

Skinner, J. E., 2012. *The Invention of Greek Ethnography: From Homer to Herodotus*, Oxford.

Skuse, M. L., 2018. 'The Arcesilas Cup in Context: Greek Interactions with Late Period Funerary Art', *ABSA* 113, pp. 221–49.

Slater, W. J., 1976. 'Symposium at Sea', *HSCP* 80, pp. 162–3.

Smith, A., 2007. 'Komos Growing up among Satyrs and Children', *Hesperia Supplements*, Vol. 41, *Constructions of Childhood in Ancient Greece and Italy*, Princeton, pp. 153–71.

Smith, H., 1992. 'The Making of Egypt: A Review of the Influence of Susa and Sumer on Upper Egypt and Lower Nubia in the 4th Millennium BC', in R. Friedman and B. Adams, eds., *The Followers of Horus. Studies Dedicated to Michael Allen Hoffman*, Oxford, pp. 235–46.

Smith, S. D., 2013. 'Monstrous Love? Erotic Reciprocity in Aelian's *De natura animalium*', in E. Sanders, C. Thumiger, C. Carey and N. J. Lowe, eds., *Erôs in Ancient Greece*, Oxford, pp. 74–90.

Soldi, S., 2012. '"Chimaeric Animals" in the Ancient Near East', in G. C. Cianferoni, M. Iozzo and E. Setari, eds., *Myth, Allegory, Emblem: The Many Lives of the Chimaera of Arezzo: Proceedings of the International Colloquium Malibu, The J. Paul Getty Museum (December 4–5, 2009)*, Rome, pp. 91–111.

Soles, J., 1995. 'The Functions of a Cosmological Center: Knossos in Palatial Crete', in R. Laffineur and W.-D. Niemeier, eds., *Politeia: Society and State in the Aegean Bronze Age*, Liège, pp. 404–14.

Sommer, M., 2012. 'Heart of Darkness? Post-Colonial Theory and the Transformation of the Mediterranean', *Ancient West & East*, 11, pp. 235–45.

Sonik, K., 2015. 'Divine (Re-)Presentation: Authoritative Images and a Pictorial Stream of Tradition in Mesopotamia', in B. Pongratz-Leisten and K. Sonik, eds., *The Materiality of Divine Agency*, Berlin, pp. 142–95.

Sorabji, R., 1993. *Animal Minds and Human Morals: The Origins of the Western Debate*, London.

Sperber, D., 1975. 'Pourquoi les animaux parfaits, les hybrides et les monstres sont-ils bons à penser symboliquement?' *L'Homme*, 15.2, pp. 5–34.

Squire, M., 2016. 'Introductory Reflections: Making Sense of Ancient Sight', in M. Squire, ed., *Sight and the Ancient Senses*, London, pp. 1–35.

Srinivasan, D. M., 1975/1976. 'The So-Called Proto-Siva Seal from Mohenjo-Daro: An Iconological Assessment', *Archives of Asian Art*, 29, pp. 47–58.

Srinivasan, D. M., 1997. *Many Heads, Arms, and Eyes. Origin, Meaning, and Form of Multiplicity in Indian Art*, Leiden.

Stafford, E., 2011. 'Clutching the Chickpea: Private Pleasures of the Bad Boyfriend', in S. D. Lambert, ed., *Sociable Man: Essays on Ancient Greek Social Behaviour in Honour of Nick Fischer*, Swansea, pp. 337–63.

Stanner, W., 1979. *White Man Got No Dreaming*, Canberra.

Stannish, S. M. and C. M. Doran, 2013. 'Magic and Vampirism in Philostratus's Life of Apollonius of Tyana and Bram Stoker's Dracula', *Preternature: Critical and Historical Studies on the Preternatural*, 2.2, pp. 113–38.

Steele, P. M., 2019. *Writing and Society in Ancient Cyprus*, Cambridge.

Steiner, D., 2015. 'From the Demonic to the Divine: Cauldrons, Choral Dancer and Encounters with the Gods', in S. Estienne, V. Huet, F. Lissarague and F. Prost, eds., *Figures de dieux: Construire le divin en images*, Rennes, pp. 153–74.

Stephens, S. A., 2003. *Seeing Double: Intercultural Poetics in Ptolemaic Alexandria*, Berkeley.

Stephens, S. A., 2016. 'Plato's Egyptian *Republic*', in I. Rutherford, ed., *Graeco-Egyptian Interactions Literature, Translation, and Culture, 500 BC–AD 300*, Oxford, pp. 41–59.

Stoneman, R., 2019. *The Greek Experience of India: From Alexander to the Indo-Greeks*, Princeton.

Storey, I., 1998. 'Poets, Politicians and Perverts: Personal Humour in Aristophanes', *Classics Ireland*, 5, pp. 85–134.

Streck, M. P., 2003. 'Oannes', in O.E. Dietz, ed., *Reallexikon der Assyriologie und Vorderasiatischen Archäologie* (vol. 10), Berlin, pp. 1–3.

Strøm, I., 1992. 'Obeloi of Pre-or Proto-Monetary Value in the Greek Sanctuaries', in T. Linders and B. Alroth, eds., *Economics of Cult in the Ancient Greek World. Proceedings of the Uppsala Symposium 1990* (Boreas: Uppsala Studies in Ancient Mediterranean and Near Eastern Civilizations 21), Uppsala, pp. 41–51.

Stronach, D., 1978. *Pasargadae: A Report on the Excavations Conducted by the British Institute of Persian Studies from 1961 to 1963*, Oxford.

Strong, A. K., 2010. 'Mules in Herodotus: The Destiny of Half-Breeds', *CW*, 103.4, pp. 455–64.

Strootman, R., ed., 2019. *Empires of the Sea: Maritime Power Networks in World History*, Leiden.

Stroszeck, J., 2010. 'Das Heiligtum Des Tritopatores Im Kerameikos Von Athen', in H. Frielinghaus and J. Stroszeck, eds., *Neue Forschungen zu griechischen Städten und Heiligtümern: Festschrift für Burkhard Wesenberg zum 65. Geburtstag: Beiträge zur Archäologie Griechenlands* Bd. 1, Münster, pp. 55-83, taf. 25-33.

Stroud, R. S., 1968. *Drakon's Law on Homicide*, Univ. Cal. Pub. Classical Studs. 3, Berkeley.

Surbeck, M. and G. Hohmann, 2008. 'Primate Hunting by Bonobos at LuiKotale, Salonga National Park', *Current Biology* 18.19, pp. 1-2.

Surtees, A., 2014. 'Satyrs as Women and Maenads as Men: Transvestites and Transgression in Dionysian Worship', in A. Avramidou and D. Demetriou, eds., *Approaching the Ancient Artifact: Representation, Narrative, and Function*, Berlin, pp. 281-93.

Süss, W., 1910. *Ethos: Studien zur älteren griechischen Rhetorik*, Leipzig.

Suter, A., 2015. 'The Anasyrma: Baubo, Medusa, and the Gendering of Obscenity', in D. Dutsch and A. Suter, eds., *Ancient Obscenities: Their Nature and Use in the Ancient Greek and Roman Worlds*, Ann Arbor, pp. 21-43.

Sutton, P., 2003. *Native Title in Australia: An Ethnographic Perspective*, Cambridge.

Svenbro, J., 1993. *Phrasikleia: An Anthropology of Reading in Ancient Greece*, Ithaca.

Swancutt, D. M., 2007. '*Still* before Sexuality: "Greek" Androgyny, the Roman Imperial Politics of Masculinity and the Roman Invention of the *Tribas*', in T. Penner and C. Vander Stickele, eds., *Mapping Gender in Ancient Religious Discourses*, Leiden, pp. 11-62.

Sweetman, R., 2003. 'The Roman Mosaics of the Knossos Valley', *ABSA* 98, pp. 517-47.

Szabo, M., 1994. *Archaic Terracottas of Boeotia*, Rome.

Szegedy-Maszak, A., 1978. 'Legends of the Greek Lawgivers', *GRBS* 19, pp. 199-209.

Szepessy, V. L., 2014. *The Marriage Maker. The Pergamon Hermaphrodite as the God Hermaphroditos, Divine Ideal and Erotic Object*. Unpublished Master of Arts thesis: University of Oslo. https://core.ac.uk/download/pdf/30901964.pdf.

Sztybel, D., 2006. 'Can the Treatment of Animals Be Compared to the Holocaust?' *Ethics and the Environment*, 11.1, pp. 97-132.

Tamvaki, A., 1974. 'The Seals and Sealings from the Citadel House Area: A Study in Mycenaean Glyptic and Iconography', *BSA* 69, pp. 259-94.

Tandy, D. W., 1997. *Warriors into Traders: The Power of the Market in Early Greece*, Berkeley.

Tartaron, T. F., 2013. *Maritime Networks in the Mycenaean World*, Cambridge.

Thomas, R., 2021. 'Writing and Pre-Writing in Early Archaic Methone and Eretria', in R. Parker and P. M. Steele, eds., *The Early Greek Alphabets: Origin, Diffusion, Uses*, Oxford, pp. 58-73.

Thompson, W. R., 2004. 'Complexity, Diminishing Marginal Returns, and Serial Mesopotamian Fragmentation', *Journal of World-Systems Research*, 10.3, pp. 613–52.

Thumiger, C., 2014. 'Metamorphosis: Human into Animal', in G. L. Campbell, ed., *The Oxford Handbook of Animals in Classical Thought and Life*, Oxford, pp. 384–413.

Tookey, H., 2004. '"The Fiend that Smites with a Look": The Monstrous/Menstruous Woman and the Danger of the Gaze in Oscar Wilde's *Salomé*', *Literature and Theology*, 18.1, pp. 23–37.

Topper, K., 2007. 'Perseus, the Maiden Medusa, and the Imagery of Abduction', *Hesperia* 76.1, pp. 73–105.

Topper, K., 2010. 'Maidens, Fillies and the Death of Medusa on a Seventh century Pithos', *JHS*, 130, pp. 109–19.

Topper, K., 2012. *The Imagery of the Athenian Symposium*, Cambridge.

Trahman, C. R., 1952. 'Odysseus' Lies (*Odyssey*, Books 13–19)', *Phoenix*, 6.2, pp. 31–43.

Tran, H., 2018. 'When the Nereid became Mermaid', *Shima*, 12.2, pp. 82–103.

Trevett, J., 1992. *Apollodoros, the son of Pasion*. Oxford.

Trimble, J., 2018. 'Beyond Surprise: the Sleeping Hermaphrodite in the Palazzo Massimo, Rome', in B. Longfellow and E. E. Perry, eds., *Roman Artists, Patrons and Public Consumption: Familiar Works Reconsidered*, Ann Arbor, pp. 13–37.

Tritsch, F. J., 1957. 'The Lycian Chimaira', in Z. V. Togan, ed., *Proceeedings of the Twenty-Second Congress of Orientalists*, vol. II *Communications*. Leiden, pp. 67–77.

Tsiafakis, D., 2003. 'Πέλωρα: Fabulous Creatures and/or Demons of Death', in J. M. Padgett, ed., *The Centaur's Smile: The Human Animal in Early Greek Art*, New Haven, pp. 73–104.

Turner, S., 2016. 'Sight and Death, Seeing the Dead through Ancient Eyes', in M. Squire, ed., *Sight and the Ancient Senses*, London, pp. 143–60.

Uhlig, A., 2018. 'Sailing and singing: Alcaeus at Sea', in F. Budelmann and T. Philips, eds., *Textual Events: Performance and the Lyric in Early Greece*, Oxford, pp. 63–91.

Updegraff, R., 1988. 'The Blemmyes I: The Rise of the Blemmyes and the Roman Withdrawal from Nubia under Diocletian (with Additional Remarks by L. TÖRÖK, Budapest)', in H. Temporini, ed., *Aufstieg und Niedergang der römischen Welt: Geschichte und Kultur Roms im Spiegel der neueren Forschung*. Teil II *Principat*. Bd. 10. Politische Geschichte, Berlin, pp. 44–106.

Updike, J., 1963. *The Centaur*, New York.

Ustinova, Y., 2022. 'Apolline and Dionysian Ecstasy at Delphi', in D. L. Stein, S. K. Costello, K. P. Foster, eds., *The Routledge Companion to Ecstatic Experience in the Ancient World*, Abingdon, pp. 332–50.

Valla, F. R., 2019. 'More on Early Natufian Building 131 at Eynan (Ain Mallaha), Israel', in H. Goldfus, M. I. Gruber, S. Yona and P. Fabian, eds., *'Isaac went out to the field': Studies in Archaeology and Ancient Cultures in Honor of Isaac Gilead*, Oxford, pp. 302–15.

van Alfen, P., 2016. 'The Beginnings of Coinage at Cyrene: Weight Standards, Trade, and Politics', in M. Assolati, ed., *Le monete di Cirene e della Cirenaica nel Mediterraneo: Problemi e prospettive*, Padua, pp. 15–32.

van der Sluijs, M. A. and A. L. Peratt, 2009. 'The Ourobóros as an Auroral Phenomenon', *Journal of Folklore Research*, 46.1, pp. 3–41.

van Dijk, J., 1962. 'Die Inschriftenfunde', *Vorläufiger Bericht über die von dem Deutschen Archäologischen Institut und der Deutschen Orient-Gesellschaft aus Mitteln der Deutschen Forschungsgemeinschaft unternommenen Ausgrabungen in Uruk-Warka* 18, pp. 43–52.

Van Dommelen, P., 2005. 'Colonial Interactions and Hybrid Practices: Phoenician and Carhaginian Settlement in the Ancient Mediterranean', in G. L. Stein, ed., *The Archaeology of Colonial Encounters: Comparative Perspectives*, Santa Fe, pp. 109–41.

Van Rookhuijzen, J. Z., 2021. 'Seascapes of War: Herodotus's Littoral Gaze on the Battle of Salamis', in B. Reitz-Joose, M. W. Makins and C. J. Mackie, eds., *Landscapes of War in Greek and Roman Literature*, London, pp. 213–28.

Vansina, J., 1985. *Oral Tradition as History*, Madison, WI.

Venit, M. C., 1989. 'Herakles and the Hydra in Athens in the First Half of the Sixth Century BC', *Hesperia*, 58.1, pp. 99–113.

Verde, F., 2020. 'Momenti di riflessione sull'animalità nel Kepos: Epicuro, Lucrezio, Ermarco e Polistrato', in S. Gensini, ed., *La voce e il logos: Filosofie dell'animalit: Nella storia delle idee*, Pisa, pp. 53–78.

Verderame, L., 2016. 'Pleiades in Ancient Mesopotamia', *Mediterranean Archaeology and Archaeometry*, 16.4, pp. 109–17.

Vernant, J.-P., 1988. 'The Myth of Prometheus in Hesiod', in *Myth and Society in Ancient Greece*, tr. Janet Lloyd, New York, pp. 183–201.

Vernant, J.-P., 1991. 'Death in the Eyes: Gorgo, Figure of the Other', in F. I. Zeitlin, ed., *Mortals and Immortals: Collected Essays*, Princeton, NJ, pp. 111–38.

Vernant, J.-P. and F. Frontisi-Ducroux, 2006. 'Features of the Mask in Ancient Greece', in J.-P. Vernant and P. Vidal-Naquet, *Myth and Tragedy in Ancient Greece*, trans. Janet Lloyd, Brooklyn.

Versnel, H., 2011. *Coping with the Gods. Wayward Readings in Greek Theology*, Leiden.

Vespa, M., 2020. 'Presenting the Divine in Ancient Greek Tales: Human Voices in Animal Bodies', in H. Schmalzgruber, ed., *Speaking Animals in Ancient Literature*, Heidelberg, pp. 402–25.

Veszy-Wagner, L., 1963. 'The Bearded Man', *American Imago*, 20.2, pp. 133–47.

Villing, A., 2018. 'Wahibreemakhet at Saqqara. The Tomb of a Greek in Egypt', *Zeitschrift für Ägyptische Sprache und Altertumskunde*, 145.2, pp. 174–86.

Villing, A. and U. Schlotzhauer, 2006. 'Naukratis and the Eastern Mediterranean: Past, Present and Future', in A. Villing and U. Schlotzhauer, eds., *Naukratis:*

Greek Diversity in Egypt. Studies in East Greek Pottery and Exchange in the Eastern Mediterranean, London, pp. 1–10.

Virgilio, B., 1988. *Epigrafia e storiografia: Studi di storia antica, Volume 1*, Pisa.

Visintin, M., 1997. 'Di Echidna e di altre femmine anguiformi', *Mètis. Anthropologie des mondes grecs anciens*, 12, pp. 205–21.

Visser, M., 1982. 'Worship Your Enemy: Aspects of the Cult of Heroes in Ancient Greece', *HTR*, 75, pp. 403–28.

Vittmann, G., 2003. *Ägypten und die Fremden im ersten vorchristlichen Jahrtausend*, Mainz.

Vogel, M., 1978. *Chiron, der Kentaur mit der Kithara*, Bonn-Bad Godesberg.

Vogt, K. M., 2017. 'Platon on Hunger and Thirst', *History of Philosophy and Logical Analysis*, 20.1, pp. 103–19.

von Stackelberg, K. T., 2014, 'Garden Hybrids: Hermaphrodite Images in the Roman House', *Class. Antiq.*, 33, 395–426.

Voskos, I. and A. B. Knapp, 2008. 'Cyprus at the End of the Late Bronze Age: Crisis and Colonization or Continuity and Hybridization?' *AJA*, 112, pp. 659–84.

Wade, P., 2005. 'Rethinking Mestizaje: Ideology and Lived Experience', *Journal of Latin American Studies*, 37.2, pp. 239–57.

Waitkus, W., 2002. 'Die Geburt des Harsomtus aus der Blüte. Zur Bedeutung und Funktion einiger Kultgegenstände des Tempels von Dendera', *Studien zur Altägyptischen Kultur*, 30, pp. 373–94.

Waldbaum, J. C., 2002. 'Trade Items or Soldiers' Gear? Cooking Pots from Ashkelon, Israel', in D. Kacharava, M. Faudot and E. Geny, eds., *Autour de la mer Noire: Hommage à Otar Lordkipanidzé*, Paris, pp. 133–40.

Wallace, P. W., 1969. 'Psyttaleia and the Trophies of the Battle of Salamis', *AJA*, 73.3, pp. 293–303.

Warden, P. G., 2012. 'Pinning the Tale on the Chimaera: Hybridity and Sacrifice', in G. C. Cianferoni, M. Iozzo and E. Setari, eds., *Myth, Allegory, Emblem: The Many Lives of the Chimaera of Arezzo; Proceedings of the International Colloquium, Malibu, The J. Paul Getty Museum (December 4–5, 2009)*, Rome, pp. 79–90.

Warner, M., 2007. *Monsters of our own Making: The Peculiar Pleasures of Fear*, Lexington.

Waters, M., 2017. *Ctesias'* Persica *and Its Near Eastern Context*, Madison.

Watson, C., 2015. 'A Sociologist Walks into a Bar (and Other Academic Challenges): Towards a Methodology of Humour', *Sociology*, 49.3, pp. 407–21.

Webb, J. and J. Weingarten, 2012. 'Seals and Seal Use: Markers of Social, Political and Economic Transformations on Two Islands', G. Cadogan, M. Iacovou, K. Kopaka and J. Whitley, eds., *Parallel Lives: Ancient Island Societies in Crete and Cyprus*. British School at Athens Studies Vol. 20, London, pp. 85–104.

Webb, V., 2021. 'Faience Found in the Recent Excavations to the East of the Great Altar in the Samos Heraion', *Archäologischer Anzeiger*, 1, pp. 1–62.

Wegner, J. H. and J. W. Wegner, 2015. *The Sphinx that Traveled to Philadelphia*, Philadelphia.

Weingarten, J., 1991. *The Transformation of Egyptian Taweret into the Minoan Genius: A Study in Cultural Transmission in the Middle Bronze Age*, Partille.

Weingarten, J., 2013. 'The Arrival of Egyptian Taweret and Bes[et] on Minoan Crete: Contact and Choice', in L. Bombardieri, A. D'Agostino, G. Guarducci, V. Orsi and S. Valentini, eds., *SOMA 2012. Identity and Connectivity: Proceedings of the 16th Symposium on Mediterranean Archaeology, Florence, Italy, 1-3 March 2012*. Volume I, Oxford, pp. 371–8.

Weinstock, J. A., ed., 2020. *The Monster Theory Reader*, Minneapolis.

Wenghofer, R., 2014. 'Sexual Promiscuity of Non-Greeks in Herodotus' *Histories*', *CW*, 107.4, pp. 515–34.

Wengrow, D., 2006. *The Archaeology of Early Egypt. Social Transformation in North-East Africa, 10,000 to 2650 BC*, Cambridge.

Wengrow, D., 2014. *The Origins of Monsters*, Princeton.

Werbner, P., 2001. 'The Limits of Cultural Hybridity: On Ritual Monsters, Poetic License and Contested Postcolonial Purifications', *The Journal of the Royal Anthropological Institute*, 7.1, pp. 133–52.

West, M. L., 1966. *Hesiod: Theogony*, Oxford.

West, M. L., 1997. *The East Face of Helicon: West Asiatic Elements in Greek Poetry*, Oxford.

West, S., 2006. 'The Amphisbaena's Antecedents', *CQ*, 56.1, pp. 290–1.

Westermann, A., ed., 1839. *Paradoxographoi: Scriptores Rerum Mirabilium Graeci*, Brunsweig.

White, R., 1991. *The Middle Ground: Indians, Empires, and Republics in the Great Lakes Region, 1650-1815*, Cambridge.

Wiggermann, F. A. M., 1992. *Mesopotamian Protective Spirits: The Ritual Texts*, Groningen.

Wilamowitz-Moellendorff, U. von, 1893. *Aristoteles und Athen* II, Berlin.

Wilkinson, T. B. A., 2000. 'What a King is This: Narmer and the Concept of the King', *Journal of Egyptian Archaeology* 86, pp. 23–32.

Williams, C. A., 2013. 'When a Dolphin loves a Boy: Some Greco-Roman and Native American Love Stories', *Class. Antiq.*, 32.1, pp. 200–42.

Wilson, A. M., 1977. 'The Individualized Chorus in Old Comedy', *CQ*, 27.2, pp. 278–83.

Wilson, E., 2021. 'Slaves and Sex in the *Odyssey*', in D. Kamen and C. W. Marshall, eds., *Slavery and Sexuality in Classical Antiquity*, Madison, pp. 15–39.

Wilson, R. E. and E. L. E. Rees, 2009. 'Sometimes a Guitar is Just a Guitar', in S. Calef, ed., *Led Zeppelin and Philosophy: All Will Be Revealed*, Chicago, pp. 63–74.

Wilson, R. R., 1986. 'Play, Transgression and Carnival: Bakhtin and Derrida on *Scriptor Ludens*', *Mosaic*, 19.1, pp. 73–89.

Winbladh, M.-L., 2012. *The Bearded Goddess: Androgynes, Goddesses and Monsters in Ancient Cyprus*, Nicosia.

Winkler, J. J., 1982. 'Akko', *CP*, 77.2, pp. 137–8.

Winkler, J. J., 1990. 'The Ephebes' Song: *Tragoidia* and *Polis*', in J. J. Winkler and F. I. Zeitlin, eds., *Nothing to Do with Dionysos?* Princeton, pp. 20–62.

Winter, I., 2000. 'The Eyes Have It: Votive Statuary, Gilgamesh's Axe, and Cathected Viewing in the Ancient Near East', in R. S. Nelson, ed., *Visuality Before and Beyond the Renaissance*, Cambridge, pp. 22–44.

Withers, C. W. J., 1996. 'Encyclopaedism, Modernism and the Classification of Geographical Knowledge', *Transactions of the Institute of British Geographers*, 21.1, pp. 275–98.

Witmore, C., 2020. 'Objecthood', in L. Wilkie and J. Chenoweth, eds., *A Cultural History of Objects: Modern Period, 1900 to Present*, London, 37–64.

Wittkower, R., 1942. 'Marvels of the East: A Study in the History of Monsters', *Journal of the Warburg and Courtauld Institutes*, 5, pp. 159–97.

Wittkower, R., 1957. 'Marco Polo and the Pictorial Traditions of the Marvels of the East', *Oriente Poliano: Studi e conferenze tenute all'Is. M.E.O*, Rome, pp. 153–72.

Wolf, D., 2020. 'Embodying Change? Homosomatic Hybridity as Transformational Response in LM II/III Crete', *Fontes Archaeologici Posnanienses*, 56, pp. 57–66.

Woodard, R. D., 2021. 'Contextualizing the Origin of the Greek Alphabet', in R. Parker and P. M. Steele, eds., *The Early Greek Alphabets: Origin, Diffusion, Uses*, Oxford, pp. 74–103.

Woodring, C., 2007. 'Centaurs Unnaturally Fabulous', *The Wordsworth Circle* 38.1/2, pp. 4–12.

Woolerton, E., 2010. 'The Roots of Lucretius' Tree-Men, *De Rerum Natura* 2.702–3', *CQ*, 60.1, pp. 255–7.

Woolf, G., 2009. 'Cruptorix and His Kind: Talking Ethnicity on the Middle Ground', in T. Derks and N. Roymans, eds., *Ethnic Constructs in Antiquity: The Role of Power and Tradition*, Amsterdam, pp. 207–18

Wormhoudt, A., 1950. 'The Unconscious Bird Symbol in Literature', *American Imago*, 7, pp. 173–82.

Woudhuizen, F., 2011. 'The Bee-Sign (Evans no. 86). An Instance of Egyptian Influence on Cretan Hieroglyphic', in W. van Binsbergen, ed., *Black Athena Comes of Age: Towards a Constructive Re-Assessment*, Münster, pp. 283–96.

Wrede, H., 1976. 'Lebenssymbole und Bildnisse zwischen Meerwesen', in H. Keller and J. Kleine, eds., *Festschrift für Gerhard Kleiner*, Tübingen, pp. 147–78.

Wright, A., 2013. *Monstrosity: The Human Monster in Visual Culture*, London.

Wynn, T., F. Coolidge and M. Bright, 2009. 'Hohlenstein-Stadel and the Evolution of Human Conceptual Thought', *Camb. Archaeol. J.* 19, pp. 73–84.

Xagorari-Gleißner, M., 2008. *Meter Theon: Die Göttermutter bei den Griechen*, Ruhpolding/Mainz.

Yalouris, N., 1950. 'Athena als Herrin der Pferde', *Museum Helveticum*, 7.1, pp. 19–64.

Yeates, J. W., 2017. 'How Good? Ethical Criteria for a 'Good Life' for Farm Animals', *J Agric Environ Ethics*, 30, pp. 23–35.

Yon, M. and W. A. P. Childs, 1997. 'Kition in the Tenth to Fourth Centuries BC', *BASOR*, 308, *The City-Kingdoms of Early Iron Age Cyprus in Their Eastern Mediterranean Context*, pp. 9–17.

Zambrini, A., 2017. 'Megasthenes Thirty Years Later', in C. Antonetti and P. Biagi, eds., *With Alexander in India and Central Asia: Moving East and Back to West*, Oxford, pp. 222–37.

Zatta, C., 2016. 'Plants' Interconnected Lives: From Ovid's Myths to Presocratic Thought and Beyond', *Arion*, 24.2, pp. 101–26.

Zatta, C., 2019. *Interconnectedness: The Living World of the Early Greek Philosophers*, Baden.

Zeitlin, F. I., 1985. 'Playing the Other: Theater, Theatricality, and the Feminine in Greek Drama', *Representations*, 11, pp. 63–94.

Zhmud', L., 1992. 'Orphism and Graffiti from Olbia', *Hermes*, 120, pp. 159–68.

Ziskowski, A., 2014. 'The Bellerophon Myth in Early Corinthian History and Art', *Hesperia* 83.1, pp. 81–102.

Zuchtriegel, G., 2017. *Colonization and Subalternity in Classical Greece: Experience of the Nonelite Population*, Cambridge.

Zuwiyya, Z. D., 2011. *A Companion to Alexander Literature in the Middle Ages*, Leiden.

Index

Abjection, 40, 322
acculturation, 37, 38
Acheloos, 169, 182, 183
Achilles, viii, 17, 22, 26, 27, 68, 103, 104, 108, 141, 169, 172, 183, 194, 195, 218, 248
actor–network theory, 236
adynata, vii, 260, 281
Aegean, 36, 44, 57, 61, 63, 65, 71, 73, 77, 79, 82, 88, 90, 92, 94, 95, 102, 109, 110, 111, 119, 125, 126, 129, 131, 132, 177, 203, 205, 263, 293
aegis, 204
Aesop, 81, 167
affordance, 52
Africa, 36, 83, 96, 228, 257, 258, 260, 268, 295
Agamemnon, 91, 141
Agdistis, 243, 245
Aglauros, 212, 216
Aigialeia, 198, 199
Aitete, 259, 275
Akousilaos, 249
Akropolis, x, 21, 90, 163, 187, 210, 212, 213, 214, 216, 221, 222, 223, 226, 228
Aktaion, 165, 168
Aktaios, 208
Alexander, 22, 43, 246, 265, 268, 270, 278, 279, 280, 281
Alexander Romance, 278, 280, 281
Alexandria, 117, 206, 271
Alkman, 70
allegory, 13, 100, 106, 181, 198, 240, 290
alphabet, 132
alterity, 8, 29, 61, 135, 236, 296
Amasis
  pharaoh, 117, 118, 158, 179
Amazons, 44, 228, 279
amphisbaina, 206
Amukteres, 267
anaphanda trees, 278
Anat, 134
Anatolia, 5, 48, 94, 95, 132, 196, 197, 241
Ancient Near East, 17, 31, 60, 61, 62, 71, 73, 74, 82, 196

anomalous, 8, 22, 28, 45, 174, 211, 251, 257, 262, 268, 269, 275
anomaly, 17, 21, 23, 26, 45, 61, 65, 92, 107, 151, 183, 188, 244, 262, 269
Antheadai, 218, 240
anthropinon, to, 217
anthropomorphic, 14, 15, 42, 60, 61, 64, 65, 80, 104, 137, 168, 206, 216, 245, 285
Antifa, 294
Antiochos III, 274
ants
  gold-digging, 266, 267
Anubis, 82, 83, 277
Apedamak, 205
Aphrodite, 22, 42, 82, 120, 134, 234, 238, 239, 241, 242, 247
Apkallu, 65, 124
Apkallū, 64
Apollo, 5, 43, 106, 117, 133, 134, 163, 164, 169, 170, 174, 181, 195, 198, 213, 246
Apollodoros, 86, 100, 101, 207, 209, 245, 246, 292, 293
Apple-Eaters, 278
Apsu, 64, 65
Argolid, 177, 199, 319
Argos, viii, xi, xii, 94, 198, 199, 257
Aristonothos, ix, 114, 115
Aristophanes, 150, 162, 173, 193, 209, 237, 242, 244
Aristotle, 43, 53, 54, 70, 100, 155, 174, 233, 234, 252, 264, 278, 283, 292, 294
Aristoxenos, 202
Arkadia, 164, 168
Arkesilas, Cup of, viii, 83, 84
Arnold, Matthew, 236
Arrhephoroi, 212, 216
Arrinoi, 267
Artemidorus, 288
Ashurbanipal, 67, 91
Assyria, 7, 46, 58, 62, 64, 66, 69, 70, 82, 91, 95, 123, 124, 125, 126, 127, 132, 178, 205
Astomoi, 267

Athena, x, 18, 21, 83, 102, 116, 120, 134, 139, 141, 144, 146, 163, 169, 179, 197, 204, 210, 211, 212, 213, 214, 215, 216, 219, 222, 223, 242, 244, 245
Atthidographers, 209, 225, 227
autochthony, 21, 207, 211, 212, 213, 218, 225, 226
Avaris, 87

Baalmilk
  king of Kition, 134
baboon, 80, 83, 84
Bakhtin, 30, 31, 56
Balios, 194
Bataille, Georges, 11
Baubo, 148, 151
Bellerophon, x, 179, 196, 197, 199, 200, 218
Berossos, 65, 124
bestiality, xii, 61, 173, 181, 191, 194
Bhabha, Homi, 29, 30, 31, 32
binarism, 21, 233, 235, 239, 242, 251
Blemmyes, 23, 263, 268, 269
Bluebeard, x, 21, 221, 222, 223, 225, 226, 227, 228, 230, *See* Tritopateres
blue-eyed soul, 32
Boreas, 227, 282
Borysthenes, 35, 180
Botany Bay, 36
Bouplagos, 274
bull-leaping, 87, 88
Burke, Peter
  Hybrid Renaissance, 34
Burkert, Walter, 18, 57, 67, 164
Buto, 206

Caliban, 262
callicantzaros, 16
caste system, 265
Çatalhöyük, 14, 45
cauldron, 137, 140, 187
centaur, ix, x, xi, 16, 20, 23, 26, 55, 65, 107, 130, 131, 142, 143, 144, 147, 152, 171, 172, 173, 174, 175, 176, 180, 181, 182, 183, 185, 186, 187, 188, 189, 190, 191, 192, 193, 194, 275, 276, 277, 282, 283, 284, 285, 286, 287, 289, 294
Centaurides, x, 284, 286
Centauro de Royos, ix, 186, 187
centaurs, ix, x, xi, xii, xiii, 1, 20, 26, 42, 44, 55, 60, 107, 130, 152, 171, 172, 173, 174, 175, 176, 180, 181, 182, 183, 184, 185, 186, 187, 188, 190, 191, 192, 193, 201, 202, 228, 250,
253, 273, 275, 277, 279, 282, 284, 287, 289, 296
cephalomancy, 274
Chaireas and Kallirrhoe, 294
Chairemon, 283
Chandragupta, 265, 267
Chaoskampf, 59, 60, 91, 254
Chauvet Cave, 10
Cheiron, x, 20, 26, 65, 99, 172, 183, 185, 190, 192, 193, 201, 209, 281
chersydras, 203
cherubim, 4
childbirth, 52, 130, 147, 148
Chimaira, 98, 149, 196, 197, 198, 199, 231, 281
Chimbu
  women feeding piglets, viii, 11, 12
chorus, 70, 71, 144, 159, 161, 162
Christ, 14, 170, 290
Chrysantas, 180, 282
Chrysaor, 146, 228
Circe, ix, 58, 98, 99, 166, 167
colonization, 36, 37, 43, 105, 266
contrafactual, 20, 23, 55, 100, 111, 174, 193, 287
Corinth, x, 17, 43, 165, 197, 198, 199, 200, 201, 248
Crete, 17, 71, 77, 78, 79, 80, 86, 87, 88, 94, 110, 116, 129, 131, 165, 199, 204, 310
Crielaard, Jan Paul, 37, 39, 40
Cyllarus, 285
Cynocephali, 263, 264, 270, 278, 296
Cypriot Elaborate Style, 129
Cyprus, ix, 17, 19, 39, 74, 89, 92, 94, 125, 126, 127, 128, 129, 130, 131, 132, 134, 176, 177, 186
Cyrus, 35, 180

Daphne, 42, 166
Darwin, 232, 288
Deianeira, 182, 183, 192, 194
Deir el-Medina
  satirical papyrus, viii, 80
Deleuze, Gilles and Félix Guattari, 51, 54, 55
Delphi, 5, 47, 106, 165, 167, 199, 213, 223, 274
Delta, Nile, 85, 117, 119
Demaratos, 40
Demeter, 146, 151, 169, 204, 256, 266
  Black, 164, 169
diaspora, 36, 96, 106, 262
diffusionism, 18, 57, 58
dildo, 156
dinos, 104, 112, 157, 186
Diodorus Siculus, 173, 234, 255, 289

Dionysos, ix, 47, 82, 83, 146, 150, 153, 160, 168, 170, 205, 206, 220, 248, 266, 276
dithyramb, 96, 161
Dodona, 25, 82
Dog-Heads. *See* Cynocephali
dolphin, 41, 52, 160, 161, 168, 200
Doppelgänger, 189, 212
Dougherty, Carol, 34, 36, 96, 101, 105, 115
Douglas, Mary, 28, 29
Drako, 214, 219
dreadlocks, 32
Dreaming, 9, 12
Dryads, 42
dysphoria, 21, 248

Echidna, 24, 55, 66, 98, 149, 196, 197, 198, 231, 285
Egypt, viii, 5, 17, 31, 43, 59, 71, 72, 77, 78, 79, 80, 82, 83, 85, 86, 87, 97, 106, 116, 117, 118, 119, 120, 123, 131, 134, 204, 205, 206, 263, 268, 275, 276, 277, 333
Eleusis, ix, 138, 139, 140, 142, 147, 150, 151, 210, 211, 215, 219
Eliade, Mircea, 218
Empedokles, 42, 55, 86, 232, 288
Empousa, 148, 150
Enotokoitai, 267
entanglement, 9, 11, 15, 20, 29, 32, 36, 39, 42, 50, 57, 78, 92, 131, 132, 162, 224, 281, 285, 291
Enuma Elish, 18, 63, 64, 66, 104
episemata, 200
epistemology, 8, 53
Eratosthenes, 211, 268, 269
Erechtheion, 211, 214
Erechtheus, 202, 207, 208, 209, 210, 211, 213, 214, 215, 219, 225
erection, 19, 153, 154, 155, 157, 158
Erichthonios, 21, 202, 207, 208, 209, 210, 211, 212, 213, 214, 216, 218, 221, 244
Erinyes, 150, 196, 229, 232, 294
Erisychthon, 208
Esarhaddon, 205
eschatology, 295
Eteoboutadai, 21, 215
ethnography, 260, 262, 263, 264, 265, 269
Etruscan, 39, 40, 69, 107, 113, 115, 147, 160, 185, 186
Euboia, 39
Eurynome, 169
Eusebios, 289
ewúúm, 11

exchange, 18, 29, 37, 39, 51, 58, 74, 75, 82, 93, 96, 97, 111, 116, 120, 121, 126, 135, 196, 228, 238, 242
exotic, 7, 19, 22, 46, 52, 65, 73, 75, 77, 83, 96, 103, 108, 109, 121, 125, 151, 154, 260, 262, 263, 265, 266, 271, 277, 278, 296
extromission, 140

faience, 73, 78, 119, 120
foetus, with two heads, 277
Fondo Artiaco
  Kyme, Campania, 39
François Vase, ix, 171, 172
Freud, 17, 29, 48, 144, 189, 190, 212, 244
Furies, 162, 163

Gary Larson, 24
gegenes, 207, 215
Gello, 148
genre, 23, 81, 83, 194, 271, 272, 273, 283
Gerontius, 295
Geryon, 31, 102, 146, 222, 228
ghost, 163, 273
ghosts, 258, 273, 274
Gilgamesh, 18, 67, 68, 69, 71, 82, 91, 168
globalism, 31, 44
goat, 5, 60, 61, 65, 83, 107, 110, 196, 197, 198, 199
Göbekli Tepe, 14, 15, 45
Godzilla, 230
gorgon, ix, 1, 17, 19, 50, 69, 138, 139, 140, 141, 142, 143, 144, 145, 146, 147, 151, 163, 164, 168, 176, 200, 294
gorgoneion, 144, 147, 200
gorgons, xiii, 1, 3, 19, 42, 44, 112, 139, 140, 142, 144, 147, 158, 162, 171, 193, 202, 204, 296
Gorillai, 261
Graiai, 98, 231
griffin, ix, 57, 61, 71, 72, 109, 137, 138, 290
Griffin Warrior
  Pylos Burial, 87, 109
griffins, 1, 19, 73, 108, 130, 279
Gryllos, 167
Gymnosophists, 279

Halikarnassos, 21, 43, 218, 237, 238, 239, 240, 241
Hanno, 22, 260, 261, 262, 279
Harsomtus, 205
Hekate, 105, 218
Hektor, 141, 179, 195
Hello Kitty, 121
Hephaistos, 21, 108, 137, 140, 153, 210, 212, 213, 216, 244

Hera, 85, 117, 120, 149, 165, 167, 168, 173, 195, 217, 244, 246, 247
Heraïs, 255, 256
Herakleitos, 170
Herakles, viii, ix, 31, 52, 67, 82, 100, 101, 102, 103, 104, 106, 126, 133, 168, 170, 182, 183, 184, 185, 186, 188, 198, 222, 223, 227, 248, 263, 266
hermaphrodite, 21, 57, 233, 234, 235, 236, 237, 241, 244, 248, 254, 255, 258, 259, 274
hermaphroditism, 233, 234, 243, 247, 248, 258, 274
Hermaphroditos, 21, 234, 237, 238, 239, 240, 241, 245
Herodotos, 34, 35, 82, 101, 117, 118, 123, 180, 206, 208, 223, 247, 263, 268, 270, 291
Herse, 212
Hesiod, 1, 19, 24, 44, 63, 64, 65, 66, 81, 83, 98, 99, 104, 105, 106, 178, 197, 198, 215, 218, 220, 223, 225, 227, 231, 232, 233, 244, 254, 260, 285
heteronormativity, 245, 259
hieroglyphic thinking, 73
hippocentaur, 185, 187, 188, 191, 192, 275, 277, 284, 287
hoaxes, 262, 276
Homer, 34, 58, 61, 68, 83, 98, 116, 132, 137, 167, 172, 179, 194, 195, 196, 197, 218, 246, 260, 264, 265, 272, 275, 313
horses, ix, 17, 20, 41, 54, 163, 173, 175, 176, 177, 178, 180, 181, 187, 188, 194, 195, 267, 278, 284, 287
humanimality, 11, 55, 183, 201
Humbaba, viii, 57, 68, 69, 70, 71, 91, 127, 140
humour, 24, 154, 162, 167, 253
hybridism, 36, 37, 38, 288
hybridization, 7, 35, 36, 37, 38, 126
Hylonome, 285

Iambe, 151
Idalion Bilingual, 132, 134
Iliad, 169, 179, 194, 218
India, 22, 263, 265, 266, 267, 268, 269, 270, 278
indigenes, 31, 37, 44, 96, 102, 126, 135, 263
initiation, 12, 15, 20, 46, 105, 127, 145, 150, 160, 164, 165, 243
International Style, 18, 73, 75, 77, 122
Io, 85, 165, 168
Iobates, 197
Isis-Thermouthis, 205
isonomia, 164
Ixion, 173, 175, 176, 275

John Malalas, 289

Kaineus, x, 22, 188, 249, 250, 274
kainotes, 250
kalathoi, 204
kalos k'agathos, 26, 183
Karian, 22, 43, 118, 131, 206, 239, 240, 241
kawaii, 121
Kekrops, x, 202, 207, 208, 209, 210, 211, 212, 214, 216, 218, 219, 220, 221
Kentauros, 173
Kerameikos, 5, 227
Kerberos, 24, 98, 281
Kikkuli, 176
Kingship in Heaven, 63
Klazomenai, 187, 188
Kleisthenes of Sikyon, 199
Klytaimnestra, 163
Knossos, viii, 87, 88, 89, 107, 110, 203
Koko, lowland gorilla, 262
Kolainos, 208
komasts, 156
korai, 143
kouros, 123, 174
Kranaus, 207
Kreousa, 213
kriol, 32
Kristeva, Julia, 11, 40
Ktesias, 22, 197, 263, 264, 265, 269
Kychreus, 207, 219, 220, 221

Lamia, 148, 149
Lapiths, ix, 172, 173, 175, 181, 184, 188, 194, 249, 250, 275, 285
Leaina, 248
Leang Bulu' Sipong 4, Sulawesi, 13
Leang Tedongnge Sulawesi, 13
Lefkandi, 39
Lerna, 198
Lernaian hydra, 198
liquid continent Mediterranean, 95
littoral, Mediterranean, 92
locked-in syndrome, 166
Locri, 38
Löwenmensch, viii, 9, 10
Lucian, 149, 150, 248, 270, 272, 283, 284
Lucretius, 7, 42, 232, 242, 243, 287
ludic, 56, 156, 161, 251

magic, 22, 52, 78, 140, 205, 206, 253, 254, 257
Magna Graecia, 36, 115
Mahabharata, 81, 206
Makrai Petrai, 213
Makroskeles, 267
Malkin, Irad, xv, 36, 82, 95, 106, 118, 133
Marduk, 60, 61, 63, 64, 66, 69
Mares of Diomedes, 20
marriage, 22, 38, 43, 54, 98, 104, 144,
    145, 147, 148, 173, 182, 213, 239, 245, 275
martichora, 264
masks, 49, 69, 71, 88, 127, 140, 145, 147, 153,
    161, 162, 164, 254, 291
Medea, 140, 248
Medusa, ix, 24, 27, 30, 69, 102, 136, 139, 140,
    142, 143, 144, 145, 147, 148, 281,
    See gorgon
Megasthenes, 22, 265, 266, 267, 279
Megilla, 248
Mehen, 204, 205
Mekone, 217
Melqart, 82, 126, 133
Menelaus, 97, 98, 100, 123, 168
mercenaries, 116, 118, 131, 132, 205, 206
Meroe, 205, 268
Mesopotamia, 18, 59, 64, 73
metamorphosis, 93, 148, 159, 160, 164, 165,
    169, 239, 242
Metis, 244, 245
métissage, 35, 36, 93
Middle Ages, 269, 278, 295
middle ground, 36, 78, 126, 240, 242
Minoan Genius, 77, 78, 79, 80
Minotaur, viii, 18, 86, 88, 89, 90
mirabilia, 206, 263, 273, 275, 277, 278
Mischwesen, 60, 66, 85, 313
misogyny, 151
mnemotope, 228
modes of perception, 286
Monocoli, 264
Monommatoi, 267
Monophthalmoi, 267
monsters, xi, 1, 5, 6, 7, 11, 16, 17, 19, 20, 21, 24,
    25, 26, 27, 29, 31, 44, 53, 55, 56, 59, 60, 61,
    63, 64, 65, 66, 68, 70, 71, 86, 88, 90, 91, 98,
    101, 102, 103, 104, 106, 107, 110, 131, 134,
    135, 142, 145, 146, 147, 148, 151, 159, 188,
    194, 197, 198, 199, 200, 206, 213, 216, 217,
    220, 222, 223, 228, 229, 231, 232, 233, 234,
    242, 254, 260, 262, 277, 278, 281, 282, 283,
    289, 295
Moreau, 1, 2, 5
Mormo, 148

mormolykeion, 149
Mušḫuššu, viii, 62, 64

Narmer palette, 72, 73
Naukratis, 19, 116, 117, 118, 119, 123, 131
Nectanebo, 278
Nektanebis, Stele of, 118
Nemea, 198, 199
Nemean Lion, 98, 198, 231
Neolithic, 9
Nephele, 173, 175, 176, 183, 275, 277
Nereids, 19, 42, 103, 104, 105, 108, 162
Nereus, 19, 98, 99, 100, 103, 106
Nessos, 182, 183, 184, 185, 192
Nikander of Kolophon, 203
Nikostratos, 292
nomos, 35, 169, 183
Notos, 227

oath of Plataea, 26
object-oriented ontology, 236
Ochlitai, 278
Odysseus, ix, 58, 67, 68, 97, 98, 99, 101, 116,
    123, 138, 166, 167, 263
Odyssey, 58, 68, 96, 106, 116
Okeanos, 65, 66
Okypodes, 267
Olympia, 123, 124, 125, 168, 171, 181, 188,
    250, 253
Olympias, 278, 280
Opisthodaktyloi, 267
Orangutan, 261
Orthia
    Artemis, 71, 127
Ovid, xvi, 42, 166, 173, 238, 239, 240, 241, 249,
    250, 285

Palaiphatos, 175, 176, 276
Panchaia, 170
Pandion, 207
Pandrosos, 212
paradox, xiv, 22, 35, 49, 51, 71, 144, 168, 170,
    221, 224, 262, 264, 267, 272, 281, 289
parrot, 264
Pasion, 293
Pataliputra, 265, 266
Patroklos, 17, 68, 194, 195, 265
Pedon, 123
Pegasos, x, 17, 20, 27, 29, 42, 63, 146, 159, 179,
    196, 197, 200, 201, 281
Peisistratos, 223
Pelasgians, 213
Pelion, Mt, 173, 175, 176, 275, 284

Pella hydria, x, 219, 220
Peloponnese, 94, 125, 165, 166, 198, 199
penetration, 156, 158
penis, 19, 152, 153, 154, 155, 156, 157, 191, 234, 255, 256
Perachora, x, 120, 221
Periplous, 260, 261, 262
Perseus, ix, 102, 106, 139, 140, 141, 142, 143, 144, 145, 147
phallos, ix, 154, 155, 156
phallos-bird, ix, 155, 156
Phano, 237
Philinnion, 274
Philotis, 259, 274
Phlegon, 245, 246, 258, 273, 274, 275, 276, 277, 278
Phoenician, 19, 36, 37, 39, 40, 58, 71, 85, 93, 115, 116, 126, 127, 128, 132, 133, 134
Pholos, ix, 26, 183, 184, 185, 186
Phorkys, 55, 98, 231
Physika
  Orphic text, 227
Phytoi, 278
Piccinini, Patricia, viii, 40, 41
Pithekoussai, 39, 116, 132
Plato, xvi, 53, 85, 97, 149, 155, 159, 164, 185, 252, 253, 269, 281, 282, 294
platypus, 262
Pleiades, 70, 88
plupast, 21, 217, 218
Polykritos, 273, 274
Poseidon, 86, 103, 107, 146, 150, 169, 177, 179, 196, 208, 210, 211, 213, 215, 218, 219, 240, 249, 250
post-human, 235
predators, 9, 140, 165
Psamtik, pharaoh, 118, 123, 205, 206
Ptah, 5, 6

Rainbow Serpent, 203
Ramses II, viii, 5, 6, 76
rape, xii, 21, 157, 183, 191, 197, 213
reciprocity, 75, 96, 121
Remus, 213
Renenutet, 204, 205
revenant, 274
Rhegion, 38
Rock and Roll, 32
Romans, 261, 264, 269, 274, 276
Romulus, 213

Sahlins, Marshall, 252
Salamis, 219, 220

Salmacis
  Ovidian nymph, 238
Salmakis, 238, 239, 240, 241
Samos, 19, 81, 116, 117, 119, 120, 124
satyrs, 1, 19, 44, 50, 152, 153, 154, 155, 156, 157, 158, 162, 171, 172, 188, 191, 194, 202, 236, 253, 283, 294
Saune, 275, 276, 277
scala naturae, 174, 260
Sciapodes, 264
scorpions, flying, 88, 266
sea, 93, 96, 97, 98
seal, 62, 69, 70, 87, 104, 109, 129, 168
Semnai Theai, 163, 218
Semonides, 151, 152
Senegal, 11, 33
Serres, 266
sexuality, 20, 21, 145, 150, 156, 158, 164, 173, 190, 191, 237, 241, 242, 243, 245, 294
Shalmaneser III, 132
shaman, 9, 12, 46, 72
Sibylline oracle, 275
Sicily, 19, 37, 99, 101, 102, 114, 115
Sikyon, x, xvi, 165, 198, 199, 201
Sisyphos, 207
Sitz im Leben, 42, 215
Skamander, 169
Skyles, 35
Skylla, viii, 17, 19, 29, 55, 97, 98, 99, 103, 149, 206, 280, 281, 285, 288
Skythia, 35, 247, 263
slasher movies, 229
snake goddess, 203
snakes, 21, 103, 136, 198, 200, 202, 203, 204, 205, 207, 209, 212, 214, 219, 245, 246, 247, 249, 254, 263, 266, 267
sophrosyne, 155, 156, 184
Spain, 38, 93, 186
spatium historicum, 218
spatium mythicum, 218
species, 7, 9, 28, 42, 50, 51, 52, 53, 61, 141, 151, 162, 164, 174, 203, 206, 215, 232, 249, 261, 287, 296
spells, 11, 61, 204, 253
Sphinx, vii, viii, 1, 2, 3, 4, 5, 6, 7, 16, 80, 98, 130, 149, 157, 197, 231, 281
sphinxes, viii, xiii, 1, 2, 3, 5, 7, 73, 112, 136
sphyrelaton, 125
sub-human, 259, 260, 261, 262, 270
Sympherousa, 274
symposium, 26, 108, 113, 152, 156, 161, 184, 292

Tanagra, 276, 277
Taweret, viii, 77, 78, 79, 80, 82, 91
taxidermy, 276
Taxonomy, 292
Teiresias, 22, 101, 167, 245, 246, 247, 248, 249, 258, 274
Tell el-Farkha, 72, 306
Testamentum Porcelli, 167
Tethys, 65, 66
thauma idesthai, 136
thaumata, 262, 263, 271, 273
The Shipwrecked Sailor, 58
Thebes, 7, 84, 198, 200, 206
Theogony, 63, 98, 197, 227, 231, 254
Theophrastos, 228, 237
theoria, 142
therianthropes, 55
theriomorphic, 13, 80, 128, 166, 168
Theseus, 86, 90, 104, 106, 208, 213, 220, 226, 228
Thetis, ix, 103, 104, 107, 108, 137
Tiamat, 64, 65, 66, 69
Tiryns, viii, ix, 79, 145, 146, 147, 164, 178, 197
Tok Pisin, 32
transformation, ix, 10, 16, 20, 22, 46, 47, 69, 78, 79, 85, 87, 88, 104, 106, 121, 127, 140, 145, 149, 151, 152, 159, 164, 165, 166, 168, 170, 188, 190, 229, 239, 242, 246, 249, 250, 251, 274
Triton, viii, 100, 101, 106, 107, 222, 224, 227, 263, 276
Tritopatores, 21, 225, 227
Trojan War, 194, 218
Two Dog Palette, viii, 72, 73

Typhoeus, viii, 66, 67, 69, 91, 206
Typhon, 66, 222, 282

Ugarit, viii, 60, 71, 75, 76, 125
Unheimlich, 29, 90, 189
unicorns, 264

vagina dentata, 99
vampires, 149, 274
vision, cathected, 141
Vulci, 90, 157, 185, 186

Wahibbreemakhet, 119
Wappenmünzen, 200
Wengrow, David, 14, 59, 72, 73
Werbner, Pnina, 30, 31
werewolf, 8, 16, 149, 164, 274, 294
West Africa, 33, 260
West, Martin, 18, 31, 57, 58, 63, 66, 67, 68, 81, 102, 105, 205, 263
wheat
  hybridized grains, 7, 222, 224
wolves, 8, 164

Xanthos, 194, 195, 196
Xenophon, 43, 52, 148, 179, 180, 282
Xouthos, 213

Zephyros, 227
Zeus, viii, 18, 42, 63, 66, 67, 69, 82, 85, 91, 104, 117, 146, 150, 164, 168, 171, 173, 181, 182, 195, 206, 208, 222, 225, 232, 243, 244, 245, 246, 249, 253